AFRODIASPORIC FORMS

AFRODIASPORIC FORMS

Slavery in Literature and Culture of the African Diaspora

RAQUEL KENNON

Louisiana State University Press
Baton Rouge

This publication was subsidized in part by Harvard Studies in Comparative Literature.

Published by Louisiana State University Press
lsupress.org

LSU Press Paperback Original

Manufactured in the United States of America
First printing

DESIGNER: Michelle A. Neustrom
TYPEFACE: Calluna
PRINTER AND BINDER: Sheridan Books, Inc.

COVER ILLUSTRATION: *Gates of Return,* 2006-7, by Julien Sinzogan. Acrylic on canvas, 4.65 × 10 meters. Courtesy of the artist and October Gallery, London. Photograph copyright © Jonathan Greet.

LIBRARY OF CONGRESS CATALOGING-IN-PUBLICATION DATA

Names: Kennon, Raquel, author.
Title: Afrodiasporic forms : slavery in literature and culture of the African diaspora / Raquel Kennon.
Description: Baton Rouge : Louisiana State University Press, 2022. | Includes bibliographical references and index.
Identifiers: LCCN 2021048344 (print) | LCCN 2021048345 (ebook) | ISBN 978-0-8071-7681-8 (paperback) | ISBN 978-0-8071-7763-1 (pdf) | ISBN 978-0-8071-7764-8 (epub)
Subjects: LCSH: Slavery in literature. | Slavery in mass media. | Literature—Black authors—History and criticism. | African diaspora.
Classification: LCC PN56.S5765 K46 2022 (print) | LCC PN56.S5765 (ebook) | DDC 808.803552—dc23/eng/20211118
LC record available at https://lccn.loc.gov/2021048344
LC ebook record available at https://lccn.loc.gov/2021048345

To my cherished mother, Andrea Deborah Kennon

To the loving memory of my father, Dr. Tom L. Kennon (1952–2003)

And to my ancestors who fought and sacrificed

You can't put the past behind you. It's buried in you; it's turned your flesh into its own cupboard.

—CLAUDIA RANKINE, *Citizen: An American Lyric*

Contents

Acknowledgments

This book has dwelled with me for many years and taken on numerous forms. My interest in the literary forms and genres of the African diaspora began with animated stories my father told at home and the inspiring genealogy work of my mother. Wordplay fueled our imaginations and attuned us to the power of word work. My father's oral histories—about family members, names, and places known and unknown—prompted a lasting curiosity. The story of our enslaved ancestor Peter, separated from his two brothers, who could only sign his name with an *X*, intrigued me as I pondered what inheritance and family reunion might mean across the vast locations and languages of diaspora, and what those unknowable silences and ruptures of slavery signified across these shores over time.

I would like to express my gratitude to the first readers of this project for their support, guidance, and recognizing promise in what would become this book. I wish to thank Werner Sollors for his wisdom, inimitable calm, kind encouragement, careful readings, and commentary on my work. His insights, recommendations, stunning wealth of intertextual references, and editorial suggestions helped me to shape my arguments and make connections between my work and existing scholarship in the field.

I extend my gratitude to Biodun Jeyifo for his trenchant critiques and thought-provoking conversations about diaspora from the initial seedling of an idea and as my project began to take shape. Our discussions about theory and critical approaches to the study of slavery were invaluable.

I am also deeply grateful to Karen Thornber for her mentorship, words of advice about the craft of academic writing and establishing writerly voice, thoughtful close readings of early versions of this work, and astute feedback. I am thankful for questions that pushed me to conceptualize the threads of my research as an organic whole in its earliest form.

In grateful memory of the late Professor Joaquim-Francisco Coelho for his intellectual generosity, advisement, and his explanations of the nuances of the Portuguese language and the joys of studying Brazilian poetry, in his course on Manuel Bandeira and Carlos Drummond de Andrade during my first semester of graduate school.

I must thank my colleagues in the Department of Africana Studies at California State University, Northridge, for stimulating conversations and modeling activism, teaching, and scholarship. Thanks to the remarkable students whose determination, creativity, and imagination inspire me so much. I am grateful for research grant support and a semester-long sabbatical leave from the College of Social and Behavioral Sciences, which enabled me to complete the final stages of this book.

Earlier versions of chapters 1 and 2 appeared in *Studies in Latin American Popular Culture* and *African American Review.* I am grateful for permission to reproduce sections from those essays here. My thanks to the Harvard Department of Comparative Literature's Schofield Fund. This publication was subsidized in part by Harvard Studies in Comparative Literature.

I offer my sincerest thanks and appreciation to James Long at Louisiana State University Press for his incredible support and his belief in this book. I am also tremendously thankful to the editorial board. This book has benefited from the incisive feedback of the anonymous reader who offered generous comments around the book's conceptualization, which helped to bring out its current form. I also thank anonymous reviewers of earlier versions of essays, whose thoughtful comments and suggestions greatly improved the work. Any shortcomings or errors that remain are my own.

I am indebted to the scholarly generosity of Caroline A. Brown, Kimberly Juanita Brown, Monique-Adelle Callahan, and Therí Pickens, who have, at various times and in different ways, supported me along this intellectual journey, selflessly giving their guidance, support, and encouragement. To Porsha Cropper and Christina Ramos: your friendship, beautiful spirits, laughter, and reading of drafts propelled me forward as we traveled along this academic road together from California to Cambridge.

I am thankful for the unwavering support of my family, who have always rooted for me and never tired of saying they were proud. For my grandmothers, Essie and Flavy, tender strong towers, whose bold intergenerational prayers live on as I think about the lives of their own grandmothers and great-grandmothers, who would have been enslaved in their not too distant era.

Enormous gratitude is reserved for my sister, Taja, who faithfully believed in what I could accomplish from the beginning.

To my parents, who wrapped me in unconditional love and instilled the value of education and work in the community, for their visioning of a better future, which was always cast in the language of what might be achieved over generations, I owe a debt I cannot repay. To my extraordinary mother, Andrea, a boundless bastion of daily care, my earliest literature instructor, for reading groups, modeling a practice of archival work, fierce advocacy, and unceasing spiritual and emotional support, I give my thanks, always. And to the loving memory of my father, Tommy, whose astounding hard work, sacrifice, words of encouragement, vision for the future, dazzling spinning of tales, orature, fits of laughter, and guitar strumming enlivened our everyday lives. Although he did not live to see me attend graduate school, he gave me the practical advice to write just one paragraph a day, long before I ever imagined writing a book.

For his unfaltering love, patience, humor, always believing, and so much more that sustained me on this path, I offer immeasurable thanks to Corey. And to our dearest sons, William Ayodele, in heaven, and Marcus Ayorinde, whose arrival while I finalized this book has brought immense joy.

Finally, I wish to thank the brilliant writers, poets, musicians, artists, and scholars whose enthralling work has shaped my thinking and compelled me to venture to write about slavery's memory and the complex genres of the African diaspora.

American Popular Culture, Volume 35, pp. 138–159. Copyright © 2017 by the University of Texas Press. All rights reserved.

A portion of chapter 2 was published as "Subtle Resistance: On Sugar and the Mammy Figure in Kara Walker's *A Subtlety* and Sherley Anne Williams's *Dessa Rose*" *African American Review* 52, no. 2, pp. 143–164. Copyright © 2019 by Johns Hopkins University Press. All rights reserved.

AFRODIASPORIC FORMS

Introduction

TRAVELING THROUGH FOG

Slavery's Memorial Expressions in the Black World

Looking back, we cannot see,
except for its blurring lights
like underwater stars and moons,
our starting-place.

—ROBERT HAYDEN, "Traveling Through Fog"

Look for me in the whirlwind or the storm, look for me all around you, for with God's grace, I shall come and bring with me countless millions of black slaves who have died in America and the West Indies and the millions in Africa to aid you in the Fight for Liberty, Freedom and Life.

—MARCUS GARVEY, "First Message to the Negroes of the World from Atlanta Prison"

Afrodiasporic Forms considers the epistemological possibilities of the "Black world" paradigm, however polemical, illusory, and unstable, and sketches a literary and cultural cartography of the "monde noir" and its constitutive African diasporas, amid infinite poetic, visual, and cultural permutations, vis-à-vis the transatlantic slave trade, modern racial slavery, and its afterlife. Construing slavery's memory in a diasporic, transtemporal context is akin to "traveling through fog," as the epigraph from Robert Hayden's eponymous poem brings to light, the vertiginous sensation of walking in quicksand, guided only by "blurring lights," with "our starting-place" a flickering location in the past "we cannot see."[1] This book analyzes divergent texts and artistic forms engaging slavery's memory, spanning from the 1830s to the twenty-first century across wide-ranging genres and geographies, to trace contradictions, ambiguities, and contestations within diasporic narratologies of slavery.

Revisiting the contested notion of history's "usable past,"[2] this book explores how varied literary and cultural products of slavery's afterlife—poetry, prose, plays, painting, telenovelas, music, sculpture, and photography—shape understandings of the African diaspora. This is an old history, as Colin A. Palmer argues, in which "African peoples have been in constant motion for over 100,000 years, traveling all over the globe, transforming it in many ways and being transformed themselves" ("African Diaspora" 56). While recognizing at once the fiction of a cohesive "Black world" (or elaborating on what Benedict Anderson calls an "imagined community," in reference to the nation-state) and its theoretical and strategic necessity, and the cultural and political imperatives of Pan-Africanism, "an uneven and wide-flung phenomenon" as Olakunle George asserts,[3] *Afrodiasporic Forms* considers, through studying these variations of genre and form, the complicated connections and divergences of peoples of African descent in this "monde noir." I propose the transatlantic slave trade as one framework that links Africans on both sides of the Atlantic Ocean, the trauma of the slave trade as the space where they intersect, and the New World as the location where African, European, Asian, and Indigenous peoples and histories collide.[4] This, of course, is not the singular story of African diaspora(s), nor the historical point at which the history of African descendants in the Americas commences.[5]

The "African imagination," as F. Abiola Irele defines it, provides a foundational point of commonality among the literary corpus he terms "Black texts." It is "a conjunction of impulses that have been given a unified expression in a body of literary texts. From these impulses, grounded both in common experience and in common cultural references, Black texts have come to assume a particular significance that is worth attempting to elucidate" (*African Imagination* 4). Irele's foregrounding of "unified expression," "common experience," and "common cultural references" simultaneously insists on "an African imagination as a general perspective for apprehending in a single vision the various dimensions of Black expression" (xv).

One such commonality is the shared anticolonialist struggle for the emancipation of Black people, or what Marcus Garvey calls the "Fight for Liberty, Freedom and Life." Recognizing the complex dimensionality of Black expression is a crucial feature; rather than collapsing difference, Irele's theory offers a unifying term that enlarges the field to encompass the "African world" while acknowledging the distinctiveness of Black expression within it. The significance of a real or imagined relationship to an ancestral homeland, Hayden's blurry "starting-place," emerges as a defining feature of diaspora communities. Scholars such as Kim D. Butler, Paul Gilroy, Robin D. G. Kelley, Michael A. Gomez, Lisa Lowe, and others emphasize "intimacies" forged by the forced scatterings and dispersals, bloodied and brutal ruptures, that led to the making of New World modernities born from European imperial projects.[6]

This comparative work requires bridging difference to envision a vast panorama of heterogeneous poetic creation in the African world. As Brent Hayes Edwards argues in *The Practice of Diaspora,* "The cultures of black internationalism can be seen only *in translation.* It is not possible to take up the question of 'diaspora' without taking account of the fact that the great majority of peoples of African descent do not speak or write in English" (7). According to Edwards's conjecture that translation is the mode by which we must apprehend Black globality, the striving toward transnational, African diasporic exchanges exists precariously between abstraction and "anti-essentialism," articulating "discourses of cultural and political linkage only through and across difference in full view of the risks of that endeavor" (13). Christel N. Temple similarly issues a call for transtemporal "comparative studies of global black literatures" to yield "dynamic new comparisons."[7]

The earliest text explored here, Juan Francisco Manzano's *Autobiografía de un esclavo* (1839), for example, is the only extant slave narrative from the Spanish colonial archive, well known within Latin American studies, but perhaps less so outside this disciplinary realm. Published nearly fifty years before abolition on the island in 1886, and sixteen years before Cuba's independence, Manzano's memoir reveals the significance of formal elements in narratives of slavery in which redactions, ellipses, and omissions are as salient as the written words.[8] Notably, Manzano self-identifies as a "refined mulatto" and occupies a hybrid position within the racial designations of the period and region.[9] Similar themes emerge within the literary and cultural forms investigated here, a selected cross section of the imaginative infinitude that constitutes the poetic monde noir, one that profoundly complicates readings of race across spatiotemporalities.

SLAVERY AS THE LIVING WOUND

Slavery is the living wound under the patchwork of scars.
—KWADWO OPOKU-AGYEMANG, *Cape Coast Castle*

La nación es el más hollado y a la vez el más impenetrable de los territorios de la sociedad moderna. Todos sabemos que esas líneas negras en los mapas políticos son como cicatrices de innumerables guerras, saqueos y conquistas; pero también sospechamos que, además de la violencia estatal fundadora de las naciones, hay antiguas y extrañas fuerzas de índole cultural y psíquica que dibujan las fronteras que nos separan de los extraños.

[The nation is the most tread upon and at the same time most impenetrable of the territories of modern society. We all know that those black lines on political maps are like scars of countless wars, plunders, and conquests; but also we suspect that, in addition to the foundational state-violence of the nations, there are ancient and strange forces of a cultural and psychic nature that draw the borders that separate us from foreigners.]
—ROGER BARTRA, *La jaula de la melancolía*

Turning to the literary and cultural production of transatlantic slavery—one of many African diasporic foci—as phenomenological grounds for comparison within the Black world, I approach the question through the prism of the enduring imprint of slavery, the "living wound under the patchwork of scars," or "cicatrices de innumerables guerras, saqueos y conquistas" (scars from innumerable wars, plunders, and conquests). In Homi K. Bhabha's introduction to *Nation and Narration,* language itself becomes ambivalent in the construction of national discourse and modernity.[10] The process of composing diaspora, with its multiple manifestations often emerging before official nation formations, is marked by this ambivalence, in which textual meanings are extracted in ongoing states of transition and liminality. Drawing upon a scholarly tradition that problematizes facile understandings of diaspora and the very notion of the transatlantic itself broadens our conceptions of these terms. Like the recent work of Yomaira Figueroa-Vásquez, which decolonizes diasporic reading practices by centering what she terms "peripherized" Afro-Atlantic Hispanophone subjects, this book assembles an archive of slavery in and around the monde noir that occupies the space of ambivalence.[11] Christina Sharpe's *In the Wake* calls the "Trans*Atlantic" that "s/place, condition, or process that appears alongside and in relation to the Black Atlantic but also in excess of its currents," in which the asterisk marks "a range of configurations of Black being" and powerfully points to the commodification and fungibility of Black life.[12] Yogita Goyal's urgent call for "new diasporas" further evidences the significance of liminality: "The varied routes of migration that have generated the new diaspora helpfully counters the hegemony of any single genealogy of blackness."[13]

Even as contemporary waves of African migrations and relocations outside the historical context of transatlantic slavery must be accounted for, "the ambiguities of diaspora," as Brent Hayes Edwards argues, "do not resolve" (118). Considering crucial questions around translation and print culture reveals the "uneasy space" and "décalage of diaspora," a disjointed, ambivalent model, as Edwards puts it (14–15, 116). Samantha Pinto relatedly employs the titular critical term "difficult" to characterize a practice of diaspora literary studies that exposes "the critical values of failure, distance, disconnection, and displacement" around a "diaspora feminist aesthetics" (16). I am interested in engaging with these terms—*trans*Atlantic, difficult, uneasy, disjointed, liminal, ambivalent, failure, decolonial*—to think through the complexities and contradictions of imagining how transatlantic slavery continues to construct and reconstruct literary and cultural diasporic archives of an aspirational and ephemeral Black world that is always already in a process of cohering and unraveling, becoming lost in the interstices of translation that, as Aarthi Vadde contends, "invites readers to dwell in those impasses, though it makes no guarantee of getting through them" (3).[14]

Opoku-Agyemang and Bartra's metaphorical invocations in the two epigraphs of this section further call to mind the patchwork of scars resembling a chokecherry tree knotting Sethe's back in Toni Morrison's *Beloved,* the intricate pattern of lacerated skin that transformed her back into a "sculpture" that Paul D first tenderly kisses like "the most expensive part of himself" but soon after, his desire hastily quenched, views as a "revolting clump of scars" (17, 21).[15] As a paradigmatic visual icon of slavery's abhorrent violence, the scourged back encodes what Kimberly Juanita Brown in *The Repeating Body,* following Mary Ann Doane's theory of the photographic afterimage, calls the "the proliferation of imagery seeking to address the impossible duality between black women's representation and slavery's memory" (3).[16] What Brown argues is "a repetition of imagistic concern" in Morrison's classic novel reveals the inexhaustible, widely disseminated visual iterations of the 1863 photograph of the formerly enslaved Gordon's viciously whipped and scarred back. The chokecherry tree violence inscribed on Sethe's back, and the prior sexual and maternal violation of her lactating breasts, complicate the gendered graphic brutality seared into the enslaved male's back.[17]

Intervening in contestations around the monde noir as a heuristic, *Afrodiasporic Forms* explores how the constraints and expansiveness, difficulties, disjointedness, incompatibilities, and irresolvabilities of the notion of African diaspora inform transnational concepts of Blackness and projects of freedom.[18] Comparatively reading global genres, subgenres, and forms of slavery unsettles dominant, US-centered, Anglophone narratives of slavery and refuses a definitive or singularly authoritative narrative of slavery. This line of inquiry moves beyond merely seeking transnational analogs to the North American classic slave narratives, yet it simultaneously recognizes the difficult impasses and disjointedness that linguistic and cultural translation often yields.

Despite the risks of comparative literary studies of slavery, relational readings of the literary and cultural archive of slavery's past—transfigured in myriad ways across variegated geographies, historical periods, genres, and forms—unveil the wide-ranging possibilities of Afrodiasporic memorial expression and slavery's intertexts. The expansive terrain of comparative genres of slavery wrestles with putative high and low art forms, canonical, popular, irreverent, and lesser known, to foreground how the global implications of slavery's memory, in pre-emancipation texts and postslavery literature and culture, are at various times and in disparate spaces obscured, redacted, sanitized, transfigured, and sentimentalized in the pauses, punctuation, and innovative material construction of these texts. Although prose, and particularly the novel, has predominately been the literary domain of the first-person memoir or novelistic form in African American and Anglophone Caribbean fiction—traditions with their own respective literary figurations—which Arlene Keizer in *Black Subjects* terms the "contemporary narratives of slavery," this book attends to the variegated archive of transtemporal prosaic, poetic, dramatic, televisual, filmic, sculptural, and monumental representations that, taken together, uncover how comparative study of genres and forms of slavery structure a version of the Black world in its multifocal, polyvocal, and multilingual global dimensions (2–10).

Centering literature of and concerning African descendants in the diaspora, *Afrodiasporic Forms* considers the discursive cartography of the Middle Passage waterways and the mythology around the mapping of the so-called triangular trade as foundational to thinking through oceanic metaphors of motion: *flows, currents, crosscurrents, streams, waves, crossings, passages, arrivals, departures, trodding* (3).[19] As Katherine McKittrick has observed, specifically regarding Black women's geographies and domination, "We produce space, we produce its meanings, and we work very hard to make geography what it is" (*Demonic Grounds* xi).[20] These socially produced Black geographies, which refer to both "physical materiality and imaginative configurations," to borrow McKittrick's phrase, signal the movement—crisscrossing and zigzagging—of people, ideas, histories, cultures, languages, and knowledges across spatiotemporal borders and the Black aesthetic performances they engender (x). I argue that the vectors of slavery's memory extending through Black geographies, or sites of slavery[21]—crossing over and returning—are multidirectional, though not equivalent. Rather, these crosscurrents often reveal complex incongruencies and gradients of influence within the literature of the diaspora by highlighting canonical texts that have maintained a substantial impact on the shaping of comparative slavery studies.

The Afrodiasporic literary and cultural outpouring attests to the fraught, confounding, romanticized, and complicated relationships to and between homeland and host lands. Paul Gilroy cites the founding of the journal *Présence Africaine* as a pivotal moment "in the developing awareness of the African diaspora as a transnational and intercultural multiplicity" that joins together Africans and diasporic Africans "in a new and potent anti-imperialist configuration" (195). In his 1993 classic *The Black Atlantic: Modernity and Double Consciousness,* Gilroy charts the tensions between the critical political geographic term he calls "the black Atlantic," modernity, tradition, and what he names the "restless discontinuity" and "cultural mutations" that constitute "the stereophonic, bilingual, or bifocal cultural forms originated by," but not the exclusive territory of, Black people dispersed in the "black Atlantic world" (2–3). J. Lorand Matory, in the context of diasporic syncretic religious practice, provides an apt temporal and spatial metaphor to emphasize the slave trade's transoceanic nature across the Atlantic Ocean and the resultant displacement and dispossession of Africans into the New World.[22]

I employ the broader term "African diaspora" as an analytic framework for an aspirational comparative, multilingual, multifocal method, to the extent possible here, to underscore the exchanges, linkages, and "restless discontinuities" between peoples in Africa, Europe, and the Americas vis-à-vis the global touchstone of slavery (map 1).[23] I am concerned with the diverse ways the memory of this transnational atrocity comes to bear on literary and cultural panoramas and shifting racial representations.[24]

Many literary studies of slavery have focused disproportionately on the

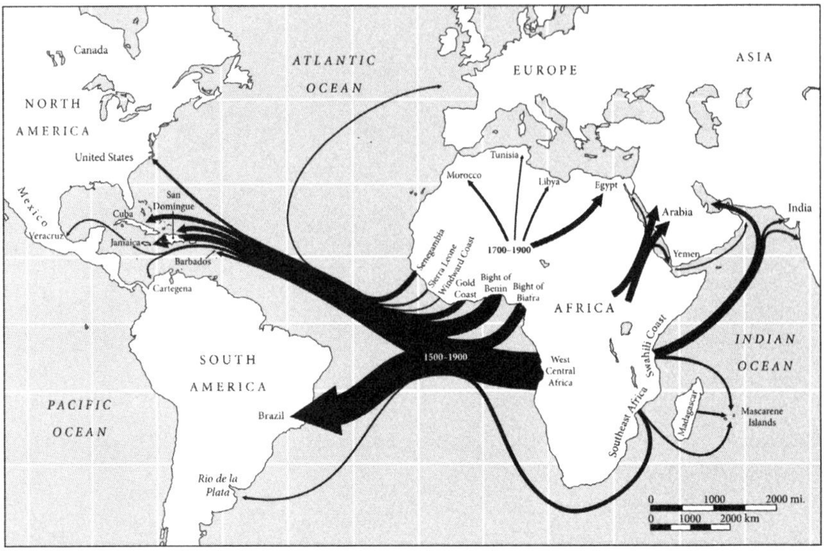

MAP 1. Overview of the Slave Trade Out of Africa, 1500–1900. Map adapted from David Eltis and David Richardson, *Atlas of the Transatlantic Slave Trade* (Yale University Press, 2010).

United States context. Historian Paul Tiyambe Zeleza urges us to consider the field of African diaspora studies from a global perspective, warning against the hegemonic dominance of "the African American model in which the US experience and modes of racialization and identity formation are often generalized to the rest of the Americas" ("African Diasporas" 8).[25] Similarly, Palmer insists that "scholars must be careful not to homogenize the experiences of the diverse peoples of the modern diaspora," specifically pointing out that "North American scholars in particular must avoid the temptations to impose paradigms that reflect their own experiences upon other areas of the diaspora" ("Defining and Studying the Modern African Diaspora" 30).

Literary studies of slavery that venture outside US geography most often focus on canonical Anglophone Caribbean narratives of slavery. Moreover, Tina Campt and Deborah A. Thomas alert us to the hegemonies embedded in diasporic formations, using a transnational feminist frame to interrogate a "general masculinism in the conception of diasporic community" (1–2). To trouble these hegemonies of geography, gender, and reified binaries of "home/host or displacement/homeland," following Campt and Thomas, I attempt here to bring together a selection of Afrodiasporic literary and cultural texts, broadly construed, across space and time.

To underscore how ruptures of transatlantic slavery's afterlife variously imprint in transatlantic texts, the overarching aim of this post-Eurocentric, post-Americanist comparative book, in light of recent reconsiderations of the critical turn toward transnational, transatlantic, and diaspora studies, is to move beyond the centricity of the "American" paradigm of remembering and forgetting slavery (and where *American* is usually understood as pertaining to the United States), by exploring selected inter-American representations, eschewing the prominence of the United States as the prevailing analytic template for literary slavery studies. Drawing from VèVè Amasasa Clark's concept of "diaspora literacy," which "demands a knowledge of historical social, cultural, and political development generated by lived and textual experience" (42), I argue for *relational* cross reading that juxtaposes texts as an effort both to begin to unsettle US primacy in this field and to think through the varied textual transmutations of remembering and forgetting, through and across difference. How does the diasporic literary panorama engage with prevalent readings of *resilience* and *resistance* emergent in "post-traumatic poetics," to use Houston Baker Jr.'s term, and represent racial violence as both a direct and indirect legacy of slavery, from the atrocities of the Middle Passage to the brutality of plantation punishments to the horrific American ritual of lynching? Other scholars also have challenged the pervasiveness of the plantation framework as an overindexed representation of slavery.

Afrodiasporic Forms explores a vast range of slavery's genres and forms, including drama, poetry, prose, varieties of visual culture, popular culture, and the sculptural and monumental in three symbolic loci of the African diaspora, or "sites of slavery" in the Atlantic World: Brazil, the United States, and Cuba.[26] Geographies of the Global South are the focus of this study, constituting a central pillar of inquiry that returns to the capacious notion of the monde noir. Relatively late dates of emancipation mark the locations in the Americas: the United States, Cuba, and Brazil continued legal enslavement of Africans in the Western Hemisphere until emancipation in 1865, 1886, and 1888, respectively.[27]

The majority of the texts here are from the postbellum era, the mid- to late twentieth century. A few, however, were published around the 1830s and reference a period before nation-state formation. Although the texts travel over vast stretches of space and time, spanning more than 150 years and three countries, the study is not meant to be comprehensive, but only to suggest an approach to interdisciplinary literary studies of slavery to cultivate "diaspora literacy."

Following Binyavanga Wainaina's poignant critique, I am not suggesting that these geographies are discrete, contained, or fixed entities or that the appellation "Africa" represents an undifferentiated land mass without distinctive cultures, languages, literatures, and histories.[28] Conversely, the present book argues that each region is interconnected and overlapping, while eschewing restrictive significations of diaspora. I argue, along with others, that diaspora connotes multidirectional flow and bilateral vectors of influence, as Kwame Essien has demonstrated in his work on the Brazilian presence in Ghana.[29] To read literary and cultural representations of slavery in the Americas, or "transnational Black dialogues," as Markus Nehl calls them, is to challenge overly aestheticized interpretations that diminish or flatten the specificity of the reverberations of enslavement in each spatiotemporality. Instead, it discusses how the accumulation of memories of slavery might be intergenerationally and transnationally transmitted, omitted, and reworked through text to produce what Ira Berlin calls the "creative legacy of slavery" ("Coming to Terms with Slavery" 6).

ON MEMORY AND TEXT

To remember is to have a memory
or to set off in search of a memory.
—PAUL RICOEUR, *Memory, History, Forgetting*

Afrodiasporic Forms sets off in search of textual and cultural memories. The work of Paul Ricoeur and Michel-Rolph Trouillot on memory and archival silences, supplemented by Maurice Halbwachs's classic notion of "collective memory," shape the memorial aspect of this project.[30] New analytic grammars afford us ways of exploring what it means to be a person of African descent moving in the world in the wake of this historical atrocity. I am interested in the ways the interplay of remembering and forgetting slavery across the diaspora is textualized and conceptualized to investigate how slavery and its afterlife compelled transnational transformation, improvisation, and artistic creation.

This book rests on a number of vital presuppositions: first, that transatlantic slavery constitutes a global atrocity; second, that memorial engagements are transmitted transnationally, transhistorically, and intergenerationally; and third, that the memory of slavery lurks, sometimes latently, and expresses itself—not exclusively, of course, and sometimes not at all—textually and artistically. I pursue, in particular, how inter-American representations of and engagements with slavery are a function of temporal distance and shifting cultural specificity. What do these commonalities and disjunctures reveal about the vastly different geographic locations and cultural contexts? To what exchanges between these groups are we privy? What do these cross-cultural interactions reveal about broader notions of global blackness and of African and African diasporic identity?

The chapters in *Afrodiasporic Forms* follow, and even require, asynchronous presentation. As Tavia Nyong'o posits, "The study of blackness can rearrange our perceptions of chronology, time, and temporality."[31] Selected texts reach out diagonally, noncontinuously, tousled to reflect and refract the discontinuity and dislocation inherent in the rupture of slavery. Specific texts might be canonical within their respective national traditions, yet they might not be usually read alongside other works presented here. Following scholars such as Nyong'o and Michelle Wright, I am concerned less with establishing a rigid historical or literary chronology or suggesting that racial formation is articulated through linear, teleological narratives of Atlantic slavery. I am more interested in enacting contrary ways of assembling, reading, and juxtaposing divergent African diasporic literature from a comparatist scope and multilingual perspective.[32]

The far-flung aim of this book confronts Stuart Hall's notion of "the positions of *enunciation*"—my positionality as a Black scholar trained in comparative literature in the United States—underscoring the risks and limitations of a single study attempting to perform this decentering work and look across and between, which is always an unfinished task.[33] While this book incorporates texts in the original languages—primarily Spanish, Portuguese, and English—it attempts to present a methodology for comparative literary slavery studies, precarious textual juxtapositions, informed by other fields such as sociology, anthropology, Black feminist thought, performance studies, and history. The field is open to fruitful multilinguistic and cross-disciplinary comparisons using a number of African and European languages, especially studies moving beyond European imperial languages.[34]

Conceptually, this book functions as a collection of interrelated readings organized around a theme rather than tracing a traditional narrative arc. Silence, elision, gaps, discontinuities, and reimaginings mark these texts. Heterogeneity becomes the instructive mode of reading slavery in the African diaspora as it exposes the impossibility of a linear, cohesive narrative of slavery, the "living wound." However, the wound metaphor does not function to pathologize the enslaved; rather, it exposes the global festering wound that reopens and bleeds. *Afrodiasporic Forms* brings into view corporeal forms—often surveilled and scrutinized—that have shaped the genres and forms of Black literary and cultural expression. This method of inquiry would be useful for future extensive thematic studies (perhaps of African diasporic music or new media or dance) or intensive studies (of, say, African diasporic drama or poetry). While historicized close reading lies at the center of this book, I consider a broad range of Afrodiasporic texts, broadly defined, engaging with Stephen Best's "wanton" practices of reading in *The Fugitive's Properties,* untethered from an insistence on chronology but propelled more by "associative logics" to unearth "hybrid formation" (21–23).[35] However, I depart from Best's use of analogy in the sense of his emphasis on nineteenth-century property and law by seeking out points of variation and difference beyond the analogic as signal features of my readings.

Each chapter centers on a specific African diasporic geography, excavating a transatlantic archive of slavery that includes art, public space, newspaper clippings, telenovelas, monuments (both imagined and actually built), and song, then delves into a more traditional cross section of literature from each national and regional context, juxtaposing canonical and noncanonical works with one another. It attempts to dismantle designations of high and low, literary and popular art forms. As these chapters move in multiple directions, with texts considered canonical in their respective national and linguistic traditions but perhaps lesser known outside of those disciplinary boundaries, it has most often been the work of anthologies to bring these diasporic voices together. Breaking from chronological order, each chapter traverses geographies and spatiotemporalities to focus on how transnational sites of slavery are reimagined in and through texts over time, and how the relationship between remembering and forgetting reconfigures these manifestations.

Chapter 1 examines nineteenth-century Brazilian author Bernardo Guimarães's classic antislavery novel *A Escrava Isaura: Romance* (1875) and its widely successful twentieth-century televisual adaptation, the 1976 eponymous telenovela, as a fascinating kitsch use of slavery's memory. This popular culture product continues to travel globally in translation and exports an uncommon narrative of slavery that centers the harrowing life and freedom pursuits of a *quase branca* (nearly white) enslaved woman deemed exceptional. Revisiting the famous "Retirantes" telenovela theme song and iconic Jean-Baptiste Debret lithographs of imperial Brazil as paratextual framing, I address the scopic economies that render Isaura, and enslaved women more broadly, perpetually vulnerable to physical and sexual abuse, always subject to public and private punishments. The chapter then focuses on the specific ways in which the Romantic conventions of the pre-emancipation text index slave status through skin color difference, language, culture, education, and manners. The pernicious mechanisms of patriarchy, racism, and sexism are grandly spectacularized in the telenovela, a century later. Emphasizing Isaura's near whiteness as the locus of the tragedy of her enslavement in fact undermines the abolitionist purpose of both works by denouncing slavery only for those who, like Isaura, contravene beliefs that naturalize the connection between blackness and bondage.

In chapter 2, I discuss monumentality, memorialization, and the stakes of a seemingly irrepressible cultural investment in creating and circulating new textual and sculptural permutations of the mythic Mammy figure. I analyze Kara Walker's 2014 *A Subtlety,* the ephemeral Mammy-sphinx sugar-coated installation at the now defunct Domino Sugar Refinery, looking at this artwork as a stunning twenty-first-century rejoinder to the infamous 1923 US congressional proposal to erect a statue in honor of the generations of "faithful, colored southern Mammies" on the National Mall. The early twentieth-century nostalgic recollections of Mammy in the congressional record and the defense of Mammy's children against racial violence, found in the African American press, constitute an instructive dialogic pair. The chapter then shifts to representations of the Mammy figure in fiction, reading a striking scene involving naming, identity, and misrecognition in Sherley Anne Williams's contemporary narrative of slavery, *Dessa Rose* (1986), and George S. Schuyler's 1931 satirical novel, *Black No More,* which parodies the embeddedeness of white supremacist thinking and extreme attempts to contain and control the imaginative Mammy figure.

The third chapter addresses routinized racial violence, and specifically the vicious US lynching ritual, in African American literature as a brutal extension of slavery's legacy in the contemporary period. Drawing on Saidiya Hartman's theory of emancipation as a "nonevent," I engage texts representing the Black cultural afterlife of slavery. Using Billie Holiday's performance of "Strange Fruit" as a point of departure, I consider the intersection of racial terror, public spectacle, and the photographic image that emerge in a study of the 1930 lynching of Thomas Shipp and Abram Smith in Marion, Indiana. Next, I read Jean Toomer's "Kabnis" and "Portrait in Georgia" in *Cane* (1923) to address slavery's memory as tied to southern geographies and organic substances such as sugar and cotton. The chapter closes with a close formal analysis of the poetic strategies in Robert Hayden's epic poem "Middle Passage" (1962, 1966).

Opening with an examination of Pelourinho, in Salvador da Bahia, Brazil, as both an officially designated UNESCO World Heritage space and former site of the pillory, chapter 4 provides a close textual analysis of nineteenth-century Romantic poet Castro Alves's canonical "O navio negreiro" from *Os Escravos* (1883). I turn to a constellation of genres of slavery, including shorter readings of poetry by Francisco Alvim and Afro-Brazilian women Esmeralda Ribeiro and Alzira Rufino, to explore the significance of an Afro-Brazilian poetic movement. Carolina Maria de Jesus's remarkable diary of favela life, *Quarto de Despejo* (1960), evidences writing as liberatory practice. The chapter ends with Dudda Seixas's *Mãe África Pai Brasil* (2007) and interprets the African diaspora through the lens of familial, national, and transnational kinship. Bringing together disparate genres, I consider how these selected Brazilian narratives of slavery have evolved over time in ways that persistently challenge Gilberto Freyre's myth of racial democracy.

The final chapter returns to a discussion of sugar as an enduring link to slavery in Cuba, a slave sugarocracy. Music legend Celia Cruz's "Azúcar!" incantation and its multilayered resonances function as a clarion call, connecting slavery's past of commodification and forced labor with the popular culture present. Fernando Ortiz's personification of the sugar refinement process in his classic *Contrapunteo cubano del tabaco y el azúcar* provides illuminating context for close readings of two well-known Cuban slave narratives, separated by more than a century—Juan Francisco Manzano's *Autobiografía de un esclavo* (1839) and Esteban Montejo's narrative, *Cimarrón: Historia de un esclavo* (1966), recorded by writer Miguel Barnet—to consider how questions around authorship, memory, omission, mediation, censorship, fabrication, silence, and self-abolition figure prominently in these testimonials of enslavement.

As Irele argues, literature "communicates a structure of feeling" and "also reflects a climate of thought" (*African Imagination* xviii). This idea of literature at once conveying a structure of feeling and a climate of thought animates my readings of texts from the canonical to the kitsch in *Afrodiasporic Forms* as I argue for the enduring significance of affect. If we banish or disregard structures of feeling from our experience of reading and interpreting literature from the monde noir—specifically, the literature examined here, which delves into the variegated forms and textual engagements with slavery—then we have lost that which makes us human. James Baldwin famously cautions against the "wet eyes" of sentimentality, which he characterizes as "the ostentatious parading of excessive and spurious emotion" and "the mark of dishonesty, the inability to feel" (14). Saidiya Hartman's similar exhortation against the "precariousness of empathy" in *Scenes of Subjection* warns against a kind of voyeuristic complicity in Black suffering that often leads to inaction (4).

Heeding these important warnings, I am not suggesting that we, as readers, abandon ourselves to maudlin expressions or mawkish romanticism as we embark on what Evie Shockley in *a half-red sea* calls "dreaming the lives of the ancestors" (4), nor am I prescribing a uniform reader response. Rather, I am questioning a scholarly practice of distant reading necessitated by a cool critical remove that renders the efflorescent imaginative literature of slavery's era and afterlife, and the historical reality of the embodied experiences of those enslaved Africans symbolized by that patchwork of scars, as mere literary devices, or that reduces the African people listed on slave trade ledgers and bills of sale to arithmetic abstractions. Although we cannot lay claim to a definitive conceptualization of the African diaspora or the poetics of the monde noir as cohesive, immutable, or stable, by studying disparate genres of slavery, might we, rather than presuming a sentimental, white audience, consider the surprising and instructive interactions when bringing these diasporic texts together in conversation with one another? This is a risky comparative procedure, as reading the genres and forms of the African diaspora induces the sensation of "traveling through fog," to use Hayden's poetic image from the first epigraph. In *Afrodiasporic Forms,* I offer "close readings" in this sense and, I hope, a place for feeling, witnessing, and thinking that compels us to act.

1

WHITE SKIN, BLACK SLAVERY

Bernardo Guimarães's *A Escrava Isaura* and the Global Telenovela

A escrava negra de maior sucesso da tevê brasileira era branca.
[The most successful enslaved black woman on Brazilian TV was white.]

—JOEL ZITO ARAÚJO, *A negação do Brasil: O negro na telenovela brasileira*

Broadcast weekly at six o'clock in the evening between October 11, 1976, and February 5, 1977, the first televised serial drama inspired by Bernardo Guimarães's classic nineteenth-century abolitionist romance *A Escrava Isaura* (1875)[1] exploded onto the telenovela scene in Brazil.[2] Produced by the largest Brazilian television network, Rede Globo, this famous telenovela, which novelist Gilberto Braga adapted from the original text, rapidly gained international success, eventually being exported to more than 120 countries in condensed format, starting with Italy in 1982 as *La Schiava Isaura,* and later including Cuba (1984), as the immensely popular Spanish language version, *La esclava Isaura,* Poland (1985), China (1985),[3] and the Soviet Union (1989). It also was overdubbed in multiple languages, including Galician, earning it the title of the "most dubbed program in the history of world television."[4] Scholars of the telenovela genre note that Fidel Castro rearranged his meetings and conference schedules around the show's broadcasts.[5]

By 2005, it was estimated that approximately 2 billion people worldwide regularly watched telenovelas. As globally circulating cultural products exporting national myths abroad, the telenovela represents a televisual contact zone of interweaving languages, dialects, translations, subtitles, and colliding cultural contexts. The dispersal of Latin American narratives abroad via telenovelas, as Ibsen Martínez argues, was a phenomenon of "reverse cultural imperialism" or, simply put, "Montezuma's Revenge" (49).[6]

However, other telenovela scholars, such as Jesús Martín-Barbero, Michèle Mattelart, and Ana M. Lopez, have resisted correlating international telenovela commercial success with an indication of shifting hegemonic powers. For these scholars, the viewing experience highlights the process of mediation between production and reception.[7] This echoes Harold Hinds's sentiment that "through consumption consumers are themselves partially responsible for creating the cultural context within which future popular texts are produced."[8] The producers of the televised fiction craft narratives to meet the demands of the consumers, sprinkling a dash of exoticism over a narrative that presents the universal themes of loss, love, betrayal, personal maturation, and most often, the rags-to-riches story, through an unexpected windfall like the discovery of an unknown inheritance or marriage providing social mobility as a fringe benefit.[9]

The telenovela, then, enacts persistent questions often posed about world literature, and fundamental to literary study, recast in a popular culture context: How do we communicate in the age of globalization? What languages might we use? What is lost in the process of translation (as telenovelas often are two or three levels removed from the original language and cultural context through layers of overdubbing and subtitles)?[10] In what ways do these translations tell the viewer more about the country of the translator than the country and cultural context of the original production? And what histories are obscured in the renarrativizing of an epic interracial telenovela, itself a twentieth-century televisual translation of a nineteenth-century romance of slavery?

The transnational impact of Latin American telenovelas, a medium that is kitsch by design, reconfigures these puzzling theoretical questions in the accessible language of popular culture, circulating, to borrow David Damrosch's definition of world literature, "a mode of reading, a detached engagement with a world beyond our own" (297). The mass-media phenomenon of *A Escrava Isaura* introduced global audiences to a world beyond their own, however detached and mediated the engagement may have been. Telenovela scholars Antonio C. La Pastina and Joseph D. Straubhaar argue that cultural proximity, similar cultural-linguistic markets, and the creation of subgenres may account for the booming transnational exportation of televised serial fiction (271–273). Paula Halperin posits, "The authoritarian state created a vast array of agencies in an attempt to secure control of the production of the symbolic and to reinvent a Brazil that suited their modernizing aspirations" (165).

Reading two divergent Afrodiasporic forms over and against each other—

Bernardo Guimarães's pre-emancipation Romantic novella, *A Escrava Isaura,* and the popular culture televisual product reconfigured for a global mass entertainment market in the 1970s—I am most fascinated by the enduring cultural capital of this particular representation of Brazilian slavery and the resounding worldwide success of this telenovela, which adapts Guimarães's plot of the beautiful, nearly white slave ultimately thwarting the sexual advances of her despicable master by finding love and independence through marriage to another white man. This narrative choice is even more intriguing given the scale of slavery's era in Brazil, where slavery was not abolished until 1888, where close to 40 percent of enslaved Africans were transported, and where slavery's indelible imprint on the cultural, spiritual, and material life of Brazil is widely acknowledged (Reis and Gomes 9).[11]

The topos of markets and global currencies intersect with the economic imperatives of world circulation, doubling the geopolitical economic engine of transatlantic slavery, to expose how multiple generic and scopic economies of enslavement function globally.[12] The question of why various televisual iterations of the Isaura narrative continue to be such a profitable commodity of the entertainment industry prompts a discussion of the extent to which Guimarães, and later the producers of the telenovela, remain deeply invested in exporting a certain memory of Brazilian slavery and crafting a triumphalist narrative of liberation while also generating a major profit. The complex narratological stakes emerge when we consider, for example, that the military dictatorship mandated a major revision to the script.[13] At some point during filming, Gilberto Braga was prohibited from using the word *escravo* (slave) and instead replaced it with the word *peça* (piece), which signifies a unit of value used for quantifying Africans held captive during the slave trade. Rather than silencing the global economies of slavery, this script change in fact emphasizes the linguistic, social, cultural, and economic reduction of African-descended people to property within the slavocracy, and the racial capitalist making of the modern world.

In this chapter, I probe the immensely popular 1976 telenovela and closely read the contours of Guimarães's 1875 romance to explore why this historical fiction of racialized slavery in Brazil, and its most iconic televisual adaptation, continue to captivate an international viewing public. In this analysis, I consider the scopic economies that operate in Guimarães's original novella and their translation into a kitsch filmic representation of slavery to expose how the sexual vulnerability and exploitation of the enslaved woman and the hypervisibility of her body are imbricated in long-held beliefs about slavery and skin color, corporeal difference, class, education, and family lineage.

Global audiences maintain a collective memory of this 1970s televised drama, and Brazilian and worldwide viewers feel *saudade* (melancholic nostalgia, or a yearning for that which may not return) for this enthralling story of the enslaved nearly white woman and the masterful cast of actors.[14] Many remain familiar with the actors, the unforgettable "lerê lerê" chant of Dorival Caymmi's "Retirantes" soundtrack, and the famous Jean-Baptiste Debret images from his three-volume *Voyage Pittoresque et Historique au Brésil* (1834–1839), cycling in the opening title sequence.[15] Isaura's name, for many, alternately exemplifies the dominant narrative of the experience of the enslaved woman in Brazil, the rags-to-riches fairy tale of a beautiful princess who evades the evil master to enjoy eternal love with her prince, and the advocacy work of abolitionists. So enshrined was her name in the Brazilian popular imagination by the first third of the twentieth century that modernist poet, musicologist, and essayist Mário de Andrade (1893–1945) ironically titled his critical study of modernist poetics in Brazil *A Escrava que não é Isaura: Discurso sobre algumas tendências da poesia modernista,* composed in 1922 but not published until 1925.

Just as Mário de Andrade deploys the name Isaura to counter the sentimentality of Guimarães's text and frame his critical treatise on the Brazilian modernist tradition, using the metaphor of the enslaved woman to discuss poetics, contemporary authors have seized the narrative yet again to create sardonic parodies and gory spinoffs. The latest popular iteration of this famous story that looms so large in the Brazilian and global consciousness is Jovane Nunes's 2010 fiction *Escrava Isaura e o Vampiro* [Isaura the Slave and the Vampire], which rewrites Guimarães's classic, adding horror and a humoristic twist in the fashion of the literary mash-up of a classic plot. Kitsch begets more kitsch in these pop reconstructions, which are "um tipo de renovação pouco ortodoxa de grandes clássicos, inspiraram versões brasileiras que se apóiam em cânones da nossa literatura e acabam de chegar às prateleiras" (a type of unorthodox renovation of great classics [the literary mash-up], inspired Brazilian versions that depended on canonized works from our literature and just arrived on the shelves).[16]

In Nunes's version, part of a special series called "Coleção Clássicos Fantásticos" [Fantastic Classics Collection], he draws from the wildly popular (especially among adolescents and young adults) cast of undead characters—vampires, zombies, and werewolves—and interweaves them with sensational plotlines and references to Brazilian popular culture, politics, and social critique to reconstruct the evil Leôncio as a vampire (who was actually turned into a vampire by Count Dracula while he was studying law in Europe), who not only lays claim to Isaura as one of his properties as a slave owner but also wants to suck her blood. Nunes plays with the conventions of Brazilian Romanticism, the Gothic genre, and vampire literature in his literary hybrid and challenges the notion of a classic by deconstructing and then reconstructing it with bizarre, disparate literary parts. He even credits Guimarães with coauthorship, listing the famous writer's name first in bold letters with his own name in smaller letters underneath.

This text falls into the camp of "weirdo noir" uses of the memory of slavery. Using these textual and paratextual devices, Nunes at once troubles the notion of fixed literary value and relies on the authorial name recognition of Guimarães and the cultural capital of Isaura to turn a profit. The incorporation of the nineteenth-century narrative of Isaura into the twenty-first-century reawakening of vampire literature evidences the possibilities of stitching together texts, genres, and styles while simultaneously rejecting categorical distinctions between "high" and "low" art.[17] The trajectory of the shifting *Escrava Isaura* narrative, from the work of Guimarães (political propaganda) to that of Herval Rossano/Gilberto Braga (telenovela) to that of Jovane Nunes (satirical literary mash-up), demonstrates how slavery recedes into a minor subplot or a superficial literary backdrop by the twenty-first century, revealing the new economies of slavery. Now, the trade of marketable stories about slavery for entertainment displaces the trade of Africans. On a larger scale, Nunes's incorporation of the Isaura narrative into a gore tale and vice versa discloses the new historicist notion of "culture under capital."[18] Producing work in the age of capitalism, with the existing market imperatives of the publishing industry, compels artists to adapt the form and content of their work to maximize its profitability, affecting cultural production and the ways in which the public engages with the memory of slavery.

Within global media, the telenovela emerged as an exceedingly marketable cultural export; it is constantly being remade and rewritten. Before the enormously popular 1970s version, at least two films from the first half of the twentieth century were released. The first cinematic version was the Antônio Marques Costa Filho–directed silent film, released in 1929, followed by another film in 1949, directed by Eurides Ramos, with Robert Stam suggesting the existence of a third feature-length film in some sources (77). In 2004, Rede Record debuted the most recent telenovela remake. Although the same director, Herval Rossano, directed both the 1976 and 2004 versions for TV Globo, the 1970s version remains the fan favorite and cult classic.

With international revenue streams stretching to Asia, Africa, and Eastern Europe, the commercial success of *A Escrava Isaura* signals that slavery still sells. Arguably the most popular telenovela to date in world television history, the enthusiastic reception of the 1976 version, broadcast a year before the classic miniseries based on Alex Haley's *Roots* appeared on television in the United States, raises a crucial question: What is it about *this* fictional narrative of slavery, and this particular representation of an enslaved woman, that continues to captivate a global viewing public?

SCRUTINIZING THE SOURCE TEXT: GUIMARÃES'S NINETEENTH-CENTURY VISION OF ISAURA

Melodrama connects the literary vision of Guimarães's original romance with the eponymous telenovela, the plot and action in both genres operating within the scopic economies of enslavement. A premier writer in the Brazilian Romanticism movement, Bernardo Joaquim da Silva Guimarães (1825–1884) produced both poetry and prose.[19] I turn now to narrative features of the text to set the stage for an understanding of the ways in which the optical register, kitsch, and narratology cohere to produce a captivating export. Scholar Norwood Andrews classifies *A Escrava Isaura* (1875) and *Rosaura, A Enjeitada* (1883) as Guimarães's two "polemics."[20] While Andrews considers the text "a good pamphlet and no novel at all except superficially" (237), Antonio Cândido and Raymond S. Sayers similarly designate *A Escrava Isaura* an abolitionist text that exposes the atrocities of slavery and finds an eager audience during the height of the Brazilian abolitionist movement of the 1870s.[21]

A common critique, however, is the romance's inconsistent setting: "Obra predominantemente de imaginação, dela está ausente o cuidado regionalista de fixar a ambiência física e social em que se desenrola a ação dramática" (Predominantly an imaginative work, absent from it is the regionalist care to establish the physical and social environment in which the dramatic action unfolds) (Paes and Moisés 182). Wilson Martins echoes this critique of the unfounded flights of imagination and lack of Aristotelian unity of place and a fixed "physical and social environment," offering an even harsher appraisal of the novel's shortcomings: "*A Escrava Isaura* é o exemplo, talvez único na literatura mundial, de um romance em que *todos* os dados são inverossímeis, para nada dizer do estilo, que é pobre, rasteiro e declamatório" (*A Escrava Isaura* is an example, perhaps unique in world literature, of a novel in which *all* of the data lack verisimilitude, to say nothing of the style, which is poor, crawling, and bombastic) (484). This lack of verisimilitude, Martins charges, strips the novel of any persuasive qualities.

I would counter, however, that it is not the inconsistent setting, absence of realism, or flawed dramatic structure that weakens the text, but rather the troubling ways in which it reaffirms racialized and racist justifications of slavery even in its attempt at abolitionist propaganda. Writing in 1875, Guimarães employs a conservative thematic approach, and as Giorgio Marotti has pointed out, has the abolitionist character Álvaro abide by the legal practices of the time and liberate Isaura only through her purchase, thereby reinforcing the property status of enslaved people undergirding the slavocratic regime (34). Yet, for the twenty-first-century reader, the most frustrating narrative limitation is perhaps its failure to provide a unilateral denunciation of slavery. If one probes beneath its abolitionist veneer and condemnation of Isaura's enslaved condition, one finds only feeble attacks on the larger institution of slavery.

The text employs melodramatic plotlines and Romantic conventions to present an antislavery narrative using the common motifs of obscure family origins, miscegenation, passing, and tragedy. The opening line introduces the omniscient third-person narrator—"Era nos primeiros anos do reino do D. Pedro II" (It was during the first years of the reign of Don Pedro II)—and historically situates the drama during the reign of this second emperor of Brazil, two decades after independence from Portugal in 1822. Martins cites this temporal staging as "um anacronismo absoluto entre os personagens 'bons' e o tempo em que viviam" (an absolute anachronism between the "good" character and the time in which they live) and the existence of the character Álvaro, a staunch abolitionist willing to sacrifice his wealth and high social status to marry an enslaved woman, as inconceivable in 1840, a period during which Brazil was still a bustling slave economy (483). Perhaps this obvious anachronism is only permissible in the revisionist historical fantasyland of telenovelas to enhance emotional impact.

A practical reason for Guimarães's anachronistic historical setting may have been the shifting laws around slavery. It is important to note that, had the narrative taken place thirty years later, the story would be altered by the passage of the Lei do Rio Branco (Law of the Free Womb) in 1871, one of the first liberatory laws on the gradual road to final emancipation in 1888, which granted freedom at the age of twenty-one to the children born of enslaved mothers (Callaway). Legal ambiguity would have supplanted the racial ambiguity of the narrative, as Isaura would have occupied the status of an *ingênuo* until she came of age, living in the boundary between slavery and freedom, in many ways not unlike the melodrama constructed around Isaura's liminality (racial, social, and cultural) depicted in the novel.

Both the novel and the telenovela present the following basic narrative arc: a beautiful white-presenting, mixed-race enslaved woman laboring within a domestic setting receives an elite education far beyond her station as a captive, which essentially renders her a social misfit, vunerable to the quotidian threats of sexual assault of her villainous master, Leôncio. The caring and wealthy abolitionist, Álvaro, eventually falls in love with and "rescues" her, even after finding out she is a fugitive from slavery. Because she was born previous to the Law of the Free Womb, Isaura inherits her slave status through maternal descent, and her "African blood" represents an invisible blot precluding the life of a free (white) woman, which the narrator convinces the reader she rightfully deserves, by virtue of her beauty and talent as an "*escrava especial.*"

Scholars Martins, Marotti, and Bosi associate Isaura's phenotypic whiteness with the implausibility of her enslaved condition, maintaining the same logics of slavery advanced in the novel one hundred years earlier. Martins, for example, offers a racialized interpretation of the novel's main flaw: "Contudo, o romance não poderia existir se Isaura fosse realmente escrava, isto é, uma negra analfabeta e primitiva, brutalizada pelo trabalho e certamente divergente dos padrões ocidentais de beleza" (However, the novel would not exist if Isaura were really a slave, that is, a primitive and illiterate black woman, brutalized by work and certainly divergent from Western standards of beauty) (483). Martins's proclamation that Isaura is not really a slave foreshadows the questions later posed about the casting of Isaura in the telenovela, and particularly about what an enslaved woman should look like. By equating a "real" slave with being *negra,* or a Black woman who is illiterate, primitive, a victim of the brutalities of work and unattractive by Western standards, Martins not only highlights certain stereotypes about the appearance and condition of an "authentic" enslaved woman but also seemingly reaffirms beliefs that naturalize the connection between Black skin and slavery.

As the casting controversy of the telenovela also reflected, Isaura's beauty derives from her white skin, or, as Alfredo Bosi remarks, "Toda a beleza da escrava é posta no seu não parecer negra, mas nívea donzela" (All of the beauty of the enslaved girl is placed in her not appearing like a black woman, but a snowy-haired damsel) (143–144). It is precisely this "não parecer negra" (not appearing black) and veneration of the white-skinned slave that makes Isaura such a complicated figure to carry the abolitionist mantle. Reaching a similar conclusion to Martins's regarding the popularity of the text, Marotti calls her the "nonslave slave" who is "similar in every aspect to any white young lady of the time, whose freedom of action was very much limited by her father and brothers' will and who was often compelled to marry an old and disagreeable husband" (29–38). Focusing on the axis of gender, *A Escrava Isaura* serves as a cautionary tale, for women of all colors, about the perpetual vulnerability of her body to sexual abuse and about the danger of being an orphaned child.

The pastoral setting of the *fazenda* (a farm estate with enslaved laborers, analogous to the space of the plantation) in Campos dos Goitacazes in Rio de Janeiro establishes sharp spatial contrasts: the rigors of slavery for those enslaved people working inside the masters' house versus those outside the house and living in the *senzala* (slave quarters). The reader encounters the first description of Isaura's physical beauty as she is playing the piano and singing melodiously in the opening scene:

> Acha-se ali sozinha e sentada ao piano uma bela e nobre figura de moça. As linhas do perfil desenham-se distintamente entre o ébano da caixa do piano, e as bastas madeixas ainda mais negras do que ele. São tão puras e suaves essas linhas, que fascinam os olhos, enlevam a mente, e paralisam toda analise. A tez é como o marfim do teclado, alva que não deslumbra, embaçada por uma nuança delicada, que não sabereis dizer se é leve palidez ou cor-de-rosa desmaiada. . . . Na fronte calma e lisa como mármore polido, a luz do ocaso esbatia um róseo e suave reflexo; di-la-íeis misteriosa lâmpada de alabastro guardando no seio diáfano o fogo celeste da inspiração.
>
> [One finds there alone and seated at the piano the beautiful and noble figure of a young girl. The lines of her profile take shape distinctly between the ebony of the case of the piano, and her tresses of hair even blacker than it. So pure and smooth are these lines that they intrigue the eyes, enrapture the mind, and paralyze total analysis. Her skin color is like the ivory of the keyboard, daylight that does not dazzle, darkened by a delicate nuance, that one is unable to call a light pallor or faint pink. . . . On her brow calm and smooth like polished mar-

ble, the light of sunset casts a blushing and soft reflection; mysterious lamp of alabaster guarding on her delicate breast the celestial fire of inspiration.] (8–9)

As the omniscient narrator describes her extraordinary beauty, the reader is complicit in the voyeuristic act of spying on the young woman who sits *sozinha* (alone) at the piano. The hyperbolic language of this passage describes her beauty using familiar Black–white conceits of interracial literature: her skin, which seems to be sculpted out of marble, is like the ivory of the keyboard and contrasts dazzlingly with the ebony of the piano. Cloaked in an understated style of dress, Isaura is an idealized vision of elegant repose. She is completely good while the predatory and wholly evil Leôncio exercises, as Cristina Helena Carneiro argues, "um duplo poder sobre Isaura" (a double power over Isaura) as both "o patriarca e também o colonizador" (the patriarch and also the colonizer) (7). Guimarães employs allegory to paint an unambiguous morality tale about the innocent young enslaved woman and the sinister enslaver to denounce the institution of slavery while also exposing its patriarchal, sexist, classist, and imperialist underpinnings.

There is an important moment when Isaura laments the inextricable burden that is manifested in the incommensurability of her nearly white skin and her condition as a captive, which renders her a target in the various spaces of the *fazenda:*

> Ah! meu Deus!—pensava ela; nem aqui posso achar um pouco de sossego! . . . em toda parte juraram martirizar-me! . . . Na sala, os brancos me perseguem e armam mil intrigas e enredos para me atormentarem. Aqui, onde entre minhas parceiras, que parecem me querer bem, esperava ficar mais tranqüila, há uma, que por inveja, ou seja lá pelo que for, me olha de revés e só trata de achincalhar-me. Meu Deus! meu Deus! . . . já que tive a desgraça de nascer cativa, não era melhor que tivesse nascido bruta e disforme, como a mais vil das negras, do que ter recebido de céu estes dotes, que só servem para amargurar-me a existência?
>
> [Oh! my God!, she thought. Not even here can I find a little peace! . . . Everywhere they pledge to martyr me! . . . In the living room, the whites pursue me and set up a thousand intrigues and plots to torment me. Here, where I am among my partners, who seem to love me well, I hoped to be calmer, there is one who, because of envy, or who knows what, looks at me upside down and only tries to ridicule me. My God! My God! . . . since I already had the disgrace of being born

> captive, wouldn't it have been better to have been born brute and disfigured, like the most vile of Black women, than to have received from heaven these riches, which only serve to make me resentful of my existence?] (32)

For all her self-abnegation, this glimpse into Isaura's interiority indicates that she holds herself in high esteem (or at least believes that she deserves better treatment) and indeed imagines herself set apart from the "mais vil das negras" (most vile of the Black women). In effect, she believes in the fiction of her exemplarity and laments the impossibility of living between the Black and white worlds, the light tasks of the domestic place and the arduous work outside the *casa-grande* (big house), the world of slavery and the world of freedom, luxury, and the possibility of finding love. This proclamation stands out, too, as a singular glimpse into Isaura's subjectivity as she remains relatively passive and silent in the text (in comparison to the telenovela). Her reticence underscores her status as an object; men make decisions *for* and *about* her.

THE MARKED BODY: UM PEQUENO SINAL PRETO (A LITTLE BLACK SIGN)

Perhaps the most salient theme of the novel is the logic of racial surveillance, which reveals the scopic economies of enslavement. Just as the third-person narrator and the reader are complicit in this constant watching of Isaura, beginning with spying on her playing the piano in the opening scene, the constant observation intensifies when Isaura passes for white. In another quirky anachronism, Guimarães has these characters flee north in what some critics have called a *navio negreiro* (slave ship). As Raymond Sayers argues, Isaura's climactic flight from Minas to Recife mirrors Eliza's flight in Harriet Beecher Stowe's *Uncle Tom's Cabin* (316–317). Even though they have secluded themselves in a faraway cottage on the outskirts of the town in Recife, Isaura and her father live with an intense fear of discovery. The greedy opportunist, Martinho, recognizes her as the slave described in a wanted reward poster:

> Fugiu da fazenda do Sr. Leôncio Gomes da Fonseca, no município de Campos, província do Rio de Janeiro, uma escrava por nome Isaura, cujos sinais são os seguintes: Cor clara e tez delicada como de qualquer branca; olhos pretos e grandes; cabelos da mesma cor, compridos e ligeiramente ondeados; boca pequena, rosada e bem-feita; dentes alvos e bem dispostos; nariz saliente e bem

talhado; cintura delgada, talhe esbelto, e estatura regular; tem na face esquerda *um pequeno sinal preto,* e acima do seio direito *um sinal de queimadura,* mui semelhante a uma asa de borboleta.

Traja-se com gosto e elegância, canta e toca piano com perfeição. Como teve excelente educação e tem uma boa figura, pode passar em qualquer parte por uma senhora livre e de boa sociedade. Fugiu em companhia de um português, por nome Miguel, que se diz seu pai. É natural que tenham mudado o nome. Quem a apreender, e levar ao dito seu senhor, alem de se lhe satisfazerem todas as despesas, receberá a gratificação de 5:000$000.

[Fled from the fazenda of Mr. Leôncio Gomes da Fonseca, in the township of Campos, province of Rio de Janeiro, a female slave by the name of Isaura, whose signs are the following: Clear color and delicate skin like any white woman; large black eyes, hair the same color, long and slightly wavy; small mouth, rosy and shapely; teeth white and straight; nose prominent and well-shaped; thin waist, svelte figure, and standard height; she has on the left side of her face *a little black sign,* and on her right breast *a burn mark,* very similar to the wing of a butterfly.

She dresses with taste and elegance, she sings and plays the piano with perfection. Since she has excellent education and a nice figure, she could pass in any parts for a free *senhora* of high society. She fled in the company of a Portuguese man, by the name of Miguel, who says he is her father. It is natural that they have changed their names. Whichever person finds and returns her to said *senhor,* will receive a reward of 5 million réis.] (59; emphasis added)

Ironically, Leôncio, and all the other men and women who gaze upon her, fall captive to Isaura's extraordinary beauty. Even Martinho's companions doubt that the description he reads to them corresponds to a fugitive slave and not "o retrato de Vênus" (the portrait of Venus). This comparison of Isaura to Venus repeats the analogy employed in her first physical description, in which the narrator likens her melodic singing at the piano in her simple attire to "Vênus nascendo da espuma do mar, ou como um anjo surgindo dentre brumas vaporosas" (like the birth of Venus from the foam of the sea, or like an angel arising amongst vaporous fog) (9). To counter their disbelief, Martinho tells them "reparem naquela bonita moça . . . e vejam se não combinam perfeitamente os sinais?" (notice the beautiful young woman . . . and see if the signs do not match perfectly) (59). Upon looking at her, they are incredulous; one comments, "O céus! E possível que uma moça tão linda seja uma escrava!" (O heavens! It is possible that a young woman so beautiful be a slave!) (59). In the exchange between Martinho and his friends after he points out the "sinais pretos" (black signs), they exclaim:

"É assombroso! Quem diria, que debaixo daquela figura de anjo estaria oculta uma escrava fugida!" (It's amazing! Who could tell us, that beneath that figure of an angel there could be, veiled, a fugitive slave woman!)

"E também quem nos diz, que no corpo da escrava não se acha asilada uma alma de anjo?" (And also who tells us, that in that body of an enslaved woman one would not find a refugee, the soul of an angel?) (60)

The familiar chiastic structure of this dialogue—(*anjo* → *escrava*) and (*escrava* → *anjo*) and (*figura* → *alma*)—recalls Henry Louis Gates Jr.'s theory that chiasmus is "the central trope of the slave narrative, in which a slave-object writes himself or herself into a human-subject through the act of writing." He continues, "The overarching rhetorical strategy of the slave narratives written after 1845 can be represented as a chiasmus, as repetition and reversal" (*Signifying* 186). The difference here is that Isaura does not speak (or write) these words and therefore does not gain agency and subjectivity from this moment. Instead, the men watching her at the dance pronounce these words of reversal and repetition, in effect reinscribing her in the status of thing-object because she lacks the power to speak for herself. She remains a "figura" (figure) and a "corpo" (body) oscillating between the descriptors *anjo* (angel) and *escrava* (slave), circumscribed in the dehumanizing reduction of a person to property.

The multiple digressions of the nonlinear narrative only offer glimpses into the interiority of Isaura and the cast of characters surrounding her. The exclamatory surprise at Isaura's beauty, then, operates against cultural expectations about the appearance of an enslaved woman. The recurring motif of Isaura's beauty and nearly white skin, then, normalizes the formulation: Black skin = ugly = enslaved, whereas white skin = beauty = free. The onlookers are aghast not because they find the system of slavery repugnant but because Isaura's presence undercuts its prevailing racial and gendered logic. As Leôncio reveals in the announcement, Isaura "pode passar" (can pass) for white. Even when it seems the text is on the verge of decoupling the assumed natural connection between skin color and slavery, it recoils into the safety of the discourse of exemplarity and the conventions of the genre. Both men and women at the dance attempt to read race onto Isaura's seemingly unmarked body (that is, a body lacking a glaring signal of her few drops of "African blood") but find her white skin and slave status incomprehensible.

Yet there is the striking *pequeno sinal preto* (little black sign) and *sinal de queimadura* (burn mark) on her nearly white skin. These dark markers are the only features that differentiate her from "qualquer branca" (any white woman). In fact, the women at the party, jealous of Álvaro's attention to Isaura, criticize her simple style of dress, ironically commenting that "a minha mucama tem melhor gosto para se trajar" (my [enslaved] house girl has better taste in dressing), not knowing that Isaura has fled her position as a *mucama* after being banished to hard labor. These young women notice "aquele pinta negra, que tem na face" (that black spot she has on her face), which one woman says detracts from her beauty, while another says it gives her a "graça particular" (particular grace) (45). Divided on the question of Isaura's aesthetic appeal, they decide to *estudar* (study) her further throughout the evening. Even as the women scrutinize her almost white body, performing the quotidian scopic economies of slavery, Isaura's skin color negates the correlation between legible racial signifiers of blackness and enslavement while simultaneously revealing the fallacy of any binaristic racial calculus dividing branco (white) and negro (black) in Brazil, and in Latin America more broadly.

Interestingly, the telenovela only alludes to this singular corporeal detail of a dark patch of skin. In a moment of sexual aggression, Leôncio invades the privacy of Isaura's bedroom while she is dressed in her nightgown and touches this spot of hyperpigmentation on her breast, thereby touching her breast, too. Instead of the bluish tinge on the half-moon of her fingernail, which Werner Sollors has shown is the revelatory hallmark of the "tragic mulatto" narratives, Isaura's *sinais* (signs) seem to concentrate all evidence or proof of her "African blood" in one spot of hyperpigmentation on her otherwise nearly white skin. This little black sign, a symbolic drop of melanin, indexes racial difference in a pattern reminiscent of the "magpie" metaphor in Wolfram von Eschenbach's medieval epic knightly romance, *Parzival.*[22]

The burn mark, too, takes the shape of a lovely butterfly's wing, harking back to this notion of Isaura as angel, Venus, or ephemeral princess from a fairy tale. However, the narrative, even with all its digressions to provide backstory on various characters, never indicates the (possibly violent) source of Isaura's burned chest. Although Isaura combats the constant surveillance of her body through self-concealment, she ultimately blames herself for her condition of enslavement.

When Isaura finally speaks publicly, it is only to criminalize her self-protective action of fleeing. By situating herself as a criminal, she implicitly reinforces the legality of the enslaver's ownership claims to human beings detained as private property. Before this emotional scene, while at the dance, she privately expresses fear and guilt to her father about the so-called treason of her self-liberation:

> É um crime que cometo, envolvendo-me no meio de tão luzida sociedade; é uma traição, meu pai; eu o conheço, e sinto remorsos . . . Se estas nobres senhoras adivinhassem que ao lado delas diverte-se e dança uma miserável escrava fugida a seus senhores! . . . Escrava!—exclamou levantando-se—escrava! . . . afigura-se-me que *todos estão lendo, gravada em letras negras em minha fronte, esta sinistra palavra!* . . . fujamos daqui, meu pai, fujamos! esta sociedade parece estar escarnecendo de mim; este ar me sufoca . . . fujamos.
>
> [It is a crime that I commit, involving myself in the middle of such shining society; it is treason, my father; I know it, and I feel remorseful. . . . If these noble women guessed that at their side a miserable slave has fun and dances, fugitive from her masters! . . . Slave!, she exclaimed, raising up. Slave! . . . It appears to me that *everyone is reading, carved in black letters on my forehead, this sinister word!* . . . Let's flee from here, my father, let's flee! This society seems to be mocking me, this air suffocates me . . . let's flee.] (48; emphasis added)[23]

This candid view into Isaura's interiority rarely occurs in the novel. She is the silenced center around which all the action radiates. Furthermore, dialogue and third-person narration predominate the novel, so there is even less opportunity to discern Isaura's inner thoughts, or any other character's, for that matter. The melodramatic exclamation marks—"Escrava!"—foreshadow the seamless adaption of this text into the telenovela genre. Isaura's belief that everyone is reading the word *Escrava* engraved onto her forehead is reminiscent of Hester Prynne's moment of public humiliation when she stands on the pillory, baby Pearl in her arms, with the judgmental crowd gazing upon the ignominious scarlet letter *A* emblazoned on her breast.[24]

While Hester acquired her *A* through a purported "sinful" deed, Isaura, by contrast, acquired her marking by the chance of birth. After Martinho identifies the signs on Isaura's body as those of the fugitive slave, Isaura publicly confesses her identity. Here, Isaura speaks aloud to an audience, and she begins in the apologetic mode, stating that she should not speak. In one of the most melodramatic scenes of the novel, Isaura stands before the entire crowd at the party, where she has just impressed them with her dancing, and confesses all:

> —Não é preciso que me toquem,—exclamou com voz angustiada. —Meus senhores, e senhoras, perdão! cometi uma infâmia, uma indignidade imperdoável! . . . mas Deus me é testemunha, que uma cruel fatalidade a isso me levou. Senhores, o que esse homem diz, é verdade. Eu sou . . . uma escrava!
>
> ["It is not necessary to touch me," she exclaimed with an anguished voice. "Ladies and gentlemen, forgive me! I committed an infamy, an unpardonable indignity! . . . But as God is my witness, a cruel fatality drove me to this. Gentlemen, what this man says is true. I am . . . a slave!"] (64)

Here, *escrava* becomes a transformative word, even after Isaura announces her enslavement: "Alguns, a despeito da evidência dos indícios e da confissão de Isaura, ainda duvidavam da verdade que tinham diante dos olhos" (Some, despite the evidence of the traces and Isaura's confession, still doubted the truth that they had before their eyes) (64). But, one wonders, what is the "truth before their eyes"? Isaura's revelation at this spectacle of the high society dance, which incidentally Álvaro convinced Isaura and her father to attend because it is important to "ser vista" (be seen), dispels the presupposition that slavery registers itself on the body. Yet, as is the case throughout the novel, there is a disconnect for the viewers at the party who refuse to abandon the natural equation between Black skin and slave status, thereby undermining its abolitionist force.

The dénouement of the novel presents another commercial exchange. After Leôncio assigns a monetary value to Isaura's life in a fugitive slave announcement, reinscribing her in the transactional logics of enslavement, Isaura in effect exchanges one sexual master for another of her choosing. As a target of racialized sexual violence from libidinous men throughout the narrative, Isaura must find Álvaro a welcome replacement for Leôncio, because at least this relationship is based on love, the narrative suggests, and not force.[25] It seems doubtful, however, that Isaura could have rejected Álvaro in the last instant, after receiving her liberty. As Jenny Sharpe argues in *Ghosts of Slavery,* regarding the tactics of enslaved women in the eighteenth-century West Indian context, "the existence of sexual exploitation does not diminish the mobility black and racially mixed women were able to acquire for themselves within the coercive relations of slavery." One of these tactics includes "the ability to establish conjugal relationships with white men who were not their owners," which "allowed them to move out of the households to which they belonged" (44–45). Jessica Callaway notes, too, that the conclusion to Isaura's tale and her fate "is perhaps the least overtly 'tragic' of the characters who might be associated with [Sterling A.] Brown's concept [of the tragic mulatto stereotype]."[26]

While the reader may conclude initially that this is a happy ending for an enslaved mixed-race woman, one is reminded of Marotti's analysis of Isaura as the embodiment of the domestically incarcerated nineteenth-century white woman. There is a sense that marriage represents another sexual and spatial binding for women of this period, in which she is, as Carneiro argues, "duplamente colonizada" (doubly colonized), "escravizada pelo sistema e, ao mesmo tempo, pelos paramêtros da sociedade patriarcal" (enslaved by the system and, at the same time, by the parameters of the patriarchal society) (11).[27]

IS ISAURA A "TRAGIC MULATTO"?

Guimarães's concise novel transfers seamlessly to the conventions of the television serial. The nineteenth-century melodrama is a literary precursor to the exaggerated emotion of the telenovela genre, with the love story and marriage plot taking primacy over any political message. *A Escrava Isaura,* upon first inspection, seems to conform to one of the most popular melodramatic plotlines of nineteenth-century sentimental abolitionist literature: the narrative of the tragic mulatto.[28] As Sollors outlines in *Neither Black nor White yet Both,* a focus on ambiguous racial identity rather than the slave status of the child of an interracial union is a salient feature of the tragic mulatto figure (211). While the narrative does focus on the titular Isaura, the product of an interracial relationship, both the textual and telenovela Isaura complicate and depart from established conventions of this narrative stereotype in fascinating ways. Unlike the US origin of this stereotypical literary type, the Brazilian *mulata* figure, as Nubia Hanciau argues, possesses both positive and negative attributes. She is "exótica, bela, alegre, solidária, dotada de irresistível sensualidade, hábil cozinheira, com vocação para a música, a dança e o canto" (exotic, beautiful, happy, supportive, endowed with irresistible sensuality, skillful cook, with a vocation for music, dance, and singing) and possesses traits of a "mulher libertina" (licentious woman), characterized by "imoralidade" (immorality).[29] Giovana Xavier likewise contends that Isaura's "caráter e sua beleza representam o sucesso da fusão entre as raças branca e negra" (character and her beauty represent the success of the fusion between the black and white races), personifying, as a *boa mestiça* (good *mestiza*) the image of "Brasil em construção" (Brazil in construction) (92–94). A defining feature of brasilidade is in fact the triumph of *mestiçagem* (interracial relationships resulting in mixed-race children); thus, the *mulata* or *mestiça* would not be characterized as an inherently tragic figure but rather as a marker of burgeoning national identity.

In both versions, Isaura, though nearly white, is born into slavery because her deceased mother, a mixed-race woman herself, was enslaved. Isaura never knew her mother, who in both the telenovela and the original text dies after childbirth, during a flashback sequence, after being exiled from her domestic work as a *mucama* to the hard labor of the *senzala*—punishment for repeatedly refusing the sexual advances of the Comendador Almeida. She only later meets her working-class Portuguese father, Miguel, who was the *feitor* who loved her mother but was fired by Almeida after the latter learned of his relationship with Isaura's mother. Isaura is aware of their racial classification and social standing, and therefore she recognizes "o seu lugar" (her place). Furthermore, she does not experience a dramatic revelation of her racial background or attempt to conceal it for the sake of an advantageous marriage to a white suitor, nor does the protagonist seem to possess any of the stereotypical pathologies (madness, suicide, depression) of the doomed literary personage.[30] In Sollors's explication of the six elements that constitute Brown's tragic mulatto complex, he summarizes the defining features of the stereotype, which appear in the literature of a wide range of national traditions: "Conceived for white readers, these characters invite empathy because they are so much like whites and so little like blacks; the internal conflict they experience is explainable as a result of racial forces; therefore, no wonder white writers were far more eager to develop them" (*Neither Black nor White* 223–225).

Indeed, Isaura seems to occupy the space of the white characters more than of the Black ones—the enslaved laborers, field hands, the cook, and the cloth spinners who make up the large cast of supporting characters in the telenovela, though they play an even smaller role in the novel. The assertion holds that Isaura's near whiteness and exceptional beauty render her identifiable and "invite empathy" from the white nineteenth-century reader. In fact, her whiteness is never contested in either the novel or the 1976 telenovela. In the latter production, even her harsh owner, Comendador Almeida, and other characters (both Black and white) emphasize that she is "quase branca" (almost white).

Nor are her striking beauty and sophisticated attributes denied; she speaks French, Italian, and a little English and is a skillful pianist.

Where Isaura departs from the "Negro character type," however subtly, is in her relative reticence on the issue of her inherited Blackness in the telenovela. While Guimarães's text certainly conforms to the stereotype, making his Isaura utter a version of the quintessential tragic mulatto lamentation, the center of gravity of the telenovela deemphasizes this topos and foregrounds the plot of Isaura's sexual vulnerability and desire for true love. The televised version of Isaura expresses an angelic resignation to her slave status, minimizing the internal conflict caused by her fractional possession of "African blood," although this may be due to the lack of subjectivity given to the character and the creative direction of the series.

What we can infer from both Guimarães's text and the telenovela is that Isaura is tragic not because of internal or external conflict due to her racial liminality but because all those around her recognize her almost white status and superb education as antithetical to her slave status. Brazilian racial tabulations allow for more differentiation, with the census officially recognizing a difference between *preto* (Black) and *pardo* (brown).[31] In contrast to a tension stemming solely from "racial forces," Isaura's struggle in the television series derives in large part from the relentless sexual pursuit of Leôncio, her master's lascivious son, based on his claims of legal possession over her body as property. In a complex conundrum, Isaura's racial composition matters only to the extent that it is the source of her lamentable status as a slave.

The focal point of the drama and narrative tension, then, springs from the seeming oxymoron of her being both visibly white (exquisitely beautiful, no less) and in bondage. Thus, returning to the central question about the reason for the global popularity of *A Escrava Isaura,* it seems that, paradoxically, the most popular telenovela about slavery extols the beauty of its enslaved, phenotypically white protagonist, and it seems that it is commercially successful precisely because the protagonist is visibly white. This ironically circumvents an overt treatment of "Black themes" (beyond the enslaved Afro-Brazilians, like the cunning Rosa, jealous of Isaura's white beauty, who act as props in the background) in a globally circulating tale of modern racial slavery.[32]

While Guimarães's aim to write a widely popular abolitionist narrative in 1875 explains the use of the protagonist who shares, as Brown puts it, a "common humanity with whites,"[33] it is curious that in all the modifications and addenda Braga made to the original text, he did not alter this element, even nearly one hundred years later. This is not to suggest that the story of the nearly white enslaved woman should not be told or that the main protagonist of a slavery narrative ought to be discernibly Black or mixed race, but Guimarães's premise of Isaura's exceptionality due to her white skin not only makes her the anti–Black Is Beautiful heroine—in the moment of burgeoning racial pride for Blacks in Brazil in the late-1970s—but also implicitly reinforces the dangerous correlation between Black skin and slavery.[34]

Within the context of Guimarães's literary world and Braga's adapted script, Isaura's enslaved condition is tragic only because she is nearly white, not because slavery itself is deplorable. Of course, there are a few general lines denouncing slavery thrown into the telenovela for good measure, communicated mostly by Isaura's kindly mistress, Dona Ester (who is given quite a substantial role in the telenovela and makes a pet of Isaura, although she is unnamed and killed off rather quickly in the source text), the abolitionist Tobias, and lastly Álvaro, the man who ultimately rescues Isaura from her condition by buying, emancipating, and then marrying her (a triumphant marriage scene is depicted in the telenovela, with the picturesque, mostly Black ensemble cast encircling the happy couple). One can only hope that Álvaro does not renege on his promise and abandon Isaura in the life after the text, as is often the case in the tragic mulatto plot. These critical anxieties around race—Isaura's blackness or lack thereof—rekindle questions about the appearance of an enslaved person and the legibility of the enslaved status, and problematize the memory of slavery deemed "representative" and worthy of retelling to the world.

Yet this question of the "representative" enslaved woman is a complex one. Sollors argues that "'mulatto identity' has often been considered as a (not representative) part of 'black identity,' mixed-race self-images have in many cases been 'themed away' . . . making *any* representation of biracial characters appear to be 'unrealistic' and potentially dangerous heterostereotypes."[35] Following this observation, if literary critics such as Brown and J. H. Nelson deemed biracial characters "unrealistic" and not representative of an "authentic" Black experience—only selected because they arouse pity, sympathy, and serve as a point of identification for the (white) readers—then does not their line of argument implicitly reinforce essentialist notions of Black identity? For the purposes of this discussion, perhaps the more compelling question is not why Isaura is a white-skinned, mixed-race enslaved woman played by a white actress in the telenovela but rather why she should *not* be. One cannot help but speculate about the commercial viability of a reimagined *A Escrava Isaura* with the title character praised for the beauty of her Black skin and African heritage.

It is clear that race plays a significant role in the kitsch arts of slavery; the two cannot easily be disentangled in a study of the commercial success of this telenovela. The element of race, from interracial mixing to the casting of the actors, is doubly complicated in the production of this drama. Isaura's racial classification reveals itself through her mother, a "*mulata clara*" in the telenovela and a "*linda mulata*" in Guimarães's text (12). Thus, the reader can assume that she only possesses one-fourth "African blood," positioning her in the subgenre of "quadroon" narratives of the interracial literature genre.[36]

Both versions of the narrative adopt a common motif of this genre: the mixed-race protagonist, though mostly white, maintains some telltale sign on her body belying her African heritage. Unlike the recurring "fingernail motif," in which the only vestige of a mixed-race character's tiny drop of "Black blood" is found in a slightly darker hue in the half-moon shape of the nail bed,[37] Isaura's markings appear as small, dark-colored birthmarks (one on her left breast and another on the side of her face) and are tied up with the scopic economies—the connection between sexuality and surveillance—in both the text and its most famous television adaptation. Isaura's ancestry further complicates the question of mixed-race representation on film.

"DESIGN IN MOVEMENT": DEBRET'S LITHOGRAPHS AND "RETIRANTES" IN A ESCRAVA ISAURA TITLE SEQUENCE

The general cultural and theoretical context of the hugely popular 1976 telenovela set the stage to explore the salient discursive features—both in form and content—from which the intriguing phenomenon of its popularity and international cultural capital emerge. As reflected by its history of vastly different permutations, from the nineteenth-century original romance to the twenty-first century pastiche, the text is malleable. Yet there is an essential appeal that withstands the number of authorial revisions. In the close reading that follows, I explore the ways in which its cinematic features and central themes capture the melodramatic spirit of the original.

The excessive sentimentality of the concise source text lends itself splendidly to the melodramatic capabilities of the televised narrative form. The most noticeable change is the length of the story. Depending on the printing style, the original text only numbers between 100 and 150 pages, while Gilberto Braga's version expands the narrative to epic proportions with one hundred episodes running sixty minutes each in the final version, although this was reduced to as few as thirty episodes for some international exports. Braga amplifies all aspects of the narrative arc, inventing new characters (most notably including a new love interest for Isaura, called Tobias, whom the hateful Leôncio sadistically burns to death in an abandoned windmill—along with his own wife, Malvina, whom he did not realize was also in the barn with Tobias, in a shocking moment that seems borrowed from an Alfred Hitchcock film), minor plots, dramatic musical interludes and theme music, and alternating extreme close-ups and panoramic views that heighten the high drama of the tale. When Leôncio confesses to his father, for example, that he has not received his degree in physics while studying in Paris and has been squandering the money his father sent him over the last three years, an ominous melodramatic sound effect plays, coupled with a close-up of Almeida's distressed facial expression.

So, there is a synchronization of dramatic music and dramatic points of the story, giving it that ultra kitsch aesthetic in which the music calls the audience's attention to the next melodramatic turn in the drama. A number of visual anchor symbols subliminally set a tone as well; for example, the foregrounding of the grandfather clock in the scenes in the drawing room to indicate slow passage of time in the domestic settings, and the wide panoramic views of nature, especially Isaura standing under the trees, seeking her place between the inside and outside spaces. Of course, it is no surprise that the televisual format allows for the addition of these compelling audiovisual elements. Let us examine, then, the iconic introduction to the telenovela, which establishes an audiovisual rhetoric that brings together the drama as a cohesive whole.

The title sequence situates the story in the setting of the *fazenda,* with orderly scenes of submissive Black servitude. Dorival Caymmi performs the song he cowrote with Jorge Amado, "Retirantes" [Migrants],[38] featured on the original soundtrack album, *Escrava Isaura Som Livre* (1976), which is used in the opening credits (N. Xavier). Arranged by Waltel Branco, the lyrics and choreography of musical instruments from the *Som Livre* band and chorus blend drumming, bass, keyboards, violin, wind instruments, and haunting soprano background vocals singing "Lerê lerê lerê lerê lerê lerê lerê,"[39] which sets up a striking contrast with the content of drama:

Vida de negro é difícil
É difícil como quê! (× 2)

Eu quero morrer de noite
Na tocaia me matar
Eu quero morrer de açoite
Se tu negra me deixar

Vida de negro é difícil
É difícil como quê! (× 2)

Meu amor, eu vou me embora
Nessa terra vou morrer
O dia não mais vou ver
Nunca mais eu vou te ver

Vida de negro é difícil
É difícil como quê! (× 2)

[The life of a Black is difficult
So difficult it is! (× 2)

I want to die at night
In an ambush I will be killed
I want to die from whipping
If you, Black woman, leave me

The life of a Black person is difficult
So difficult it is! (× 2)

My love, I'm going away
In this land I'm going to die
The day I won't see again
Never again will I see you

The life of a Black person is difficult
So difficult it is! (× 2)]

In some exported versions of the telenovela, the language of the opening song is not in the Portuguese of the original soundtrack but is a mixture of Nagô (the generic Brazilian term for the ancient form of the Yoruba language and its speakers) and a racialized sonic imitation of unspecified African languages overlaying the indelible percussion arrangements.[40] These sounds code "exotic" for the foreign viewer and introduce the question of African origin as a locus of the narrative's drama arc, an element largely absent in the novel.

The irony of selecting "Retirantes" as the opening song, with lyrics underscoring the difficulty of life as a Black enslaved person, lies in its divergence from the crux of drama of *A Escrava Isaura,* which revolves around the seemingly incompatible status of possessing white skin and being enslaved. While the song laments the suffering of the enslaved male with Black skin living under the constant threat of physical violence and impending death, employing words like *tocaia* (ambush) and *açoite* (whipping), the telenovela centers on the distinct and less common experience of the enslaved woman who could pass for white and whose chief danger is sexual violence at the hands of her master. This experience is less common, not because she is subjected to frequent sexual advances, which was the norm for the enslaved woman, but because her nearly white skin afforded her the slightest bit of agency in repelling her master's advances. It seems, in fact, that he hoped she would love him.

With the infectious drums and Caymmi's simple verses, the song takes the form of both a battle hymn and a funeral march, emphasizing the archetypal aspects of the slave's narrative—strenuous life of toil and fear of murder—to surprise the viewer by its contrast with the story of an enslaved woman who could pass for white, were her maternal origin not known. Her daily struggle is not to stave off death by beating but to cope with the horrendous aftershocks of her mother's rape, with sexual exploitation, and with the ambiguity of her racial and social classification following generations of miscegenation.

A familiar montage of slavery imagery, which by the mid-twentieth century was embedded in the Brazilian national consciousness and collective memory, complements the high emotion of this musical introduction. The series of images by French artist Jean-Baptiste Debret (1768–1848) in the title sequence of *A Escrava Isaura,* together with the opening song, stir the audience and set a mournful tone. Significant, too, is the fact that these images are lithographs, contributing to the sense of reproduction central to the multiple retellings of the narrative and the proliferation of authors. Luz García Neira terms the telenovela title sequences "design in movement" and notes that they promote the plot using "ícones de tão fácil entendimento quanto a própria trama" (easily understood icons in relation to the plot). Although the images are not complex signs, Neira concedes that it is impossible to "resumir as tramas em uma única imagem" (summarize the plotlines in one single image) (3995).

Thus, the layering of sound and image requires the reader to interpret their joint significance. Together, the joining of image and sound represents the creative framework. The objective of the montage is to orient and prepare the viewer for the narrative action, using the "identificação dos símbolos da escravidão" (identification of symbols of slavery). These symbols of slavery establish a visual language, like the famous images used by British abolitionists, explored earlier, to locate the viewers in a certain period and place in Brazilian history: in the sixty-year period between independence (1822) and the formation of the first Republic (1889), when slavery still flourished (until 1888).

The visual language and historical narrative established in the Brazilian voyage paintings of Debret transport viewers to this transitional moment in Brazilian history. Debret traveled with the French Cultural Mission and lived in Brazil for fifteen years, from 1816 to 1831, during which time he founded the Escola Nacional de Belas Artes (National Institute of Fine Arts). After returning to France, Debret published the three-volume *Voyage Pittoresque et Historique au Brésil, ou séjour d'un artiste français au Brésil* [Picturesque and Historic Voyage to Brazil, or the Sojourn of a French Artist in Brazil], between 1834 and 1839. Comprising 153 lithographic prints accompanied by descriptive text, the volumes illustrate quotidian scenes of labor and leisure in domestic and natural settings in the early nineteenth century during the imperial reign of Dom João VI of Portugal. Debret endeavors to categorize racial types in several of these lithographs and creates "scientific" charts defining Portuguese, Brazilian, and mulatto, and distinguishing classes of Indians ("savage," "pure," or "civilized") and Blacks (born in Africa or outside of Brazil; Brazilian-born *creole* versus intermixing of Blacks and mulattoes, called "goats" or "she-goats"; and Blacks and Indians, called *curiboca*) (Sadlier 112–114). In one illustration from 1830, he presents a variety of faces and costumes of Black women in *Esclaves Nègres de Différents Nations* [Black Enslaved Women from Different Nations]. Citing Debret's constant chronicling of major events in his lithographs as one of the significant ways Brazil has been imagined, Sadlier argues that Debret was aware of the market value of the illustrated travelogue and the public hunger for "exotic" landscapes (124).

Several paintings from these volumes complete the creative design of the opening sequence by priming the audience with a familiar visual lexicon of slavery. If Debret's lithographs were not considered kitsch before they were appropriated by the telenovela, they quickly occupied that space of popular consumption following their broadcast. A series of ten images spliced together highlight common sites and sights of Brazilian society: interior spaces and the interracial cast of people found working and living in them, free Black vendors on the streets selling their wares to richly dressed European nobility, and a tattooed free Black woman sitting pensively outside, selling cashews. The reworked still images appear almost cartoonish, with rudimentary visual effects creating an illusion of movement: enslaved Black laborers dragging a heavy load across the screen, a light flickering in a lamppost, cutouts from one painting superimposed on another scene, each image flashing one after the other like a modern viewfinder, situating the spectator temporally and spatially in the scene.

Debret's lithographs operate in an observational mode and present the viewer with a window into scenes of racial and cultural difference. These paintings depict the varied costumes and interracial interactions and social hierarchies between Afro-Brazilians, Portuguese courtesans, white Brazilians, and Indigenous people. For cultural historians, Debret's classifications demonstrate early representations of the mythic formation of the "Brazilian race." As Livio Sansone describes in *Blackness without Ethnicity,* racial formation in Brazil centers on the myth of the "three races" that triumphantly merged to form what sociologist Sílvio Romero calls "a alma brasileira de hoje" (the Brazilian spirit of today).[41]

There was a shift around the 1940s from a "purging" of African traits to an embrace of this Brazilian spirit, which signaled an "incorporation of certain aspects of Black culture into the national self-image together with their commodification and commercialization." The Indigenous, the African, and the Portuguese "melted to create a new potentially color-blind race, [that] had already been celebrated over the last decades in poetry and the fine arts," and this cultural amalgam was upheld as representative of the national image (Sansone 72). Along with the increasingly commodified celebration and exportation of certain aspects of Afro-Brazilian religion, history, and culture, such as *candomblé, capoeira,* and local dishes like *acarajé,* this commercialization also has included selling a distinct narrative of enslavement and liberation.

A tale perfectly devised to garner the global commercial appeal that it did, *A Escrava Isaura* features an all-Black supporting cast of ingratiating minor characters and dialogue peppered with enough Afro-Brazilianisms to satiate the international viewing public's desire for the exotic Other. For instance, the memorable character of Januária, the stereotypically sharp-tongued, assertive enslaved Black cook, a maternal figure to Isaura and closely related to the Black Mammy figure in the United States—a *mãe preta,* in this context—is one of Braga's telenovela additions as she does not appear in Guimarães's original text. And then, of course, there is the leading lady with the nearly white skin whose beauty, cultivation, and exemplarity stand in high relief against the course manners of the nameless enslaved people who exit in the margins.

Surprisingly, though Debret's description indicates that he intends to depict the mulatto in the paintings, the lithographs omit the skin color variation of the spectrum of mixed-race enslaved inhabitants in these scenes. These lithographs do not depict the resistance of the enslaved, the celebrated *quilombo* (maroons), Palmares, or the agency of the captives. Instead, the audiovisual codes feature scenes of submission, orderly domestic environments with enslaved workers "in their place"—on the floor, serving, and sewing for their *senhora*—or free slaves in the marketplace.[42]

There are two poignant illustrations in the title sequence that depict domestic scenes and warrant closer inspection (figures 2 and 3). Reminiscent of the seventeenth- and eighteenth-century Casta paintings, which depict scenes of every conceivable combination of racial mixing in the Spanish colonies and document the racial classification and nomenclature of the offspring, each of these images presents the two races (European and African) in close proximity in domestic spaces. Notably, and perhaps because of his romantic notions of "Indian savage primitivism," Debret only displays Brazil's "third race," the Indigenous figures, ornately adorned in traditional costume and in natural settings, never in enclosed environments.[43] However, no images of Indigenous peoples appear in most versions of the opening credits.

Notably, Debret's artistic vision of colonial Brazil emphasizes the boundaries among the three races, underlining their separate spheres even when they appear together, as well as the social and labor divisions, based on skin color, between enslaved and free. Like the Indigenous figures, the presumably free Black people appear only in exterior settings, selling their wares to Europeans and white Brazilians on the street. In the watercolor illustrations where Debret depicts Indigenous people, he uses a shade of brown between the pearly white skin of the Portuguese courtesans and the monotone dark brown hue of the enslaved Blacks. However, Debret does not endeavor to show the spectrum of *mestiçagem.* Even the lithograph with the word *mulato* in its description, *Negros e Mulatos Coletando Esmolas para Irmandades,* does not differentiate among skin colors beyond the Black–white dichotomy. The Black figures are all nearly the same shade of black. As I noted earlier, the *mulato* or *pardo* (brown) seems to be missing from these paintings. This is a salient point, because the focus on the enslaved Black figures in these lithographs ironically exposes the absence of the enslaved Black person in the foreground of the drama in the telenovela. The enslaved Afro-descendants in the televised fiction exist on the periphery of the action, and when they attempt to enter the central drama, they die.

The Brazilian woman in *Uma senhora brasileira em seu lar* (figure 1), occupies the largest space in the painting. Each of the images presents the toiling and service of the enslaved Afro-Brazilians and the inactivity and consumption of the white Brazilians. The *senhora* with her rosy cheeks and flower in her hair is spatially larger and higher than the other figures in the image. All the dark figures are on or close to the ground. The nude and seminude babies—chocolate putti—crawling around or seated on the floor appear nearly identical to those in the foreground. The adults, even, become infantilized, sitting on the floor, each with his or her manual assignment.

Interestingly, no one looks up toward the viewer. All eyes are concealed, in profile, or oriented downward, consumed in their work, as all figures, except for the baby in the center, have an object of work or leisure in their hands. The young girl seated with her back to the viewer is the one figure that could potentially represent a mixed-race character. She is in the chair, reading to her *senhora,* just as Isaura often does in the telenovela. This scene of reading is important because it signals that Isaura has received a first-class education, thereby rendering her even more ill-suited for her official status as *escrava,* or property of the family.

In figure 2, an elaborately dressed man and a woman (presumably the Portuguese or white Brazilian owners of the domicile and estate), their backs arched over the dining table, consume fruit and roasted fowl and drink wine, with their enslaved Black laborers surrounding them in the background. Given the number of enslaved people present in this scene, it is likely an expansive *fazenda.* The enslaved woman, likely the *mucama* (house girl)—herself adorned in fancy clothes and accessories, probably donated to her by the lady of the house, including a two-strand necklace, dangling earrings, and a hair clip—fans the mistress of the house while two enslaved male figures stand behind the man to the right. One of the male figures stands on the threshold between the kitchen and the dining area, more a faint outline than a definitive figure. The other stands directly behind the *senhor* (who appears oblivious to the scene) with his arms folded, his facial expression a mixture of disgust, sadness, and anger—or perhaps stoic restfulness, since he is inactive at the moment.

In the opening of the telenovela, the camera slowly focuses on the European feasters, who are the largest figures and occupy the most pictorial space, therefore signaling to the spectator that we should consider them the most important in the image. Then the camera slowly moves down to the foreground of the painting, displaying the two nude, bald children, nearly identical to the two chocolate putti in figure 1, who sit and stand near their *senhora*'s feet, receiving scraps from the table like family pets.

The most striking aspect of this segment of the opening montage is the way the camera lingers and zooms in on the enslaved man's face. The focus on his disgruntled face is the only indication we have of the discontent of the enslaved people, who otherwise seem blindly and contentedly attending to their work, in Debret's artistic imagination of the Brazilian social world. With this close-up, furthermore, the viewer learns that all is not well in this household, for simmering enslaved Afro-Brazilians are not living comfortably under this mantle of "racial harmony."

Overall, image and sound function reciprocally to reveal the complexities of slavery in nineteenth-century Brazil; the sonic and the visual highlight the disconnect between seemingly pacific interior settings populated by obedient slaves and the fatalism of slave life represented by the "Retirantes" song. The ambiguous identity of the white-skinned sitting girl in figure 1 and the expression of quiet outrage from the enslaved Afro-Brazilian with arms folded in figure 2 give the viewer a peek into the scenes that follow.

Isaura's exemplarity emerges in two central themes in the telenovela: identity (legal, familial, or racial) and sexual liaisons and exploitation. Of course, the medium of television also makes possible dramatic film effects to enhance the melodrama of the opening title sequence. As the narratives of enslaved women so often present, in both coded and explicit ways—as we see in the classic *The History of Mary Prince: A West Indian Slave* (1831) and Harriet Jacobs's *Incidents in the Life of a Slave Girl* (1861)—sexual vulnerability is the defining feature of the life of the woman in bondage. What distinguishes Isaura's situation is her nearly white skin. Instead of raping her, Leôncio attempts to coerce Isaura over time, suggesting that he wants her to surrender to his relentless advances.

For these women, surviving in the midst of their sexual predator/owners' pursuit equates to bargaining with their bodies and leveraging the only capital they have in this system: their sexuality. This often translates to forming a sexual relationship with one man in order to forestall the forceful advances of others. Indeed, the womb of the enslaved woman represents both the locus of sexual desire and the vehicle for the continuity of the slave regime, thereby rendering the sexual exploitation of enslaved women economically profitable.

This pattern continues for Isaura, whose beauty and slave status in both the original text and the telenovela render her particularly vulnerable. The latter production, however, emphasizes her youth (she appears to be quite young), casting an even stronger predatory slant on the attention she receives from older men, and from Leôncio in particular. Since Rubens de Falco (Leôncio) was more than twenty years older than Lucélia Santos (Isaura) at the time of filming, this age difference introduced an almost Isaura-as-nymphet dimension to the serial drama (although she is postpubescent), reminiscent of Nabokov's *Lolita.* At the whim of a seemingly endless series of libidinous men, Isaura endeavors to maintain her Christian piety, evading their sexual overtures while hoping for a love of her own. Her simple attire of plain dress with a prominent cross around her neck provides a visual cue of young Isaura's virtue.[44]

PROJECTING ISAURA AS AN EXCEPTIONAL ENSLAVED WOMAN

The opening scenes of the telenovela draw out the complexities of these narrative strands of sex and identity while also marking Isaura as exemplary. As *mucama* and surrogate daughter to the lady of the house, Dona Ester, wife of the Comendador Almeida, Isaura lives in the land of *quase branca.* She is almost white and almost treated as the daughter of D. Ester, whom she refers to as *madrinha.* The first dramatic moment of the introductory scenes surrounds the sharp contrast between the apparent tranquility and luxury of the domestic space of the drawing room for the white Brazilians (although there are emotional struggles and familial strain beneath this facade) and the torment and misery of the slave auction for the Afro-Brazilians, as the eerie "lerê lerê" chant of "Retirantes" is mounting, building the dramatic suspense, and identifying the location of the auction block as the space that animates the lyrics "Vida de negro é difícil / é difícil como quê!"

The comendador and Coronel Sebastião (Malvina's father) inspect the bodies and teeth of the enslaved Afro-Brazilians on display at the auction. In an ambiguous moment, after a close-up shot of Isaura's face in the kitchen, the scene switches to the slave auction. Both male characters face the camera directly as they comment on the beauty and attractiveness of an enslaved woman whom the comendador calls "quase branca" (almost white) and the coronel declares strikingly beautiful, exclaiming "Que formosura" (What a beauty) and citing her beauty as "obras dos feitores" (work of the overseer). This nearly white enslaved woman whom we never see—the viewer stands in her position and sees these two men from her point of view—becomes a double for Isaura and foreshadows the oversexualized sentiments about her appearance. The comendador comments, "Não me faria mau ter em casa uma criaturinha dessas" (It would not hurt to have such a little creature at home) and then jokes that if he had one, the coronel would not see him for days. The cruel humor in his lewd joke and the implied sexual exploitation is that he *does* have a "creature" like her in his house, the daughter of the enslaved *mulata* he relentlessly pursued unto her death.

Professing that she knows "o seu lugar" (her place), Isaura seeks answers to the puzzle of her familial roots as a way to understand her identity and enslavement. Fittingly, Isaura possesses two surrogate mother figures who stand in for her absent biological mother, one white and free (Dona Ester) and one Black and enslaved (Januária).[45] From each mother figure, Isaura continues to probe for information about her parents. D. Ester only tells her that her mother's name was Juliana and she was "mestiça clara" (a light-skinned mixed-race woman). With Januária, Isaura maintains a more familiar and emotionally open relationship, and she often begs the feisty cook, who plays the role of the mãe preta, to tell her about her birth and origins. However, Januária withholds information about her mother and father until she deems it absolutely necessary.

For instance, Januária intervenes in a moment when Leôncio demands a kiss from Isaura in the kitchen. The fact that she is able to rescue Isaura in the kitchen is salient because this space is depicted as her domain throughout the telenovela. In fact, the viewer rarely sees Januária outside of this domestic sphere. Leôncio's blatant sexual advance prompts the protective cook to finally recount to Isaura the story of her birth.[46] Januária—well aware that an enslaved woman's most significant vulnerability is her female body and the constant threat of sexual violation—shields Isaura in the only way she knows: by introducing her to another man—her father, Miguel. In the framework of this telenovela, and likewise in the original text, men can save women through coercion and forced sexual transactions.

Notably, discussions challenging or confirming Isaura's exemplarity recur during the drama. After Malvina piques his curiosity, Henrique asks the comendador about Isaura's origins before concluding that she is a "singular" character. It is this very notion of Isaura as exceptional that the villain and evil core of the house rejects. In a crucial conversation that ties in the uncertainty of racial designation, family relations, and the definition of slavery, the couple heatedly debates Isaura's identity. The head of the house views the attention and elevated education Isaura has received as an eccentricity of his wife that he can no longer tolerate. In preparation for the return of their son, Leôncio, from studying abroad in France, the family despot forbids D. Ester from permitting Isaura to sit and eat at the dinner table with them, "como se fosse uma pessoa da família" (as if she were a family member), as she customarily did. Instead, Isaura is to eat in the kitchen with the other enslaved laborers. He insists that D. Ester no longer treat Isaura like a favored child, allowing her to walk around with "ares de princesinha" (airs of a little princess). Attacking the notion that Isaura's ability to read and her extensive education in music and foreign languages confers an exempt status, he barks to his wife, "Se trata de uma escrava, Ester. Tão escrava quanto o mais nojento negro da senzala mais suja!" (We are dealing with a slave, Ester. She's as much of a slave as the most disgusting nigger in the dirtiest slave quarters!). Since D. Ester fails to convince her husband that Isaura's superb education makes her exceptional and deserving of special treatment, she relies on the argument of blood. With surprising courage and strength, D. Ester loses her demeanor of a timid, oppressed, and lonely housewife and boldly counters her husband in this exchange:

> Comendador Almeida: Comendo a mesma conosco como se em suas veias corre o mesmo sangue que corre nas nossas.
>
> D. Ester: Você sabe muito bem que a maior parte de sangue de Isaura é exatamente como nosso.
>
> . . .
>
> Comendador Almeida: Não tem cabimento impedir a mesa de nosso filho a figura de uma escrava.
>
> D. Ester: Mas Isaura não foi criada como uma escrava. Recebeu uma educação mais esmerada do que a maioria das moças aqui.
>
> [Comendador Almeida: Eating the same food with us as if the same blood runs in her veins that runs in ours.

D. Ester: You know very well that the major part of Isaura's blood is exactly like ours.

. . .

Comendador Almeida: It is not suitable to obstruct our son's table with the figure of a slave.

D. Ester: But Isaura wasn't raised as a slave. She received a more extensive education than most of the girls here.]

Although D. Ester's "same blood" argument for Isaura's exemplarity infuriates her husband even more, it also reminds him of his pursuit and failed seduction of Isaura's mother. Almeida is the only character who denies Isaura's exemplary status, telling his wife that the young enslaved girl must return to "seu lugar" in the kitchen with the other enslaved Black women. The scenes showing Isaura looking pensive while standing under a tree in the garden heighten the sense of undefined place for Isaura. To depict graphically this tension between the two worlds, the telenovela includes scenes of Isaura wandering through nature, talking long walks, and finding solace in natural environments.

Throughout the dramatic arc, Isaura's status as exemplary justifies the claims for her liberation. When D. Ester petitions her husband for Isaura's emancipation, she does not ask for the emancipation of *all* slaves but just of Isaura. Likewise, Malvina never tries to undo the entire slave-based labor structure but only to rescue Isaura from the tyranny of her condition. When the working-class Portuguese man Miguel finally reveals to Isaura that he is her father, after receiving encouragement from Januária, he comments, "Você e uma moça excepcional" (You are an exceptional girl).

The rhetoric of Isaura's exceptionalism also emerges as Miguel dedicates himself to purchasing his daughter's freedom. It is clear that when he categorically denounces slavery as "um mal social," he truly is only concerned with the individual emancipation of his nearly white daughter. Ultimately, through the monologues of the newly invested character of Tobias, a legal scholar, we learn the philosophical arguments against slavery and hear an unequivocal denunciation of the dehumanization of enslaved people and a condemnation of Leôncio for his harsh treatment of his slaves. Before his eventual murder, Tobias discovers a law that fines slave owners who leave their slaves moribund and protects the health interests of sick slaves. Tobias's love does not impede this abolitionist commitment to all enslaved Afro-Brazilians.

Bound in a complex knot with issues of Isaura's identity is her sexual vulnerability to the men who own her and live around her. From the moment the letter arrives from the wayward son, Leôncio, announcing his return from Paris, the drama focuses on Isaura's struggle to avoid Leôncio's obsession with possessing her sexually and cornering her in secluded domestic spaces. This narrative strand speaks to a whole tradition in antislavery literature of descriptions of the sexual vulnerability of enslaved women, revealed in the narratives they wrote or dictated to others. After hearing this news, Isaura immediately flashes back to an early childhood scene when, as a boy, the rebellious Leôncio demanded a kiss from Isaura when she was a little girl, reasoning that if she is the slave of his father, she is his slave too. Upon his return to his family's house, having disgraced his father because he has not received his degree in physics and has only further squandered the family finances, Leôncio seems to salivate when he first sees Isaura working as his mother's *mucama.*

Leôncio's initial vindictive moment of subjection and shaming comes when he demands, "Tire minhas botas!" (Take off my boots!). Even though Isaura does not usually perform manual labor in the house, she complies with his cruel demand, kneeling to the floor and removing his heavy boots from his feet, in a position of submission and supplication. The camera zooms in and the sound track mounts as Leôncio grabs Isaura's face and tells her she is beautiful, as she places his boots on the floor.

This scene is the first of a series of Leôncio's increasingly sadomasochistic sexual advances. One of the most violent scenes involves having Isaura tied to the *tronco* (tree trunk), which was common practice for punishing rebellious enslaved people; he had earlier punished her by forcing her to witness the brutal whipping of an enslaved man. He chooses not to rape her but instead engages in this prolonged process of public and private humiliation, perhaps hoping that Isaura will willingly surrender. In his most blatant act of sexual aggression, Leôncio tracks down Isaura in the expansive gardens (her place of escape between the interior and exterior settings) and traps her under a tree branch, brazenly embracing her. Isaura tells him that she knows "her place" and that there exists a "social barrier" between them. In this instance, Isaura leverages the rules of slave society in her favor, pleading for Leôncio not to traverse the boundaries of their social and class division.

In a daring act of resistance, Isaura deploys the notion of her "African blood" to repel Leôncio. This is a significant departure from Guimarães's text, in which Isaura remains relatively silent while action happens around her. Here, Dona Ester asks Leôncio if he thinks it would be acceptable for her beloved Isaura to accompany them to the visit to the home of Tobias, who lives with his widowed mother and his sister, Dona Teresa. Although Leôncio tells his mother that he will consider it, he later enters the private space of Isaura's bedroom when she is dressed for bed and explains to Isaura that the choice is with her, insinuating an exchange of sexual activity for permission to attend the trip. Yet, giving consent within the system of domination, violence, and power that structures a slavocratic society is impossible, and as Emily A. Owens elucidates, "enslaved women in particular lacked the capacity to consent or withhold consent from sex" (151).[47]

Again, Leôncio argues that any other enslaved girl would gladly receive his attention, and like Rosa, consider a sexual relationship with her *senhor* (master) an honor. What most infuriates him, and perhaps even makes him wildly jealous, like his father Comendador Almeida with her mother, is the collective investment in Isaura as a novelty. He asks her cruelly, "Você se considera uma escrava especial?" (Do you consider yourself a special slave?). Although Isaura replies that she simply considers herself an enslaved woman who knows "o seu lugar" (her place), Leôncio does not believe that Isaura behaves like "qualquer escrava" (any enslaved woman); he, too, is invested in her exemplarity, even as he attempts his regular practices of sexual coercion.

Despite his efforts to undercut Isaura's exemplary status and reposition her as "qualquer escrava," he treats her differently. Before Leôncio ever subjects Isaura to the typical physical punishments reserved for the humans he holds as property, he first creates a public spectacle to show her how he handles enslaved people he deems disobedient. Amid this aggression, Isaura struggles to maintain a personal code of conduct and Christian morality—visually signaled by the large cross necklace—while not being allowed to fully possess her own body. Just as Leôncio pins Isaura against the wall in her bedroom, on the brink of sexual violation, Isaura calls upon the power of her potent "African blood" to assist her in fighting back. Isaura proclaims she will scream "com cada gota de seu sangre Africano" (with every drop of her African blood). Screaming, Isaura warns, is the one thing that the enslaved woman can do. Isaura ultimately gains mobility by evoking societal perceptions of her whiteness to pass while fleeing with her father, Miguel, to northern Brazil. As she uses racial stereotypes and presumptions to her advantage, race becomes a veil under which Isaura strategically hides and protects herself.

▲▲▲▲▲

NEVER-ENDING STORY

It seems the answer to the opening question of this chapter—What accounts for the global popularity of this serialized fiction of slavery?—can be found in the general principles of kitsch and narratology. The parameters for this elusive concept of success in the televised narrative world relate to economic measures: the number of countries to which the telenovela is exported, the number of translations—in short, the amount of money the product generates. While on the one hand, there is a sense of culture under siege by these market pressures, on the other hand, there is the possibility that the reverse is true, that market forces are under siege by culture.

Clearly, this telenovela represents a melodramatic, "Disneyfied" version of Guimarães's already overly sentimental narrative of slavery, yet the international viewing public adores it. The 1976 telenovela transforms *A Escrava Isaura* into a fairy tale in which Isaura becomes the princess rescued from the villain, Leôncio, by her knight(s) in shining armor (first Tobias, then Álvaro). Fairy tales, like telenovelas and the cinematic afterlife of *A Escrava Isaura,* "circulate in multiple versions, reconfigured by each telling to form kaleidoscopic variations with distinctly different effects," as Maria Tatar puts it (ix). Even so, reconfiguring the sexual exploitation of an enslaved woman as a sentimental love story is dangerous at best and a violently sinister rewriting of the history of slavery at worst. This reconceptualization fails to recognize the impossibility of a consensual sexual relationship between slave owner or free white man and enslaved woman within the slavocratic regime, that it is always de facto rape, a process of material exchange and domination.

However, this telenovela requires the reader to suspend disbelief and hurry past these doubts around hegemonic power and racialized gender relations to enjoy the universal appeal of the love story. Besides the startling murder of Tobias, the plot is predictable, the evil characters are easy to hate because they are wholly evil, and the good characters do no wrong and easily win our support. In short, it is the definition of kitsch: mass produced, conventional, not surprising, and yet incredibly pleasurable to watch and consume—as long as you do not look too deeply or ask too many questions. Finding this telenovela problematic on the grounds of its inadequate antislavery stance, reification of white beauty, or gender trouble is, in a way, asking it to be more than it ever set out to be: a commercial success. As Thomas Kulka notes, "Kitsch comes to support our basic sentiments and beliefs, not to disturb or question them" (27). That the most successful slavery telenovela would feature a white actress depicting a nearly white enslaved woman whose travails become diluted into a series of thorny love entanglements within the scopic economy bears out this expectation of kitsch.

As an instructive point of comparison on the issue of the apparent race of the enslaved protagonist, it is important to consider briefly that 1976 also marks the year of the release of another popular Brazilian film that features an eighteenth-century enslaved woman as the lead character. The chief difference is that in Carlos Diegues's historical feature-length film *Xica da Silva,* based on João Felício dos Santos's novel *Memórias do Distrito Diamantino da Comarca do Serro Frio* [Memories of the Diamond District of the Serro Frio Region] (1868), the main protagonist, although also a *mulata,* is clearly marked as a racial Other (Stam).[48] Unlike the virginal white-skinned Isaura, Xica is sexually attainable, and the "sensuous" film, according to Niyi Afolabi, "betrays far-ranging stereotypes and misconceptions about blacks and mulattas" (183–192). The myths swirling around Xica combine the following factual elements: she was an eighteenth-century enslaved mixed-race woman living in the diamond mining district of Tejuco during Brazil's colonial period, who gained her freedom and became a queen, as legend has it, through a strategic sexual liaison and social relationship with the Portuguese high court judge of the diamantine estate, João Fernandes. As Kimberly Juanita Brown contends, "It is her race, gender, and slave status that situate her body as both with and *without* power" (48). By wielding her sexual prowess, or "the construction of the mythology of sexual supremacy" of the enslaved woman, as Brown calls it (45), Xica advances in society and sheds her past in bondage in exchange for concubinage (it would be impossible for a Black woman or *mulata* to gain legal wife status under Portuguese law), which won her social and economic gain.

Similar to the controversial La Malinche figure in Mexican history, whom critics doubly interpret as whore and transcultural intermediary for her relationship with the Spanish conquistador Hernán Cortes, scholars and historians impose multiple interpretations and value judgments on Xica da Silva's actions. As Júnia Ferreira Furtado argues in *Chica da Silva: A Brazilian Slave of the Eighteenth Century,* the symbolism in this famous figure in the Brazilian popular imagination, and the conflicting stereotypes of "witch, seductress, heroine, queen, or slave," cover the most intriguing aspect of her history, her agency as an eighteenth-century woman (xix). Diegues's carnivalesque film moves the story to the nineteenth century and inserts comedy into the narrative, parodying the myth of racial democracy.

The Xica da Silva story firmly implanted in Brazilian collective memory the notion of racial democracy through the example of rewarding social ascension as a result of the intermixing between *brancos* (white men) and *mulatas,* and the beguiling hypersexuality of the Black or mixed-race woman. In terms of the importation of Black images, Alex Haley's *Roots* was the first and most popular US-produced "Black series" broadcast on free Brazilian television channels (Sansone 82). Although the film version of *Xica da Silva* was released in the same year as *A Escrava Isaura,* it was not transformed into a telenovela until 1996, when Taís Araújo starred as the first Afro-Brazilian lead role in a telenovela and the global public was finally ready to consume a complicated Black heroine of slavery. In contrast to what we have seen in the United States, in which reimagined cinematic tales of slavery, for the most part, center around the lives of men as the main characters (excluding Kizzy's storyline in *Roots*), the prevailing fictions of slavery propagated in television and cinema in Brazil from the late 1970s onward focus on the conditions and experiences of the enslaved woman (the most famous examples being Isaura and Xica da Silva).

A Escrava Isaura and its 1976 telenovela permutation offer presuppositions to the reader/viewer that undermine its political pamphlet aims. Isaura's story is a travesty not because she is an enslaved woman but because she is an enslaved woman who is nearly white. From a retrospective twenty-first-century reading, Guimarães's short novel fails as an effective abolitionist treatise because it does not in any way challenge the corrosive logics of enslavement that devalue Black skin and equate it with captivity. It is Isaura's exemplarity—possessing white skin, high education, and cultivated manners—that enables the nineteenth-century white readership to sympathize with her by looking at her, thereby replicating the same scopic economies of enslavement. Guimarães's novel only emancipates Isaura from the burden of her minuscule "African blood"; it does not excoriate slavery in a general sense except on two passing occasions. As Heloisa Toller Gomes observes, "The denunciation of slavery is allied to the ethnocentric vision of society peculiar to the Europeanized Americas of those days, the actual life of the enslaved black community in the slave quarters being utterly ignored" (166).

As with the telenovelas it generated, perhaps the modern reader expects too much of the novel and should appreciate its internal logic and the qualified denunciation of slavery it offers, even if the antislavery sentiments are particular to the anomaly that is Isaura. Perhaps this is, in fact, the genius of Guimarães's original text. While the erasure of Isaura's minuscule Blackness and promotion of her near whiteness may seem to skirt the issue of racial discourse in Brazil, it in fact exposes the racialized logic of skin color spectral hierarchies (*branco, pardo, moreno, preto,* and so on).

Where *A Escrava Isaura* falls short as an abolitionist text, it succeeds as a narrative that debunks the premise of Freyre's racial democracy, ultimately demonstrating that a white-skinned slave and a Black-skinned slave are not treated equally. Yet skin color difference does not tell the complete story. Just as much as her white skin, Isaura's superb education and refined manners separate her from the majority of Black people enslaved at the *fazenda.* As Cuti argues about Afro-Brazilian literature more broadly, "As diferenças de raça estão presentes juntamente com as diferenças de classe e que há contradições, sim, a serem superadas pelo diálogo e pela transformação social" (The racial differences are presented along with class differences, and there are contradictions, yes, to be overcome by dialogue and social transformation) (114).

The story of Isaura, in both late nineteenth-century abolitionist prose and twentieth-century televisual forms, brings together this complicated intersection of race, gender, sexuality, and class, which continue to shape the conversation around social inequalities and the possibility of social and economic transformation and liberation in Brazil. The extraordinary popularity of *A Escrava Isaura* as the global telenovela and symbol of slavery's kitsch arts par excellence reveals the desires, melodramatic fantasies, and scopic economies of slavery, in which the audience is at once complicit in observing scenes of brutal violence and sexual attack and delighted when the enslaved Africans, in the final triumphalist scene of emancipation in the telenovela, celebrate and sing, "Liberdade! Liberdade! Liberdade!" (Liberty! Liberty! Liberty!). I turn now to questions of the monument and monumental in US genres of slavery to discuss a rejection of the predictable narrative pleasures located in mythic figures of enslavement.

2

SUBTLE RESISTANCE

On Sugar and the Mammy Figure in Kara Walker's *A Subtlety* and Sherley Anne Williams's *Dessa Rose*

I could never arrive at the heart of the thing through placards or language.

—KARA WALKER, in "The Un-Private Collection"

Mammy ain't nobody name, not they real one.

—SHERLEY ANNE WILLIAMS, *Dessa Rose*

Kara Walker's 2014 installation *A Subtlety, or the Marvelous Sugar Baby* offers a stunning twenty-first-century artistic rejoinder to the infamous 1923 proposal to erect a statue "in memory of the faithful colored mammies of the South" on the National Mall.[1] Renowned maker of the provocative cut black paper silhouettes depicting seething antebellum scenes of racial violence and affixed to sprawling white gallery walls, Walker claims agency over a haunting tradition of racist imagery and stereotypical caricatures embedded in US visual culture.[2] Considering the Mammy figure as a "floating signifier" is central to tracing the mediated memory of transatlantic slavery.[3] Extending beyond the memorialization of slavery, the mythic Mammy telegraphs shifts in national identity formation, or "the cultural practice of 'writing' the national body vis-à-vis the black body in our nation's public forums and printed materials."[4]

In this chapter, divergent forms of the monumental—in visual art, public memory, and the novel—suggest the expansive generic permutations encoded in Afrodiasporic representations of slavery. Analyzing the hybrid representational valences in *A Subtlety* within and against the peculiar historical precedent of white southern congressmen's nostalgic longing to memorialize the enslaved African American woman caretaker in a monument for posterity in the capitol of the United States reveals the stakes of remembrance, race, representation, and resistance. I also will revisit a pivotal scene in Sherley Anne Williams's *Dessa Rose* (1986) to interpret a moment of contested identity of a Mammy figure that is hotly debated by two main characters, Dessa and Rufel, enslaved and free, and that renders possible interracial collaboration against patriarchal systems during slavery. Reading these two vastly distinct genres together—Walker's monumental sugar-coated Mammy–Sphinx sculpture, *A Subtlety,* alongside Williams's novel *Dessa Rose*—presents a strong critique of the cult of Mammy and larger memorialization projects articulated in the 1923 congressional Mammy monument proposal.[5]

Neo–slave narratives, or contemporary narratives of slavery, rework, reimagine, and "reinvigorate the slave narrative form," according to Aliyyah Abdur-Rahman, *Against the Closet,* "to provide more complete accounts of slave life[,] at times us[ing] the trope of silence or impossible disclosure to get at the sexual violence at the heart of slaves' experience" (30). While Williams's *Dessa Rose* clearly falls within this recuperative genre, Walker's oeuvre famously commingles image and textual influences and visually embodies the neo–slave narrative, revealing and revising the perverse subtexts and contexts of classic literature, historical records, and personal experience, or as Gwendolyn DuBois Shaw contends in her masterful *Seeing the Unspeakable,* Walker creates "a fantastically horrific narrative out of racial stereotypes, nostalgic themes, and historical mythology" (5).

Walker's large-scale, evanescent public sculpture and the complex scene in Williams's novel, then, problematize enduring impulses to memorialize a fictive icon of the loyal, enslaved Black woman. This resistance exposes the Mammy figure as "a sign that should be interrogated, a locus of contradictions," to borrow Hazel V. Carby's insightful formulation, and registers the intriguing ways in which producers of imaginative literature and visual culture at once transgress and reconfigure Mammy by denying her existence in racist iconography (15).

The magnitude and iconic urban setting of Walker's *A Subtlety* at once engage cartographies of suffering and resistance. Walker constructs this monumental structure, measuring a towering 75 1/2 feet long by 35 1/2 feet tall—its hypervisibility a coy play on its title—to occupy nearly the entire thirty-thousand-square-foot space of the legendary Domino Sugar Refinery located on the industrial waterfront of Williamsburg, Brooklyn.[6] Built in 1884, shuttered in 2004, and already set to be demolished from the inception of

Walker's piece, this cultural landmark, with the neon forty-foot rooftop Domino Sugar sign, was once the world's largest refinery, processing 60 percent of the nation's refined sugar and receiving its raw material from various sugar-producing countries, including Jamaica and Cuba.[7] Installing *A Subtlety* at this symbolic location, then, invokes the antebellum history of sugar as a dominant consumable good, and the geopolitical slave economies of labor, cultivation, refinement, and circulation that rendered it profitable.

Walker's installation strikingly presents the stereotypical visage of an enslaved domestic servant, her head wrapped in a bandanna, atop a mammoth Mammy-Sphinx hybrid figure, assembled with eighty tons of sugar donated from Domino Foods, sitting in perfect repose, with head held high and gaze fixed into the distance.[8] The front of the installation foregrounds her prominent bare breasts and erect nipples, enclosed on either side by outstretched leonine arms and gently balled fists, with her left thumb tucked between the pointer and middle finger (figure 3). An upraised bottom reveals the figure's vulva in the back of the sculpture (figure 4). Attendant boys carrying bananas and baskets surround the *Marvelous Sugar Baby,* at her service (figure 5).

The theatricality of *A Subtlety,* evocatively staged as an open-access, interactive experience in a crumbling relic to sugar refining and processing, brilliantly lends itself to the expansive reach of the social media age. Viewers attended in droves to meditate, blush, or stand in awe of its monumentality.[9] Thus, Walker's first sculptural project subverts the mythic Mammy figure—a symbol Kimberly Wallace-Stevens argues is "part of the lexicon of antebellum mythology that continues to have a provocative and tenacious hold on the American psyche" (2)—by complicating the simplistic dichotomy of post-Reconstruction white sentimentality and Black nationalist revulsion.

To be clear, Walker is certainly not the first artist to reclaim, repurpose, or radicalize Mammy. In the decades between 1923 and 2014, a rich archive of artistic production flourishes, most notably during the Black Arts Movement, aimed to dismantle what Patricia A. Turner calls the "insidious iconography" and "contemptible collectibles" constituting racist American popular culture (1, 9). Artists such as Kay Browne, Carole Byard, Murray DePillars, Jeff Donaldson, Jon Lockard, Dinga McCannon, Joe Overstreet, Faith Ringgold, and Betye Saar, among others, produced powerful revolutionary art of political struggle in the 1960s and 1970s that revolts against the specter of pancake Mammy memorialization, racist stereotypes more generally, societal and gender inequalities, and white supremacy.[10] Remarkably, it is the Aunt Jemima advertising trademark, the most commodified and circulated Mammy image of the widely grinning, servile Black cook, used to sell pancakes, that many of these artists so exquisitely transgressed.[11]

Building on this radical, counterhegemonic African American artistic tradition, however indirectly, Walker's *A Subtlety* is exceptional precisely because of its "profound indeterminacy," to use Arlene Keizer's phrase, but also because of its postmodern stickiness and ingenious defiance of the fixity of the Mammy myth, evidenced by its own transient materiality.[12] If the Mammy statue proposal reflects a state-sponsored nostalgic desire for the immutable symbolic subjugation of the Black woman's body, publicly fixed in stone as romanticized enslaved woman of Southern Plantation lore, then Walker's *Marvelous Sugar Baby* brilliantly evades confinement. Her twenty-first-century Mammy monument, in fact, melts away. Existing now only in the digital photographic record and on countless social media accounts, this is a fugitive sculpture, fabricated to be deconstructed, always already in ruins, an ephemeral monument persuasively countering what Paule Marshall calls "the use of the Negro woman as an embodiment of myth and fantasies."[13]

On a literary level, Williams's *Dessa Rose* similarly acts to undermine the racial typographies and hegemonies of the antebellum South, undoing rigid distinctions between white mistress and enslaved woman, fugitive and freeperson, and the mythologies naturalizing the contented Black Mammy figure as wet nurse to white babies. M. M. Manring emphasizes the fictions around Black female servitude: "No single person named mammy ever existed; an idea about Black female servants was negotiated among whites, Blacks, men, women, historians, diarists, and novelists. *Mammy* is shorthand for a set of behaviors used to explain diverse concepts such as slavery, love, service, motherhood" (59).

As we will see when analyzing the scene in which Dessa and Rufel passionately debate the "authentic" identity and name of Mammy, Williams subverts slavery-era matrices of domination by transgressing language and colloquial kinship naming practices, wherein Rufel's blithe remembrances of her Mammy echo the sentimentality of the southern congressmen. In this dazzling rhetorical exchange between these two women, Williams's Dessa opposes what Michele Wallace derides as "a hated figure in black history," situated in a pernicious catalog of degrading stereotypical imagery, including the obsequious Uncle Tom and rambunctious pickaninnies, by humanizing the specific histories of Black women's lived experiences while also dismantling color-coded myths about the Mammy figure, breast-feeding, and child care (21). Just as

Walker's Mammy sculpture melts away, Williams's novel discursively demolishes Rufel's Mammy and replaces her with the shared maternal experiences of two women—one Black and enslaved and the other white and abandoned—living astonishingly proximal lives in the antebellum South.

As we will see, the transgressive themes in both creative works topple cultural monuments to the mythic Mammy figure. Using the stickiness of Walker's *A Subtlety* as both the point of departure and central subject of investigation, I argue that visual and literary figurations of Mammy at once (re)produce the misery of the African woman's captivity and dispossession of her body while complicating facile interpretations of her resistance. Although I focus solely on reading Mammy within a US context here, the mythologized Black wet nurse circulated broadly within slavery's archive in the Americas.[14] *A Subtlety* remakes her body in large, cheeky proportions, while *Dessa Rose* counters the caricature by imbuing Black domestics with humanity. Both works reckon with notions of domination, power, and remembrances of slavery's past. Gwendolyn DuBois Shaw posits that Walker's images represent "detailed excavations of the visual history of multiple genres of American raced and gendered representation" that signify on, following Gates, racist caricatures (9, 42).

In the next section, I turn to the 1923 *Congressional Record* to contextualize the Mammy monument proposal and explore contemporary reactions, including W. E. B. Du Bois's sentiments in *The Gift of Black Folk,* to establish how this memorialization project engenders the titillating subversive undercurrents in *A Subtlety* and *Dessa Rose.*

MEMORY, MAMMY, AND MONUMENTS

On January 9, 1923, when Charles Manly Stedman, a Democrat from North Carolina, introduced H.R. 13672 to the House of Representatives, it was identical to Senator John Sharp Williams's December 8, 1922, bill "to erect a monument in memory of the faithful colored mammies of the South" (S. 4119).[15] During this session, Stedman and Bill Green Lowrey (1862–1947) of Mississippi delivered what I would like to call a series of poignant "Mammy monologue confessions," though I will focus here on a salient passage from Stedman's remarks. Echoing the authors of plantation literature, and adding another layer in the chain of mimetic voicing, the southern congressmen seemed compelled to present a public account of their childhood recollections of their mammies in the lyrical, sentimental idiom of the genre.

What's striking, though, is that these extended Mammy monologues took place during sessions of Congress. Although the monument proposal passed in the Senate before stalling in the House, their heartfelt testimonies and speech acts perform discursive monuments to Mammy. After Stedman thanked the chairman for "the privilege of diverting for a brief interval the attention of the House," he delivered a persuasive speech extolling the virtues of the national monument, the United Daughters of the Confederacy, the Confederate Veterans' Association, the Old South, and Mammy's place. His fervent appeals for the memorialization of Mammy in stone presage urgent twenty-first-century public debates around the significance and necessity of Confederate monuments and flags.[16]

However, on this January day in 1923, in his grandiloquent opening lines, Stedman explained the historical purpose of the monument in society and attempted to convince the representatives, by first appealing to their personal generosity and benevolence, that memorializing Mammy would make the United States the first country to erect a monument to honor a person of a different race. Second, he attempted to combat lingering sectionalism by invoking an American identity (though nonwhites are excluded from this citizenry), stating that the Mammy monument proposal "should find a responsive echo in the hearts of citizens of this great Republic"; that is, it is not just a southern vanity project. Moreover, he foregrounds both the Western expansionism of the previous century and the postbellum unification of all states with the phrase "They are all Americans," regardless of the region in which one is born.

After praising the United Daughters of the Confederacy, Stedman launched into a romanticized history of the Old South to set the stage for describing Mammy's laudable work. In anticipation of northern criticisms, Stedman speaks for the "misrepresented and misunderstood" South and offers this sentimental description of Mammy:

> The colored mammies of the South lived in and were a part of this civilization. No one, except the youth of that generation, can realize the mutual devotion of the colored mammies of the South and those they served. They were educated by their young mistresses, and their characters molded by them. The fidelity of these colored mammies was scarcely a parallel in history. The safety and comfort of "their children," as they called the boys and girls whom they nursed, gave them contentment and happiness. They watched them with tenderness

> and care, and sang them to sleep with their plantation songs. They could not be seduced from their love and loyalty by either promise of reward or threats of violence. Numerous instances of their fidelity are recorded in the traditions of the South.

For Stedman, the "colored mammies of the South" emblematize the pinnacle of southern civilization. Recycling the tropes of plantation literature, Stedman claimed a "mutual devotion" between Mammy and the white children she nursed with "tenderness and care," "love and loyalty," singing "plantation songs" as they fell asleep. Those traits alone deserve adulation from all American citizens and memorialization in stone. Puzzling is the next sentence, which says that mammies "could not be seduced from their love and loyalty by either promise of reward or threats of violence." Stedman seems to reveal too much with this statement, which hints at a more complex vision of Black womanhood, beyond unerring fidelity.

As the southern white cultural imagination sought to sanctify Mammy in statute, the African American community vociferously rejected it. The Black press called the proposal a "mockery" and "disgrace" in an era of rampant racial terror and violence.[17] Distinguished leader and intellectual W. E. B. Du Bois simultaneously elevated the Mammy figure while admonishing the legislative proposal. Praising Mammy as the ultimate gift of the Negro to the New World, Du Bois concludes *The Gift of Black Folk* (1924) with a magisterial flourish:

> Above all looms the figure of the Black Mammy, one of the most pitiful of the world's Christs. Whether drab and dirty drudge or dark and gentle lady she played her part in the uplift of the South. She was an embodied Sorrow, an anomaly crucified on the cross of her own neglected children for the sake of the children of masters who bought and sold her as they bought and sold cattle. Whatever she had of slovenliness or neatness, of degradation or of education she surrendered it to those who lived to lynch her sons and ravish her daughters. From her great full breast walked forth governors and judges, ladies of wealth and fashions, merchants and scoundrels who lead the South. And the rest gave her memory the reverence of silence. But a few snobs have lately sought to advertise her sacrifice and degradation and enhance their own cheap success by building on the blood of her riven heart a load of stone miscalled a monument. (123–124)

Du Bois's deification of the Black Mammy as "the most pitiful of the world's Christs" and "an anomaly crucified" emphasizes her maternal sacrifices to care for the master's children before her own. Indeed, Du Bois's pathos in this passage seemingly echoes the sentimentality of the congressmen, as he even repeats the caricaturized description of her stout body by describing her "great full breast." Yet, within his hagiography of Mammy as an "embodied Sorrow," long-suffering and degraded, Du Bois issued a sharp critique of American racial terror and the tragic history of lynching when he also characterized Mammy as surrendering all her mental and spiritual strength to those who enslaved her and "lived to lynch" her biological children. This rhetorical juxtaposition exposes how the Mammy proposal sinisterly trivializes the brutalized, tortured, maimed Black bodies on display; every lynching constitutes a ghastly public monument to human violence, depravity, and racial hate. The unbearable contradiction between Mammy's exaltation and the physical and psychic destruction of her sons and daughters via lynching and rape compels Du Bois to assail the proposal with this piercing imagery: "building on the blood of her riven heart a load of stone miscalled a monument."

This argument reflects the key oppositional refrain in the Negro newspapers as well. In the aftermath of what James Weldon Johnson called the "Red Summer" of 1919, the horrific spike in lynchings, the passage of women's suffrage with the Nineteenth Amendment, and the defeat of Dyer's antilynching bill, first introduced in 1918, the Mammy monument proposal gained momentum.[18] The African American press, as a whole, swiftly denounced it.

Before examining the scathing response of the press, however, I look briefly at one of the most significant literary examples of the denunciation of the Mammy figure. George S. Schuyler's satire, *Black No More* (1931), attacks the Mammy figure through a complicated and humorous plot in which the African American medical doctor, Dr. Junius Crookman, develops a scientific process called Black-No-More that turns Black people white, and is even capable of turning a Senegalese into "the most Nordic looking person in the room" (12). Of course, hilarious escapades ensue as Schuyler uses the racial passing motif ad absurdum. As Jeffrey B. Ferguson provocatively argues in *The Sage of Sugar Hill,* "Few concepts appear more deserving of satirical treatment than race," and "the irreverent force" of Schuyler's parodic novel brilliantly achieves this combining humor and incisive social commentary as "a mock race novel aimed like a precision-guided weapon at the central features of popular 1920s race mythology informing the perspectives of whites and blacks alike" (vii, ix, 213).

Dr. Crookman explains to his eager patients that literature, drama, the arts, and cartoons propagate cultural inaccuracies or reductionism that the public generally accepts without challenge. A biting scene parodies the popularity of blackface minstrelsy and "America's premier black-faced troubadour," as Sollors argues, likely critiquing "Al Jolson and the sentimental mammy cult of *The Jazz Singer*."[19]

Here we have a fictional rebuttal to the primacy of popular caricatures of the Mammy figure like the one forever emblazoned in film history in Jolson's song "My Mammy": "Mr. Jack Albert, the well-known singer and comedian, has kindly consented to render his favorite among the popular songs of the day, 'Vanishing Mammy,'" over the radio waves:

> Vanishing Mammy, Mammy! Mammy! of Mi—ne,
> You've been away, dear, such an awfully long time
> You went away, Sweet Mammy! Mammy! one summer night
> I can't help thinkin', Mammy, that you went white.
> Of course I can't blame you, Mammy!
> Because you had so many troubles, Mammy, to bear.
> But the old homestead hasn't been the same
> Since I last heard you, Mammy, call my name.
> And so I wait, loving Mammy, it seems in vain,
> For you to come waddling back home again
> Vanishing Mammy! Mammy! Mammy!
> I'm waiting for you to come back home again. (114–115)

Inverting the longing in Walter Donaldson, Joe Young, and Sam Lewis's "My Mammy," in which the departed singer hopes to one day rejoin his faithful Mammy, the singer of "Vanishing Mammy" hopes that the departed Mammy will return home. He speculates that his Mammy has crossed the color line ("I can't help thinkin', Mammy, that you went white") by using Dr. Crookman's race-changing procedure, yet he understands why she might want to escape because she "had so many troubles to bear" (115).

Although most of the lyrics could integrate seamlessly into the Donaldson et al. or Berlin Music Publishing versions of "My Mammy," the parody works because the reader is left to speculate about why she has vanished. Unlike other musical figurations of Mammy as the "happy darky," this one admits that she lived a hard life. The subtext of the song is that the circumstances of the "many troubles" of her life may have motivated her to run away or disappear through Dr. Crookman's race-change procedure. What's more, the idea of vanishing Mammy satirizes the rampant fears, as published in major national newspapers, about the terrible loss to the South of the Old Mammy and her superb cooking technique. Finally, the use of the word *waddling* in the lines "And so I wait, loving Mammy, it seems in vain, / For you to come waddling back home again" adds the comedic indictment of the strange deification of this racial stereotype, whose body is always coded as excessive.

This disdain for the minstrel performer first emerges early in the novel, during a New Year's Eve celebration scene in which two main characters, Max Disher and Bunny Brown, attend an integrated New York nightclub called the Honky Tonk Club. Before the clock strikes midnight, the narrator describes the main entertainment for the evening: "The floor show came on. A black-faced comedian, a corpulent shouter of mammy songs with a gin-roughened voice, three chocolate soft-shoe dancers and an octette of wriggling, practically nude, mulatto chlorines" (7). The racial designations of the entertainers in this show, and especially of the "black-faced comedian," reveal the complicated racial structure of this "integrated" New York club. While a blackfaced performer apes the well-worn Mammy trope, scantily clad biracial women dance in the background and three African Americans tap dance. That this performance style, most famously popularized by Bojangles, eventually became shorthand for racial performance of submission and obeisance does not escape Schuyler's 1931 satire.[20]

The blackfaced minstrel singer of Mammy tunes is at the heart of a scene that exposes the cracks in the architecture of the "democracy of night life" (5). Max and his friend Bunny are still called "boys" when a white man in a white group of revelers enters the club and asks them where they can find some alcohol (6). After Max fetches the alcohol for them, in the hopes that he will be invited to join their table, the man simply gives him the change from the purchase without including him.

The ultimate insult and destruction of the veneer of the nightclub as a site of placid interracial socializing, however, comes when Max approaches an attractive young blond-haired white woman from the party to which he has just provided the liquor and asks her to dance, to which she icily replies, "I never dance with niggers!" (8). Schuyler highlights the absurdity of the blackfaced minstrel singer of Mammy songs to deliver a deeper critique of the contradictions of race relations even in the integrated northern city of New York: adoration for Mammy, emulation of African American performers by using blackface, attendance at "Negro resorts," as Max calls them, yet refusal to see them as more than the racial Other.

Resurrecting the specter of Mammy seemed little more than a halfhearted attempt by Congress to prove their cordiality toward African Americans within the tumultuous political context of unchecked lynchings. For several of the major African American newspapers of the time, the juxtaposition of the Mammy movement with the brutal disregard for human life was irreconcilable. The political volley between the benevolent intentions of the United Daughters of the Confederacy and US congressmen, on the one hand, and the indignant Black press, on the other, attests to the fact that Mammy remained imprinted in the consciousness of the nation.

Four of the major African American newspapers—the *Chicago Defender, New York Amsterdam News, Baltimore Afro-American,* and *Philadelphia Tribune*—reveal the organized and immediate community effort to oppose the construction of such a monument. With varying degrees of disapproval and indignant disbelief, each paper published a series of articles rejecting the proposal and suggesting that the construction of a monument to the fictional Mammy, both in stone and in public sentiment, was akin to erasing the atrocities of enslavement and ignoring the ongoing violence of lynching by stuffing the charred, lifeless remains of the lynching victims' corpses—her own children—underneath Mammy's capacious calico frock. In response to the statuesque Mammy, the reporters reminded readers of the lynching victim who also became an icon for many southerners in the form of a photographic postcard.[21]

Paradoxically, the Mammy monologues and public narratives of affection were the very ones invoked to counter the Dyer Anti-Lynching Bill in debates. Explicit in many of the southern congressmen's public speeches that express loving devotion to the African American nurse is an insistence on recognizing this particular period as the golden era of the South, a nostalgic romanticization of the days of slavery, and an unwillingness to accept the rapidly changing present. Take Congressman Percy L. Gassaway of Oklahoma, for example, who recounted a touching "Mammy story" in a radio address before using the word *nigger* six times and stating that the greatest ambition of an African American was to become a barber, adding, aware of the northern environment, "Of course, niggers up here are different."[22] Two years later, after proclaiming that the South is "the best friend of the Negro race," Senator Ellison DuRant Smith of South Carolina professed his love for Mammy on the Senate floor: "As a baby boy I was nursed in the arms of a Negro woman, whom I loved as devotedly as possible. Then, later on, old Uncle Bill, who lived to be 103 years old, was my shelter in the time of storm. . . . Oh, I loved him with devotion."[23] Smith uttered this proclamation of love only moments before he argued that it would be good if northern African Americans were disenfranchised, as they were in the South. Neither of these politicians saw any inherent contradiction in using their "love of Mammy" monologue to oppose enfranchisement or the antilynching bill. Thus, the deification of the Mammy clouded attempts for justice, racial equality, and full citizenship.

An author from the *Philadelphia Tribune* expressed radical indignation and a refusal to assume the "position of humility," in an article republished in the *New York Amsterdam News:*

> A monument to "black mammies" is a mockery, a farce, and a disgrace to the intelligence of the United States Senate. Likewise it is an affront to every American citizen that descends from those saintly women who were sacrificed to the avaricious beastly natures of southern gentlemen.
>
> These men would erect a monument to commemorate, what? A position of humility, subserviency, meniality, servility is the idea they desire branded and scorched into the brain and heart of every American who happens to be of African lineage. The only thing the Negro has done worthy of note in the estimation of Congress is the suffering and sacrifices endured by the "Black Mammies" who were willing to suffer for the brutes who held them in bondage.[24]

This article refuses to accept a commemoration of the servile figure and this revisionist interpretation of slavery's past. However, when the Mammy statue bill passed the Senate and African Americans believed it would pass the House as well, they dismissed it as a meaningless symbolic gesture that provided an escape clause from grappling with inequalities plaguing the African American community:

> The future of the Negro in Harlem, New York State and the Nation is at stake. Urgent questions are pressing for a solution. Colored men and women are being driven out of towns by the hundreds each week. Our fellow men are still being lynched and burned at the stake. Unless one would call the "Mammy" Monument Bill a piece of favorable legislation, not a single measure looking to the emancipation of the colored citizen, was passed by the last Congress.[25]

Despite the Phillis Wheatley YWCA and other clubwomen protests against the Mammy monuments, which these news articles both stirred and reflected, the bill passed the Senate vote on March 6, 1923, though it was stalled in the House of Representatives the following year. The article titles tell it all. A lengthy headline from the *Chicago Defender* excoriates the bill: "Senate OK's 'Mammy' Monument: Insults Race—Monument to 'Mammy' Wins Senate Pays Respect to Uncle Tom's Wife; Refuses to Give a Man's Job to W. L. Cohen." Other headlines state the reaction simply. *The Afro- American* stated "Mammy Statue Disgraceful Insult," and *The New York Amsterdam News* wrote "Oppose Monument."[26]

Bolder still, the *Chicago Defender* published the punchiest reactions to the monument. Roscoe Simmons's editorial hit a comic note:

> A dozen letters came to this writer with the word: "Please write on the 'Mammy Statue' proposed for Washington." But for these requests this writer would not waste your time, nor his.
>
> "Do you favor the erection?" one lady asks. Maybe so; then maybe not. Our white people lose a lot of valuable time trying to bring slavery back.
>
> "No, we are not," they say.
>
> Well, they try to bring back the flavor without the dish. That is good, isn't it?
>
> Suppose a "mammy statue" stood in Washington. You might take the children there and say to them: "There is a memorial to a lady, a woman of your Race, who had it so easy in bondage that she didn't want to break up bondage. Look on her quiet, peaceful features, then, children, think how far God has brought your people since both she and the people she loved and who loved her lost out."
>
> This writer could sit around half a day under that statue and read "My Life and Times" by Douglass; "Up From Slavery," by Booker T. Washington, and three or four poems by Dunbar, and think on the power of God in the affairs of men.
>
> Don't worry, no "mammy statue" will adorn the Capital.
>
> Two great southern papers, the Columbia State and the Montgomery Advertiser, are stirred up because Colored people oppose the statue.
>
> No use answering them, for they stand on sentiment. This writer would favor any monument that would make it easier for you. Stone crumbles. ("Mammy Statue")

Simmons's irreverent tone assails the Mammy monument proposal by trivializing it. When he writes, "Our white people lose a lot of valuable time trying to bring slavery back," he dismisses this nostalgia for the idyllic plantation era as laughable. In short, Simmons's use of humor assures his readers that there will never be a return to slavery. Moreover, the phrase "our white people" inverts the standard possessive relationship in which Black people belong to white people, but it also indicates a familiarity, interconnectedness, and sense that all people in the United States must figure out this "race problem" together. The line stating that white people are trying to "bring back the flavor without the dish" puns on Mammy as cook. Simmons continues his humor, not "wasting" his time by dignifying the proposal with a serious article, through speculation of what the monument might signify for African American children. He sarcastically paints a picture of taking children there to explain this "woman of your Race," content in bondage, and then reading famous slave narratives under the statue. In case his readers miss the parody, he ensures them that a Mammy statue will never "adorn the Capital."

The *Chicago Defender* also published the most forthright and scathing rejection of the Mammy statue. One article asks of the Mammy proposal: "Thus do the southern whites cling to an illusion. Who is deluded?"[27] More than five years before the bill proposal, this paper urged its readers to "boycott" any paper that uses *wench, negress,* and *Mammy,* which is called "the gravest insults that any living mortal can offer another, and it should be resented even if it should cost one their life."[28] As these articles of the Black press seek to demonstrate, the fixation on the Mammy character not only discloses a yearning for the bygone Dixieland era and a complete distortion of North American slavery but also diverts attention from the pervasive violence against African Americans at the time, particularly rituals of lynching.

Nathaniel Williams's poem, also published in the *Chicago Defender,* points out that the erection of a Mammy statue equates the exemplary African American with enslaved property, a woman in bondage. The second half of the poem calls for justice for the offspring of Mammy, playing upon the metaphor of the statue:

> Her memory's sacred to us; please don't build,
> A statue of, or to her as a slave.
> To us she was a mother, dear and true,
> By her our fears could always be allayed;

While memories recalled of her by you—
Are of chattel you can barter, sell or trade.
If you must build a monument for old
mammy,
Don't build it of cold granite, bleak and
gray,
Just give her little Ephraim and Sammy,
The same old sunny smile she gave away.
And since all your childhood cares were
lightened,
By smiles that mammy gave you, always kind;
Try making all the cloudy days seem
brightened,
By giving justice to the brood she left behind.

Give them the change to know life's worth
the living.
Give back some kindness mammy gave to
you;
And you'll add a black, each day you're
giving
To a monument that mammy would like to
view.[29]

In the first six lines of this excerpted poem, the speaker debunks the notion of Mammy's maternal neglect of her own children: "To us she was a mother, dear and true / By her our fears could always be allayed." The speaker announces that African Americans possess a "sacred" memory of Mammy as mother. The line "By giving justice to the brood she left behind" encapsulates the moral of this protest poem, that is, that justice is due to her children, whom he names Ephraim and Sammy. Appealing to a belief in justice as a universal right, Williams instructs the proponents of the Mammy statue that a better way to demonstrate their gratitude is by "giving" to her descendants: "Give them the change to know life's worth / the living. / Give back some kindness mammy gave to / you." With the suggestion of giving to Mammy's children, Williams closes the poem by coming full circle, returning to the imperative not to build a monument "of cold granite, bleak and / gray," but instead to build a living monument to moral and uplifting behavior, which would, "add a black, each day you're / giving / To a monument that mammy would like to / view." Williams's plea in this poem, and the criticisms in the Black press, reflect Joan Marie Johnson's argument that the rejection of the Black Mammy statue equals a rejection of "the symbol of slavery and subservience" and of the myth of African American contentment and containment in slavery (79). A representative headline from the *Chicago Defender* blasts, "Thus do the southern whites cling to an illusion. Who is deluded?"[30]

MAMMY RECONFIGURATIONS: MILK, SPHINX, AND MONUMENTALITY

Walker's *A Subtlety* provides a multilayered twenty-first-century artistic rejection of the congressional proposal that Du Bois dismissed in 1924 and that Micki McElya characterizes as "an obviously political effort to legitimize this distorted version of the southern past" (117). These legitimization efforts crystallize in the wistful remembrances of Representative Stedman in Congress. As Deborah Gray White elucidates, Mammy "personified the ideal slave and the ideal woman, the centerpiece in the antebellum Southerner's perception of the perfectly organized society. She was at once Black and female, and thus in reality and mythology was subservient to white men" (168).

Intriguingly, some of Walker's detractors have accused her of reinforcing distorted histories and racist antebellum imagery for the delight of white audiences and the mainstream art establishment.[31] Walker's artwork defies what Keizer, "Gone Astray" calls the reverent "attitude of mourning and outrage" that senior African American artists consider "appropriate" for the subject matter (1656). However, I assert that the radicality of *A Subtlety* lies precisely in its disavowal of convention, its monumentality, its material impermanence as rejection of confinement, and its charged semiotics—pronounced breasts, Mammy-Sphinx hybrid figuration, excess—which insist upon the viewer performing the difficult hermeneutic work. *A Subtlety,* constructed entirely of bleached sugar, with the head of a bandanna-wearing, stoic Mammy figure and the body of a crouching woman–lion hybrid, in a position of supplication or ready to pounce, at once announces the commodification of the "marked" enslaved women's body and transgresses the power structure that supports it. As Hortense Spillers brilliantly argues in "Mama's Baby, Papa's Maybe: An American Grammar Book," "The captive female body locates precisely a moment of converging political and social vectors that mark the flesh as a prime commodity of exchange" (75).

Walker acknowledges the "Artisans" whose "marked" flesh was transformed into commodity, in the subtitle of her work: "An Homage to the unpaid and overworked Artisans who have refined our Sweet tastes from the cane fields to the Kitchens of the New World on the Occasion of the demolition of the Domino Sugar Refining Plant." These forty-four words in the full title of *A Subtlety*—characteristic of Walker's playful parody of nineteenth-century sentimental fiction and slave narrative title conventions—give the spectator the only directed language with which to interpret the sculpture and the attendant Black boy molasses figures.[32] Gwendolyn DuBois Shaw insightfully elaborates that Walker's "recurrent self-inclusion in titles and textual material," which includes "various personae" (such as "Nigger Wench," "Missus K.E.B. Walker, Colored," or "a Negress"), evidence the "constant self-referentiality" of her work and allows Walker to "rewrite the white voice of the nineteenth-century sentimental novel" (6, 26). Designating "the unpaid and overworked" enslaved people as "Artisans" rather than "slaves" honors their physical and creative labor; they not only harvest the sugar but also transform it into delicious confections.

Walker pays homage to the creative work of these Artisans on a monumental scale, registering what Patricia Yaeger calls "thematic excess." The colossal size and multiple signifiers allude to Yaeger's compelling argument that "circum-Atlantic artists of color engage in an aesthetics of excess," which becomes "a virtuoso act" (774). The corporeal exposure in Walker's sugarcoated sculpture, its "thematic excess," lays bare the slave system's reliance on the Black woman's body—arms, hands, breasts, womb—each reduced to a source of physical and reproductive labor. Staging *Marvelous Sugar Baby*, its scale already emblematic of the "aesthetics of excess," at the Domino Sugar Refinery, with sugar stalactites dripping from its pipes, a site laden with historical resonances of slavery and industry, underscores its radicality, its presence "taking up property, reclaiming space" (774). Furthermore, the inclusion of these organic commodities in the material substance of the work locates the enslaved African woman not only in the United States but also in an inter-American context where bananas, sugar, rum, and tobacco, for example, are cultivated and circulate on the market.

Walker's work opposes the statue proponents' steadfast insistence on Mammy as a historically accurate figure to be captured and contained—*fixed* in a state of eternal domination—in immutable stone or marble on the Washington Mall. Refusing the suggestion of a permanent, realist representation of an imaginary figure, Walker instead casts her temporal, colossal project in the form of mixed mythologies: a Mammy–Sphinx sculpture coated in the elusive, ephemeral substance of refined sugar. Toni Morrison's term "American Africanism" is instructive here as a theoretical framework to think through this saccharine mythic Mammy, by exploring "the ways in which a nonwhite Africanlike (or Africanist) presence or persona was constructed in the United States, and the imaginative uses this fabricated presence served" ("Playing in the Dark" 6). As Morrison reminds us, Blackness functions as a trope in literature, and by extension in visual culture, that illuminates a range of dichotomies: "to say and not say, to inscribe and erase, to escape and engage, to act out and act on, to historicize and render timeless. It provides a way of contemplating chaos and civilization, *desire and fear,* and a mechanism for testing the problems and blessings of freedom" (7; emphasis added). *A Subtlety,* then, forces the audience to confront the dialectic of desire and fear, to act out and act on the historical and timeless Mammy–Sphinx figuration.

The Mammy–Sphinx hybrid sculpture boldly announces her presence instead of diminishing herself, revealing the sticky interplay between the historical enslaved Black women who labored in the kitchen and "big house" of the southern plantations, carrying out domestic and lactation work, and her mythic representation as stereotypical Mammy.[33] Fulfilling the work of surrogate maternal care—breast-feeding white charges—constituted a significant portion of her unpaid domestic labor. The enormous breasts and prominent nipples on display, a mythic site of comfort and nourishment in Stedman's congressional Mammy monologue, register her charge to perform the most intimate of maternal biological functions, to suckle the white infants of her "master and mistress," a few of whom grew up to become the nostalgic senators who sought to memorialize the "faithful Mammy" that animated their romantic childhood remembrances of slavery (see Map 1).[34]

Moreover, the centering of the full breasts and nipples forcefully confronts the viewer with the historical context of the lactating Mammy, her maternality constructed as always available for nursing white children, to the detriment of her own (Collins 80).[35] Yaeger offers an illuminating reading of Walker's uses of Black women's breasts, lactation, and milk in her earlier silhouette work, which proves useful here. Black women's breast milk converts into commodity, a "superfluid," and their labor as wet nurses becomes an integral part of circum-Atlantic networks of production in which Black women's bodies are classed as "hyperproductive" and a "superabundant" site of "plentitude" (Yaeger 782, 795). *Marvelous Sugar Baby,* with its monumental stature, remarkably illustrates these themes of superfluidity, excess, and superabundance reflective of nineteenth-century pseudoscientific theories of racial difference encoded in the body.[36] The prominent placement of Mammy's anatomy also challenges the fiction of her asexuality and undermines the notion that the only function of her voluptuous breasts is to give nourishment and not to give or receive pleasure.[37]

Yet *A Subtlety* merges the mythologies of the Sphinx with the Mammy trope, two figures conceived and socially constructed to occupy different geographies, to subvert Mammy memorialization. Although characterized by excessive girth and by sternness with the white children she raises, Mammy is constructed as an endearing rather than an imposing character, as the Mammy proposal nostalgia underscores (McElya 8–9). Conversely, the Sphinx figuration encodes an illustrious ancient Egyptian civilization, massive by design, signaling dynastic power and innovation while also implicated in a long-standing cultural war around the racial representation and origins of the creators of these great feats of architecture.[38] By blending this iconography, Walker transmutes our understanding of the geographies of the enslaved Black body and reaffirms the existence of Black subjectivity even in the "belly of the whale."[39] As Katherine McKittrick, *Demonic Grounds* contends, intersecting "geographies of domination" and "geographies of black women" permeate the transatlantic slave trade, the Middle Passage, the Atlantic Ocean, and the plantation.[40] Although the dominant narrative of the Black woman's body often imagines it solely as a colonized space repeatedly violated in "geographies of domination," as McKittrick indicates, the "geographies of black women" represent spaces where their subjectivity emerges *in spite of* the geographies of domination. Walker's *A Subtlety* conveys, in part by its absolute size and hybrid figurations, Black women's subtle modes of resistance.

The subversive monumentality of the sculpture, furthermore, signals the emergence of Black women's subjectivity despite attempts to enshrine her degradation as a Confederate memorial statue. Here we can benefit from Spillers's reading of the ways in which the spatiality of the Middle Passage enacts Black corporeality. Spillers's "Mama's Baby" explicates the notion of "ungendering" of African persons, that is, the "displacement of genitalia" for the male and female African captives on the slave ship during the Middle Passage. Analyzing the infamous sketch of the *Brookes* slave galley, Spillers notes how the space allotted the enslaved was gender-based, with the enslaved men receiving more space than the women, who were expected to occupy "less room" (72–73).

Walker disrupts this racial economy in several ways. First, she undoes the "ungendering" by exposing the Mammy icon, presenting her in the nude, highlighting her female genitalia, regendering and commingling her image with that of the Sphinx. Second, she counters the mandate that the enslaved African woman occupy "less room" by designing her to inhabit the immense space of the Domino Sugar Refinery. Thus, Walker's *A Subtlety* decolonizes the Black woman's body from the geographies of domination of the slave ship and plantation, enlarging her dimensions where she was once forced into small spaces, centering her where she was once marginalized, and problematizing her representation where it was once captured in a fictive icon.

On a linguistic level, a significant part of what this sculpture challenges are what Spillers calls the "overdetermined nominative properties" of terms marking Black women, such as *Peaches, Aunty,* and *Brown Sugar.* Together with *Mammy,* these terms "demonstrate a sort of telegraphic encoding" as "markers so loaded with 'mythical prepossession' that there is no easy way for the agents buried beneath them to come clean" (65). Yet the grand stature of the *Marvelous Sugar Baby* mocks the misguided suggestion of the Mammy statue proposal that sought to memorialize in perpetuity the African American woman as the docile, devoted enslaved domestic worker. Instead of attempting to extricate the referents "buried beneath," *A Subtlety* sardonically disrupts the mythical prepossession at the intersection of the figuration of Mammy and Brown Sugar by making it at once playful and sticky with cultural identity and history.[41] I call on the primary significance of *sticky* as "having the property of sticking or adhering, adhesive," but also the colloquial definition related to both a person or a situation: "difficult to cope with, uncooperative," "tending to make difficulties," and "disagreeable owing to hardship or danger." *Marvelous Sugar Baby* is sticky, then, because she summons the viewer's personal histories, anxieties, and presuppositions but also resists knowability. She is dangerous, disagreeable, and difficult to decipher.

A SUBTLETY AS SWEET REVOLT

In Alice Walker's "In Search of Our Mothers' Gardens," she writes of Black women's bodies: "Instead of being perceived as whole persons, their bodies became shrines: what was thought to be their minds became temples suitable for worship. These crazy Saints stared out at the world, wildly, like lunatics—or quietly, like suicides; and the 'God' that was in their gaze was as mute as a great stone" (232). Kara Walker's *A Subtlety* conjures the enshrinement of Black women's bodies and evokes the pernicious history of the Black female body on display, exposed for public consumption, once considered "property" for sale on the auction block.[42] However, while the sculpture summons the violent exploitation of slavery and colonization, it also demands a consideration of the interlacing concepts of history, power, memory, generational trauma, and specifically, the simultaneity of the past and the present.[43]

While southern congressmen's plantation romance portrays Mammy as the asexual, corpulent, deeply devoted enslaved domestic, the foregrounding of her anatomy in *Marvelous Sugar Baby* forces the viewer to recognize her as a sexual and sexually vulnerable being.[44] As Abdur-Rahman convincingly argues, "the myriad ways" that enslaved bodies "were hideously and repeatedly violated became apt metaphors for revealing the gruesome and violent nature of American slavery itself" (28). The physiognomy of Walker's sculpture highlights what Abdur-Rahman describes as slavery's "collective 'raped' subjectivity" (41). Moreover, the overt placement of the nearly anatomically correct figure (there is no anus shown) compels the audience to reckon with the sexual violation of the enslaved African woman—her forced breeding and the resultant progeny—which was precisely the violent mechanism by which the slavocratic system was propagated and sustained (figures 4, 5, and 6).

One of the most significant colonial decrees that impacted the Black mother's body was codified in a 1662 Virginia law: "All children borne in this country shalbe held bond or free only according to the condition of the mother," thereby relegating the children of enslaved women to lifelong bondage.[45] Colonial Virginia assemblymen enacted this hereditary slavery law, explains Jennifer L. Morgan, "to guide them through the emerging morass of racial identities" resulting from interracial sex, criminalized as "fornication with a negro man or woman" (72). The duality of the enslaved woman as producer and reproducer "created tensions that perplexed their masters and injured their children," writes Dorothy Roberts, which was heightened after the abolition of the British transatlantic slave trade in 1807 (39).

Protean representations of the Black woman's body and her sexuality underscore the subversive undercurrents in *A Subtlety* and invoke "afterimages of slavery," a useful framework for interrogating neo-slave narratives. Viktoria Schmidt-Linsenhoff defines these as "images after images of slavery, passed down to the artists as a genealogy of pictures, which have been distorted, stereotyped and fragmented, but are nevertheless transporting visible traces of historical experience." These inherited images, Schmidt-Linsenhoff argues, "repeat and transform, reframe and translate old ones into the contemporary" (64). Following Saidiya Hartman's use of the "afterlife of slavery," Kimberly Juanita Brown astutely elaborates on the representational valences of the Black female body, mapping out the "afterimages of slavery" as "the place where black women's endurances have been used against them, and their bare survival is reconfigured as a strength that cannot be altered, damaged, or destroyed" (3). A salient shade of difference emerges with Walker's afterimage of slavery: the figure's body is cast in white bleached sugar.

A Subtlety, then, complicates the chiaroscuro of racial representation. This sculpture signifies Blackness yet ironically is constructed of white organic material, precisely the substance that drives the slavocracy in various regions of the New World, and especially the Caribbean. Thus, it plays with a spectrum of racial signifiers that emerge distinctly in the literature and visual culture of the Americas. Historians of slavery commonly note the contemporaneous development of slavery economies and sugar production in the New World.[46] Walker's medium and the occasion of the Domino Sugar Refinery demolition recall the sugar mill process of bleaching that transforms sugar from dark to white, as famously outlined in Cuban anthropologist Fernando Ortiz's *Contrapunteo* and referenced in one of Walker's handwritten notes.

If Morrison emphasizes race as metaphor in *Playing in the Dark* (63), then Christina Sharpe in *Monstrous Intimacies* specifically analyzes the allegories of color in Walker's black silhouettes and notes a particular (white) critical blind spot: "the *black* black figures in her silhouetted work nonetheless tend to become the sole site on which the signifying power of slavery in the past and the present is put to work." Sharpe posits that Walker's later silhouettes counter such myopic readings by adding "white figures and gray backgrounds and used light and overhead projection" to disrupt the "erasure" of the *white* black figures (154). What interests me here is the Black–white color reversal in *A Subtlety,* whereby this large-scale public monument of, to, and seemingly about the Black woman's body is in fact constructed of white sugar (that is, it is a *black* white figure, to use Sharpe's language). While this use of sugar as artistic material functions within the historical context of the medieval sculptural sugar subtleties that Walker cites as one of her inspirations, it also highlights the complex power exchanges through its reversal of Black–white color designations. Existing Mammy iconography portrays her as a Black woman with dark brown skin; however, Walker constructs her sculpture of the very material that fuels Mammy's enslavement in many loci of the Americas: sugar from the plantation.

Within the immersive exhibit space of the Domino Sugar Refinery, already a ruin, the politics of the gaze, audience, and reception emerge. Critic Jamilah King laments the "overwhelming whiteness" of viewership of *A Subtlety,* and of Black art in general.[47] As thousands of viewers solemnly observed the gigantic sculpture and from various angles, others made lewd gestures, publicly simulating the vulgar motions of sexual assault while taking selfies to share on social media.[48] Nicholas Powers recalls how he shouted in protest, "You are recreating the very racism this art is supposed to critique!"[49]

Interestingly, this representational contestation has plagued Walker's work itself, with critics arguing that it replicates the imperial gaze and reinforces stereotypical images of white supremacy while pandering to a white audience.[50] However, I suggest that *A Subtlety* propels the critical viewer to grapple with the racist, sexist, capitalist legacies of colonization and enslavement referenced in the semiotics of the hybrid sculpture. The indignation that Powers vocalizes over the pantomimed sexual and racial violence in the contact zone of the Domino Sugar Refinery (21–39) congeals with bell hooks's apt conceptualization of "eating the Other," the consumption and prompt forgetting of the subaltern.[51] Although the sugary substance of the sculpture lends itself to this metaphor, with its obvious resonances with the sugar commodity of slave economies, it also encourages slower digestion and absorption of notions of alterity, demanding recognition of viewer complicity in this process of Othering. Thus, when Powers calls for "guidelines on how to interpret" Walker's work, the suggestion undercuts the work's exegetic power, embodied in the preliminary concept sketch, which shows the Mammy-Sphinx in her full oracular power, with the words "Go ahead, Ask" emanating from her mouth.[52]

Walker deliberately avoids a didactic framing and remarks in later interviews, "I could never arrive at the heart of the thing through placards or language" and "People had to make the piece have meaning. They had to connect the dots between sugar, worker, slavery. Where does it come from? Who has produced this?" ("Un-Private Collection").[53] The reenactment of racism and sexism Powers admonishes, in fact, evidences the persistence of these systems of domination, the necessity for dialogue in the historically exclusionary space of the public art exhibit, and a reexamination of how and why we engage with and move through this installation, while confronting the proposed memorialization of Mammy and the violent histories it attempts to cover.

MULTIPLE MAMMIES IN WILLIAMS'S *DESSA ROSE*

I have addressed the sticky politics of reception and purposeful collisions engendered by the immersive viewer experience at the Domino Sugar Refinery, in light of Walker's refusal to provide an official didactic framing for *A Subtlety,* as evidence of its subversive strands. Notably, Mammy nomenclature belies the complexity of racialized maternal identity in the construction of this derogatory image. Just as the congressmen refer to the "colored mammies of the South" in the 1923 proposal, Du Bois, too, uses "Black Mammy" in *The Gift of Black Folk* to distinguish this African American domestic servant from the general colloquial usage of *mammy,* which might refer to a mother of any race.[54]

This linguistic slippage around the archetypal Mammy appellation challenges the racially inscribed fictions fueling it. As we see in this final section, on *Dessa Rose,* Sherley Anne Williams artfully complicates, shifts, and inverts the southern congressmen's Mammy conceptualizations to counter the fixity of this disturbing image in American mythology. This literary mode of resistance, a neo–slave narrative, convincingly opposes Mammy's memorialization. Scenes of cross-racial breast-feeding disrupt the romanticized Black wet nurse and introduce the *white Mammy,* that is, a white woman who breast-feeds a Black baby.

The eponymous protagonist in *Dessa Rose* endeavors to forge a liberatory space by *talking back* and destabilizing structures of domination, even as she survives clandestinely within them, in her precarious status as a fugitive enslaved woman, pregnant and then mother. This upending of rigid constructions of power/subordination in the US South predicts the Mammy iconoclasm of Walker's sugar sculpture. In the novel's three-act structure—"The Darky," "The Wench," "The Negress"—the reader gleans the violence of naming from an Orientalist, colonialist positionality. Williams intersperses the third person limited omniscient narration with alternating points of view, transporting the reader into the "most private thoughts" of her characters (S. Williams 108).[55] The shifting narrative voices dramatize an extraordinary chronicle of an imaginary encounter between two early nineteenth-century women, one Black and enslaved (Dessa/Odessa) and one white (Rufel/Ruth Elizabeth), both oppressed, to varying degrees, by the patriarchy, sexism, racism, and physical exploitation of the slavocratic regime.

Another polyvocal textual register is its anachronistic vocabulary, which ruptures the plausibility of an 1847 narrative world. Dessa, her lover Kaine recently killed in a slave rebellion, courageously escapes the coffle while heavily pregnant, and simultaneously enacts stereotypical assumptions about her unbridled, animalistic wickedness to slip in and out of spaces of containment. Rufel, conversely, exaggerates a helpless naïveté after her husband's physical and financial abandonment to act out interracial sexual desires with Nathan, one of the runaway captives who sought refuge at her farm.

Much like the appellation *Mammy,* the titles of the three sections signal the inescapable dangers of Othering vis-à-vis imposed naming and renaming practices common during colonization and enslavement. Returning to Spillers's notion of "overdetermined nominative properties" illuminates the nexus between giving name and claiming property; "the names by which I am called in the public place render an example of signifying property *plus*" ("Mama's Baby" 65). The names hold signifying power in both public and private spaces. Challenging dominant power structures, the novel discloses how both the enslaved *and* the free participate in naming and renaming, undercutting figures of authority with epithets whispered in secret. For instance, in private conversations, "scheming" Ada, the formerly enslaved woman who finds refuge on Rufel's property, derisively refers to the mistress of the property as "Miz Ruint," a nominative alluding to Rufel's unstable societal position. She is living in an unfinished house in ruins—there is a staircase to nowhere—discarded by her husband and considered "crazy," "touched," and "strange in the head" by the Black people living on her land (S. Williams 115, 118). The epithet also forecasts her "ruined" corporeal status after her sexual relationship with a Black man, Nathan, which, if made public, would render her socially dead and might even lead to her physical death as punishment for the crime of interracial sex.

Consider her other appellation, "Miz Rufel," also a "slave-given name, discarded by white people when they reached adulthood" (99). As Ada ridicules Rufel through transgressive naming, she also negates the possibility of ever belonging to her as property. The narrator suggests that "neither of them belonged to her, that in fact they did her a favor by working for her at all!" (100). Ada later reassures Dessa, "Didn't none of us never belong to this place"; the *never* in the double negative construction emphasizes their slippery in-between status—runaways, yet free from being classified as Rufel's property (116). However, it is her beloved Mammy who first bestows upon her the name Rufel and its diminutive form, 'Fel, as a pet name, a result of her inability to pronounce her official name, Ruth Elizabeth. As Odessa is abbreviated to Dessa, Ruth is transliterated as Rufel.

Even in the tender remembrance of her pet name's origin, the narrator conveys an undercurrent of racial disdain: "The darkies never could get her name straight, slurring and garbling the syllables until the name seemed almost unrecognizable" (124). Yet even in her critique of Black vernacular, Rufel admits that to snuggle on her Mammy's "pillowy bosom" and to hear those names, 'Fel and Rufel, "was to hear, to know herself loved" (124). Williams's characters understand the synchrony between naming, owning, kinship, and belonging as they negotiate official and unofficial names to enforce or resist social order.

These transgressive acts of naming occur in the liminal territory of Sutton's Glen, a property already remotely located on the outskirts of a northern Alabama district "hidden again by the trees" (105). Rufel, in denial about her husband, Bertie's, abandonment, is uncertain of her survival as a white woman left alone without white male patriarchal protection, while Dessa and the other "runaways" are considered violent fugitives according to governing slavery laws; they are without a proper "owner" yet are not owned by Rufel, occupying the outlaw territoriality of the neither enslaved nor free. Dessa's maternality and recent difficult childbirth experience in the woods render her doubly vulnerable and in desperate need of safety as she awakens in Rufel's house and fears "the white woman would kill her kill her and . . . the baby. Baby. Her ba—" (82). The repetition in these half-formed utterances—that she might be doubly obliterated—divulges her maternal fear of corporeal annihilation and infanticide, and, by extension, the omnipresent fear of the enslaved woman that her own flesh is always susceptible to racial violence and destruction, that the fruit of her womb does not belong to her and might be sold away or murdered at any moment.

In Rufel's feigned bewilderment, she not only permits a group of unknown "darkies" to stay on her property but also regularly breast-feeds (hesitantly at first, and then willingly, even pleasurably) a Black baby, Dessa's newborn son. I posit that Rufel performs confused naïveté to maintain a semblance of the cult of white womanhood even as her interior thoughts recognize Dessa's humanity, as she astonishingly becomes her wet nurse and, in turn, the Black baby's *white Mammy.* The narrator repeatedly informs us that Rufel is hyperaware of their skin color difference: "Dessa looked down. The brown baby was in her arms, his dark eyes staring up at her unwinkingly" (89). She temporarily regards

FIG. 1. Jean-Baptiste Debret, *Uma senhora brasileira em seu lar* [*A Brazilian Senhora in Her Home*] (1823), from *Voyage pittoresque et historique au Brésil.*

FIG. 2. Jean-Baptiste Debret, *Le Dîner* [*A Brazilian Dîner*] (1827).

FIGS. 3 AND 4. Kara Walker, *A Subtlety* (2014). Front view (*left*), rear view (*right*). Photographs by Jason Wyche. Courtesy Creative Time.

FIG. 5. Kara Walker, *A Subtlety* (2014). Adjacent figure.
Photograph by Jason Wyche. Courtesy Creative Time.

FIG. 6. Frederico Guilherme Briggs, *Negros que vão levar açoutes* [*Negroes Going to Be Whipped*] (1832), lithograph.

FIG. 7. Julien Sinzogan, *Gates of Return* (2007). Acrylic on canvas, 4.65 × 10 meters. Courtesy of the artist and October Gallery, London. Photograph copyright © Jonathan Greet.

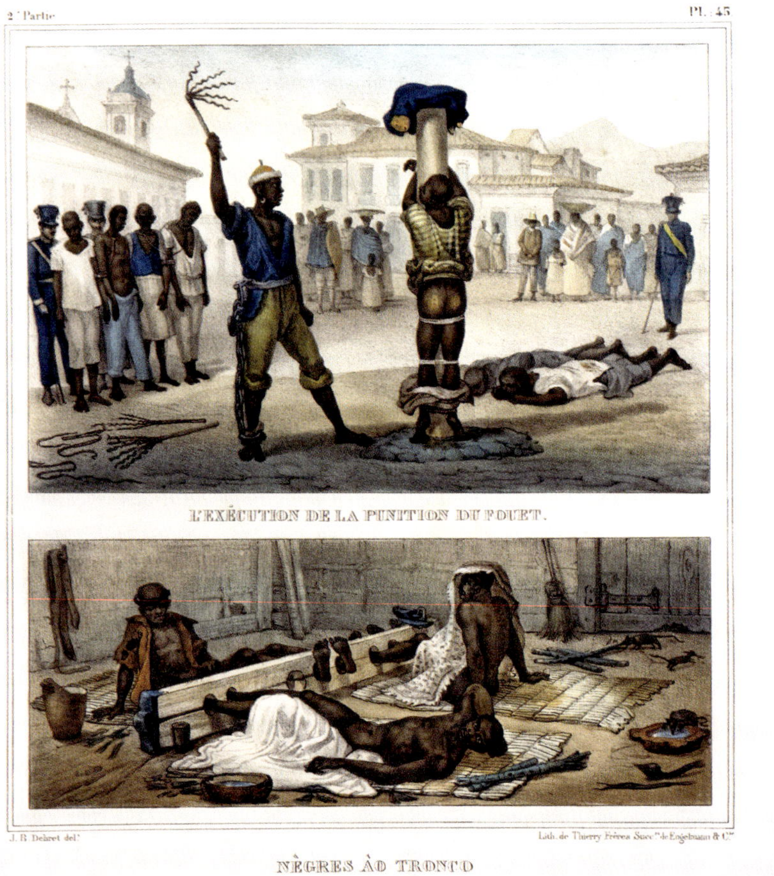

FIG. 8. Jean-Baptiste Debret, *Nègres ào tronco* [*Blacks in the Stocks*] and *L'exécution de la punition du fouet* [*The Execution of the Punishment of the Whip*], from *Voyage pittoresque et historique au Brésil.*

the Black baby as animalistic Other upon speculating about her neighbor's reaction to the shocking scene of her nursing the Black child: "a *pickaninny* . . . his dark skin might as well be fur" (127; emphasis added).

Although the narration intimates that Rufel "had felt some mortification at becoming wet nurse for a darky," a sense of obligation compels her to continue "of necessity to suckle the baby" as the "only nursing woman on the place" (102). Most often, she fetishizes the Black–white skin color difference:

> Rufel sank gratefully into the rocker in the parlor and freed her breast to the baby's searching mouth. The baby planted a tiny fist on her breast, sucking hungrily, his shoe-button eyes glittery with tears. She turned her head from his stare, uncomfortable under his unwinking gaze. Almost of their own volition, her fingers stroked his silken curls, so different from the bald heads of her own newborns, the utter brownness of him a striking contrast with the pallor of their skins. Willfully, she closed her eyes and, sighing, gave herself over to the sensual rhythm of his feeding. (128)

Although she exoticizes the baby's racial difference and contrasts his physical attributes to her own children's—"shoe-button eyes," "silken curls," and "utter brownness"—Rufel cannot and does not allow the baby to die from starvation, though Dessa is no longer producing milk. Rufel identifies with Dessa via common bonds of motherhood, from the initial moment she springs to clean and clothe the bloody infant upon their arrival on her property. Yet Rufel's inability to make eye contact indicates a reluctance to acknowledge this brown-skinned baby, to embrace an interracial bonding experience, and her role as wet nurse for a Black child.[56] Williams poignantly reverses the conventional racial typologies of the Mammy figure, subversively rendering Rufel a white Mammy to a Black baby.[57]

However, Rufel's resolve to "do something about this" is fraught; she vacillates between regarding Dessa with empathetic maternal allegiance and upholding the white supremacy upon which racialized slavery is based (95). Dessa, too, agonizes over Rufel's assistance. Her guttural lament upon viewing Rufel nursing her newborn—"Naaaaaawwwww!" (88)—reveals not only her fright at this implausible vision, what Jennifer Griffiths calls "an unfathomable intimacy" (24), but perhaps also a registering of her baby's treason, latching on to a white woman's breast for sustenance after Dessa has nearly lost her life to escape the coffle and fight her slave trader. This fascinating moment subverts racial configurations of child-care provider and recipient during slavery, foreshadowing the semiotic multiplicity embedded in the gigantic *black* white sugar-coated breasts of Walker's *Marvelous Sugar Baby.*[58] Despite her internal vacillations, Rufel conspires with Dessa in acts of interracial breast-feeding against a patriarchal system that has left them both materially stranded. While breast-feeding is Dessa's first conscious encounter with Rufel, the Mammy debate is their first contentious dialogue.

In these powerful dialogic exchanges between the main protagonists, particularly "the passionate argument over Mammy," Dessa outwits and instructs her *almost* mistress through semantic and lexical contortions (S. Williams 141). Against the backdrop of her perilous liminality and her strategic refusal to speak to the white interlocutor Nehemiah during her confinement, in "The Darky," Dessa strikingly carves out a liberatory space through language. As the new mother convalesces, battered, bedridden, and silent, Rufel dreamily reminisces out loud about her affluent upbringing in Charleston, before the ill-fated marriage to Bertie and financial ruin in Alabama, nostalgically recalling her Mammy's devotion and the beautiful clothes she dutifully sewed for her. Suddenly, Dessa rouses from sleep and hurls a biting series of accusations: "Wasn't no 'mammy' to it"; "Mammy ain't made you nothing!"; "Mammy ain't nobody name, not they real one" (118–119).

This critical exchange evidences a bold moment of oppositional speech. Reversing Dessa's initial inarticulation upon the sight of Rufel nursing her baby, it is now Rufel who cannot complete her thoughts or demonstrate any intimate knowledge of her beloved Mammy's life. When asked to state Mammy's "real" name, she responds, "Why, she—"; "My, my—*My* Mammy—"; and then only sheepishly, "Mam—" (118–119). The repetition of *my* here indicates that Rufel is only certain of her possession of Mammy, that she belongs to her. Dessa excoriates Rufel:

> "See! See! You don't even know 'mammy's' name. Mammy have a name, have children."
>
> "She didn't." The white woman, finger stabbing toward her own heart, finally rose. "She just had me! I was like her child." (119)

Through a marvelous sequence of rhetorical moves and incisive interrogation—"What was her name then? . . . Child don't even know its own mammy's name. What was mammy's name?" (119)—Dessa not only probes the extent of Rufel's knowledge of "her" Mammy, but also exposes lacunae in Rufel's notions about Mammy's "true" identity, effectively nullifying any claimed kinship ties. Being "like her child" does not equate to knowing Mammy as she was: the living and breathing Black woman with a family and history.

Angelo Robinson Rich insightfully argues that Dessa rejects the conflation of "Mammy" and "mothering," and insists on distinguishing between "the work of an enslaved Black female and the emotional attachment of a mother's love (54). Indeed, Dessa shouts that Mammy's name was Rose and describes her identifying physical features, including her "smooth black" skin and mouth "slick as butter, her kiss tangy as clabber" (S. Williams 119). When she recounts her mother's story and the painful history of the ten children who were sold away into slavery, she maps out a genealogy and calls them all by name. In this verbal confrontation, Dessa steals power away from Rufel by giving Mammy a name, distinctive facial features, describing the taste of Mammy's kiss, and providing a personal life history as a corrective to Rufel's misguided notions of a rootless Black woman called Mammy who only existed to serve and please her.

With these proclamations, Dessa, the woman who strategically enacts silence after surviving brutal physical punishment, defiantly corrects this white woman who is not her mistress but who has housed her and breast-feeds her baby. Exposing the absurdity of Rufel's assumption—that her Mammy was the same woman as Dessa's Mammy, that only one Mammy could possibly exist—she reclaims the complexity of Black womanhood, rejecting a monolithic formulation of the women who perform this servile role of enslaved wet nurse. Like Walker's *A Subtlety,* Dessa's words reveal the figuration of Mammy to be nothing more than another shimmering imaginary figment, liable to dissolve in one's hands. Thus, Dessa counters the history of "*African-American* female's misnaming" by disavowing Mammy's memorialization (Spillers, "Mama's Baby" 66).

In this climactic moment, Dessa simultaneously reveals the mythology around the fictitious Mammy of southern lore and confiscates Black women from this white woman's imagination: "And Mammy—Rufel burst into tears. Of course she knew Mammy's name, she told herself, and she would think of it as soon as she got over being so upset" (S. Williams 122). This revelation creates an epistemological fissure in Rufel's understanding of an antebellum racialized societal order. Ashraf Rushdy notes that their conversation "provides Rufel with a sense of how a simile of 'family' is an oppressive structure under the conditions of plantation culture" (368). The loving, dedicated Mammy of her memories vanishes, with Rufel "finding no comfort in the familiar image. It was as if the wench had taken her beloved Mammy and put a stranger in her place" as she now envisions a face that "seemed that of a stranger" (S. Williams 128, 125).

Dessa asserts authority in her relationship with Rufel by estranging her from the fondest remembrances of her Mammy, simultaneously revealing to her that she was more than the silk handkerchief–wearing, white-aproned caricature of her imagination. Dessa's forceful instruction succeeds, as Rufel acknowledges Mammy was in fact a woman who possessed a name—Dorcas—and had her own personal history of sorrows, triumphs, loves, hopes, and desires. Although the pain of her personal experiences may not be easily legible on her neatly presented body, it may exist, hidden just like Dessa's own mutilated body and scarred inner thighs.

Griffiths locates in Dessa's trauma a representation of resilient feminine empowerment in the midst of victimhood that "bears witness to suffering without condemning the survivor to silence" (32). The narrator concedes, "But Mammy might have had children and it bothered Rufel that she did not know" (S. Williams 128). As Dessa's interrogation lingers in her mind, Rufel reenvisions Mammy as an enslaved woman who may have had a sweetheart or children, may have been subjected to brutal beatings, and she "wanted desperately to believe that Mammy had loved her not only fully, but freely as well" (138).

Dessa's destruction of the Mammy myth forces Rufel—entranced by Old South plantation romanticism just like the proponents of the 1923 Mammy statue proposal—to confront a startling reality: "her" Mammy was a multidimensional woman with a life outside her own. As Deborah Gray White summarizes, "black subservience and faithfulness had been the product of white power and imagination" (167). Dessa's word work is generative in that she finds a place to go and be free in the intimate knowledge and cultural understanding of Mammy's personhood and in her relentless insistence that Rufel recognize her full humanity. Dessa's arguments render Rufel speechless, and in so doing, rehabilitate and honor, at least for those fleeting moments, the story of her mother's life, reasserting the complexity of Black womanhood and powerfully resisting misguided Mammy memorialization projects.

"NEVER ARRIVING AT THE HEART OF THE THING"

Walker's *A Subtlety* provocatively subverts the congressional Mammy statue proposal, a proposition sinisterly haunting the annals of history for nearly the last century. As viewers visually and corporeally consume the gigantic confection with its intersecting politicized, racialized and gendered signifiers, what emerges is the complex dyad of desire and fear animating twenty-first-century engagements with the legacy of slavery. Defying the notion that the Black woman might be enshrined in a derogatory representation, the Mammy–Sphinx hybrid represents a complicated Black subject, evading her capture and containment in an immutable monument. As Darlene Clark Hine incisively theorizes, "Black women, as a rule, developed and adhered to a cult of secrecy, a culture of dissemblance, to protect the sanctity of inner aspects of their lives," appearing to publicly disclose "while actually remaining an enigma" (915). Sticky, unknowable, already melting away, *Marvelous Sugar Baby* dissimulates.

Similarly, Williams's *Dessa Rose* gives voice and name to the enslaved woman, Dessa, who straddles the boundary between slavery and freedom, while leaving space for her to debate and contradict her *almost* mistress on the meaning and interpretation of Mammy, of her lived experiences, painful and triumphant. Both works transform the trauma linking sugar and the Mammy figure by creating what Judith Herman in *Trauma and Recovery* calls a "survivor mission" in which the women "transform the meaning of their personal tragedy by making it the basis for social action" (207). Often this social action takes the form of provocation and disruption of neat interpretations, which Walker achieves with her visual art and Williams with her neo-slave narrative of misery, survival, and resistance.

Hilton Als posits in a 2014 *New Yorker* article "The Sugar Sphinx," that "Walker's sphinx is triumphant, rising from another kind of half world—the shadowy half world of slavery and degradation as she gives us a version of 'the finger'" due to the placement of the fingers in the figure's left hand, the only element Walker saved from the now destroyed *Marvelous Sugar Baby.* A defiant hand gesture with the thumb slightly protruding between the pointer finger and middle finger, the *figa* is a symbol of fertility and eroticism with European origins, which assumed new meaning in New World contexts. It is perhaps a curse to the viewer, an amulet, a symbol of resistance, protection, and good fortune.

These visual and literary representations of misery and resistance empower because they come out of their grief to "give the finger" to singular interpretations of history and demand continued interrogation of representations of the Mammy figure. If the reactions from the African American press, Schuyler's *Black No More,* and the work of Walker and Williams disclose at turns cautious and defiant reimaginings of the imposed "symbols of slavery and subservience" exemplified by the Mammy cult, then in the next chapter we shall see direct creative challenges to two of the most heinous rituals and events in African American history: lynching and the Middle Passage. The poetry of Jean Toomer and Robert Hayden affirm that a thing of beauty can be created even in the face of inexplicable human suffering.

3

BLACK FLESH AFTER FLAME

Lynching, Resistance, and the Legacy of Slavery in the Poetry of Jean Toomer and Robert Hayden

Day dawned, and soon the mixed crowds came to view
The ghastly body swaying in the sun:
The women thronged to look, but never a one
Showed sorrow in her eyes of steely blue;
And little lads, lynchers that were to be,
Danced round the dreadful thing in fiendish glee.

—CLAUDE MCKAY, "The Lynching"

There was a design of white bones slumbering forgottenly
    upon a cushion of ashes.
There was a charred stump of a sampling pointing a blunt finger
    accusingly at the sky.

—RICHARD WRIGHT, "Between the World and Me"

At a performance in a Los Angeles nightclub, a boisterous patron shouted to legendary jazz singer Billie Holiday (1915–1959), "Billie, why don't you sing that sexy song you're so famous for? You know, the one about the naked bodies swinging in the trees." Holiday flatly refused, later calling the anonymous woman a "bitch" in her 1956 autobiography, *Lady Sings the Blues.* However, Holiday recalled a vastly different reception from a fan after a New York performance at the Downbeat Club on Fifty-Second Street. Depleted from the emotional intensity of the performance and crying backstage in the ladies' room, a woman approached her and tearfully said, "I never heard anything so beautiful in my life. You can still hear a pin drop out there" (Holiday and Dufty 84–85).

These contrasting episodes, which took place sometime between 1939 and the mid-1950s, index the problem of representing the horror of the lynching spectacle, the ritualistic practice of anti-Black violence, and the coupled legacies of slavery and white supremacy in literature and song.[1] I have thus far focused on manifold literary and visual direct representations of enslavement, and I expand the analysis here to poetic echoes of slavery, with specific attention to the overt and oblique resonances of lynching in Jean Toomer's *Cane,* followed by a reading of the stunning imagery and lyrical experimentation in Robert Hayden's "Middle Passage." As Saidiya Hartman argues in *Scenes of Subjection* in reference to the 1892 US Supreme Court ruling in *Plessy v. Ferguson,* the "insidious ascription of place under the guise of equality resurrected the subjugation of slavery" (193). The post-Reconstruction resurrection of the subjugation of slavery—of keeping the Negro in her place—and the reproduction of the "legal subjection of blacks" under *Plessy* empowered the most pernicious practices of extrajudicial subjection of Black citizens. The ensuing white supremacist violence in the public domain serves as a corrective to any alleged breach of the social order rigidly organized around the fiction of immutable racial distinctions and the prohibition of "encounters between scandalously proximate bodies" across the color line (206). Without the incentive of property preservation under the racial capitalist logic of chattel slavery, the lynch mob and their accomplices enact postbellum white violence as a mode of replicating the racialized power hierarchies of slavery and perpetuating a pervasive state of racial terror.

Drawing on Hartman's theory of emancipation as a "nonevent," I first turn to renderings of lynching in poetry and song as exemplars of the cultural afterlife of racial slavery, "transformed rather than annulled," to excavate the "tragic continuities" of white violence and Black degradation across time and space (116, 10, 7). How might we account for the poet's compulsion to create art—to reveal the enduring beauty of the human spirit that dares to seek liberty—in the wake of this unspeakable history of Black torture and suffering, or what Sharpe in *In the Wake* calls the "continuous and changing present of slavery's as yet unresolved unfolding" (14)?

Scholars from the postbellum period to the present have recounted the tenuous, unfinished project of postemancipation freedom, or "slavery by another name," to use Blackmon's term, and the enactment of public humiliation, intimidation, and brutal acts of racial violence and the prevailing "reign of terror" to reassert sociopolitical control and uphold the racial order (Du Bois,

Black Reconstruction 671; Kendi 259). As James H. Cone summarizes: "The sufferings of black people during slavery are too deep for words. That suffering did not end with emancipation . . . The lynching tree is the most potent symbol of the trouble nobody knows that blacks have seen but do not talk about because of the pain of remembering" (2–3).[2] This chapter focuses on literary renderings of the monstrous US rituals of lynching in the postbellum period in Toomer's "Kabnis" and "Portrait in Georgia," and the terrors of the transatlantic journey in Hayden's "Middle Passage" to pose the question: What is the task of the poet who writes in the aftermath of public spectacles of human torture and inexpressible suffering?

Holiday's April 20, 1939, recording under the Commodore label and her subsequent live dramatic performances of the chilling song "Strange Fruit," which jazz critic Leonard Feather declared "the first significant protest in words and music, the first unmuted cry against racism," elicit manifold reactions and push the boundaries of representation (Margolick, *Biography of a Song* 4). Holiday, too, recognized its tremendous significance—politically, socially, and personally—in fact, calling it her "personal protest" in *Lady Sings the Blues,* which incidentally she proposed to title *Bitter Crop,* the final two agonizing words of the song (16–17). Her book publisher, however, denied her request. Nevertheless, "Strange Fruit" became her signature ballad and the poignant centerpiece of a carefully crafted musical repertoire that catapulted her from local talent to major player in the international jazz scene (A. Davis 187).[3]

Returning, then, to the divergent reactions from the women during and after Holiday's performances, one observes that the vocalist omits race from her recollection of these events. This is notable because she does not avoid pejorative language, nor does she hold her tongue with racial slurs in her autobiography, at various points even referring to disruptive audience members and racist white folks she encountered on tour as "crackers."[4] Since she withholds the race of either woman who approached her in each anecdote, we are left to read race into this ambiguity. Given the fact that Café Society was one of the only integrated jazz clubs in early 1940s Greenwich Village, it is not an unfounded presupposition that Holiday performed in front of a segregated (all-white) crowd in both instances (Panish 38).[5] For the woman in the New York club who approached her after the performance, the song transmitted astonishing and incomparable sounds of beauty. But how could this searing musical rendition of the painful American tradition of pernicious disregard of African American life, which a 1939 *New York Amsterdam News* review article calls a "plea to fight mob law," and required listening for "every American who abhors lynching," at once be a thing of sonorous beauty (Chase)? Is it dangerous to locate beauty in "the slow majesty of a dirge," a song about vicious rituals of lynching, one of the grisly continuing legacies of slavery in the United States?

The exchange with the woman from the audience in the Los Angeles club is both troubling and illuminating. In her mocking request for the song about the "naked bodies swinging in the trees," the female audience member draws attention to the racial order without explicitly naming it. Her willful misreading of the iconic song's content, erroneously naming it a "sexy song," not only trivializes African American suffering and effaces the Black body in pain (and the explosive white mob that propagated the violence) but also reinscribes the Black male body in the fiction of the hypersexual "brute" swinging from trees like a beast in the jungle. In a potent perversion of the song's significance, the heckler erases the murderous gravity of the lynching act and attempts to make Holiday complicit in her verbal effacement by calling her to perform on command, reasserting her power as patron over Billie as the mere Black entertainer.

Far from an innocuous parody, the comment announces the painful sexual politics and history of US antimiscegenation laws, the very sanctions and accusations that caused so many Black men to be lynched in the first place, sometimes for the crime of "reckless eyeballing," or merely looking at a white woman.[6] The woman's charged words expose the disturbing underbelly of the exuberance of the racial mingling, or "black and tan" atmosphere, in the jazz club scene. Thus, to call a song about lynching "sexy" and to satirize it as a song about swinging Black "naked bodies" overlays a distinctly frivolous interpretive violence, trivializing the polemical connection between race, rape, and lynching that Sandra Gunning calls attention to when she argues that "we tend to ignore automatically the very different manner of participation engaged in by Black and white women writers when they approach the subject of lynching," which extends beyond the common narrative of white/Black male homosocial fears and desires over the white female body (9). The brief exchange between Holiday and the raucous patron exhibits the complex tensions between a Black and white female intervention in lynching discourse that is overwhelmingly coded masculine (though there were Black female victims as well).

The "strange fruit" of the song in question, of course, is the organic metaphor of the tree that bears not nutritive sustenance but dead, mutilated Black bodies. The corpses hang not from a tree of life but of death and heinous torture:

Southern trees bear a strange fruit,
Blood on the leaves and blood at the root,
Black body swinging in the southern breeze,
Strange fruit hanging from the poplar trees.

Pastoral scene of the gallant South,
The bulging eyes and the twisted mouth,
Scent of magnolia sweet and fresh,
And the sudden smell of burning flesh!

Here is a fruit for the crows to pluck,
For the rain to gather, for the wind to suck,
For the sun to rot, for a tree to drop,
Here is a strange and bitter crop.

The haunting imagery encapsulated in the simple couplet rhyme scheme of this song of protest (*fruit/root, breeze/trees, South/mouth, fresh/flesh, pluck/suck,* and *drop/crop*), originally written by Jewish New York public school teacher Abel Meeropol (whose pen name was Lewis Allan), offers an elegy to the named and unnamed victims in the ghastly racial theater and horrific violence of an American ritual of the Jim Crow era that predominated in the last decade of the nineteenth century and the first third of the twentieth century in the United States, what Mark Twain called the "epidemic of bloody insanities" in his essay "The United States of Lyncherdom" (1901). A basic sketch of this drama exposes an angry white mob seeking to restore order after a perceived breach of a codified or implicitly understood racial division or claims of criminality, whether fraudulent or substantiated. Standing trial was not an option for African Americans. Thus, the offending Black victim becomes the savage brute and criminal who must be annihilated via public hanging. While the Black body and the life contained within it was never valued in the United States (except for the labor that could be extracted from it), the violence of the postemancipation period rose to frighteningly insatiable levels:

> What was strikingly new and different in the late nineteenth and early twentieth century was the sadism and exhibitionism that characterized white violence. The ordinary modes of execution and punishment no longer satisfied the emotional appetite of the crowd. To kill the victim was not enough; the

> execution became public theater, a participatory ritual of torture and death, a voyeuristic spectacle prolonged as long as possible (once for seven hours) for the benefit of the crowd. (J. Allen 13)[7]

A stirring lament, "Strange Fruit" therefore points to a startling paradox: the use of nature (tree) as an instrument of murder. Yet the increased incidence of lynchings during this period normalized the tragic event of the dead Black bodies dangling from the tree limbs—lynching scenes were even captured in photographs and circulated widely as postcards—denying even the descriptor *strange* in the sense of "unfamiliar" or "hitherto unknown."

According to the mythology around the production of "Strange Fruit," Allan was inspired to write the famous political poem, which arguably became the first civil rights protest song, by one of the major historical events of racial terror: the August 7, 1930, lynching of Thomas Shipp (nineteen years old) and Abram Smith (eighteen years old) in Marion, Indiana, which was captured and reproduced by town photographer Lawrence Beitler in a now iconic lynching souvenir postcard. The next morning, Beitler sold the postcards for fifty cents in the Marion town square. The attribution to Beitler Studio is visible in the shocking photograph, which shows the bloody corpses of the two lynched Black teenagers surrounded by a white crowd, a mixture of proud mobsters and curious gawkers, including a smiling couple holding hands, a pregnant woman, elderly and young people, a man in his work clothes, and an ominous figure looking directly at the camera with an angry expression, pointing to the hanging corpses.[8] One reviewer astutely compared the countenance of the crowd to a group of people attending a county fair or other festive occasion.

As news reports and eyewitnesses to the event recount, an angry mob used a sledgehammer to break through the ironclad jail wall at the Grant County Court House on that sweltering summer evening and seized Shipp and Smith from their jail cells after their arrest for the alleged murder of Claude Deeter, a local white factory worker, and the rape of his girlfriend, Mary Ball (Madison 8–9). One newspaper, the *Albany Evening,* announced the events thusly: "Infuriated Mob Storms Jail to Kill 2 Negroes: Town Terrorized as Prisoners Taken from Cells." After stripping Smith's corpse of his pants to save as souvenirs, someone in the crowd, in a baffling inversion of morality, draped a Ku Klux Klan robe over the naked lower half of Smith's body, for the sake of decency (Adler).

The sole survivor of this lynching, who was marked to be the third victim that night, was sixteen-year-old James Herbert Cameron Jr. Cameron recalled that Shipp wanted him to demand money from an unsuspecting couple at gunpoint and use it to buy a new car. According to Cameron's account, he approached the car with the gun, but when he noticed that Deeter was a friend who came in to get his shoes shined, he refused to proceed with the robbery, fled the scene of the crime, and ran six miles to his home. Although he was later dragged from the jail cell as well, and had a noose placed around his neck under the tree, Cameron remembered a providential voice coming from heaven—or a solitary sympathizer in the crowd, who shouted that he was innocent.

Whether it was divine intervention, as Cameron believed, his small stature (he appeared to be a boy of twelve or thirteen years old), or some combination of these factors, he narrowly escaped the fate of his two friends. Amazingly, he was returned to the jail. He was later convicted and served four years in jail. Cameron found healing fifty years later through writing, distributing, and presenting his story at schools, even when no publisher wanted to support the project. As we will see in "Kabnis," the cathartic release of emotion through bearing witness and telling one's story might lead to forgiveness and renewal. Mortgaging his house in 1982, Cameron self-published and distributed his book, *A Time of Terror: The True Story by the Third Victim of This Lynching in the North Who Missed His Appointment with Death,* with its long descriptive title reminiscent of the titles of nineteenth-century slave narratives.[9] He founded America's Black Holocaust Museum in Milwaukee to tell his story, and although it closed after his death, a website has replaced it, providing a virtual museum and pedagogical tool with the capacity to reach a much broader, transnational audience. Cameron ultimately used his torture and near-death experience as a teenage boy to educate the public about the atrocities of white supremacy.

Yet this may have represented Cameron's official narrative for the public, while he continued to protect those who could no longer speak for themselves. Various competing narratives complicate a neat reading of the forensic readability and reliability of Beitler's photograph. Furthermore, the 2011 drama *The Gospel According to James,* written by Charles Smith, challenges the stability of James Cameron's account of the events preceding the lynching and creates a romantic relationship between Mary Ball and Abram Smith, seemingly not to discredit the survivor's story but to bring into crisis the possibility of a single, "official" narrative in the United States' collective memory of trauma (T. Williams).

Over the past century, scholars of criminal law and sociology have investigated this vicious American tradition and national trauma, which Patterson, *Rituals of Blood* summarizes as the "terrorization of Afro-Americans by lynch mobs and their ritualized killing in communal acts of human sacrifice" (172).[10] Consider this entry from nearly two decades before the Marion, Indiana, lynching, from the *Journal of the American Institute of Criminal Law and Criminology,* as an example of the emphasis on numerical tabulations of national lynchings:

> *Lynchings in 1912.*—The Chicago *Record Herald* has compiled interesting statistics with respect to lynchings perpetrated in the United States in 1912. Only twenty-eight are recorded. This suggests the most orderly year in the country's recent history. A year ago there were thirty-five lynchings; in 1910 the figures were 45; and in 1909, 30. The highest known number was in 1894 when the spirit of mob rule was responsible for 190 deaths. In 1903 the total was 106. (Gault 130)

Although this record indicates a downward trend in the number of annual lynchings, the "reign of terror" or "feast of blood," as one 1931 newspaper called an act of lynching, continued at a disturbing pace from the 1890 through the post–World War I period (Goldsby 25).[11] Much scholarly attention has focused on counting the lynching victims. As with the efforts to quantify the number of African captives forcibly transported across the Atlantic Ocean, determining the total number of African Americans lynched has proven extremely difficult. While sources vary, statistics estimate *recorded* lynchings in the United States from 1880 to 1930 to number roughly 4,697 (Wilkes 8).[12]

The founder of the National Association for the Advancement of Colored People, and one of the most outspoken antilynching activists, Ida B. Wells-Barnett, organized the NAACP around this campaign for justice. Some of her most prominent work for this cause included publishing the pamphlet "Southern Horrors: Lynch Law in All Its Phases" (1892), in which she argued that the rampant allegations of Black men raping white women were often instances of consensual relationships, or in her words, "African Americans [*sic*] Sampsons who suffer themselves to be betrayed by white Delilahs"—a daring biblical analogy and potentially deadly claim to make, no doubt (Wells-Barnett 19). She also produced "A Red Record: Tabulated Statistics and Alleged Causes of Lynchings in the United States, 1892–1893–1894." In 1909, Wells-Barnett also gave the speech "Lynching, Our National Crime," reinforcing her argument that lynching was not confined to the Jim Crow South. The location and elaborate details of the infamous lynching of Shipp and Smith in Marion, Indiana, for instance, exposed lynching as a national practice of racial terror.

As Robin Mitchell reminds us, "The lives of the long-dead people we write about still matter, and the way we tell these stories undeniably matters" (xv). Claudia Rankine's poetic collection *Citizen: An American Lyric* includes a variation of the widely circulated souvenir photograph displaying the tortured bodies of Shipp and Smith; however, the corpses have been digitally removed from the shot. This digital erasure of the bodies shifts the focus of the image to the atrocity of the white mob, to the accomplices, to those who gathered out of curiosity, for entertainment, or to tear away a fragment of the mutilated bodies for remembrance, to witness, and to intimidate. The white mob acts to restore a perceived affront to white supremacist racial order through the public spectacle of brutal anti-Black violence.

What remains in the digitally altered version of Beitler's photograph, produced by artist John Lucas, is the ritualistic "feast of blood," the horde of white faces, old and young, the specter of the bodies—the normalization of this vile United States practice of anti-Black violence and terror. For the viewer unacquainted with this monstrous photographic archetype of American racial terror, the revision in Rankine's book might elicit questions about the purpose of the gathering. Were people congregated to observe a rare celestial occurrence? To revel at a town fair or celebrate a family event? Removing the disfigured corpses of Shipp and Smith clarifies and ultimately enables the viewer to see more clearly the ubiquitous national practices of hunting that rely on reducing Black people to things, from slavery to its post-Reconstruction historical continuities, a system built upon the degradation of Black life, injustice, and the violent oppression that persists.

In a similar vein to the genre of plays that trouble the primacy of a singular memorial narrative, Koritha Mitchell in *Living with Lynching* argues that despite the circulation of lynching postcards that capture crowds of white onlookers surrounding Black corpses hanging from trees, and the nearly one hundred images of lynching victims published in James Allen's 1999 book *Without Sanctuary,* the sign of the hanging corpse does not contain or explicate the entirety of racial terrorism. There is a competing literary tradition, Mitchell contends, that promotes survival: "African Americans wrote plays about mob violence that tell stories strikingly different from those suggested by lynching photography" (1). Mitchell upholds the genre of the lynching play, written primarily by African American women, as the mechanism by which the African

American community maintained its dignity as well as its status as human beings and citizens of the United States while simultaneously undercutting the graphic proof of dominance, or "insignia of power," to use Elaine Scarry's phrase, that was the lynching photograph (55).[13]

HORROR, BEAUTY, AND THE LYNCHING PLOT IN TOOMER'S "KABNIS" AND "PORTRAIT IN GEORGIA"

Following Mitchell, the lynching photograph conceals as much as it reveals about the life of the African American. Imaginative literature shades in the gaps and seeks a nuanced understanding of the violence. The final two lines of Elizabeth Alexander's poem "Toomer," in the collection *Crave Radiance,* explore the condition of being a Negro in America. Invoking at once the voice and corporeality of Jean Toomer (1894–1967), premier writer of the Harlem Renaissance (also known as the New Negro Movement) and celebrated author of the brilliant 1923 American modernist volume *Cane,* Alexander's repeating pithy riddle of the poem asks:

> to be a Negro is—is?—
> to be a Negro, is. To be. (237)[14]

Part apologia, part justification of his resistance to the Negro label and his alleged eventual racial passing, Alexander sings of a Toomer who "made up a language in which to exist." What, after all, does it mean to be a Negro? What are the possible ways of being? What language must he use? Why is the verb *to be* and the state of being such a difficulty or unknown quantity for the African American? *To be* means "to exist," "to endure," "to occupy space." The final pronouncement of the poem, "To be," then, echoes that famous opening to the soliloquy from *Hamlet,* "To be, or not to be," implicitly forwarding the question of the possibility for selecting Negro-ness. It is also an infinitive. The verb remains unconjugated, ripe for manipulation and interpretation.

Alexander begins the poem with "*(Jean Toomer)*," perhaps simply to identify the Toomer to which she refers. However, the parenthesis a great purpose; it is a sign that explains and qualifies that Toomer achieves liberation from the confinement of racial categorization through his ability to cross the color line. The lyrics force the reader to contend with the materiality of Toomer, a materiality he often sought to evade or elude. Alexander evokes a Toomer who moves from disembodied poetic voice to a man who offers the following explanation: "I did not wish to 'rise above' / or 'move beyond' my race. I wished / to contemplate who I was beyond / my body, this container of flesh."

If the reader only knows Toomer as the masterful lyricist of staggering poetic tours de force, all voice and no body, then Alexander paints Toomer as a full-bodied man who in fact seeks to distance himself from "this container of flesh," and later the "complicated, milk-skinned, genital-ed body." Reducing Toomer to his corporeal self, with skin the color of milk and genitals, perfectly complicated (instead of his authorial self), presents a contrastive image to the Black male "genital-ed" bodies hanging lifeless from trees in the most poignant moments of Toomer's poetry. Toomer could transcend his Blackness and the imminent fatality it encoded in a way his characters could not.

Did the mixed-race man born on December 26, 1894, and named Nathan Pinchback Toomer, whom Darwin T. Turner describes as "a signal light for the writers of the Harlem Renaissance" (122), choose to pass as white and move from the "New Negro" author Jean Toomer to the "New American" writer, philosopher, and lecturer Nathan Jean (or N. J.) Toomer after the publication of *Cane?*[15] This is a question to which critics return repeatedly. Salient details of Toomer's biography shed light on the complexity of his racial designation and preferred identity.

He was raised in his early childhood years by his devoted mother and a wandering, often absent father; by the time he was four years old, his parents had divorced and, due to economic hardship, Toomer and his mother were forced to return to the house of his grandfather, Pinckney Benton Stewart Pinchback, the first Black lieutenant governor of Louisiana. Although Toomer lived with his mother and her second husband for three years in New York, where he attended all-white schools, he returned to Washington, DC, after his mother's untimely death in 1909. It was mostly in this multigenerational extended family environment that Toomer, whose grandfather called him Eugene Pinchback (to remove any connection to his absent namesake father), was reared, attending "colored schools" in Washington, DC, including Garnet School and the famous Paul Laurence Dunbar High School (Byrd 167). In his pursuit of postsecondary education, Toomer switched from one academic discipline to another, including agriculture, music, exercise and bodybuilding, attending six universities and colleges but always abandoning the subjects after he lost interest. He never earned a degree.

Critics debate the level of Toomer's involvement in African American literary circles.[16] For three months, as a break from providing constant care for his ailing grandparents, Toomer served as substitute principal at the Sparta Industrial and Agricultural Institute in Sparta, Georgia. It was here, in the "heart of the South," that he saw the "valley of 'Cane'" and heard for the first time "the folk-songs and spirituals" that he considered "very rich and sad and joyous and beautiful" (Toomer, *Wayward* 123). What Toomer witnessed during his three-month stay in Sparta planted a creative seed in his soul and provided the raw cultural materials and rural pastoral settings that he would later poeticize in *Cane* (Kerman and Eldridge 82). When studying the years surrounding the writing of *Cane,* biographers and critics often downplay the narrative of Toomer's correspondence with Alain Locke and Countee Cullen. However, Mark Whalan argues that Toomer, who later in life became a Quaker leader, defies racial and artistic categorization as he was more involved in the Washington, DC, literary circles as well as the Lost Generation literary groups during the years in which *Cane* was written than his own attempts at autobiography and earlier scholarship have suggested (xxxviii).

A great ideological turning point in his life came with his association with the Russian philosopher and psychologist George Ivanovitch Gurdjieff. Toomer studied under Gurdjieff, adopting his raceless worldview of the "harmonious development of man" and eventually spent ten years lecturing to others on the principles of this psychological system (Kerman and Eldridge 143–44; Byrd 70–71). The constant pursuit of intellectual stimulation he had sought in other disciplines he finally found in Gurdjieff's teachings, which, according to Byrd "would endow his life with order, purpose, and direction as well as renew his belief in the existence of a transcendent reality" and finally provide for him that elusive "intelligible scheme."[17] However, his writing became much more didactic and dogmatic during this period of prolific literary production, and consequently, few publishers were interested in his later works. Toomer resented publishers' request that he produce literary clones of *Cane,* calling this "one of the queer misunderstandings of [his] life" (*Wayward* 123).

His 1931 book of aphorisms, *Essentials,* includes the much-quoted dictum "I am of no particular race. I am of the human race, a man at large in the human world, preparing a new race" (xxiv).[18] Whalan argues that scholars' readings of Toomer's letters tend "to isolate and fetishize the issue of racial identity in Toomer and *Cane,* even as Toomer's status as a social constructionist of 'race' *avant la lettre* is acknowledged" (xvii). Scholars have seized upon this aphoristic statement to make sense of the man who delighted in reinventing himself and evading labels. Nevertheless, Toomer's later works and his letters enrich and contextualize the historical moment in which this groundbreaking text was written. The four sentences that follow the oft-cited aphorism further illuminate Toomer's advanced notions of identity:

> I am of no specific region. I am of earth.
> I am of not particular class. I am of the human class,
> preparing a new class.
> I am neither male nor female nor in-between. I am of
> Sex, with male differentiations.
> I am of no special field. I am of the field of being. (xxiv)

Taken together with the first statement, "I am of no particular race," this sequence of aphorisms presents a sophisticated theory of race, class, and gender as social constructions. These aphorisms are similar in structure to the proclamation in the unpublished essay "The Americans," in which he writes, "This new race is neither white nor black nor red nor brown. These are old terms for old races, and they must be discarded" (Rusch 107–108).

Not only does Toomer banish the binary oppositions that constituted traditional understandings of race, gender, and class, but also he advocated a discursive stance of self-fashioning and performance decades before Michel Foucault's and Judith Butler's theories transformed the discipline with elaborations on these ideas.[19] In "A New Race in America," Toomer rearticulates this theory: "There is a new race in America. I am a member of this new race. It is neither white nor black nor in-between. It is the American race, differing as much from white and black as white and black differ from each other" (Rusch 105).

The irony of Toomer's oeuvre, of course, is that despite his greatest efforts at endorsing "new Americans" that transcend race, the very poems, short stories, and poetic prose in *Cane* that secured his lasting reputation in American and African American letters were the texts that most concretely dealt with race. What factors led Toomer to renounce his Black identity, as the official narrative of the Toomer papers assert? Although Toomer would most likely be frustratingly disappointed that scholars are still asking both his landmark text and the author himself to answer the race question, nearly a century later, race continues to be a salient point in terms of contextualizing his work during the bloody mob law of this period and the peak of racial violence. In the end, Toomer was a man ahead of his time in his claims for belonging to the human race only, and he therefore was not passing for white, in his opinion, because he completely eschewed racial categorization. However, one must note that it was precisely his fair skin color and appearance that afforded him the space to renounce race in the first place.

Here, I explore the theme of lynching in two works in Toomer's *Cane*—"Kabnis" and "Portrait in Georgia"—to interrogate the interplay of horror and beauty in poetry and prose depicting one of the most searing legacies of slavery: the trauma of lynching. *Cane,* a landmark, generically hybrid text of the Harlem Renaissance—whose exuberant reception the twenty-eight-year-old author would never be able to duplicate with his later works—brilliantly presents a confluence of signs, sounds, and images of northern and southern life, interracial relations, and gender dynamics, if it can be said to have unifying themes at all. While Mitchell argues that the lynching dramas present evidence of admirable African American survival, I contend that the longer-form poetic prose in "Kabnis" and the staggering short poem "Portrait in Georgia" protest and poeticize the heinous crimes and unspeakable violence of the lynching act while painting the complexity of African American subjectivity.

What most intrigues me about these representations of the horrific is their lyricism and poetic devices, their—dare I say, ever so cautiously—*aesthetic beauty.* But how could such an odious and repellant historical legacy be transformed into a literary "masterpiece"? Is this dangerous? Can a poignant depiction of the domestic terrorism of the lynch mob and the resulting lynched body indeed be beautiful? One is reminded of Adorno's oft-quoted (if only partially) dictum about the barbarism of poetry after Auschwitz.[20] McKittrick, too, warns about metaphors, particularly of violence and Black life, that become "delinked from their material underpinnings or histories" (*Dear Science* 11). What are the ethical considerations at stake, then, when poeticizing, or rendering into poetry, one of the most painful and shameful moments in US history?

In "Kabnis," Toomer achieves an apogee of poetic and prosaic experimentation. Its protean generic form—is it a "novelette-drama" as Darwin Turner terms it, a short story, a folk play?—resists labels, just as Toomer later resists racial designation (134). The literary experimentation that enlivens this acclaimed text foreshadows his renunciation of labels in aphorism LXI in *Essentials:* "We assume that because we have the label we have the understanding." Rejecting the perceived security of an immutable label, Toomer forces the reader to search, to probe, and to excavate understanding separate from prevailing racial assumptions and taxonomies.

Waldo Frank, a prolific novelist to whom the author dedicates this final section of *Cane* and author of the foreword to the first edition, was not only his literary mentor and friend but also his travel companion during his second trip south to Spartanburg, South Carolina, in 1922.[21] Interestingly, Toomer alerts his mentor, whom he lovingly refers to as "brother," that he will "have to be known as Negro" during said sojourn to South Carolina because "only by experiencing white pressure can the venture bear its fullest fruit for me" and "because the color of my skin (it is nearly black from sun) at the present time makes such a course a physical necessity" (Whalan 63). In effect, Toomer acknowledges a certain materiality of race based on skin color perception, a set of racial signifiers that may be read and deciphered, that supersede a theoretical aspiration for "racelessness" that he later articulates.

A December 12, 1922, letter to his unofficial advisor elaborates the dedication: "Kabnis, the spirit and the soil, to you" (Whalan 101). In a later letter, dated approximately 1922 or 1923, Frank refers to "Kabnis" as "big stuff" and "quite perfect as the expression of man" (Whalan 153). Although the reader encounters in this poetic narrative a northern Negro, to use the parlance of that day, the eponymous Ralph Kabnis, lying in his bed in an ethereal or dreamlike state, in a candlelit wooden cabin deep in the woods on an autumn Georgia night, Frank reads in the protagonist an uneasiness generalizable to humanity.[22] In a plainspoken admission in a letter to Frank, Toomer writes, "Kabnis is me."[23]

This short sentence destroys the theory that the reader should not conflate author and protagonist; Toomer aligns himself with his restless mixed-raced northern character who lives in the anxiogenic atmosphere of the spiritual-laden South. In a letter to Kenneth MacGowan, editor of *Theatre Arts Magazine,* on March 15, 1923, he writes one of the more precise descriptions of his conception of the text and its relation to him:

> Kabnis is a drama of Negro life. While the body of the work is dialog, I have incorporated narrative and descriptive passages, for it will form the third section of my book CANE (Boni and Liveright—summer publication). As the piece now stands, it makes better reading. The ms is forty seven pages, double spaced. There are six sections to it. Kabnis is really the story of my own real or imaginary experiences in Georgia. The central figure reacts with a certain intensity to the beauty and ugliness of southern life. His energy, dispersed and unchanneled, cannot push him through its crude mass. Hence the mass, with friction and heat and sparks, crushes him. (Whalan 141)[24]

The narrator renders the cabin in flickers of light and bland colors, visualizing it through the poor lighting of the oil lamp near the bed. Kabnis sits in the nucleus of the cabin room, with two concentric circles surrounding him. Propped in bed (as Toomer's Uncle Bismark often studied), the oil lamp and books form the first orbit, with the walls of the cabin delineating the other circle. Painting the room in blurry, impressionistic brushstrokes, the narrator describes the "hearth and chimney, black with sooty saw-teeth," and the "cracks between the boards are black . . . the lips the night winds use for whispering" (*Cane* 83). Even the room reveals itself in disconnected body parts. When the narrator announces, "Kabnis is a dream," this statement again predicts Toomer's later aphoristic writing: "We do not have states of being; we have states of dreaming" (*Essentials* LV). We encounter Kabnis in one of these states of dreaming, from which he does not awaken until the ultimate scene with Father John.

It is not a stretch to note, while remaining cautious about committing the intentional fallacy, an autobiographical connection between the author and his restless protagonist, as both express anxieties over an unfamiliar southern location—Toomer during his brief stint as head of an industrial and agricultural institute in Sparta, Georgia, in the fall of 1921, and Kabnis as a temporary lead teaching at a Negro school in the fictional town of Sempter, Georgia. In fact, from Toomer's letters, we know that he wanted to be anything but dead to his readership and set about the task of carefully crafting his public persona. Notably, the opening sentence tells us he "tries to read" (*Cane* 84).

When the narration switches to the dramatic conventions denoting dialogue from a play, with the character name followed by a colon (Kabnis:), we hear the protagonist's inner thoughts. Even here, though, the narration alternates between first person and third person. In this opening scene, we hear Kabnis think, "No use to read" (83). Reading and attempting to read become the central tropes of the short six-part narrative, recalling the antebellum legal sanctions against the literacy of slavery, as Kabnis attempts to read his foreign southern surroundings—the haunting and inspirational old spirituals wafting through the air, the southern vernacular, the animal sounds, the immense sky, the whispering wind, the moon peeking over the treetops, the red mud—and the people with whom he interacts there. Striking, too, is the main protagonist's name, an imperfect anagram of cabin(s), primarily associated with the slave cabins or location of the slave quarters.

The poetic language of the opening paragraphs introduces the reader to the main protagonist and mimics the bodily objectification and fragmentation of the lynching victim. The use of abstracted body imagery, with Kabnis's emotional state initially presented to the reader through the language of isolated body parts and segmented limbs, alludes to the cleavage of the mangled lynching victim's body and the incomprehensible system of mob law in which "white folks . . . sometimes mixes um [good and bad niggers] up when it comes t lynching" (89). Kabnis meets us in divided parts:

> Kabnis' thin hair is streaked on the pillow. His hand strokes the slim silk of his mustache. His thumb, pressed under his chin, seems to be trying to give squareness and projection to it. Brown eyes stare from a lemon face. Moisture gathers beneath his arm-pits. He slides down beneath the cover, seeking release. (83)

The narrator provides close-up images of a constellation of Kabnis's body parts: hair, hand, thumb, chin, eyes, face, arm-pits. However, we cannot perceive the man as a unified whole. Again, his mental discontent, evidenced through disjointed body parts, predicts the societal evil and the reduction of the lynching victim to a collection of disconnected, broken body parts. As noted, Frank identifies the universality of this fragmentation as "the perfect expression of man."

Yet the sobering reality of lynching violence comes to us in the dialogue in section 2, when one of Kabnis's new southern friends, Layman, explains,

> I've seed th time when there werent no use t even stretch out flat upon th ground. Seen um shoot an cut a man t pieces who had died th night befo. Yassur. An they didn't stop when they found out he was dead—jes went on ahackin at him anyway. (90)

Even before Layman's horrifying description of this event, the analogy of the dissected body foreshadows this thematic focus. Adding complexity to this act of violence and underscoring its psychological reverberations, Toomer here fills out the outlines of the lynching act he more crudely and hurriedly depicts in "Blue-Burning Moon," his other lynching sketch that appears in section 2 of the book, though it was written later. In the passage revealing Kabnis's interiority in the opening scene, alternating stream of consciousness and free indirect discourse repeat the body analogy: "And dreams are faces with large eyes and weak chins and broad brows that get smashed by the fists of square faces. The body of the world is bull-necked. A dream is a soft face that fits uncertainly upon it." Violence shockingly flares here, as a corporeal depiction of dreams "get[s] smashed by the fists of square faces" (83). Even though the possessor of both the dreams and the "square faces" is unclear, there is an intrusion of inexplicable violence ("smashed by the fist"). Thus, the main protagonist and visitor to the South, Kabnis, is a man "cut t pieces" emotionally, left to make meaning of those brutally "cut t pieces" physically.

But why write about this violence? It is instructive to turn here to Scarry, *The Body in Pain* to explore how Toomer's "Kabnis" and "Portrait in Georgia" contend with the heinous racial violence of the lynching ritual in productive ways. Scarry explains that physical pain is marked by "unsharability," that it "does not simply resist language but actively destroys it, bringing about an immediate reversion to a state anterior to language, to the sounds and cries a human being makes before language is learned" (4). She later elaborates that physical pain "deconstructs [language] into the pre-language of cries and groans. To hear those cries is to witness the shattering of language" (172).

While the witnesses to the spectacle of lynching were forced to hear the last cries of the victim, the lynching photograph souvenirs, on the other hand, silence the already dead victim, denying the physical pain she endured, emphasizing her complete submission unto death, where even unintelligible cries for mercy are hushed. As with the newspaper advertisements announcing the time and location of a lynching in advance of the event, the lynching photographs exhibit and publicly declare absolute power and order restored. What's more, the photographs take the destruction of language a step further than other forms of torture. By not depicting the process of torture—the victim being dragged for miles, or screaming, half alive, while tied to a stake enveloped with flames; a woman in the process of being raped; or the last gasps for air before the noose tightens (while paradoxically "sanitizing" or "censoring" the scene by covering the genitals of victims who were stripped and/or castrated)—the torturers deny even the vocalization of the prelanguage of cries and groans, thereby denying the physical pain. The lynching victim is always dead and silent in the still images of conquest. This focus on the icon of the mutilated corpse and the outside venue of the torture are salient departures from Scarry's formulation.

Unlike Scarry's explication of the structure of torture (usually during war), in which the events take place in a designated torture room, in the US lynching ritual, there is no interior torture room, as it were. The power of the lynching spectacle derives precisely from it occurring out of doors, in open air, visible to the public, and as Amy Louise Wood observes, with lifeless bodies often fastened not to a tree but to symbolic objects of technology and machines, exposing a "fraught connection to modernity" (5). This corresponds with what Scarry outlines as the third phenomenon in the structure of torture, that is, "the translation of the objectified attributes of pain into the insignia of power" (51).[25]

The insignia of white power, of course, is not only the violent act itself and the trophy of the corpse, often left hanging for days, but its replication through the mass production and circulation of photographs, via sale of the lynching postcards, which were dispersed through the United States Postal Service, indicating a disturbing governmental complicity in the crimes. Rallying against the inexpressibility of pain, "Kabnis," "Portrait in Georgia," and other works representing racial violence bear witness and "speak *on behalf of* those who are [in pain]" and silenced by vicious murder (Scarry 6).

Toomer's texts, then, like the lynching plays in Mitchell's study and Billie Holiday's rendition of "Strange Fruit," valorize the physical pain of the sufferers and thereby their existence. By attempting to speak on the behalf of the dispossessed—"to express someone else's pain" and "to imagine other people's pain"—these poetic works do not just name the pain of that fleeting moment but also attest to the fullness and complexity of the lives lost, restoring to them a language that torture and murder obliterated (Scarry 17).

In a realist interruption of the poetic mode of the opening paragraphs, a rat scurries across the thin ceiling boards, startling Kabnis and releasing some dust into the room.[26] The description of the red dust that seeps through the cracks between the wooden boards in his cabin wall as "dust of slavefields, dried, scattered" reinforces the connection to slavery's past (*Cane* 84). As the narrator brings the reader into Kabnis's interiority, we witness his journey to discover the significance of the South to him. Foreshadowing the tormenting angst over origins experienced by William Faulkner's protagonist Quentin Compson in *Absalom, Absalom!* (1936), who, after reconstructing and reinventing his family story with his Harvard roommate, Shreve, responds to the latter's question, "Why do you hate the South?," with this exclamation, the closing words of the text: "*I dont. I dont! I dont hate it! I dont hate it!*" (303). For Kabnis, even the mysterious whispering song of the wind in Sempter, Georgia, rattles him and dredges up fears over regional difference, race, violence (namely, lynching), and the fiction of the Old South:

> White-man's land.
> Niggers, sing.
> Burn, bear black children
> Till poor rivers bring
> Rest, and sweet glory
> In Camp Ground. (*Cane* 84)

This refrain repeats three times throughout the narrative, setting the sonic and visual backdrop to Kabnis's anxiety over his temporary life as a teacher in the South. Along with other references to distant singing and the shouting sounds and spirituals of church, this refrain punctuates the gritty dialogue between Kabnis and his two friends, Halsey and Layman. The two verbs, *sing* and *burn*, reveal the shocking juxtaposition between pain and pleasure, burning and singing, and the possibility for "rest" and "sweet glory," perhaps even beauty, in "White-man's land." It is precisely the stunning beauty of the Georgia night sky that Kabnis curses that first night, when, after violently killing a chicken by wringing its neck, he laments, "God Almighty, dear God, dear Jesus, do not torture me with beauty." "Take it away," he continues:

> Give me an ugly world. Ha, ugly. Stinking like unwashed niggers. Dear Jesus, do not chain me to myself and set these hills and valleys, heaving with folk-songs, so close to me that I cannot reach them. There is a radiant beauty in the night that touches and . . . tortures me. Ugh. Hell. Get up, you darn fool. Look around. What's beautiful here? (85)

Although Kabnis attempts to deny it, a breathtaking beauty exists in the Georgia countryside. The same gorgeous, sleepy, tree-lined landscape also bears the weight of the victims of racial aggression. This coexistence of the horrific and the beautiful confounds Kabnis; Georgia is not simply "hell," the word he frequently repeats as a curse or a direct description of the town of Sempter in his dialogue and monologues. It is a land of contradictions too, a place that contains the cellar or "hole," as the local place of congregation for drinking and relaxation. Yet even when Kabnis, Halsey, and their two female companions descend into this infernal hole with the delusional old man repeating the word *sin*, there is a beauty to be found, even there, in the process of creating something new with words. It is also a land of idyllic majesty that disrupts a dichotomous relationship between horror and beauty.

However, there is one emblematic moment that rises above all others as the most gruesome depiction of racial violence in the narrative (and perhaps one of the most despicable in literature).[27] The relation of this story confirms all of Kabnis's deepest fears about the irrational cruelty enacted against southern Blacks. The event is the double homicide and mutilation of Mame Lamkins and her unborn fetus at the hands of an unnamed white mob after she refuses to disclose the location of her husband, for whom they are searching.[28] The deplorable events become the symbol for the height of vicious brutality against African Americans. What is salient about the incorporation of this lynching is the fact that the victim is a woman and a mother-to-be, not the typical case.[29] Layman relates:

> They killed her in the street, an some white man seeing th risin in her stomach as she lay there soppy in her blood like any cow, took an ripped her belly open, an th kid fell out. It was living; but a nigger baby aint supposed t live. So he jabbed his knife in it an stuck it t a tree. An then they all went away. (92)

The terrifying brutality of this moment, cutting an unborn child from the womb of his murdered mother, slaughtered like a cow, seems utterly incomprehensible, an act that can never be understood or reasoned. The cavalier indifference of this execution recalls Kabnis's impulsive wringing of the chicken's neck, simply for being a chicken, in the first section of the story. In other words, the pregnant woman is killed just as thoughtlessly as if she were a wild country chicken.

Before the men can delve deeper into this horrible injustice or elaborate on the circumstances surrounding it, the dialogue is broken by another intrusion, suggesting that violence of this magnitude is unspeakable. The disruption is a stone wrapped in a note and thrown through the window, though the intended recipient of the message is unclear: "You northern nigger, its time fer y t leave. Git along now" (92). The past, it seems, is too painful to discuss, and only the imminent danger of the present is possible to address.

As we shall see, however, the story does not end with the impossibility of African American motherhood or the inevitability of violent death at "the hands of persons unknown."[30] Later, section 6 opens, "Night, soft belly of a pregnant Negress, throbs evenly against the torso of the South" (105). This lyrical line counters the senseless brutality of the murder of Mame and her barely born baby with the hope for consolation through a natural order. The sun will rise and set again. The beauty of this image of night as a pregnant Black woman is palpable. The fecund metaphor promises the restorative peace of night and the rebirth of daylight. Here, in sharp contrast to the symbolism of Mame Lamkin's horrific death, the pregnant Black woman signals the possibility of life itself. The passage continues:

> Night throbs a womb-song to the South. Cane- and cotton-fields, pine forests, cypress swamps, sawmills, and factories are fecund at her touch. Night's womb-song sets them singing. Night winds are the breathing of the unborn child whose calm throbbing in the belly of a Negress sets them somnolently singing. (105)

The metaphoric pregnant African American woman enriches the South with her touch, making nature ("cane- and cotton-fields, pine forests, cypress swamps") and technology ("sawmills, and factories") fruitful and productive. Nonetheless, it is a tentative hopefulness. This characterization of the pregnant Black woman, furthermore, inverts the association with death, as the night provides the proper atmosphere for creativity and allows the women of the town to sing their chanting folk songs. Just as Kabnis attempts to read books in his dimly lit cabin in the beginning of this narrative, he tries to read and interpret this horrendous violence but cannot make sense of it. In contradistinction to the immobility and muteness of the lynching postcard, the narrative nearly begins (instead of ending) with the recollection of this senseless, cold-blooded murder of mother and child, and in so doing allows the readers, alongside the characters, the opportunity to work through this trauma in the hopes of reaching a place of healing.

If the lynching ritual thematized most poignantly in "Kabnis" through the relation of pregnant Mame Lamkins's horrific demise symbolizes the utter failure of Reconstruction in the aftermath of the Civil War, then the former slave Father John represents a liminal figure who lays bare the ways in which the past wreaks havoc and continues to repeat itself in the present. "The failure of racial reconciliation," as David W. Blight argues in *Race and Reunion,* "so crucial to any ultimate working through of the meaning of the Civil War, took root in the Klan's reign of terror in 1868–71." According to Blight, "The contested legacy of Klan violence deformed understandings of history, unsettled black memories for decades, inspired white southerners in their struggle for self-determination and local rule, and most immediately, played a pivotal role in the electoral politics of the 1870s" (122). Brutal events like the gruesome murder of Mary Turner (drawn out in "Kabnis" by the story of Mame Lamkin and her child) evidence the depravity of a wounded nation and the failure of postwar racial reconciliation that devolved into the vilest form of racial violence.

In *Rituals of Blood,* Orlando Patterson echoes Blight's point about a nation trying to make sense of its deadliest war. Worsening socioeconomic, political, and cultural status contributed to the escalating lynching of African Americans during this period, because "Euro-American Southerners were faced with a vast mass of domestic enemies, an army of masterless slaves in their midst." Economic decline, post–Civil War violence, and "the fundamentalist religious fanaticism of the region," in turn, positioned "the masterless slaves of the postbellum South [as] the perfect scapegoats, the ultimate sacrificial victims" (192). Even though we know lynching was not solely a gruesome ritual of the South, Patterson compellingly argues for the aggregation effect, that is, overlapping forces, acting in concert, which created the maelstrom that would eventually give rise to these abominable acts of violence.

With this analysis in mind, I return to the drama in question. Bridging the gap between anger over the demise of the slave regime and tensions over the straggling reunification process is the figure of Father John. The physical embodiment of the memory of slavery, Father John, a former slave who lives in the basement of Halsey's workshop, hovers between the past and the present, life and death, silence and speaking. His inclusion in the narrative represents one of the most direct literary devices for engaging with the memory of slavery in Black Atlantic literature.[31]

However, he is not a mere transplanted Uncle Tom figure come to life in the early twentieth century. Appearing in the last three sections of the text, Father John, "the old man," at first seems to be a barely living relic of slavery, immobile and reduced to incomprehensible mutterings. When Lewis questions Halsey about the mysterious old man, Halsey brusquely replies, "Ask Kabnis. He blows off t him every chance he gets" (*Cane* 104). Curious Kabnis, who by this point has already been fired from his teaching job for drinking in his room on school property, uses the old man as a mute sounding board while his caretaker, Carrie K. (Fred Halsey's younger sister), finds his behavior strange: "Brother Fred, father hasnt eaten now goin on th second week, but mumbles an talks funny, or tries t talk when I put his hands ont th food. He frightens me, an I dunno what t do" (104).

Slavery's past and lynching's present, it seems, have driven Father John mad. His characterization in the next section echoes the sense of stasis surrounding the old man: "To the left, sitting in a high-backed chair which stands upon a low platform, the old man. He is like a bust in black walnut. Gray-bearded. Gray-haired. Prophetic. Immobile." Like a shrine or a relic or another piece of furniture in the basement, Father John sits frozen in time—or so the cast of characters around him assume. The astute Lewis probes, "Black Vulcan? I wouldnt say so. That forehead. Great woolly beard. Those eyes. A mute John the Baptist of a new religion—or a tongue-tied shadow of an old" (106).

Here, Lewis rehearses the binary oppositions between Old Negro and New Negro, slave and freedman, southerner and northerner, and questions where Father John falls in this dichotomous system. Lewis then names the old man Father John and imagines the narrative of his life in slavery:

> Father John it is from now on . . .
>
> Slave boy whom some Christian mistress taught to read the Bible. Black man who saw Jesus in the ricefields, and began preaching to his people. Moses- and Christ-words used for songs. Dead blind father of a muted folk who feel their way upward to a life that crushes or absorbs them. (Speak, Father!) Suppose your eyes could see, old man. (The years hold hands. O Sing!) Suppose your lips . . .
>
> Halsey, does he ever talk? (106)

In almost mocking tones, Lewis disparages both the classic slave narrative plot of the kindly mistress who educates her property and the trope of the slave's overzealous (even blind) adherence to the Christian faith, especially the popular Moses plot. However, Father John proves them wrong. He is neither dead nor mute, and although physically blind, his perception extends far beyond their capacity; life has not "crushed or absorbed him" (106).

This fiction of the Old South permeates throughout this group of friends. For example, when Kabnis discloses his fears about being chased by hounds after the rock-throwing incident, Halsey chides him: "These aint th days of hounds an Uncle Tom's Cabin, feller. White folks aint in fer them theatrics these days. Theys more direct than that. If what they wanted was t get y, theyd have just marched right in an took y where y sat" (94). Halsey's comments reveal two crucial points. First, the reference to *Uncle Tom's Cabin* shows that Stowe's best seller was by then already part of the cultural memory of slavery in the United States, more pervasive and well known than testimonies from the formerly enslaved. Second, it reaffirms Kabnis's fear of random mob violence.

Although members of this younger generation begin to impose their fears and desires onto Father John in an attempt to reconcile the past with the present, the elder survivor of slavery finally lifts his voice in a coherent fashion and captures their attention. For Lewis, Father John represents a "symbol, flesh, and spirit of the past," and he reminds Stella, one of the women in the coed group of companions, of how her "father used t look" after a white man took her mother from him (109). While the lynching victims cannot tell their story, Father John finally communicates, and in so doing, defies the portrayals (dead, dull, and useless relic of the past, left to rot in the cellar) that the younger "New Negroes" try to affix to him. In the climactic dénouement of the poetic drama, Kabnis rails against Father John in an intoxicated rant in which he asks him two key questions: "When you had eyes, did you ever see th beauty of the world?" and "Do y think youre out of slavery?" (114–115).

The first question elevates the problem of finding beauty in the midst of the horrific national abuses and racialized crimes against humanity, recalling the earlier scene when Kabnis asks God to make things ugly in Georgia to reflect the monstrosity of the acts of lynching. The taunting question, "Do y think youre out of slavery?," again raises the issue of the passage of time since the end of bondage. What, after all, has changed in three generations since slavery? When Kabnis interrogates Father John in this final wild speech, he really seems to be interrogating himself: Is he really out of slavery or any different than Father John? When Kabnis compares the "clammy floors" of the cellar (also called "the hole") to the "place they used t stow away th worn-out, no-count niggers in th days of slavery . . . that was long ago; not so long ago" and the "damp clammy floor of a dark scum-hole" (115), he is unable to say whether slavery was long ago or not, or if mob rule isn't only a cruel extension of it by another name.

At last, Father John expresses his theory of storytelling and makes them hear his voice. "Th sin whats fixed . . . (Hesitates) . . . upon th white folks— . . . —f telling Jesus—lies. O th sin th white folks 'mitted when they made th Bible lie." Although Kabnis interjects during Father John's powerful announcement, demanding that he "give us somethin new an up t date," the patriarch speaks, assuming the role of prophet Lewis assigned to him (117). In this performative act of speaking from his perch, Father John, now the archetypal wise old man, teaches Kabnis the somewhat clichéd lesson that he cannot understand the present ("new an up t date") without first comprehending slavery's past. Exemplifying the rhetorical device of the wise fool, or the literary convention of the impaired character who, through a climactic narrative reversal, is proven to be the wisest of all, Father John ultimately overcomes his seeming aphasia and inarticulate ramblings (such as his nonsensical repetition of the words "sin and death") to reveal his "truth" to the younger generation.

His lesson is a literary one. He teaches them about the unreliability of the text, even a sacred text like the Bible, and alerts them to the agendas of the mediators of these texts, who made the Bible "lie." Father John's instruction about labels and the dangerous constructedness of dominant narratives in the United States echoes Toomer's own disdain for imposed categories. While the conclusion of the short story allows Father John to finally speak for himself and interpret a sacred text, Kabnis reasserts his power as author.

In an intersecting concluding plotline, Kabnis reappropriates the horrific image of impalement and ends on a note of measured victory over the unfathomable acts of lynching in a narrative strategy that brings the story full circle. In effect, it finally closes the circle of the arc graphic that opens various sections of *Cane.* During an evening of revelry and drinking with his newfound southern friends, who he suspects are making fun of him, he announces his superiority over the lynchers of the South through his writing. He proclaims, "I've been shapin words after a design that branded here. Know what's here? M soul." Sometimes these words are "beautiful and golden" and other times they are "misshapen, split-gut, tortured, twisted words." Kabnis produces words that display the intricacies of horror and beauty, but he owns them. This empowers him to assert, about the "form that burned into [his] soul," "I wish t God some lynching white man ud stick his knife through it an pin it to tree. An pin it to a tree" (111). William Andrews succinctly summarizes the foundational theory of African American literature, that there is a "lasting tradition in African American fiction of the hero as master wordsmith, a liberator through language" (quoted in Battenfeld 1238). In his intoxicated state, Kabnis paradoxically reaches the highest level of clarity. Words, he ultimately reasons, form the greatest defense against the lynch mob. The words he shapes and births cannot be lynched or impaled on a tree.

Like the dissected arc segments of a whole circle that visually introduce the three sections and formal design of *Cane,* Toomer's "Portrait in Georgia" offers a distilled poetic still life of the atrocities of lynching embodied in a composite figure. Influenced by the Imagist style, the seven-line free verse poem that precedes "Blood-Burning Moon" operates on a visceral and repellent visual register to present the lynching spectacle:[32]

Hair—braided chestnut,
coiled like a lyncher's rope,
Eyes—fagots,
Lips—old scars, or the first red blisters,
Breath—the last sweet scent of cane,
And her slim body, white as the ash
of black flesh after flame. (29)

Scholars have debated the identity and gender of the subject of this evocative poem that precedes "Blood-Burning Moon," a longer poetic prose piece about lynching and the final longer narrative of the last section, "Kabnis," which also grapples with a history of violence. These insightful close readings situate the central personage alternately as the archetypal white woman dissolving into the lynched Black male body (J. Callahan); a superimposition of the white woman, the lynching, and the Black male body (Hutchinson, "Toomer"); a "murderous *femme fatale* . . . [who] demands the sacrifice of the Black man who undergoes a race change from black flesh into white ash because of a fiery consummation" (Gubar 103); or "a woman whose braided hair is likened to a lyncher's rope and whose slim white-skinned body is actually made of the ash of burned black flesh" (Griffin, "*Who Set You Flowin'?*" 24).

There is a comingling of mangled bodies. Certainly, the grafting of the white female body onto the Black male body foregrounds miscegenation as both the coming together of the races and the ultimate cause of the dismemberment at the hands of a bloodthirsty mob of white men, implicitly present in the poem. Then there is also the possibility that the pronoun *her* in "her slim body" refers to a lynching victim who is a Black woman, whose "black flesh" has turned "white as the ash." The reference to ash here also resonates with the poetic "ashes to ashes, dust to dust" liturgical phrase from the *Book of Common Prayer,* used in Christian funeral rites, underscoring the morality of all human beings and the promise that all bodies will one day become ash (Cummings). It simultaneously highlights the terrifying strangeness of the fate that has befallen this gender-bending victim and subject of the poem, thereby indexing the abominable and unnaturalness of death by lynching.

These personages are all present in this portrait. The list of dissected body parts—hair, eyes, lips, and "slim body"—invokes the image of the hanging burned corpse, having expressed the last biological function of life, "Breath," and representing only a spiritless cadaver, a hodgepodge of inanimate body parts, literally, a "still life" portrait. That the "Breath" smells like "the last sweet scent of cane" echoes the title, "Portrait in Georgia," situating the location of the violence in the South, perhaps somewhere around the sugarcanes of Texas or Louisiana, with Georgia standing in for all of the South.

In this perverse Petrarchan love sonnet, Toomer uses images of each grotesque body part, beginning with the abrupt swing from the beauty of the image of "Hair—braided chestnut" to the shocking comparison of "coiled like a lyncher's rope," employing the conventions of a metaphysical conceit to repel the reader and provide graphic evidence of the horrific violence of the lynching scene. The breath of the "last sweet scent of cane" is the only reminder of vitality, of a life once lived, and also an invocation of the slave-based sugar economy of the South. And yet, the scent is sweet. Even in the midst of the memory of slavery, there is still sweetness in nature and in the memory of consuming this sugarcane, a naturally sweet and unadulterated resource. In that line, Toomer gives a glimmer of hopefulness, that the South is not completely depraved, that sweetness might be found again in this braided heap of bodies.

In "Portrait in Georgia," Toomer presents a lynching postcard poeticized. This may be one answer to the controversy around the Mammy statue and the larger question of how the United States remembers slavery. In 1911, W. E. B. Du Bois already thought an explanation of American slavery was a "trite" subject, and yet in "The Economics of Negro Emancipation in the United States" he stated that it requires further investigation. "Few of us realise," he wrote, "how much a visual image influences our thought even when we know the image to be fanciful or misleading" (303). To exemplify its fanciful and misleading possibilities, Du Bois discusses how the visual image of the moment of emancipation is often imagined: "Large numbers of people involuntarily visualize some sudden dramatic movement in the freeing of the American slave—the rattle of broken shackles, the trooping forth of myriads of singing men, and the like." While Du Bois refutes this ecstatic vision of emancipation, he concedes that construing a national memory of slavery, given its "apparent contradictions," is difficult work. Acknowledging both ends of the spectrum of representation, from the Mammy monument to Toomer's "Portrait in Georgia," he clarifies:

> We hear on the one hand of the staid and gentle patriarchy and the wide and sleepy plantations with lord and retainers, ease and happiness; we hear on the other hand of barbarous cruelty and unbridled power and wide oppression of

men. *Which is the true picture? The answer is simple: both are true. They are not opposite sides of the same shield; they are different shields.* (303; emphasis added)

Following Du Bois's question "Which is the true picture?," I ask, How could the lynching postcards exist and lay claim to representing slavery and its legacy? Each of these images resonates or repels, depending on the spectator. In short, "both are true." If the figure of Mammy, was the salient cultural object onto which were projected southern shame and anxieties, African American outrage, pain and rejection, hopes for national compromise and unification, then Toomer's "Portrait in Georgia" offers the kaleidoscopic "true image," an abstraction of the braided nature of slavery's memory and postbellum, post–World War II racial violence that binds together the whole country, Black and white, men and women, in a reconciliatory struggle.

Toomer's titular reference, *Cane,* signals the product of the sugarcane and symbolizes one of the major cash crops and exports of slavery, which sweetened the tea of consumers, from southern planters to British aristocrats, through forced labor and later through underpaid sharecroppers, a vicious enterprise. Instead of patently rejecting Georgia, the metonym for the South, Toomer disavows its bitter and violent history against African Americans yet allows for the possibility of beauty in nature and the preservation of a natural order that cannot be tainted, for the vicious crimes of an angry mob cannot, in the end, turn nature against their enemies. That the lynching victim consumed a last sweet piece of cane exposes the painful contradictions of life: the cane still smells sweet, even in the midst of the horror of lynching. What "Kabnis" and "Portrait in Georgia" achieve is a dismantling of binary oppositions of ugly and beautiful, pain and pleasure, the world and I/me, and laughter and tears to return to Wright's dichotomies, or the process of "thingification" in McKay's poem.[33] People have long spoken about the redemptive power of art, about its power to heal, to awaken a higher consciousness, to empower, to sing the travails and triumphs of life that transcend and overpower the static hopelessness of the lynching photograph.

Just as Holiday infused her interpretation of "Strange Fruit" with unforgettable emotional verve, Toomer experiments with form and language in the search for understanding, beauty, and wholeness. Both artists redeem and transcend, if only for the suspended time of the song or the reading of the text, the horrific historical reality of this bloody interregnum from 1880 to 1930 when nearly five thousand lynchings were reported, denying it the ability to suffocate and consume its victims. Using those raw materials and emotions, Holiday makes her audience contend with the staggering imagery of violence and compels them to fight for peace, understanding, and the possibility of beauty. Toomer, too, uses the lynching plot to present the persistent fear and threat of death for Negroes living under mob rule, but he also manages to deploy lynching as a metaphor of modernist fragmentation and splintering in which the wholeness at the end of "Kabnis," with the final words of Father John, signal the potential for wholeness and beauty through artistic expression. Or, as Goldsby explains, "Lynching urges writers to breach new depths of creativity because, I think, they need to explore the limits of literary form to express what the violence means to them" (293).[34]

NEW NEGRO, MEMORY, AND MODERNISM IN THE POETRY OF ROBERT HAYDEN

Oh, blackskinned epic, epic with the black spear,
I cannot sing you, having too white a heart,
And yet, some day, a poet will rise to sing you
And sing you with such truth and mellowness,
Deep mellow of the husky, golden voice
Crying dark heaven through the spirituals,
Soft mellow of the levee roustabouts,
Singing at night against the banjo-moon
That you will be a match for any song
Sung by old, populous nations in the past,
And stand like hills against the American sky,
And lay your black spear down by Roland's horn.
—STEPHEN VINCENT BENÉT, "John Brown's Body"

In a February 14, 1923, address entitled "What the Negro Can Give to Literature," author and poet Clement Wood urged members of the Booklovers Club at the 135th Street branch of the New York Public Library, a notable gathering place and intellectual hub of the Harlem Renaissance, to give "an interpretation of himself to the white man" ("Noted Author Talks").[35] Railing against the myth of the "old-time Negro" that many southern whites and some northerners attempted to crystallize and preserve in perpetuity—such cultural remains from slavery as the characters of Mammy, Uncle Tom, pickaninnies, and Black Buck—Alain Locke offered "an interpretation of himself to the white man" in his transformative edited volume *The New Negro* (1925), which aimed to "register the transformations of the inner and outer life of the Negro in America" (xxv).

To dislodge the cultural primacy of these mythologies, Locke reminded his readers that the "'Old Negro' was a creature of moral debate and historical controversy . . . a stock figure perpetuated as an historical fiction partly in innocent sentimentalism, partly in deliberate reactionism" (3). By the time of its publication in 1925, *The New Negro* declared Mammy and her cast of plantation characters dead. Locke promoted bold self-expression and artistic agency with his publication of a dazzling collection of prose, music, academic essays, and poetry. This included Toomer's "Georgia Dusk," a poem as lyrically stunning as "Portrait in Georgia" and as experimental as "Kabnis," both a product of his sojourn to rural Georgia, in which he eviscerates the lynching problem by highlighting the savagery with lines like:

> The sky, lazily disdaining to pursue
> The setting sun, too indolent to hold
> A lengthened tournament for flashing gold,
> Passively darkens for night's barbecue,
>
> A feast of moon and men and barking hounds,
> An orgy for some genius of the South
> With blood-hot eyes and cane-lipped scented mouth,
> Surprised in making folk-songs from soul sounds.

Locke energized the public with this construction of the old/new dichotomy and the promotion of African American revitalization.[36]

By the time Robert Hayden (1913–1980) wrote a preface to the Atheneum edition of *The New Negro,* in 1968, he was able to reflect with critical distance on the New Negro Movement's significance for Black artists within the larger American tradition:

> Too often the Harlem Renaissance, when given any attention at all in the textbooks, is approached as though it had no organic relationship to the developments taking place in American culture generally during the twenties. That the converse was true is amply illustrated by this anthology.
>
> "The Jazz Age" was a period of *disillusionment and revolt,* of experimenta-

> tion in lifestyles and in the various forms of imaginative expression. The accent was on the "new" and untried. Old modes were either rejected or were revaluated and adapted to the uses of an often self-conscious modernism. Americans, black and white, sought to discover or reclaim their spiritual resources.
>
> . . .
>
> The Negro Renaissance was clearly an expression of the *Zeitgeist,* and its writers and artists were open to the same influences that their white counterparts were. What differentiated the New Negroes from other American intellectuals was their race consciousness, their group awareness, their sense of sharing a common purpose. (62–67; emphasis added)

Here, Hayden theorizes that the discarding of the "old" mantle for newness represents more than a Negro phenomenon, but indicates that this defined the mainstream Jazz Age, too. In other words, eschewing the old for the new and experimental during this period of "disillusionment and revolt" characterized a transracial American experience; indeed, "disillusionment and revolt" are two themes Hayden returns to in his own poetic work.

Hayden's resistance to racial classification resonates with Toomer's earlier promotion of a new American race. Furthermore, Hayden's phrase "Americans, black and white," emphasizes Americanness first and racial identity second. When he claims that both Black and white writers and artists "were open to the same influences" and that writers of the New Negro Renaissance "wanted to stress both their blackness and their 'Americanism,'" as George Hutchinson suggests, he boldly revises the dominant narrative of the Harlem Renaissance as a confined literary category (*Harlem Renaissance* 1). It is the strenuous struggle against social inequalities and the longing for harmonious race relations that are most often reflected in the literature of the first half of the twentieth century, with "apostolic" Richard Wright's *Native Son* as the exclamation point. By the 1940s, the thematic emphasis on the "plight of the Negro" was almost the only acceptable literary expression for Black writers if they hoped to get published (J. Hughes 42).

As we have seen, there was a prevalence of depictions of racial themes in contemporary scenes but rarely a backward glance to slavery. Apart from commemorations of emancipation, it seems that "slavery" was a forbidden theme at this time, a shameful reminder. Therefore, there is a gap in the literary production between nineteenth-century slave narratives and the mid-twentieth-century reinvestment in memorializing slavery, including a post-1960s surge in its literary representation.

Like Paul Laurence Dunbar, Sterling Brown, Countee Cullen, Langston Hughes, Gwendolyn Brooks, and innumerable other African American poets who came before him or were his contemporaries, Hayden sharply encountered the tension between his identity as an African American and a poet. Like Toomer before him, Hayden resisted the limitations of the Negro identification.[37] Expressing a politically unpopular view during the polarized racial era of the 1940s to 1960s, Hayden hoped to be recognized as an American poet first and a Black poet second. He strove to reach beyond the race-based praise to his first volume of poetry, *Heart-Shape in the Dust* (1940), in which William Harrison called him a "New Negro Voice" poised to make "a distinct contribution to Negro American culture and a bright augury" and Gertrude Martin noted that his topical and protest poems "evidence an awareness of the Negro and of the world and some small hope for the future" (49).

In a 1949 *New York Times Book Review* write-up of *The Lion and the Archer,* a volume that Hayden cowrote with Myron O'Higgins, another reviewer, Selden Rodman, declared it the era of the "'emancipation' of Negro poetry in America," which moves beyond "minstrel quaintness" (Goldstein and Chrisman 51; Harrison 91). With a mixture of condescension and praise, Rodman remarks, "One feels instantly behind the work of both of these very gifted poets not a persecution complex or nostalgia for the past or for a hot piano but the whole weight of modern poetry at the service of a tragic human situation" (Goldstein and Chrisman 51). Despite the insult of "persecution complex," "nostalgia for the past," and especially the condescending "hot piano," Rodman links "Negro poetry" with the universality of the larger modernist movement, deducing that "the plight of the Negro" is the quintessential modernist condition. Indeed, Hayden would later suspect that some New Negro writers may have exploited the typology of the New Negro poetry that Rodman attacks here, such as the demand "from a jaded white audience" for "fashionable exoticism" and "primitivism in arts . . . simply exchang[ing] one set of racial clichés for another" (Hayden 62–63).

In her review of his *Selected Poems* (1966), Gwendolyn Brooks calls Hayden the superior kind of poet who "'lives in life,' mixes with mud, rolls in rot, claws the scoundrels, bleeds and bloodies, and, gasping in the field, writes right there, his wounds like faucets above his page, at once besmutching and ennobling it" (58). This imagery of the ideal poet not only dirtying himself in the field of life but also allowing his blood to flow, "wounds like faucets," onto the page indicates a necessary form of self-injury for the sake of the poetic enterprise. Brooks also admonishes another sly review as "disfiguring" the cover of Hayden's book when she writes, "The jacket of *Selected Poems* is disfigured with this legend: 'Writing, of course, out of his experience as an American Negro, his lines are *NEVERTHELESS* carefully controlled and disciplined.' The furious capitalization and italics are mine." It is probable that a portion of Brooks's fury over the underestimation denoted by *nevertheless* may have stemmed from the familiar bristle of critique her own work received. In this same year, Black nationalists at the Black Writers' Conference ridiculed the poetry of both artists as not "representing" the cause.

Despite being heralded as one of the best poets of the twentieth century and serving as the first African American poetry consultant (now poet laureate) at the Library of Congress, Hayden's corpus has fallen deeper into obscurity (Rampersad 197). I offer here a brief biographical sketch, with details that may illuminate key themes in his poetry.

Born Asa Bundy Sheffey in Detroit, Michigan, on August 4, 1913, Robert Hayden experienced the acute childhood trauma of maternal abandonment at the age of two. After his biological parents separated, his mother, Ruth Sheffey (née Finn), due to financial strain, gave him up to impoverished neighbors, William Hayden and Sue Ellen Westerfield, a strict Baptist couple, whose house was also riddled with contention, bickering, and excessive discipline. Hayden's poor vision (black-and-white photographs show him wearing thick corrective lenses for his severe nearsightedness) and small stature prevented Hayden from pursuing sports as a boy. His adopted family's meager finances also precluded any cultural enrichment through extracurricular activities such as music lessons. An intensely private man, Hayden worked hard to ensure that the autobiographical could not be read in his poetry. Yet we see in his poems the gratuitous and inexplicable violence of a mother toward her son in "The Whipping," a father's familial duty in a house filled with "chronic angers" in "Those Winter Sundays," and in "Elegies for Paradise Valley," the moniker for the Detroit slum where he grew up, glimpses of what could be oppressive childhood memories of violence and poverty in the ghetto, fictionalized.[38]

Hayden's physical challenges prompted him to turn inward to an introspective life of the mind, voraciously engaging in literary studies and specifically reading poetry for escape. His academic pursuits led him first to Detroit

City College (now Wayne State University) for baccalaureate studies, and then to the University of Michigan, where he completed a master's degree and received mentorship from W. H. Auden. A recipient of the prestigious Hopwood literary award in 1938, he worked at the Federal Writer's Project and subsequently began a long career in academia, teaching for twenty-three years at Fisk University and finishing his teaching career at the University of Michigan, where he taught until his death from cancer in 1980. Although he married concert pianist Erma Morris in 1940, Hayden scholar Pontheolla T. Williams claims that Hayden may have kept secret his bisexuality throughout his life.[39]

Hayden's poem "Middle Passage," from *A Ballad of Remembrance* (1962, revised 1966), represents a revision of one of "The Black Spear" poems, which Hayden wrote in answer to Benét's call for the "blackskinned epic" in his influential "John Brown's Body." Although he won the Hopwood literary award for "The Black Spear" collection in 1942, Hayden ultimately abandoned the project in that form, though he later reintegrated revised versions of the early work into this later volume. The remembrance Hayden announces in this collection is informed by Benét's epic poeticization of the rebellion and sacrifice of John Brown. Three poems, in particular, sing of complementary insurrections in African American history: "The Ballad of Nat Turner," in which he remembers Nat Turner; "Runagate, Runagate," which memorializes Harriet Tubman; and "Middle Passage," which refashions the story of Cinquez from the *Amistad* in a layered poetic structure.

That Hayden experiments with three variations of the theme of insurrection is the great irony of his meticulously crafted, polished lyrics. It is through his method of consummate order—writing with surgical precision of vocabulary, word placement, and rhythm—that he thrillingly explores three variations of willful disorder in the act of slave revolt. Hayden mirrored this revolt in his refusal to confine himself to the "Black poet" identity and succumb to the pressures to write merely propagandistic protest poetry. Like the musical name of his poem, "Theme and Variation," each of these poems presents a variation on the theme of slavery in African American history, and particularly of rebellion and departure. He returns to this theme again in his poem "Gabriel," which presents the Gabriel Prosser insurrection in Virginia, the same subject as Arna Bontemps's *Black Thunder.* This theme repeats, too, in "O Daedalus, Fly Away Home," which represents a transatlantic departure, with the myth of the flying Africans who returned home, a myth that repeats in the Black Atlantic: "*O fly away home fly away* / Do you remember Africa? / *O cleave the air fly away home.*" We will see a version of this folk narrative in anthropologist Miguel Barnet's transcription of interviews with Cuban Esteban Montejo in chapter 5.

It is not an easy task to divide Hayden's work into early, middle, and late, as he was, as Arnold Rampersad notes, a "relentless polisher and honer" who revised and re-revised his poems (202). For instance , Hayden excluded from his later revisions and republications his first poetic collection, *Heart-Shape in the Dust.* He eschewed the restrictiveness of the label "Black poet," and scholars have spent much time tracing the influences in his work, which is heavily inspired by the European and American poets, the Greek tradition, Yeats, Auden (his advisor and mentor), T. S. Eliot, and Hart Crane. Ironically, however, the most anthologized of his works deals with arguably the most traumatic and transformative moment of the collective African American historical experience: the way in which Africans became African Americans (in all of the Americas) via the Middle Passage. It is in the specificity of this historical moment that Hayden sings most powerfully about the universality of the human struggle so central to American modernism.[40]

Hayden's powerful "Middle Passage"[41] presents a series of literal and figurative departures, from Africa to Cuba to America to Africa again, and from enslaved to liberated. Considered his magnum opus, the epic magnitude of the poem comes not from its length, for it numbers just over six pages, but from the historical ground he covers and the multiplicity of voices he integrates. Linda M. White employs Bakhtin's term *heteroglossia* in her analysis of Hayden's poem "Paradise Valley" to explain a similar sonic effect (22–32). Resonances emerge between Hayden's twentieth-century modernist "Middle Passage" and nineteenth-century Brazilian Romantic poet Castro Alves's long poem "O navio negreiro" [The Slave Ship] (1868), discussed in chapter 4.

Each of these three texts poses the larger literary question of how to represent the sadism, pain, and violence of the Middle Passage and to exceed the limits of what we consider art. What does it mean to transform the horrors of the Middle Passage into a beautifully lyrical Romantic poem, as Castro Alves does in his canonical work? What ethical questions undergird the practice of reading and deriving aesthetic pleasure from such texts? From slave narratives that attempted to document the lives of slaves (as mediated as many of these texts were through the "editing" process) to the sentimentality of Castro Alves's Romantic verse to the iconoclastic vision of postmodern fictions of slavery that dethrone and demystify the sanctity of writing about slavery lies Hayden's "Middle Passage" which combines the "realism" of the historical fact with the ethos of modernism to construct a heterogeneous, fractured pastiche of voices, scenes, and cinematic flashes.

The poem's three sections present a multiperspectival recreation of the historical slave rebellion on the *Amistad* schooner in 1839. To this end, it presents a knot of interlocking subjectivities, or as Derik Smith describes them, an "arrangement of fragmentary voices": the voices of the Spanish slave traders, prayers, chorus, and journal entries (142). Significantly, there is no direct representation of the voice of the enslaved Africans. Yet, in this poem, Hayden responds to the call of Stephen Vincent Benét's book-length poem "John Brown's Body" with an impressive economy of words. With the precision of a brain surgeon, Hayden's verse demonstrates meticulous pruning, reflecting his 1970 "Statement on Poetics": "I value form and rhythm as having an organic relationship to the theme of a poem. I am as much concerned with the sounds and textures of words as I am with their meanings. I write slowly and painstakingly; often work on a poem for several years, revising even after publication" (Goldstein and Chrisman 9).

A complex voicing works across and within each section. Amid the jarring effect of the spliced voices, a unifying design emerges. Overlaid on the traditional three-part dramatic narrative of beginning, middle, and end—with each section delineated by roman numerals—are the sounds and citations like cross talk in a play. These are voices that do not listen to each other; they are merely juxtaposed to form the landscape of the poem. In section 1, there are three beats. I describe them as "beats" because of their rhythmic quality, with various sounds moving in and out, and also for the theatrical significance of a beat as a unit of action in a scene or a deliberate pause for effect. Italics and colons mark the transitions in the otherwise sparsely punctuated poem. The first beat of section 1, roughly composed of three stanzas, reveals the way the disparate voices give the poem an overall harmonic effect:

> *Jesús, Estrella, Esperanza, Mercy:*
>
> Sails flashing to the wind like weapons,
> Sharks following the moans the fever and the dying;
> Horror the corposant and compass rose.
>
> Middle Passage:
> voyage through death
> to life upon these shores.

> "10 April 1800—
> Blacks rebellious. Crew uneasy. Our linguist says
> their moaning is a prayer for death,
> ours and their own. Some try to starve themselves.
> Lost three this morning leaped with crazy laughter
> to the waiting sharks, sang as they went under." (1.1–13)

The first stanza of the poem exposes the incongruence of the poem's title, "Middle Passage," with the names of the Spanish slave ships, *Jesús, Estrella* (Star), *Esperanza* (Hope), and *Mercy.* We know that these slavers, with their "bright, ironical names" (3.3), as the speaker calls them in the third section, is bound for Puerto Rico from Cuba, major slave posts in the Spanish Caribbean. We have entered a world ironically inverted, in which vessels carrying slaves are marked with the virtues of hope, mercy, the name of the Christian savior, and reach cosmically to the stars. A series of striking nouns dominates the first stanza that follows the slave ship names: *sails, wind, weapons, sharks, moans, fever, dying, horror, rose.* Hayden privileges the noun over the verb or adjective in this opening. Each of these three lines begins and ends with a noun, and they, along with the gerunds (*flashing, following*) and the two adjectives (*corposant, compass*), infuse this stanza with its emotion.[42]

Hayden's economical aesthetic and trimmed verses create dramatic tension and seem to answer the question I posed earlier about the problem of representing pain. His minimalist approach, from the reduced punctuation to the excision of *to be* verbs, not only renders the words present more forceful and hefty but also lays bare and vulnerable the poet's task of "singing" the horrific. The first poetic voice speaks in stripped-down lyrics, and in the restraint of this grammar, the reader sees Hayden's technique and careful crafting at work. Thus, the line "sharks following the moans the fever and the dying," a condensed list of horrors, wields a strength that propels the reader forward on the sadistic journey.

Employing ironic placement, juxtaposition, and sequencing of disparate voices instead of ornate and gilded language, Hayden conveys the complicated axis of power that constitutes the slave system. Far from internally unified in significance, each vocal strain retains a certain ambiguity. The titular reference and refrain of the poem, for instance, evoke several meanings: "Middle Passage: / voyage through death / to life upon these shores" (1.5–7). Spatially, Hayden presents these lines in a stepwise progression, another use of the three beats. In one reading, "voyage through death / to life upon these shores" connotes a sense that the Middle Passage voyage signifies the passage through death and the arrival at the "New World littoral" (3.7), in which new life begins. In this interpretation, the slave ship becomes the dark womb, which gives birth to the enslaved Africans on the shores of the Americas. There is the possibility, too, based on the unnamed referent of "these shores," that the voyage through death represents the entire diasporic loop since departure from the West Coast of Africa, a death that does not cease until the return of the Africans on *Amistad* to their shores to live once again.

In contrast to the poetic voices of the first two stanzas, which enact omniscience and the choral refrain, the third voice presumably comes from one of the Spanish slave traders in the schooner, represented like a fragment torn from his journal. Hayden uses quotation marks here to highlight this distinction. Unlike the atemporality of the first stanza with the series of nouns (*sails*, *wind*, *weapons*) and the Middle Passage refrain of the second stanza, this voice begins with the date, "10 April 1800," highlighting an attention to recording and measuring time. Once again, there is an excision of *to be* verbs, leaving only the salient details, like a terse police report: "Blacks rebellious. Crew uneasy. Our linguist says / their moaning is a prayer for death, / ours and their own" (1.9–11). Quantifying the mortalities of enslaved "cargo," the voice observes: "Lost three this morning leaped with crazy laughter / to the waiting sharks, sang as they went under" (1.12–13). The linguist interpreting "their moaning" (1.10)—a repetition of the "sharks following the moans" (1.2)—and the speaker's incredulous tone when he intimates that the African captives "leaped with crazy laughter" into shark-ridden waters, and even "sang as they went under," reveals the cross-cultural disjunction and incomprehensibility

This cultural disjunction also manifests itself in the deployment of religious references. Not only is *Jesús* the first word of the poem, but also the fourth stanza, delineated by the heading "*Desire, Adventure, Tartar, Ann:*," introduces another refrain: "Jesus Savior Pilot Me / Over Life's Tempestuous Sea" (1.20–21). The words of this poetic voice stand out because of the capitalization of the first letter of each word and the triple spacing between them. The first section ends "Pilot Oh Pilot Me" (1.69). The irony of a slave trader asking Jesus to "pilot [him] over life's tempestuous sea," essentially praying for divine assistance in "bringing home / black gold, black ivory, black seed" (1.15–16) and for "safe passage to our vessels bringing / heathen souls unto Thy chastening" (1.23–24), signals, if not an anti-Christian message then at least a critique of the dehumanization that slavery promoted under the guise of a Christian conversion and civilizing mission.[43]

The long final testimony of the surviving witness to the mutiny describes the murdered Spanish compatriots as "true Christians all" (3.52). Unlike Frances E. W. Harper, for example, who appropriates biblical tenets and characters to stand in for the enslaved African Americans in her epic poem "Moses," Hayden channels Christianity through the voice of the slave trader, disallowing any alignment between the "Jesus Savior" (1.25) of the captor and the captives. When the poetic voice recorded in the journal entry notes that "Our linguist says / their moaning is a prayer for death," one wonders if this is another cultural misreading, with the moaning not a "prayer for death" but a preparatory message with instructions for insurrection of the enslaved.

After three stanzas of two different omniscient poetic voices, the third section breaks the poetic mode and gives the details of the historic slave insurrection of the *Amistad* (again, another "ironical name," as *Amistad* means "friendship") in the prose of an eyewitness testimony, set off as a long quotation. It is in this passage that the reader learns of Cinquez, the rebel leader, as "that surly brute who calls himself a prince" (3.45). The deponent recounts that "these apes / threw overboard the butchered bodies of / our men," but "Cinquez was forced to spare the two of us / you see to steer the ship to Africa" (III.54–55). After the speaker quickly explains that they were able to escape by steering the ship to the coast of North America instead of to Africa as Cinquez had requested, he derides "so many" Americans for being "inclined / to justify the mutiny of these blacks" (3.66–67).

One of Hayden's harshest critics, David Galler, who charges the poet with being "saddled" with "sentimentality or erudition" and "oscillat[ing] from semi-dialect blues and corrupted ballads to Poundian notation," laments the fact that what he considers the strongest lines of "Middle Passage" are voiced by the Spanish sailor during his witness testimony (61):

> We find it paradoxical indeed
> that you whose wealth, whose tree of liberty
> are rooted in the labor of your slaves
> should suffer the august John Quincy Adams
> to speak with so much passion of the right
> of the chattel slaves to kill their lawful masters (3.68–73)

Although he praises Hayden as a "superb ironist," Galler ultimately calls this a problem of "frame of reference" (61). It is true that, like the Spanish sailor's voice here, the entire second section of the poem mimics the voice of another slave trader, who recalls the story of "nigger kings" from "Gambia, Rio Pongo, Calabar" (2.6, 2) who would "kill the sick and old and lead the young / in coffles to our factories" (2.19–20). Hayden does not in fact use the first person singular *I* of "The Ballad of Nat Turner," a structurally simpler poem that recounts the moments after Turner's slave uprising, when before his capture he hides in the "livid trees" of the forest, "where Ibo warriors / hung shadowless, turning in wind / that moaned like Africa" (9–12). Indeed, the first person singular subjectivity of agency in "Middle Passage" belongs only to the slave traders in their journal entries and testimony.

However, the vocal complexities and shifting frames of reference are the poem's strength. Hayden gives these incriminating lines to the speaker of the second section: "Twenty years a trader, twenty years, / for there was wealth aplenty to be harvested / from those black fields, and I'd be trading still / but for the fevers melting down my bones" (2.21–24). What Hayden presents is the reverse Mammy monologue, in which he ventriloquizes the voice of the slave trader. The trader's words possess the least poetic flare. He foregrounds them in order to expose the absurdity of their actions and words: invoking Jesus Christ in a mission to enslave and rape the "comeliest of the savage girls" (1.56–57) and chasing the wealth of the slave trade at all costs. In contrast, Hayden assigns the omniscient poetic speaker the most lyrically invigorating and challenging lines, those that Galler seems to overlook. The poignant lines flanking the testimony of the Spanish sailor issues an indictment of the whole slave trade enterprise:

> Shuttles in the rocking loom of history,
> the dark ships move, the dark ships move,
> their bright ironical names
> like jests of kindness on a murderer's mouth;
> plough through thrashing glister toward
> fata morgana's lucent melting shore,
> weave toward New World littorals that are
> mirage and myth and actual shore.
>
> Voyage through death,
> voyage whose chartings are unlove.

A charnel stench, effluvium of living death
spreads outward from the hold,
where the living and the dead, the horribly dying,
lie interlocked, lie foul with blood and excrement. (3.1–14)

Casting a judgment on the movers of the "dark ships," "murderers," in the "rocking loom of history," this voice, even more than the irony of the slave traders' voices, indexes the crux of the moral imperative of this poem. The revised refrain "Voyage through death, / voyage whose chartings are unlove" (3.9–10) universalizes the particular monstrosity of the "effluvium of living death" (3.11) to a general audience. A "voyage whose chartings are unlove" symbolizes the often heinous product of cultural incomprehension, of disparate voices talking across each other instead of with each other. The poem concludes:

The deep immortal human wish,
the timeless will:

Cinquez its deathless primaveral image,
life that transfigures many lives.

Voyage through death
to life upon these shores. (3.81–84)

Although Hayden does not articulate the voice of Cinquez or the other captive Africans, he uses the words of the slave traders against them, brilliantly juxtaposing their cruelties and insensitivities with the lyricism of the poetic voices to interrogate the barbarism of the Middle Passage and other "voyages of unlove." In these last six lines, Cinquez emerges as the hero of the poem. Unlike Nat Turner's bloody yet overturned insurrection, Cinquez's rebellion is victorious. His "deathless primaveral image" is, at last, "the deep immortal human wish . . . life that transfigures many lives." Rising above the specificity of slavery, Cinquez represents a "human" wish, not merely the wish of the beleaguered population of the enslaved. What's more, Hayden's use of the word *transfigures* here resonates with the first word of the poem, "*Jesús,*" coming full circle. Christ transforms into Cinquez, an insurrectionist who frees humankind.

To elevate Cinquez from African folk hero vigilante to life-transfiguring, immortal "primaveral image" for humanity is to recover African American heritage and history poetry from the literary margins, recalling what Hayden theorized in his preface to *The New Negro:* "Americans, black and white, sought to discover or reclaim their native spiritual resources" (62). Hayden sheds light on the universality of the Middle Passage as both a "spiritual resource" and a cultural signpost of "the voyage whose chartings are unlove"—depravity, sadism, asymmetrical power structures, and unwarranted, ghastly violence—and which plagues us all, and he positions Cinquez as a savior figure. Hayden achieves this in "Middle Passage" through the rich complexity of multiple voicing and the superb technique of a high modernist practitioner. When Harold Bloom pronounced, in May 2004, that Hayden, along with Jay Wright, was "a major American poet," omitting the racial modifier, he officially placed him in the "Western canon" (1). Rather than negating the specter of race, however, Hayden's "Middle Passage" ultimately reveals that the "blackskinned epic" and the American epic often are synonymous.

The final two chapters will consider Carolina de Jesus as a favela dweller and author, and Fernando Ortiz's metaphors of sugar and tobacco in his theories of transculturation as the theoretical background for a reading of two canonical Cuban narratives of slavery. These chapters move beyond the United States as the paragon of literary slavery studies and explore Afrodiasporic forms in an inter-American context. Traveling to South America, one finds in the public nature of the lynching ritual ties to the *pelourinho* (pillory), a device of torture for criminals, the enslaved, and the dispossessed in nineteenth-century Brazil. Most importantly, the resilience of the poetic voice in the works of Toomer and Hayden reemerges in the polyvocal poetry of slavery by Castro Alves and the protest writing of Carolina de Jesus.

4

OS LAÇOS DE LEMBRANÇA E ESQUECIMENTO

Reading Pelourinho, Castro Alves's "O navio negreiro," Carolina Maria de Jesus's *Quarto de Despejo,* and Postslavery Brazilian Literature

Meu sonho não faz silêncio
E não é apenas promessa
Planta em mim mesmo, na alma
Palmares, Palmares, Palmares
Pelo que de belo, pelo que de farto
Muitos Palmares

[My dream does not keep silent
And it is not merely a promise
It plants itself inside of me, in my soul
Palmares, Palmares, Palmares
So beautiful, So abundant
Many Palmares]

—JOSÉ CARLOS LIMEIRA, "Meu Sonho Não Faz Silêncio" [My Dream Is Not Silent] (1978)

Contam muita coisa no território livre
[They tell a lot of tales in the no-man's-land around Pelourinho.]

—JORGE AMADO, *Tenda dos Milagres* [Tent of Miracles] (1967)

In 1995, the celebrated twentieth-century Brazilian modernist author Jorge Amado (1912–2001) wrote a letter of gratitude to then Bahian Governor Antônio Carlos Magalhães praising the success of the Pelourinho neighborhood restoration project. He rhetorically mused:

> Ai, como impedir o desespero, onde recuperar a esperança e recobrar o ânimo, onde revestir-se com a força necessária para crer no Brasil e nele confiar? Pois, no Pelourinho eu diria aos pessimistas: andando pelas ruas, vendo o casario, os olhos bem abertos para poder acreditar no grandeza restaurada.
>
> [Oh, how to impede desperation, where to recuperate hope and recharge the spirit, where to vest oneself with the necessary force to believe in Brazil and trust in her? Well, in Pelourinho I would say to the pessimists: walking along the streets, seeing the rows of houses, eyes wide open to be able to believe in the restored grandeur.] (Cerqueira, Furrer, and Amado 15)

The sentimentality in Amado's discourse on the triumphant recovery of Pelourinho expresses the cultural and textual wages at stake in the restoration project of the old historic downtown neighborhood called Largo do Pelourinho in Salvador da Bahia, Brazil. In lyrical and often lofty language, Amado claims that the "força necessária" (necessary force) to trust in Brazil is intertwined with the rejuvenation of this historic coastal city. For Amado, the restoration of Pelourinho signifies the renewal of *esperança* (hope), *ânimo* (spirit), and *confiança* (confidence) in the nation. Similarly, the mission statement for the Fundação Casa de Jorge Amado (House of Jorge Amado Foundation)—a house founded in 1986 to preserve Amado's literary legacy, and ironically just steps from one of the former locations of the physical *pelourinho* (pillory)—discloses Amado's vision of Bahia and echoes his belief in the relationship between place and people: "O que desejo é que nesta casa o sentido da vida da Bahia esteja presente e que isso seja o sentimento de sua existência" (What I wish is that in this house the sense of life in Bahia is present and that this is the sentiment of its existence).[1] Amado's Pelourinho, therefore, signifies more than the site of a late twentieth-century city renovation project and the tropical Bahian backdrop to his literary world; it is at the heart of an impulse to resuscitate Brazilian pride and reinforce some of the nation's founding myths.

Amado's letter, which closes *Pelourinho: Centro Histórico de Salvador, A Grandeza Restaurada,* a celebratory volume sponsored by the Fundação Cultural do Estado da Bahia (Cultural Foundation of the State of Bahia), recounts the twentieth-century history of the region and configures the renovation project as one that rescues Pelourinho from its ruins of crumbling colonial buildings and, from 1940 to 1991, its status as a red-light district (Collins, "Melted Gold"

685; C. Smith 68–69). Amado recalls the devastation of the formerly destitute Pelourinho: "Andar no Pelourinho era uma tristeza sem tamanho, a continuar o abandono em breve já nada restaria para recordar o dia de ontem e afirmar o dia de amanhã" (Walking along Pelourinho was a sadness without bounds, to continue the neglect, before long nothing would remain to remember yesterday and affirm tomorrow) (Cerqueira 15). Following Amado's interpretation, Magalhães becomes a messianic figure who miraculously saves the city from destitution and the restoration project exemplifies a cultural imperative for *lembrança* (memory).[2]

However, Amado's congratulatory remarks emphasize history as a stable category, forestalling the possibility for competing *lembranças:* "Antônio Carlos Magalhães entrou para a História, assim mesmo com H maiúsculo, a História da Bahia e do Brasil" (Antônio Carlos Magalhães entered into History, even so with a capital *H,* the History of Bahia and of Brazil) (Cerqueira 15). But what is the official history of Brazil with a capital *H,* and how does the memory of slavery figure into this historical narrative? Which legacy is the "restoration" preserving? What, specifically, is being constructed, de(con)structed, and obscured in service of what Christen A. Smith calls "the myth of Bahia's Afro-paradise" (43)?

Interpreting Pelourinho as both a charged cultural space and a symbol provides an instructive lens for understanding Brazil's evolving national identity (most famously formulated by Gilberto Freyre) and its collective memory of slavery. It is a kind of open-air museum, or "território do saber popular" (territory of popular knowledge), that embodies at once the trauma of slavery's past and the shifting public relationship to that history.[3] This chapter uses the concept of the multivalent Pelourinho, both the region and the physical whipping post, as a theoretical touchstone to explore representations of shaming, public humiliation, punishment, and the notion of exposure, broadly conceived, as legacies of slavery in nineteenth- and primarily twentieth-century Brazilian literature. I use the term *representation* purposefully to invoke the meaning of "re-presentation," with an emphasis on the prefix *re-,* in the sense of presenting the past again or anew.[4]

The constellation of texts discussed in what follows "tell a lot of tales," or "contam muita coisa," to borrow Amado's apt phrase (*Tent of Miracles* 7; *Tenda dos Milagres* 4).[5] I read works from both canonical and noncanonical authors, and from major and minor poets, to probe how os laços de lembrança e esquecimento (the ties between remembering and forgetting) and the notion of "remembering to forget" inform this postslavery literary flourishing, which produces a version of national history.[6] Mixing "high" and "low" art, I examine Castro Alves's *Os Escravos* (1883), and one of the most widely anthologized poems from this collection, "O navio negreiro," and the short novel *Mãe África Pai Brasil* (2007) from the relatively unknown twenty-first-century writer Dudda Seixas. Other illustrative texts include Francisco Alvim's poem "A mão que escreve" (2011), the favela dweller-turned-author Carolina Maria de Jesus's *Quarto de Despejo* (1960), and two poems from self-identified Afro-Brazilian women writers: Alzira Rufino's "Verídico" and Esmeralda Ribeiro's "Fato."

THE ENDURING MYTH OF GILBERTO FREYRE'S RACIAL DEMOCRACY

Acclaimed historian, sociologist, and cultural anthropologist Gilberto Freyre (1900–1987) advanced one of the most enduring, albeit now largely contested, foundational narratives of the twentieth century. Freyre's tome *Casa-Grande & Senzala* (1933)—translated into English as *The Masters and the Slaves*—argues that a social and racial democracy exists in Brazil because of its history of miscegenation and "interpenetration of cultures" in a sugar- and later coffee-based economy.[7] This "broad democratization" is explained in the preface to the first English-language edition (1945):

> The fact of the matter is that *miscegenation* and *interpenetration of cultures*—chiefly European, Amerindian, and African culture—together with the possibilities and opportunities for rising in the social scale that in the past have been open to slaves, individuals of the colored races, and even heretics: the possibility and the opportunity of becoming free men and, in the official sense, whites and Christians (if not theologically sound, at any rate sociologically valid ones)—the fact is that all these things, from an early period, have tended to mollify the interclass and interracial antagonisms developed under an aristocratic economy. (xiv; emphasis added)

Miscegenation and interpenetration of cultures are the forces that, Freyre theorizes, not only broke down the geographic distance between the literal big house and slave quarters to which his book title refers but also eroded the emotional and social antagonisms between the masters and the slaves, symbolized by "the Big-House-and-Slave-Quarters complex in the history of Brazilian society and Brazilian culture" (xvi). Furthermore, Freyre claims that the tropical milieu and what he calls "tropical feudalism" foster an environment in which there is a "perfect fusion," that is, "one of the most harmonious unions of culture with nature and of one culture with another that the lands of this hemisphere have ever known" (xii). Amado's vision of the imagined community of Bahia resonates with Freyre's early discourse on cultural harmony.

Expanding on his aspiration for harmonious unions among different groups, Freyre develops his interpretation of Brazilian history as a utopian narrative of a nation "march[ing] toward social democracy" with a "fondness . . . for honoring differences" (xiv–xv). In his formulation, Brazil becomes the exemplary case in the treatment of African slaves in the Americas:

> The same is true of the relations between whites and blacks: those hatreds due to class or caste, extended, and at times disguised, in the form of race hatred, such as marked the history of other slave-holding areas in the Americas, were seldom carried to any such extreme in Brazil. (xii).

Thinking within an inter-American theoretical framework, Freyre sets forth this idea that, comparatively speaking, a less virulent form of racism existed in Brazil and that, after slavery, people of various racial backgrounds enjoyed harmonious cohabitation. Yet scholarship in the past forty years has disproven popular depictions of slavery in Brazil as mild and humane. Based on the high mortality rate of those enslaved in this country in the nineteenth century and the fact that they often died within three years of forced relocation, we now know that Brazil was one of the deadliest places to be enslaved (Conrad 147).[8]

Although now often critiqued and dismissed as the "myth of racial democracy" in Brazil, the persistence and defense of Freyre's unquestionably optimistic, even idealistic vision during much of the twentieth century evidences a willful national participation, to varying degrees within certain societal circles, in the propagation of a national narrative that aims for peaceful racial harmony. How does this optimistic aspiration affect reimaginings of slavery's traumatic past and, particularly, the way Brazilians have come to understand and craft their national history?

Even Freyre's concession of the traumatic role of slavery is not without rejoinder: "As a whole, Brazilians have what psychiatrists call a traumatic past. *Slavery was their great trauma.* For many, colour remained for some time the disagreeable reminder of an unhappy social situation or an injurious episode in their past" (*Brazil* 122; emphasis added). Freyre mentions Black men who were denied positions as officers in the Brazilian army as an example of an "unhappy social situation." But he quickly counters the admission of slavery's trauma with an emphatic accent on Brazilianness, or *brasilidade:*

> The general tendency in present-day Brazil is to regard slavery as an episode over and done with, having only a social bearing on the history of the total Brazilian personality. Even Brazilians with a family or individual past that has nothing to do with Africa, biologically or ethnically, join Negroid Brazilians in a feeling, now general though not universal, that nothing is honestly or sincerely Brazilian that denies or hides the influence of the Amerindian and the Negro. (122)

In Freyre's vision of Brazil, a sharp distinction exists between the trauma of slavery's past and the racial paradise of the present, to which most Brazilians lay claim, often romantically or "opportunistically," as Matory calls it—an Africanness inherent in *brasilidade* (166).[9] An exploration of the literary manifestations of slavery in Brazil, therefore, seeks to expose ruptures and blind spots in Freyre's national myth to uncover whether an exaltation of unified Brazilian national character necessarily represents a denial, an active forgetting, of the trauma of slavery.

In light of Freyre's persuasive fiction, it is important to establish briefly some key historical facts. Although slavery persisted in Brazil until the passage of *Lei Áurea,* or the Golden Law, on May 13, 1888, making it the last nation to abolish slavery in the Western Hemisphere, the foreign slave trade was abolished in 1850. Robert Brent Toplin and Florestan Fernandes observe that Brazilian abolition of slavery was not followed by social reform to integrate the emancipated Africans and Afro-Brazilians into the economic structure. Livio Sansone's *Blackness without Ethnicity* (2003) addresses the demographic statistics from the past twenty years:

> Brazil is a country in which the poor, over the last decade, have experienced little social mobility. It is also known to be one of the countries with the most unjust wealth distribution. . . . From 1992 to 1999 indices of absolute poverty, such as child mortality and illiteracy, generally reduced, but the difference in terms of quality of life between the "haves" and the "have nots" did not shift. (28)

In each of these indices, Sansone continues, "the groups officially defined as brown and even more so those defined as black are faring much worse than the group defined as white" (Sansone 331). This is a staggering statistic, given that in the 2010 census, more than 50 percent of Brazilians self-identified as Black or brown.[10]

There is one more important historical note that shapes the significance of the historic city. Led by Manuel da Nóbrega, the Portuguese Jesuits arrived in Brazil on February 26, 1549, and they founded the city of São Paulo in 1554, where there would be a pelourinho (as there would be in Rio de Janeiro) (R. Smith 8; Young and Braziel 211; Maria das Neves 104–106). São Salvador da Bahia de Todos os Santos (Saint Savior of the Bay of All Saints), called simply Bahia, was the capital of Portuguese territories in Brazil until 1763 (Simões). It served as the primary port for the importation of African slaves. John Collins insightfully summarizes its importance in the Black Atlantic:

> The restoration of Salvador's Pelourinho neighborhood, Brazil's most extensive collection of Iberian baroque architecture, its first capital, and the former administrative center of the Portuguese south Atlantic, provides a window onto a state and its citizens' negotiation of shifting meanings of race in a nation whose history has been posed repeatedly as thinkable only through mixture.... The Pelourinho, or "Pillory," holds such a special place in dominant imaginaries in part because its buildings and inhabitants, celebrated since at least the 1920s by modernist intellectuals responsible for the establishment of a federal cultural bureaucracy, stand as one of the first manifestations of the wealth and slave labor constitutive of the modern Atlantic world. Yet Bahia's preeminence ebbed as the eighteenth-century Caribbean eclipsed Brazil in sugar production. ("Melted Gold" 686)

Collins notes that the region of Pelourinho symbolized colonial power and the prosperity gained through slave labor. The historic city center is a multivalent symbol in the Brazilian cultural imagination because it is the point of intersection of socioeconomic difference, the enduring legacies of colonialism and slavery, and the market-driven impulse to commodify African heritage for tourist economies. From these fraught historical contexts and societal conditions emerge the permutations of slavery's legacy in Brazilian literature.

▲▲▲▲▲

PELOURINHO (PILLORY) IN SALVADOR DA BAHIA, BRAZIL

Você já foi à Bahia, nêga?
Não!
Então vá!

["Have you been to Bahia, black girl?"
"No!"
"Then go!"]
—DORIVAL CAYMMI,"Você já foi à Bahia?" (1957)

In a 683-page inventory of medieval Portuguese pillories published in 1997, the introductory remarks pose an intriguing question: "Was the pelourinho identified with force?" The answer given in the volume, surprisingly, is negative: "Era lugar de aplicação de penas menores e sempre de exposição ao conhecimento, ridículo e vergonha por parte dos vizinhos" (It was a place for the application of minor punishments and always to put [the charged] on exhibition to [receive] recognition, ridicule, and shame from the neighbors) (Malafala 41–42). However, a brief review of the history of Pelourinho in Brazil reveals that the identification of the pelourinho with force (or at least with the enforcement of hegemonic powers) cannot be denied within the context of its uses in Portugal's largest colony (figure 6).

Just as the skin color and status differences between the barefoot "Negros" going to be whipped (figure 8) and the taller, armed colonial officers in military uniform suggest, there is a color-based power dynamic that plays out at these locations of punishment, which perhaps was not as evident in the Portuguese metropole (as there were significantly fewer enslaved Africans and people of African descent living there). What the pillory had in common with its Portuguese precursors, however, was its prominent location. In Salvador, the original Portuguese slave port and colonial capital of Brazil from 1549 to 1793, the pelourinho stood in front of the Colégio dos Jesuítas (Jesuit College), a symbol of Portuguese authority and colonial power, until 1718. It was moved when the Jesuits "complained that the execution of sentences disrupted religious activities at their church (the present Cathedral of Salvador)" (Schwartz 246).

The word *pelourinho* comes from the Old and Middle French word *pilori* and is presumed to derive ultimately from the classical Latin *pila* + *orium.* According to the *Dicionário Priberam da Língua Portuguesa,* a pelourinho is a "coluna de pedra, erigida em lugar público, junto à qual se expunham e castigavam os criminosos" (stone column, erected in a public place, where criminals were exposed and punished). The *Oxford English Dictionary* echoes this meaning and defines the historical pillory as "a device for punishment, usually consisting of a wooden framework mounted on a post, with holes or rings for trapping the head and hands, in which an offender was confined so as to be subjected to public ridicule, abuse, assault, etc.; punishment of this kind."

Though non-Blacks were punished at this site, Black slaves, *mulatos,* and Indians received the harshest punishments, as they, of course, were considered to be the most prone to criminal behavior; there is a semantic nexus between being an *afro-descendente* (Afro-descendant) and a criminal (Schwartz 246).[11] However, as Bergad points out, being a person of color in northeast Brazil, as in the Spanish colonies, was not synonymous with enslavement: "This diversified racial structure, where to be Black or mulatto was not necessarily to be a slave, was in sharp contrast with the British- and French-controlled Caribbean and North America, where free peoples of African descent were few and far between" (61). While British and French colonial slave societies upheld a more rigid Black–white dichotomy, Spanish and Portuguese variants of slavery in the Americas maintained more flexible categories that accounted for racial intermingling.

Although it was not the most prominent model of Spanish and Portuguese slavery in the sixteenth and seventeenth centuries, gradually the "African slave-based sugar plantation complex" dominated in Brazil, and this slave/sugar model was then replicated in the Caribbean, as we will discuss in chapter 5 (Bergad 52). As the largest slave port in the Americas, Salvador experienced great prosperity in sugar cultivation, and later, tobacco production, and the maintenance of this "sugarocracy" required publicly disciplining the slaves to demonstrate power.[12] By the year 1800, there were nearly 1.8 million Africans enslaved in Brazil, providing the involuntary labor force for the lucrative sugar economy (Bergad 62; Eltis, 46).

The phallic stone monument moved four times after its initial placement and was ultimately dismantled in July 1835, following a decree of the municipal council, when such public spectacles of violence fell out of favor.[13] As Alexandra K. Brown writes, "the dismantling of pillories was accompanied by anxiety over public executions" and fear of insurrection (103). However, this created a culture of secrecy in which the beatings of slaves took place behind closed doors; the public punishment in the square moved to the private space of the jail. In effect, this is the opposite of the US lynching rituals, in which bodies were dragged from the inside of the jail to the outside to stage a public spectacle of violence.

Although the pillories in the major cities in Brazil were dismantled, Largo do Pelourinho oddly continues to bear this linguistic marker of slavery's past, triggering at first thought the violence and humiliation that enslaved Africans endured on this instrument of torture. Does the retention of the word signal public denial or amnesia or a reimagining of the past? Prominently located in Pelourinho is the Fundação Casa de Jorge Amado, which houses Amado's archive, functions as center for research, and serves as the nucleus for cultural exchange. The foundation's website gives this history of the name of the neighborhood and its symbolic location:

> O Largo do Pelourinho, oficialmente Praça José de Alencar, é assim chamado em razão de ter sido, durante muitos anos, um local de suplício, onde os condenados eram expostos, amarrados ao pelourinho, aos olhos dos passantes e à execração pública. Pelas pedras redondas de seu calçamento, polidas pelo tempo, muito sangue correu, *principalmente sangue dos negros supliciados,* que, muitas vezes, ali mesmo morriam, vítimas de sua ânsia de libertação e da crueldade dos senhores. Neste local, palco de tantas tragédias, cenário de tantas dores, mas também de intensa beleza, reproduzido em fotos pelo mundo inteiro, cartão postal obrigatório de quantos visitem a cidade do Salvador, está plantada a Casa de Jorge Amado. (Emphasis added)
>
> [The Largo do Pelourinho, officially Praça José de Alencar, is called this because of having been, for many years, a location of torture, where the condemned were exposed, bound to the pillory, to the eyes of passersby and to public execration. On the cobblestones of its pavement, polished by time, much blood flowed, *principally the blood of the tortured Blacks,* that, many times, died right there, victims of their anxiety for liberation and the cruelty of the masters. In this location, the stage of so many tragedies, the scene of so much pain, but also of an intense beauty, reproduced in photos for the entire world, the obligatory postcard of those who visit the city of Salvador, is situated the House de Jorge Amado.]

Just as this description draws out the contradiction between the physical torture enslaved Africans endured and the intense natural beauty of the location, Pelourinho continues to possess embedded, overlapping, and often contradictory histories. By the time it was recognized as a World Heritage Site by the United Nations Educational, Scientific and Cultural Organization in 1985, there existed an economic incentive to remain silent about or deemphasize the torture of Africans in order to stimulate tourism. After Magalhães's restoration project firmly established it as one of the most successful South American tourist destinations, the public landscape transformed the atrocity of slavery into a site that celebrated the African roots of the *baianos* (Bahians), even as contemporary sociopolitical reverberations of this legacy of violence manifest in both overt and coded ways (C. Smith 69). In *Um Rio Chamado Atlântico,* Alberto da Costa e Silva discloses the fluidity of the connections between Africa and the Americas that this renarrativization obscures: "As trocas deram-se nas duas direções, e a cada um dos lados do Atlântico não era de todo desconhecido e indiferente o que se passava no outro" (The exchanges took place in both directions, and on each side of the Atlantic; it was not all unknown and indifferent what was occurring on the other side) (54).

As the location known for having the largest concentration of African descendants outside of Africa, Salvador is an important cultural capital as well. It is the constructedness of roots tourism, writes Patricia de Santana Pinho, that positions Bahia as a site of joy for African Americans seeking connection to what she calls "Mama Africa." The word *Bahia* even rhymes with *alegria* (joy), while roots tourism to countries in West Africa (especially the slave castles) involves an expectation of crying, pain, and ultimately catharsis. Hence, the roots tourism industry markets to African Americans (from the United States), many of whom seek a reconnection to an ancestral African past:

> A symptomatic example of this is the manner in which Pelourinho, a historic neighborhood named after the pillory that was once located there, is currently represented by the tourism industry. With the exception of a few cases, such as Gilberto Gil and Caetano Veloso's song "Haiti," *Pelourinho is rarely associated with the place where slaves were punished.* Dotted with souvenir and trinket shops, Pelourinho today is the most popular tourist attraction in Salvador. Ironically, Bahians and visitors join each other in dance, literally and metaphorically stepping on top of "negro heads," the local term for the rounded stones that pave the streets where slaves were whipped a little over a century ago. (Pinho, *Mama Africa* 55; emphasis added)

To make sense of this dramatic recasting of the past, Kirk Savage's work on monuments and the production and construction of the past is useful: "It is true that the process of commemoration often leads to conflict, not closure, because in defining the past we define our present. Yet in choosing to remember 'historical' events or heroes we still hope to plunge them into a past secured against the vicissitudes of the present" (*Standing Soldiers* 4). One must remember, too, that the pillory is a Portuguese colonial import. The structural vestiges of the prominence of the pillory in Portugal remain, to this day, as obelisk-shaped national monuments scattered across Portuguese urban and rural landscapes, architectural reminders of the potency of the monarchal past (Malafala). That Portugal's former colony dismembers the pillory in Bahia and implants new content and a divergent narrative could then be read as a jettisoning of this colonial history.

READING THE SIGN OF PELOURINHO IN POETRY AND ART

Pelourinho becomes a malleable discursive space, constructed to reflect the presumed desires of tourists. This malleability is evident in the literature and art about the pillory as well. From the private whippings of the enslaved in American literature, such as in Richard Hildreth's *Archy Moore* (1836), or the public humiliation of the three scaffold scenes in Nathaniel Hawthorne's *Scarlet Letter* (1850), themes of flogging and the space of the pillory, the stocks, and even the slave auction block highlight climatic textual moments.[14] The grittiness of the poetry of the Brazilian "marginal poets," and especially of Francisco Alvim, elucidates the interpretative potential of this theme.

Francisco Soares Alvim Neto (Chico Alvim) was born in 1938 in the small city of Araxá, in Minas Gerais, the second most populous state in the western region of the southeastern area of Brazil. A distinguished Brazilian diplomat, his governmental career, which began in 1965, took him to France, Holland, Spain, Costa Rica, and Peru as ambassador and consul general. He published his first volume of poetry, *Sol dos cegos,* in 1968 in Brasília. However, Francisco Alvim began writing poetry during his adolescence, influenced by his older sister, Maria Ângela Alvim (1926–1959), who was also a poet. Influenced by the preceding modernist tradition, and especially the poetry of Carlos Drummond de Andrade, Manuel Bandeira, and Oswald de Andrade, Francisco Alvim joined one of the many literary groups of the generation of the so-called *poetas marginais* (marginal poets) established in the 1970s, Grupo Frenesi, along with fellow writers Chacal (Ricardo de Carvalho Duarte), Geraldo Carneiro, Cacaso (Antônio Carlos de Brito), and Robert Schwarz. Reacting to the conventions of modernism, the *poesia marginal* (marginal poetry) of Grupo Frenesi developed these common stylistic traits: the use of simple, almost *antiliterario* (antiliterary) language, colloquialisms, brevity, and humor. Critic Carlos Pereira summarizes this style as the *politização do cotidiano* (politicization of the quotidian) (Messeder 32), while Echevarría describes the genre as "pop minimalism" (Echevarría and Pupo-Walker 380).

Francisco Alvim played a significant role in the cultural movement of poesia marginal and the desire to present a *nova sensibilidade* (new sensibility).[15] He is best known as editor and organizer of the celebrated anthology *Águas Emendadas* (1977), which was the culmination of efforts to bring the poesia marginal of the 1970s to the forefront, a movement in which he was heavily involved. Several collections followed his first one, including *Passatempo* (1974), for which he won the Jabuti Award in 1982; *Dia sim dia não* (1978); *Festa* (1981); *O Copa fora* (1988); and *O Elefante* (2000). Two lines show the brilliance of his lyrical simplicity: "Quer ver? / Escuta." The poetic constant in his career, which spans more than forty years, is the endeavor to highlight and overcome Brazilian societal problems. His poetic collection *O metro nenhum* examines slavery's past and explicitly references the pelourinho as a cultural symbol (61–62).[16]

In "A mão que escreve," Alvim captures the impossibility of adequately expressing the scene of torture:

O tronco nu
contorce e grita
Na flora oblíqua

[The nude trunk
contorts and screams
in the oblique flower].

In this opening stanza, Alvim shows how even the word *tronco* overflows with meaning. *Tronco* means "trunk," and it functions as a metonym for the body, but it is also the trunk of a tree. Within the context of the brutal punishment of the enslaved, which we can assume from the second line, "contorce e grita" (contorts and screams), we are dealing with a tronco as an instrument of torture, closely related to the pelourinho. The French artist Jean-Baptiste Debret, discussed in chapter 1, depicts a scene of Black men in the tronco, secured at their ankles, barely allowing them to lie down to sleep (figure 8).[17] Their bodies become odd branches on this severed tree trunk.

In Alvim's poetic description, the tronco is nude; in the first three simple words that open the poem, "O tronco nu," the reader visualizes the collapsing of the instrument of torture and the tortured body. Is the nude trunk the stock itself, nude because it is no longer in its natural environment as a tree, or is it the Black body being tortured inside it? Although we cannot separate either of the two trunks, we learn that together they make a "flor oblíqua" (oblique flower), with the bodies positioned like petals at diagonals along the stem of the flower, the stock itself. Alvim repeats this unexpected flower analogy in the fourth stanza with these verses:

> Aqui agora
> tantos olhares
> Presos no lírio
> do pelourinho
>
> [Here now
> So many looks
> Trapped in the lily
> of Pelourinho] (lines 12–15)

The juncture of the pelourinho and the body it contains produces a strange flower, in this instance, a lily. These staggering metaphors of torture enhance their power.

The third stanza juxtaposes objects and body parts during the torture scene to make a larger statement about collective memory.

> Látego e nádega
> Um corpo cego
> emparedado
> na própria historia
>
> [Whip and buttock
> A blind body
> confined
> in history itself] (lines 8–11)

The assonance in the pairing of words in the first line of this stanza, "Látego e nádega," reminds us of another Debret lithograph depicting the execution of punishment (figure 8). There are only these objects: the whip hitting the buttock. The feeling of the scene is so strong that no verb is necessary to convey its meaning. Even though the person receiving the punishment is presumably still alive, his body parts (buttocks) become like inanimate objects, just like the whip. Although the poem stresses the materiality of slavery, on the one hand, and the execution of punishment, on the other, the scene becomes completely static and lacking animation.

The modifier *cego* (blind) is important too, as the victim is being subjected to public observation, exposure, and humiliation, yet his body is blind. One wonders, too, whether the blind body confined in history could also be the nation, jostling against certain memories of the past, resisting a confrontation with these ugly truths of slavery. Similar to the retention of the name Pelourinho for the now booming tourist center, the double meaning of *tronco* in this poem plays with the arbitrary relationship between signifier and signified. It is a poem that tells us that an instrument of torture can also transform into an odd-shaped flower with its victims locked inside it. Yet, the poetic inscription on the plaque next to Pelourinho reminds the reader to foreground the historical reality of bloodshed even as we interpret poetic legacies of slavery:

> As a memorial, we have retrieved—as in a ritual—the object that has been repressed, forever banished from local memory since the eighteenth century, the "pilori." While trying to humanize it, our look into it cannot forget this stone bled. The time has come for the baptism. The object of grief has to be named for redemption to take place. . . . From condemned matter sacred power is extracted, the sacred power of the condemned, whose sacredness is in knowing how to reinvent life through rituals, over and over, again and again. (Straile 209)

SINGING SORROW SONGS IN CASTRO ALVES'S *OS ESCRAVOS*

Ironically, the pelourinho in Salvador was first placed in Praça Castro Alves, the public square commemorating the "poet of the slaves." Much like Pelourinho's status as territory of the public imagination, contemporary Afro-Brazilian poet José Carlos Limeira's stirring 1978 poem "Meu sonho não faz silêncio" raises perennial questions about the representation of "o negro no Brasil" in relation to another symbolic and psychic location, Palmares.[18] Composed with his coauthor of *O Arco-Íris Negro,* Éle Semog, Limeira's lyrics deploy a collective *lembrança* of Palmares, a symbolic location of Black slave victory that has metonymically come to stand for Black resistance and hope. Part chant, part aspiration, the alliterative refrain "Planta em mim mesmo, na alma / Palmares, Palmares, Palmares" celebrates a proliferation of Palmareses, sites of slave resistance and settlement, not only nestled in the poetic speaker's soul but also growing in the souls of the people. The metaphor of *muitos Palmares* (many Palmareses), then, becomes a psychic *lembrança* of slavery not experienced firsthand yet knowable through a dream released from silence.

This section examines the complicated poetic interplay of *lembrança* and *esquecimento* (forgetting) and argues that it is precisely this exchange of remembering and forgetting that is the center of gravity in studies of slavery and Blackness in Brazilian literature. Through a close textual analysis of the works of two immensely contrasting literary figures—Antônio Frederico de Castro Alves (1847–1871), the nineteenth-century Bahian poet and arguably the most popular poet in Brazilian letters,[19] and Carolina Maria de Jesus (1915–1977), a twentieth-century poor Black woman and favela dweller (along with two other Afro-Brazilian poets, Esmeralda Ribeiro and Alzira Rufino), a marginalized and "underground" figure par excellence—I explore the drastically different ways each author writes about the status of Afro-Brazilians by mobilizing, to varying degrees, the memory of slavery.[20]

Alves's posthumously published late-Romantic poetic collection *Os Escravos* (1883), particularly the famous poems "O navio negreiro" (1868), "Canção do africano" (1863), "Bandido negro" (1883), and "Vozes d'África" (1868), focus the reader on the horrors of slavery in the often lofty and ornate language characteristic of Castroalvan Romantic sensibility. Conversely, Carolina Maria de Jesus's gritty, unpolished, often poetic and sometimes crude language in *Quarto de Despejo* (1960) starkly recounts the daily life of *uma favelada* who writes from a position of marginalization as a poor Black woman inhabiting the slums of Canindé in São Paulo. Examining these texts in tandem exposes the polemics of a designation such as "o poeta dos escravos." If Castro Alves is the poet of the the enslaved, then who is Carolina Maria de Jesus? How can a descendant of the enslaved sing of their own condition? Who is "authorized" to tell certain stories or assume certain subject positions? What power dynamics are at play? What can one say about authenticity, given Castro Alves's identity as non-Black? Does his voice speak for the slaves? How are these texts mediated? What is the mediating effect, for example, of the journalist Audálio Dantas, who originally edited and published Carolina's writings? Within the diary, what is the significance of the ubiquitous scenes of Carolina de Jesus writing in her notebooks?

Situating *Os Escravos* within the nineteenth-century Brazilian Romantic literary tradition at once contextualizes and sheds light on the various reasons this poetry may be considered abolitionist, antislavery, or even radical. Castro Alves, a man whose life prematurely ended at the age of twenty-four, when he succumbed to tuberculosis, indeed accomplished a literary feat through these slavery-themed poems. As Alfredo Bosi remarks, "Varela prenuncia os *condoreiros* pelo ardor nacionalista . . . pelo mito da América-paraíso-da-liberdade . . . enfim, no tratamento precoce do tema do negro em relação à literatura abolicionista dos decênios seguintes" (Varela judged the exalted by nationalist ardor . . . by the myth of America-as-paradise-of-freedom . . . finally, in the precocious treatment of the theme of the black in relation to abolitionist literature of the following decades) (119). Bosi further explains, in a footnote, "Antes da campanha [de Varela] só havia alusões esparsas ao escravo na poesia romântica. Quem precedeu imediatamente Varela e Castro Alves foi Luís Gama" (Before [Varela's] campaign, there were only sparse allusions to the slave in Romantic poetry. He who immediately preceded Varela and Castro Alves was Luís Gama) (119). Castro Alves's *Os Escravos* rescues the theme of slavery from passing allusions in Romantic poetry and places it front and center. Operating within the academy, poems like "O navio negreiro," for example, promoted a cultural paradigm shift, much like Harriet Beecher Stowe's *Uncle Tom's Cabin* (1852) did in the United States, ultimately igniting an epiphanic national recognition of the abhorrence of slavery.

Transitioning from Brazilian ultra-Romanticism to realism, or what Fausto Cunha—one of Alves's most thoughtful critics, who published his study on Romanticism in 1971 at the centennial of Alves's premature death—calls "O realismo romântico," Castro Alves's poetry teeters on the cusp of these two literary strands. Incorporated into the canon, the poetic rhetoric of "o mais popular poeta do Brasil" (the most popular poet in Brazil) reimagines notions of liberty and casts in baroque terms what it means to be a slave. As Telenia Hill asserts, "Preocupado com o existir do homem, o poeta vê a escravidão como um fato social que abrange os tempos mais afastados da humanidade e não se limita a tratá-lo apenas em relação à raça africana" (Preoccupied with the existence of man, the poet sees slavery as a social fact that encompasses the most distant times of humanity and does not limit himself to treating it only in relation to the African race) (29). Clearly, Castro Alves establishes an amplified definition of slavery that includes slavish conditions and slavery of the mind.

The critical response to his work reconfigures a new Castro Alves with each publication. As Cunha argues, "É necessário ter sempre em vista êsse estado de coisas para compreender a evolução poética de Castro Alves, medir sua importância como elemento renovador e distinguir, na sua obra, o que é resíduo e o que é fermento" (It is necessary to have always in sight this state of things in order to understand the poetic evolution of Castro Alves, to measure its importance as a reforming element and to distinguish, in his work, what is residue and what is ferment) (28). Indeed, Cunha's project is primarily concerned with categorization and identification of literary ancestors and descendants, tracing influence and literary genealogies. His literary analysis follows traditional modes of praising the individual genius of the author and locating his work within a larger literary trajectory. The scholar also notes Castro Alves's "lirismo contraditório" and claims that Alves "ergueu um mundo de contradições" (builds a world of contradictions) (29, 33). In an incisive reading, the critic introduces the question of intersection of aesthetic and social concerns in his concluding remarks: "Nas 'Vozes d'África' e no 'Navio Negreiro', a cada instante o pensamento social é soterrado pelo pensamento poético, o fato pela metáfora, o real pelo idealizado" (In 'Vozes d'África" and in 'Navio Negreiro,' at each instant social thought is buried under poetic thought, fact under metaphor, the real under the idealized) (42).

The unnamed author of a 1946 article, for example, attributes Castro Alves's wide popularity to his brave fight "pela causa da liberdade" (for the cause of freedom) ("Secção Escolar Portuguesa" 189–190). Assuming a tone at once didactic and laudatory, the anonymous author of this piece simply describes Castro Alves as "o símbolo da liberdade no Brasil" (the symbol of liberty in Brazil) and makes a case for the political power of his lyrics by historicizing Castro Alves's period:

> O vate bahiano viveu em um momento em que a pátria se achava dominada por uma sociedade patriarcal, escravocrata, monarquista, defensora de seus latifúndios, medrosa de quanto fosse progresso, a quem horrorizava a menor idéia liberal; momento também revolucionário, quando se alevantavam uns poucos jovens a clamar contra a escravidão do negro, a advogar pela republica. Castro Alves estava entre aqueles jovens, foi dos primeiros abolicionistas e republicanos, precursor, pois desde 1863 clamou pelos escravos, muitos anos,

> portanto, antes de o fazerem os mais avançados do mundo político, no Rio de Janeiro, porque estes somente depois de 1879 denunciavam com coragem o crime da escravidão.
>
> [The Bahian bard lived in a moment in which the country found itself dominated by a patriarchal society, slave owning, monarchist, defender of its agricultural estate, timid in what was progress, to whom the least liberal idea horrified; this was a revolutionary moment also, when they elevated a few youths, precursor to the first abolitionists and republicans, since 1863 they clamored for the slaves, for many years, therefore, before the most advanced of the political world did it, in Rio de Janeiro, because they only after 1869 denounced with courage the crime of slavery.] (Cunha 190)

The author argues that there is a causal relationship between "O navio negreiro" and "Vozes d'África" and the abolishment of slavery; the poetry spurs social change. This generation of critics generally praises Castro Alves as a beacon of social change instead of viewing him as a man of vapid flair, as some modernists might describe him.

What, then, is the significance of dedicating an entire poem, "O navio negreiro," which Amy Peterson translates as "Tragedy at Sea: The Slave Ship," to the subject of the Middle Passage and the slave ship at a time when captive Africans are no longer being transported to Brazil? Cunha charges Castro Alves with poetic ahistoricism: "sòmente um artista absolutamente desinteressado da validade histórica de sua obra poderia construir um dos seus mais arrojados e mais valiosos trabalhos sobre um anacronismo" (only an artist absolutely uninterested in the historic validity of his work could construct one of his most daring and most valuable works about an anachronism) (42). Yet Castro Alves's thematic anachronism seems to challenge the limits of temporality around conceptions of slavery's abolition and urges the reader to consider what the Middle Passage as a continual present might signify.

Consider the opening stanzas of the poem, "O navio negreiro":

> 'Stamos em pleno mar . . . Doudo no espaço
> Brinca o luar—dourada borboleta;
> E as vagas após ele correm . . . cansam
> Como turba de infantes inquieta.

'Stamos em pleno mar . . . Do firmamento
Os astros saltam como espumas de ouro . . .
O mar em troca acende as ardentias,
—Constelações do liquido tesouro . . .

[We are on the high seas . . . moonlight
Plays on the water—golden butterfly;
And the waves running behind . . . sing
Like mobs of restless children!

We are on the high seas . . . constellations
Leap from the night sky like golden sea-foam
And the ever-changing sea ignites
—Constellations of liquid treasure.] (*Major Abolitionist Poems* 11)[21]

The opening line of this poem divided into six parts. "Stamos em pleno mar" (We are on the high seas) becomes the poetic refrain that opens the first four stanzas. From the beginning, the language sets a tone of grandeur like the beginning of a creation myth, with references to the firmament, constellations, the moon, and the sea, and with adjectives (*dourada, de ouro*) depicting gilded nature. There is an exaltation of nature and natural elements, and the ellipses after each "'Stamos em pleno mar" hint at the inexpressibility of the beauty of nature.

The line in which the speaker contemplates the infinities of the sky and the sea—"Azuis, dourados, plácidos, sublimes . . . / Qual dos dous é o céu? qual o oceano?" (Blues, golds, the placid and sublime . . . / Which is the sky, which is the sea?)—is emblematic of the Romantic style. Indeed, the *majestidade* and *imensidade* of the open sea evoke a maritime sublime: "Meu Deus! como é sublime um canto ardente / Pelas vagas sem fim boiando à toa!" (My God! How sublimely sounds the love / Song from the endless waves as we float on). The punctuation throughout the poem is replete with ellipses and exclamation marks, indicating on a grammatical level its poetic melodrama.

By the eighth stanza, however, there is a slight shift in the tone of the poem: "Homens do mar! ó rudes marinheiros, / Tostados pelo sol dos quatro mundos!" (Men of the sea! Oh illiterate sailors, / Browned by the sun of four worlds!). And then "Esperai! Esperai!" (Wait! Wait!), perhaps foreshadowing the nefarious scheme of the sailors on the ship, later revealed to be an ill-fated slaver. This is the same tonal shift present in the fifth section of the poem, in which Castro Alves sets up a series of dichotomies comparing *ontem* (yesterday) with *hoje* (today): "Ontem simples, fortes, bravos. / Hoje míseros escravos" (Yesterday, simple, strong, brave / Today, miserable slaves). The reader knows from the outset, with the subtitle "Tragédia no mar," that Castro Alves's project is to tell the *tragedy* of slavery.

Is this extravagant poem simply anachronistic, as Cunha argues? Although the beatific scene of nature works nicely as a discursive strategy to reveal, by contrast, the horrors of slavery, what is the effect of the seeming aestheticization of slavery? Does this dangerously create a poetics of suffering? How does one square Castro Alves's altruistic, libertine agenda—underscoring the present suffering of the formerly enslaved—with the possibility that he, to some extent, returns to the subject of the Middle Passage in part to demonstrate his talent as a poet?

To examine how Castro Alves's imaginative leaps play out, let us turn to one of the most disturbing images of the poem, the scene in the fourth section in which the captive Africans are forced to dance on the ship:

Era um sonho dantesco . . . o tombadilho
Que das luzernas avermelha o brilho.
Em sangue a se banhar.
Tinir de ferros . . . estalar de açoite . . .
Legiões de homens negros como a noite,
Horrendos a dançar . . .

Negras mulheres, suspendendo às tetas
Magras crianças, cujas bocas pretas
Rega o sangue das mães:
Outras moças, mas nuas e espantadas,
No turbilhão de espectros arrastadas,
Em ânsia e magoa vãs!

[As in a vision of Dante,
I saw the quarterdeck, slippery with blood,
The skylight washed with crimson.
The clanking irons . . . the crack of a whip . . .
Legions of men black as the night,
Dancing their horrible death-dance . . .

Black-mouthed and listless children
Hang at their black mother's exhausted breasts
Spattered with blood
Shivering and naked girls,
A crowd of ghosts dragging
Their wretched bodies . . .] (15, 17)

With allusions to Dante's *Inferno,* the slave ship transforms into a gruesome theater with "Legiões de homens negros como a noite, / Horrendos a dançar" (Legions of men black as the night, / Dancing their horrible death-dance) (15). The nouns predominating in these stanzas—*sangue, açoite, ferros, noite*—emphasize a moribund tonal shift. Instead of the nourishment of milk, Black women's breasts drip blood to their babies. The mandate to dance on command reaches climax with the following stanzas:

Presa nos elos de uma só cadeia,
A multidão faminta cambaleia,
E chora e dança ali!
Um de raiva delira, outro enlouquece,
Outro, que martírios embrutece,
Cantando, geme e ri!

No entanto o capitão manda a manobra,
E após fitando o céu que se desdobra,
Tão puro sobre o mar,
Diz do fumo entre os densos nevoeiros:
"Vibrai rijo o chicote, marinheiros!
Fazei-os mais dançar!"

[Joined in the links of a single chain
A starving multitude staggers
Cries out in their death-dance—
One raving in delirium, another stupefied
With pain, brutalized and martyred . . .
Singing, moaning and laughing.

Yet the captain marshals this grim parade

In full view of the beautiful sky
Lying pure on the sea,
And orders, between puffs on his cigar,
"Shake the whip harder, sailors,
Make them dance more."] (17)

This language describes in poignant detail the hellish torture and public humiliation the African captives were forced to endure, at the same time "cantando, geme e ri" (singing, moaning, and laughing). It is the confluence of dissonant emotions—singing, moaning, and laughing—that exemplifies the atrocity of the slave ship voyage. Although Castro Alves, a white Brazilian, reimagines through his third-person speaker of the poem the ghastly transatlantic journey, his dedication to presenting the horror of this experience—"Tanto horror perante os céus?!" (Can you allow such horror beneath your heavens?!)—demonstrates an undeniable sense of empathy and commitment to presenting the history of slavery as a shared national history (21). His verses vilify the sailors/slave traders and martyr the enslaved Africans. To imagine the Middle Passage, albeit anachronistically, and render it in such detail, Castro Alves calls upon and crafts the collective national memory and boldly exposes the inextricable ties that link the curse of slavery to *all* Brazilians.

What, then, are the implications of Castro Alves channeling the voices and speech of the enslaved in "A canção do africano," a poem about *saudade?*[22] This ten-stanza poem transports the reader to the domestic space of the *senzala.* This location becomes one half of the subject of Gilberto Freyre's provocative sociological treatise *Casa-Grande & Senzala,* in which he argues that the casa-grande represents:

> O sistema patriarcal de colonização portuguesa do Brasil. . . . A casa-grande, completada pela senzala, representa todo um sistema econômico, social, político: de produção . . . de trabalho . . . de transporte . . . de religião . . . de vida sexual e de família . . . de higiene do corpo e da casa . . . de política. (12–13)

> [The patriarchal system of colonization set up by the Portuguese in Brazil . . . The Big House completed by the slave shed, represents an entire economic, social, and political system . . . of labor . . . of transport . . . of religion . . . of sexual and family life . . . of bodily and household hygiene . . . and a system of politics.] (Freyre, *Masters and Slaves* xxxii–xxxiii)

The opening line of the poem—"Lá na úmida senzala" (There in the humid slave quarters)—takes on greater meaning, given the significance of the slave quarters, a place that does not provide refuge from the enslaver, who on any occasion might "viesse, em meio do sono" (come, in the middle of sleep) to grab a baby from his mother's breast.

Castro Alves assigns these verses of yearning for return home to an enslaved African woman: "Minha terra é lá bem longe, / Das bandas de onde o sol vem; / Esta terra é mais bonita, / Mas à outra eu quero bem!" (My land is very far there / From the bands from where the sun comes / This land is more beautiful / But the other I love well!). In this moment, the captive woman sings about her longing for a home that is far away; she is bestowed with a voice and self-expression through song. Unlike "O navio negreiro," here the enslaved speaks. And also unlike "O navio negreiro," which mentions the specific country from which the Africans were captured, Sierra Leone, this poem's speaker is nostalgic about a generic and unspecified location, "minha terra" (my land). Notably, Africa is never explicitly mentioned in the poem itself, only the title reveals homeland as a mythic location that cannot be named precisely.

The contrasts begin with nature (the sun, the trees) in each space, culminating with this powerful stanza near the end of the poem: "Lá todos vivem felizes, / Todos dançam no terreiro; / A gente lá não se vende / Como aqui, só por dinheiro" (There everyone lives happily, / Everyone dances in the courtyard; / People there are not sold / Like here, only for money). The rhyme scheme, *abcb,* creates a certain musicality to a poem that deeply critiques the economic logics of slavery. The first two lines operate on a whimsical register; there is a tonal shift from light to grave in the third line of this stanza; and the final line, with the rhyme of *terreiro* (yard) and *dinheiro* (money), illustrates the bloody connection between land and money. The enslaved woman's critique counters the grotesque scene of dancing in "O navio negreiro" with the voluntary, joyful dancing that occurs in the speaker's homeland, where a life of happiness and full personhood is possible.

In both "Vozes d'Africa" and "Bandido negro," the reader finds iterations of the motif of the enslaved African in Brazil. In effect, Castro Alves seems to write, rewrite, and revise the same poetic song of the aggrieved enslaved African in varying keys. "Vozes d'Africa" begins with the high emotion characteristic of Romanticism, the speaker groaning in supplication to the Lord, "Deus! ó Deus! onde estás que não respondes?" (God! Oh God! Where are you that you do not answer!) (*Major Abolitionist Poems* 3), thereby channeling Psalms 22: "My

God, my God, why have you forsaken me? Why are you so far from saving me, so far from the words of my groaning?" The entire poem maintains the tone of a sacred hymn, with the speaker directly questioning God as David does in Psalms.

Similar to many of Castro Alves's *Os Escravos* poems, he employs the rhetoric of contrast to cast in high relief the extraordinary long-suffering of the Africans. The speaker outlines the glorious conditions of those in Asia—"Dorme a Ásia nas sombras voluptuosas" (Asia sleeps in the voluptuous shade)—and in Europe—"A Europa é sempre Europa, a gloriosa!" (Europe is always Europe, the glorious one!)—and then signals the upcoming contrast with the word *mas:* "Mas eu, Senhor! . . . Eu triste abandonada / Em meio das areias esgarrada, / Perdida marcho em vão!" (But I, Lord! . . . I am sad, abandoned / Wandering helplessly in the wilderness, / Lost and marching in vain!) (3, 5).

His supplication continues, like a son speaking to his father: "E que é que fiz, Senhor? Que torvo crime / Eu cometi jamais que assim me oprime / Teu gládio vingador?!" (What have I done, Lord? What horrifying crime / Have I ever committed, that you oppress me / With your double-edged vengeance?!) (7). In a tone that vacillates between prayer and wail, the speaker poetically names the vulture as the "ave da escravidão" (bird of slavery) and mobilizes the recurring blood motif: "Hoje em meu sangue a América se nutre" (Today my blood feeds America) (7). Employing the imagery of America feasting on the blood of the enslaved Africans for nourishment allows the speaker to express the atrocity of New World slavery in the stark religious language of evil versus good. Ultimately, the poem ends circularly, with the speaker's direct entreaties—"Meu Deus! Senhor, meu Deus!!" (My God! Lord, My God!!)—indicating the lasting struggle to overcome crimes against humanity (9).

"Bandido negro," in contrast, starts with a third-person narrative poetic voice, "Trema a terra de susto aterrada . . . Porque o negro bandido é quem passa, / Porque o negro bandido bradou" (Tremble earth with startled fright . . . Because the black bandit is the one who passes, / Because the black bandit shouted). The alternating repetition of this stanza creates a musical rhythm:

> Cai, orvalho de sangue do escravo,
> Cai, orvalho, na face do algoz.
> Cresce, cresce, seara vermelha,
> Cresce, cresce, vingança feroz.

[Leave, drizzle of slave's blood,
Leave, mist, in the face of the executioner.
Grow, grow, red harvest,
Grow, grow, ferocious vengeance.] (49)

Repeated eight times, this refrain exists in an intertextual relationship with E. Sue's *Cantos dos Filhos de Agar* [Songs of the Children of Hagar], the epigraph of the poem. Castro Alves connects the biblical story of Hagar, the enslaved Egyptian woman who bears a son, Ishmael, with Sarah's husband, Abraham, upon Sarah's request, with the plight of the enslaved. This parallelism reinforces the notion that God will protect the enslaved, just as He sent an angel to Hagar in the desert. Castro Alves's selection of the Hagar story as analogous to the experience of modern captives—*o cativo* (captive) in E. Sue's poem becomes *o escravo* (slave) in "Bandido negro"—echoes the appropriation of the biblical story of Hagar as a story of hope and survival for African descendants in the diaspora, in the harshest economic and social situations. This recasting of the *bandido negro* transforms him into the quintessential figure of resistance. Defiantly, he intones these words:

Somos nós, meu senhor, mas não tremas,
Nós quebramos as nossas algemas
Pra pedir-te as esposas ou mães.
Este é o filho do ancião que mataste.
Este-irmão da mulher que manchaste . . .
Oh! não tremas, senhor, são teus cães.

[It is us, my master, but do not tremble,
We broke our shackles
In order to ask you for our wives and mothers.
This is the son of the old man you murdered.
This—the brother of the woman you defiled . . .
Oh! do not tremble, master, they are your dogs.] (51)

Here, the *bandido negro* becomes a heroic figure, proudly announcing "somos negros" (we are Black), breaking the shackles of captivity and seeking vengeance for the death and rape of his ancestors. Again, there is a fascinating interplay of *lembrança* and *esquecimento.* The speaker demands the wives and mothers, to obtain revenge for atrocities committed against not only him but also the legions of enslaved people who preceded him, those he is connected to through kinship and memory.

In an illuminating essay about Black contemporary poetry in Brazil, Luciano Rodrigues Lima theorizes about these questions of *lembrança* and *esquecimento* as they relate to the contemporary boom of *poesia negra* and the history of slavery:

> Após a "abolição" oficial da escravatura no Brasil, a classe que detinha o poder, em lugar de criar políticas para a integração do negro através de um programa diferenciado de educação, parece ter utilizado a *tática do esquecimento* e da exclusão histórica. Não mais sendo escravo, por força de uma lei isolada, o negro desaparece como raça, em meio a denominações como operário ou camponês. Durante quase cem anos o negro não figura sequer como um problema social ou cultural. Se não era um problema, nas estatísticas oficiais, não justificava qualquer política diferenciada ou compensatória.
>
> [After the official "abolition" of slavery in Brazil, the class that held the power, instead of creating policies for the integration of Black people through a differentiated education program, seems to have utilized the *tactic of forgetfulness* and historical exclusion. No longer being a slave, by the strength of an isolated law, Blacks disappear as a race, in the midst of appellations like worker or peasant. During almost one hundred years, the Black did not figure even as a social or cultural problem. If he was not a problem, in the official statistics, he did not justify any differentiated or compensatory policy.] (2; emphasis added)

Most striking about Luciano Lima's analysis is the notion that those in power after the official abolition of slavery launched "a tática do esquecimento e da exclusão histórica." The systematic and institutionalized tactic of forgetting slavery, excluding the horrorific brutality from national histories (at least Freyre's histories), perhaps provides the nexus to the pervasive and enduring exaltation of Castro Alves as the symbolic poet of liberty. Castro Alves is safe. The task of the Black contemporary poets, starting in the second half of the twentieth century, after the 1971 Castro Alves centenary celebrations, has been to correct, revise, and deepen Castro Alves's poetic project. If, as Lima astutely argues, "consciência é a verdadeira abolição" (consciousness is the true abolition) (1), then it is not until a twentieth-century writer such as Carolina Maria de

Jesus emerges—an unlettered, arguably *nonliterary* diarist—that the resounding clamor of this consciousness sounds, an undeniable awareness of the persistent bonds of socioeconomic enslavement for the Afro-Brazilian.

CAROLINA MARIA DE JESUS'S *QUARTO DE DESPEJO* AND SLAVERY'S LEGACY OF POVERTY

Concurrently with the Pelourinho restoration project in the early 1990s, poet Miriam Alves and scholar Carolyn R. Durham united to assemble a poetic anthology of contemporary Afro-Brazilian woman writers. Published in a bilingual edition in 1995, *Enfim—Nós* [Finally—Us] presents the work of seventeen poets—some, such as Miriam Alves and Conceição Evaristo, already well known within Brazil literary studies and others just entering the literary scene. Durham notes in her introduction to the bilingual edition that the anthology represents "a primeira vez que as obras literárias contemporâneas das mulheres afro-brasileiras são reunidas para dar uma visão completa da realidade da mulher negra no Brasil" (the first time that the contemporary literary works of Afro-Brazilians are gathered together in order to provide a complete vision of the reality of the Black woman in Brazil) (1). As its title indicates, this project seeks, as did many of the feminist and women's studies movements of the generation earlier in the United States, to reclaim, recover, and recapture space for the distinctive voices of Afro-Brazilian women of all skin colors (in the wide color spectrum in which they self-identify, including *negra, morena, mulata, crioula, parda,* and so on).[23]

The thematic focus of this "explosão verdadeira de expressão" (true explosion of expression) coalesces around representations of and reactions to "circunstâncias sociais e políticas" (social and political circumstances) (1). While some readers might fault Castro Alves's "O navio negreiro" for its overly sentimental tone or its preoccupation with aesthetic concerns, critics would find quite the opposite in these verses, which privilege social commentary over overwrought artistic form, although most of the poems are stunning on both fronts.[24] Overall, a strategic essentialism lies at the conceptual center of this volume, similar to the totalizing narrative of Amado's Bahia. Who is equipped to express the "visão completa da realidade da mulher negra no Brasil" (complete vision of the reality of the Black woman in Brazil) (1)? How does the vision have such perfect completeness when even the category of "*mulher negra*" (Black woman) is exceedingly complex in Brazil and elsewhere in the diaspora? Durham calls on a collective identity of Afro-Brazilian femininity to contribute to establishing a formal tradition and then to allow for the expression of multiple voices within this community. Theorist Florentina da Silva Souza considers "a cultura Africana da diáspora no Brasil como uma cultura duplamente híbrida" (the African culture of the diaspora in Brazil as a doubly hybrid culture) (23).

Miriam Alves communicates a similar desire to allow Black Brazilian women writers, part of this cultural hybrid, to incorporate themselves into the canon of Brazilian literature and within the small but growing space allotted for Black authors, which usually is male-dominated and includes Lima Barreto, Cruz e Souza, Solano Trindade, and Machado de Assis.[25] Of course, it is difficult to assign even these authors to a certain color group, as these distinctions are so fluid and dependent upon the observer. Nevertheless, there are two poems by this collection of poets who do self-identity within the Afro-Brazilian spectrum, that provide a poetic prelude to Carolina Maria de Jesus's *Quarto de Despejo* and that signal the profound ways in which the consequences of slavery—abject poverty, social inequalities, persistent hunger—remain salient in the contemporary lives of Brazilians.

Esmeralda Ribeiro's "Fato" [Fact] is a concrete poem that derives power from its minimalist structure:

<table>
<tr><td>Aboliram</td><td></td><td>Escravidão</td></tr>
<tr><td></td><td>A</td><td></td></tr>
<tr><td>Não</td><td></td><td>condição (86)</td></tr>
<tr><td colspan="3"></td></tr>
<tr><td colspan="2">[They abolished slavery</td><td>as an institution</td></tr>
<tr><td></td><td>But</td><td></td></tr>
<tr><td>Not</td><td></td><td>as a condition] (87)[26]</td></tr>
</table>

The geometric structure of this poem—one could draw a box around it—parodies the neat nature of the presentation of the historical fact. Literally and figuratively, there are multiple ways to read this poem. One may read the original Portuguese poem in a V-shape: "Aboliram A Escravidão . . . não A condição" (they abolished slavery . . . not the condition); in a sideways V-shape: "Aboliram A não . . . Escravidão A condição" (they abolished it, no . . . slavery the condition); or perhaps vertically downward, as a free association of words: "Aboliram não . . . A . . . Escravidão condição" (they abolished not the slavery condition).

The words act as textual jigsaw puzzle pieces that allow the reader to discover new orderings of the words.

The rhyme of *escravidão* and *condição* interrogates the historical statement that slavery was abolished in Brazil on May 13, 1888. Ribeiro challenges the reader to look beyond the *fato* (fact) and highlights the difference between the institution of slavery and ongoing slavish conditions. Her project, which in translation loses these swappable layers of meaning and the minimalist power, deconstructs the primacy of the notion of "institution" and official history on a syntactical level.

This deceptively simple poem of five words challenges and subverts the established position of "major" literature by actively demonstrating the potential for manifold readings and misreadings, interpretations and misinterpretations, of any statement. It is through the poetic genre that contemporary Afro-Brazilian writers most vociferously assert a certain agency and racial self-fashioning. Ribeiro leaves so much blank space on the page and allows her readers to write between the lines of history alongside her.

Alzira Rufino, who also self-identifies as a *mulher negra,* became politically and poetically active in the mid-1980s in the Movimento Negro (Black Movement) and the Movimento de Mulheres Negras (Black Women's Movement). Her poem "Verídico" (Truthful), also a part of the anthology *Enfim—Nós,* attempts to understand the complexity of color in Brazil: "A minha cor apavora" (My color frightens) (40, line 6). The poetic voice identifies as a *crioula decente* (decent Creole woman) (line 1), but then goes on to ruminate about the treatment of the *negro:* "É na arte do negro / de viver / melhor dizendo / sobreviver" (It is the black man's art of / living / or better said / surviving) (lines 10–13). Again one wonders if this is an intentional strategic essentialism, grouping *crioula* and *negro* together, to combat collectively against poverty. The strongest statement of the poem emerges when the speaker explains that the Black man survives even while dragging "o tronco que tentam esconder" (the shackles that they try to hide):

> Os troncos estão nas favelas
> vejo troncos nas vielas
> nas moradias fedidas
> nas peles sem esperança
> nas enxurradas de não.

> [The shackles are in the favela.
> I see shackles in the alley
> In the fetid dwellings
> In the hopeless skins
> In the torrents of no's.] (40, lines 18–23)[27]

Even though the whipping post and its meaning (as we saw with the restoration project) are obscured, the shackles remain visible through the glaring social inequalities. One of the most shocking systemic legacies of slavery is the abject poverty of life in the *favela,* the unsanctioned shantytowns, outside of official recognition but within the city limits, populated by people with "peles sem esperança" (hopeless skins).

However, even living in the squalor of the favela, Carolina Maria de Jesus communicates, in *Quarto de Despejo,* both the suffering and momentary episodes of escape. Similar to Castro Alves's poetry, which straddles the boundaries between various subject positions and personages, Carolina's text blurs generic distinctions between testimony, fiction, anthropology, and diary to complicate what constitutes the "literary." Acutely aware of the connection between the abolishment of slavery and poor living conditions for the formerly enslaved and their descendants, she writes:

> *15 de Julho de 1955* Aniversário de minha filha Vera Eunice. Eu pretendia comprar um par de sapatos para ela. Mas o custo dos generos alimenticios nos impede a realização dos nossos desejos. Atualmente *somos escravos do custo de vida.* Eu achei um par de sapatos no lixo, lavei e remendei para ela calçar. (Carolina Maria de Jesus, *Quarto* 9; emphasis added)

> [*July 15, 1955* The birthday of my daughter Vera Eunice. I wanted to buy a pair of shoes for her, but the price of food keeps us from realizing our desires. Actually *we are slaves to the cost of living.* I found a pair of shoes in the garbage, washed them, and patched them for her to wear.] (Carolina Maria de Jesus, *Child* 3; emphasis added)[28]

In this opening paragraph, Carolina de Jesus introduces several motifs that run throughout her narrative: the constant search for shoes as a symbolic representation of an ongoing quest for mobility; a mother's inventiveness and the ability to transform trash and scraps into clothing and food for her three children; and the underlying thread of slavery that has only been abolished in term of bondage but continues now as the "custo de vida" (cost of life), or the hard life in the favelas. This theme of the continuation of slavery in a different form—poverty—is directly reflected in Ribeiro's "Fato" and Rufino's "Verídico." In a later entry, Carolina poignantly likens hunger to slavery in her journal entry of May 13:

> *13 de Maio* Hoje amanheceu chovendo. É um dia simpático para mim. É o dia da Abolição. Dia que comemoramos a libertação dos escravos . . . E assim no dia 13 de maio de 1958 eu lutava contra a escravatura atual—a fome! (*Quarto* 27)

> [*May 13* At dawn it was raining. Today is a nice day for me; it's the anniversary of the Abolition. The day we celebrate the freeing of the slaves . . . And that is the way on May 13, 1958, I fought against the real slavery—hunger!] (*Child* 23)

Here, Carolina translates the collective experience of slavery into an apt metaphor for her current condition. As Débora Ferreira notes, "Como afirmam Gilbert Joseph e Mark Szuchman, em *Quarto* a fome alcança a estatura de personagem, tal a sua dimensão nessa obra; e ela quem gira a manivela que regula o espaço da vida e da morte" (As Gilbert Joseph and Mark Szuchman affirm, in *Quarto* hunger reaches the level of a character, such is its dimension in this work; and it is she who rotates the handle that regulates the space between life and death) (110).[29] There is a sense of hopelessness, yet a determination to endure the hunger: "Eu estou triste porque não tenho nada para comer. Não sei como havemos de fazer. Se a gente trabalha passa fome, se não trabalha passa fome" (I am unhappy because I didn't have anything to eat. I don't know what we are going to do. If you work you go hungry, if you don't work you go hungry) (*Quarto* 114; *Child* 119). Through journal entries like these, Carolina presents hunger as the central antagonist in her life in the favela.

While Castro Alves's ornate lyrics paint a sumptuously detailed yet somber still life in words, Carolina's elliptical prose operates on a sensual register, eliciting a visceral reaction as she takes the reader through her daily trials. When she writes the simple yet poignant sentence "Estou no quarto de despejo, e o que está no quarto de despejo ou queima-se ou joga-se no lixo" (I'm in the garbage dump and those in the garbage dump either burn themselves or throw themselves into ruin) (*Quarto* 33; *Child* 29), the reader's heart aches for the worthlessness the narrator feels at inhabiting this "quarto de despejo" (garbage dump), yet the narrative demands much more than sentimental reactions.

This notion of the favela as receptacle for trash, the idea that inspired the original Portuguese title, is Carolina's political statement reiterated throughout the narrative: "E a favela é o quintal onde jogam os lixos" (The favela is the backyard where they throw the garbage) (*Quarto* 28; *Child* 24). Yet hers is a story of resilience and exposure, not wallowing, even though she is in the favela "respirando o odor dos excrementos que mescla com o barro podre" (breathing the smell of excrement mixed with the rotten earth) (33; 28–29). In the midst of this suffering, she still finds moments when she sings: "A Vera despertou e cantou. E convidou-me para cantar. Cantamos" (Vera woke up and sang and asked me to sing with her. We sang. Then José Carlos and João joined in) (33; 29). Most often, however, the moments when Carolina de Jesus metaphorically sings, that is, when she is able to transcend her bleak environment, occur through reading and writing.

The salience of reading and writing in Carolina's narrative is underscored by her incessant search for paper. Paper, the tool on which she inscribes her narrative, becomes the medium for her advancement in two ways. First, she sells the blank paper to make a modest profit to purchase food for her family, and eventually she also sells her manuscript, written on the pages of notebooks, to journalist Audálio Dantas, again to make a profit.[30] And it is through writing that Carolina exerts power over some of her illiterate neighbors. In one compelling exchange, a fellow favela dweller sees her writing in her notebook and protests:

> *18 de Dezembro* . . . Eu estava escrevendo. Ela perguntou-me:
> –Dona Carolina, eu estou neste livro? Deixa eu ver!
> –Não. Quem vai ler isto é o senhor Audálio Dantas, que vai publicá-lo.
> –E porque é que eu estou nisto?
> –Você está aqui por que naquele dia que o Armin brigou com você e começou a bater-te, você saiu correndo nua para a rua. (*Quarto* 126)
>
> December 18 . . . I was writing. She asked me:
> "Dona Carolina, am I in that book? Let me see!"
> "No. Who's going to read this is Senhor Audálio Dantas, and he's going to publish it."
> "Well, why am I in it?"
> "You are here because of that day when Armin fought with you and started to slap you, and you ran naked into the street." (*Child* 131)

The journalist, Audálio Dantas, similarly claims that he first encountered Carolina while she was shouting to one of her neighbors that if she continued her behavior, she would end up in one of the notebooks. Both the passage from the text and this anecdote illustrate how Carolina envisions herself wielding power through her pen, as a documenter of the human condition, while her neighbors resist, feeling like the subjects of her ethnographic experiment.

The power of the pen, and in turn of reading and writing, enable Carolina to craft her own intellectual escape from the material struggles of daily life. "Eu gosto da noite só para contemplar as estrelas sintilantes, ler e escrever. Durante a noite há mais silencio" (I like the night only to contemplate the shining stars, to read and to write. During the night it is quieter) (*Quarto* 33; *Child* 28). While literacy acquisition for Carolina, an autodidact, clearly represents educational progress since slavery, when her ancestors were denied the right to read or write, it also provides her the tools to point out vast social inequalities. Writing allows Carolina to transcend imaginatively the misery of her surroundings, if only temporarily:

> Enquanto escrevo vou pensando que resido num castelo cor de ouro que reluz na luz do sol. Que as janelas são de prata e as luzes de brilhantes. Que a minha vista circula no jardim e eu contemplo as flores de todas as qualidades. . . . É preciso criar este ambiente de fantasia, *para esquecer* que estou na favela.
>
> Fiz o café e fui carregar água. Olhei o céu, a estrela Dalva já estava no céu. Como é horrível pisar na lama.
>
> As horas que sou feliz é quando estou residindo nos castelos imaginários. (*Quarto* 52; emphasis added)

> When I write I think I live in a golden castle that shines in the sunlight. The windows are silver and the panes are diamonds. My view is overlooking a garden and I gaze on flowers of all kinds. I must create this atmosphere of fantasy *to forget* that I am in a favela.
>
> I made coffee and went for water. The stars were in the heavens. How disgusting it is to step in mud.
>
> My happy hours are when I am living in my imaginary castles. (*Child* 52; emphasis added)

In another dream, Carolina imagines she is an angel who "pegava as estrelas na mão para contemplá-las. Conversar com as estrelas. Elas organisaram um espetáculo para homenagear-me" (put stars in my hands and played with them. I talked to the stars. They put on a show in my honor) (*Quarto* 107; *Child* 111). Interestingly, Carolina seems to describe two parallel narratives. The diary becomes a discursive space in which she alternates between writing about quotidian drudgery and her fantasy writing, not included in the diary entries, which helps her to forget. There seems to be a double writing process in which she remembers in the diary and then forgets through creative writing. In contrast to the short, declarative sentences of her diary, in her fantasy writing she waxes poetic and inhabits not the slums but "castelos imaginarios" (imaginary castles).

These themes of daily struggle presented in Carolina's diary continue to permeate contemporary Afro-Brazilian poetry: "Reafirmando uma característica da literatura contemporânea, a poesia negra está ligada visceralmente à vida. Isto se inicia na linguagem, com forte apelo da língua natural, e continua na temática, retirada da vivência cotidiana" (Reaffirming a characteristic of contemporary literature, Black poetry is tied viscerally to life. This starts in the language, with a strong appeal to natural language, and continues in the theme, taken from quotidian existence) (Lima 12). In many ways, Carolina's diary is the thematic prototext for contemporary Black poetry. Despite the tremendous international success of the book—it was a best seller, translated into thirteen languages in forty countries, plus subsequent publications, though none as popular as her first book—she was unable to earn a consistent living by her pen, partially due to her outspoken political views. She ultimately died in poverty, a story too common for Black women writers across the diaspora (R. Levine 60). The congruence between the writings of her life in the favela and her inability to transcend these conditions is a sobering conclusion to her life story.

Reading selected poems from Castro Alves's *Os Escravos* collection and Carolina Maria de Jesus's *Quarto de Despejo* through the lens of the memory of slavery and the complex history of being Black in Brazil lays bare the compelling power dynamics at play within the literary canon. As a transitional literary figure beholden to "O Romantismo" (Romanticism), Castro Alves's grandiose lyrics achieve the intended cathartic effect of inducing emotion in his readers. The posthumous lionization of the author of *Espumas Flutuantes,* nicknamed "Cecéu," doubly complicates the question of Black representation in Brazil. Although contemporary readers may balk at its overly sentimental language, Castro Alves's verses succeed in confronting the reader with the significance of the theme of slavery.

The risk, however, is the possibility that his stature as literary luminary overshadows the poetic voices of unknown, nameless authors who also address these enduring legacies of slavery. The fact that the *Unedited Diaries of Carolina Maria de Jesus* was published to counter disbelief about Carolina's authorship raises fascinating questions about authenticity and recognition (of the canonized white author versus the voice of the overlooked). Returning to José Carlos Limeira's "Meu sonho não faz silêncio," it seems that contemporary Afro-Brazilian poets must negotiate the seemingly dissonant textual relationship between the work of Castro Alves and Carolina Maria de Jesus. Conjured from memory, Palmares is not just a trope but also a protestation, an aspiration, an inheritance.

LITERARY LIBERATION IN DUDDA SEIXAS'S *MÃE ÁFRICA PAI BRASIL*

Dudda Seixas's 2007 novel, *Mãe África Pai Brasil,* imagines the fate of a young African captive on perhaps the very last slave ship to make the journey of the Middle Passage from the West Coast of Africa to the northeast coast of Brazil, specifically to the city of Salvador in Bahia. In this fictionalized historical account of a mid-nineteenth-century departure of an illegal slave trader from Dahomey to Bahia, the main protagonist, Norambo—later baptized with the Brazilian name of Felipe dos Anjos, which translates to Phillip of the Angels—represents an exemplary slave figure.[31] With a pious character reminiscent of Harriet Beecher Stowe's righteous protagonist Uncle Tom, combined with the intellectual drive of Olaudah Equiano, Norambo/Felipe emerges from the darkest pits of human bondage through the attainment of knowledge, a common trope of inter-American literature of the enslaved.

The narration is deceptively straightforward, at times even predictable in terms of structure and plot. Structurally, the text is tropologically (rigorously) organized into chapters that mark the major life events of an enslaved man who has come to write his narrative. This ordering reveals the standardization of broad categories of the experience of the enslaved such as *a partida, a viagem, aprendendo a ler, a fuga,* and *a minha liberdade.* These compose five of the sixteen book chapter titles: "The Departure," "The Journey," "Learning to Read," "The Flight," and "My Liberty." However, Seixas manages to work within established inter-American cultural codes of the classic slave narrative while also playing with familiar plot points and reader expectation. As Seixas writes in the brief "Apresentação" (Introduction), his greatest fear while composing the novella was of "cair em lugar comum" (falling into commonplace) (7).

This notion of falling on common ground, which Seixas predicts in his writing, conveys an acknowledgment of the transhemispheric adoption of a set of standard plot points for the neo-slave narrative that took shape by the late twentieth and early twenty-first centuries. A transatlantic standardization of the narrative arc of the slave experience at once evidences the common ground of the psychic trauma of African slavery and the resistance to Pan-American generalization through the invention, writing, and rewriting of individual stories. While *Mãe África Pai Brasil* indeed often falls on well-trodden literary ground, it also disrupts a simple reading of the text that focuses solely on the commonalities of transatlantic slavery.

In this vein, Seixas's confabulation of Norambo's life represents a coming to terms with this past, which he offers to his twenty-first-century readers.[32] Rather than being a stylistic flaw, this communal quality of the text indicates a fascinating way in which contemporary writers of the Americas have come to think about and write about slavery. His text is a shared retelling, a reinscription atop those narratives that preceded it. To craft and design Norambo's mid-nineteenth-century story in 2007 is to write with the benefit of hindsight and collective reflection.

There is a striking moment of intertextuality and self-conscious calling forth of the slave narrative and the abolitionist movement. In the Brazilian tradition, it is not the slave narrative as such, but the *poetic* slave epic that dominates public consciousness. The enslaved protagonist (Norambo/Felipe) invokes this literary tradition when he introduces Antônio de Castro Alves as "um jovem poeta baiano, muito querido . . . um jovem mestre da estirpe de Gonçalves Dias e Fagundes Varela" (a young Bahian poet, well loved . . . a young master of the literary lineage of Gonçalves Dias and Fagundes Varela) and reads three stanzas from his *A Canção do africano,* which are quoted in full in the text (166). These poetic excerpts appear in the thirteenth chapter, "Maria Rosa," about the eponymous woman to whom Norambo/Felipe dedicates his love during his arduous life journey from slavery to freedom.

Underscoring the cultural prominence of the figure of Castro Alves, the narrator asserts that the poet "consegue expressar os sentimentos de uma forma extremamente real, real de doer. Ele toca a alma com as palavras" (managed to express the sentiments in a form that is extremely real, real with pain. He touches the soul with words) (167). This is an intriguing rhetorical ruse. Norambo, formerly enslaved and now called Felipe, reads Alves to find a *real* expression of the sentiments of slavery. Castro Alves, the artist, vocalizes for the enslaved Africans; the poetic becomes the real. The narrator emphasizes this notion of the poetic in slavery when he describes Alves as a writer who "fazia poesias tendo a escravidão como tema, *coisas belíssimas.* Fazia uma poesia descritiva, de cunho social. A crítica o comparava a Victor Hugo" (wrote poetry with slavery as a theme, beautiful things. He wrote descriptive poetry, with a social bent. Critics compared him to Victor Hugo) (166; emphasis added).

This description raises the larger ethical and aesthetic questions: Can a narrative recounting human abjection, such as a slave narrative, contain *coisas belíssimas,* or beautiful things? If so, what, then, is the role of the poet? The use of the infinitive *fazer* begins to answer these questions. *Fazer* means "to do, to make, to create" (also "to write," if used in the context of literary production). Thus, when the narrator says that Castro Alves "fazia poesias," it accentuates the craft involved in making a poem. Is the translation of the traumatic events of Norambo's captivity—and, in general, the thematization of a slave's life—into Castro Alves's gilded words a dangerous beauty or a matter of taste?

In many ways, Seixas's novella is unbeautiful. Often, the narration slips into a didactic tone, like a passage from an elementary school language arts textbook. Elaborating on the biographical background of Alves, the narrator adds, "Apesar da pouca idade, ele tinha prestígio em outros estados do país. Sua obra é muito rica e não escreve somente sobre a escravidão. Embora o chamassem de 'poeta dos escravos', era um romântico" (Despite being very young, he had prestige in other states in the country. His work is very rich and he does not write only about slavery. Although they called him the 'poet of the slaves,' he was a Romantic) (167). The teacherly voice that the narrator assumes, along with the alternation between first-person narrative and the textual equivalent of the cinematic effect of breaking the fourth wall, not only emphasizes the retrospective quality of the narration but also demonstrates the function of the remaking of histories. It is the pursuit of the emancipation of his love interest, Maria Rosa, along with his own that drives Norambo/Felipe to become a scholar of the law. His developmental trajectory follows a familiar path as he transitions from illiterate, unlettered, unspeaking object to literate, lettered, speaking subject. However, the narration moves beyond this conventional ascent of the enslaved protagonist by periodically switching to a teacherly tone. Norambo/Felipe as narrator becomes teacher to the reader.

Yes, education is the route to liberation for the male protagonist, but the reader witnesses and monitors the progression of that education as the complexity of the sentence structure increases in the novel. This narrative effect creates a temporal immediacy, as if Norambo/Felipe as narrator has been writing the book while he is growing up; therefore, the narration records the development of his language skills. This rhetorical technique alters a reading of this novel as a coming-of-age tale in the reflective mode. What happens to memory when the narration is written as if either the narrator is reliving each event as he is retelling it (and therefore assumes the psychological and intellectual maturity of that state) or the text is being composed as it is lived and yet it is constructed as a memory?

This progression of linguistic complexity is further compounded by a literary pastiche effect. In many ways, this slave narrative should be rightly called a historical novel, as it seeks to impart certain historical truths, through the fictional mode, about the mid- to late nineteenth-century Brazilian political, social, and cultural milieu—including the simultaneous transformation from monarchical rule to a republic and the dissolution of the institution of slavery—in highly accessible language. In fact, the brief biographical sketches of Castro Alves and Luis Gama, the rehearsal of the dates of the passage of certain antislavery laws, and Norambo's recollections throughout the narrative arc imitate his psychological status. In other words, the reader witnesses Norambo's intellectual maturity through the stylistic changes in his writing. Consequently, "A Partida" (The Departure) begins with choppy sentence fragments that mimic the difficulty of a child's narrative voice. This is a voice that changes, by the end of the novel, to the complex language of legalese.

The philosophical question that permeates and animates this often didactic novel is What is liberty? Expressed in Portuguese, this question, *O que é a liberdade?* (What is freedom?), emphasizes a lexical link between literacy and liberation. With a remarkable aptitude for learning, Norambo/Felipe chooses not merely to survive the daily backbreaking and spirit-sapping work in the *fazenda* but also to comprehend the social system. Although living without a grasp of the colonial language of Portuguese, in a coastal region whose astonishing beauty belies the atrocities of the experience of enslavement, the inquisitive young Norambo/Felipe perceptively ascertains that in order to be *livre* (free), he has to learn to read *livros* (books). Maria Rosa, who eventually becomes his wife, is his first Brazilian Portuguese language teacher.

The narrative voice alternates between a straightforward first-person account prevalent in the slave narrative genre and that of a seemingly omniscient narrator charged with recording the fictionalized historical record of Norambo/Felipe's travails in the New World. Although Seixas attributes his selection of first-person narration to "fruto da inexperiência deste autor" (fruit of the inexperience of this author), the literary convention of this genre dictates the autobiographical retelling of an enslaved person's life (7). Norambo/Felipe not only becomes a speaking subject but also becomes a professional, a man of the law. Thus, there is a contrast between a demoralizing slavery system that operates outside the jurisprudence of the monarchical legal system and an enslaved person who manages not only to extricate himself from this system but also to serve as the prosecutor, an authority, a counselor, and an advocate.

In a chiastic turn of events, Norambo/Felipe ensures that justice prevails against the very man, Mr. Justino (*O coronel*), who committed heinous crimes against humanity, held Maria Rosa captive, and refused to allow Norambo/Felipe to purchase her freedom—out of spite and because she has borne Justino's child (after he violated her). There is a happy ending and Norambo/Felipe prevails, of course. But, one wonders, is Mother Africa forgotten in order to embrace Father Brazil? Must our protagonist lose his mother?[33]

Even if the narrative is rewritten, it seems this mother can never be lost. I conclude this chapter by looking back (and ahead) to Africa and the haunting lyrics in a popular song by Mestre Tony Vargas, "Eu venho de Luanda," which resonates with the reverberations of slavery in Cuban song, and which we shall examine in the next chapter. Here, Vargas looks back across the Atlantic, imagining a connection with the ancestral "Mother Africa" in Luanda, Angola, the center of the Portuguese slave trade, a transatlantic cousin to Salvador da Bahia.[34]

> Quando eu venho de Luanda, eu Não venho só
> Quando cu vcnho dc Luanda, cu Não vcnho só
> Eu trago no meu peito um grito
> Um grito da vida inteira
> Um grito de liberdade, ô iaiá
> Um grito de capoeira
> Um grito de raça negra
> Uma raça perseguida
> Um grito de toda dor, oh! meu Deus
> Um grito de toda vida
> Quando eu venho de Luanda, eu Não venho só (× 4)

[When I came from Luanda, I didn't come alone
When I came from Luanda, I didn't come alone
I carry in my heart a shout
A shout for my entire life
A shout of liberty, ô iaiá
A shout of capoeira
A shout of the black race
A race persecuted
A shout of all the pain, oh! My God
A shout for my whole life
When I came from Luanda, I didn't come alone] (× 4)

5

AZÚCAR, (AUTO)BIOGRAFÍA, AND ABSENCE

Juan Francisco Manzano, Esteban Montejo, and the Cuban Poetics of Slavery

¡Azúuuuuucaaaarrrrr!

—CELIA CRUZ

Sin el negro Cuba no sería Cuba.
[Without the Black, Cuba would not be Cuba.]

—FERNANDO ORTIZ, *Los negros esclavos*

"Behold the isle of Cuba on a map," writes Dr. Scoffern in a tract on sugar in the May 1864 issue of the *St. James's Magazine*. "Consider how small it is," he continues, "and then marvel as you may, that such a little island produces nearly one-fourth of the sum total of sugar entering into commerce" (Scoffern 175).[1] The medical doctor and author of *The Manufacture of Sugar in the Colonies and at Home* (1849) argues, "It is all produced by negro labor, by *slave* labor; and negroes are not over-prone to work except driven. There must be some driving in Cuba, some sacrifice of negro life to the Spanish sugar Moloch." Indignant over the treatment of enslaved Africans in the Spanish colony, the author finally exhorts, "Despite the fiction that the negro slave trade has been suppressed, the Spaniards import the blacks they need—they even prefer importation to raising . . . The Spaniards not unfrequently impose on their male negroes the same discipline that St. Origen imposed on himself" (175).[2]

Even if his logic for recognizing physical abuses enacted on enslaved Africans was rooted in the troubling belief that they were naturally indolent and therefore must be "driven" to such an astonishing level of production, Dr. Scoffern poignantly admonishes the "sacrifice of negro life to the Spanish sugar

Moloch." This image of the sacrifice of enslaved African to the sugar god is striking. In one short paragraph, the medical professor not only excoriates the Spanish colonizers for perpetuating the harshest brand of slavery, the kind that castrates its enslaved African men because each generation is easily replaceable through importation, but also critiques the self-congratulatory stance of his natal country, reducing Britain's 1807 abolition of the slave trade to a mere "fiction." Dr. Scoffern's urgent warning came on the occasion of British Prime Minister William Gladstone's announcement of a sugar tariff increase, thirty years after the abolition of slavery in the British West Indian colonies.

In 1864, when Dr. Scoffern wrote this emphatic perspective on the shortcomings of the British abolition of the slave trade, the United States was embroiled in the bloody Civil War and the forced relocation of Africans was slowly drawing to a close in Cuba and Brazil (Klein 47).[3] In this chapter, I consider the instrumentality of autobiography and sugar as narrative, and agricultural products marking the enduring historical, literary, and cultural legacy of slavery in Cuba.[4] After probing Fernando Ortiz's treatise on sugar, tobacco, and "transculturation" in his classic *Contrapunteo cubano del tabaco y el azúcar,* translated as *Cuban Counterpoint: Tobacco and Sugar* (1940), I discuss the memory of slavery in the (auto)biographies of two Cuban authors who tell their stories more than a century apart. *Autobiografía de un esclavo* (1839), by Juan Francisco Manzano (1797–1853), is the firsthand account of a literate enslaved African who is able to write his own story and yet leaves numerous elisions in the text, and *Cimarrón: Historia de un esclavo* is the narrative of a 103-year-old ex-maroon named Esteban Montejo (1860–1973), who dictated his story to writer Miguel Barnet in 1963.[5]

The year 1830 is crucial to our understanding of Afrodiasporic forms in a broader sense because it reveals the vast differences between the shifting practices of colonial slavocratic regimes. Although the 1807 British slave trade abolition was a watershed moment, it was only "a very partial one," as Ada Ferrer argues, because the Cuban illegal slave trade was not only protected but was in fact "a key function of the colonial state." Considering 1830, with the construction of the first railroad in Cuba to support the sugar industry, forces us to confront the danger of a myopic "national or imperial focus" in slavery studies and demands a consideration of slavery's global dimensions beyond what Ferrer calls the "linear, and predominantly Anglophone conception of the rise and fall of slavery" (337, 335). The mediated (auto)biographies, too, underscore the potency of reading first-person narratives of slavery and *testimonios* at the intersection of Afrodiasporic imagination and historical record.

Miriam DeCosta-Willis, scholar of what we might call "Afro-Hispanic" or "Afro-Latino" literature and author of an early essay that directly compares the autobiographies of these two Cuban figures, considers the relationship between history and literature a primary concern with these authors. She writes, "Montejo's *Biografía de un cimarrón* and Manzano's *Autobiografía* are considered more significant as historical documents which describe nineteenth-century Cuban slave life than as literary works" (*Blacks in Hispanic Literature* 4). I hope to augment this prevailing claim by showing how these texts raise fascinating questions about the limits of and between the autobiographical and the biographical, the historical and the literary, truth and fabrication, and passivity and rebellion within the larger context of how slavery is remembered and forgotten in these slave narratives.

MEASURING THE "ABOMINABLE INGREDIENT"

The colonial powers tussled with the meaning of sugar. Early in the "trade" of Africans across the Atlantic, slavery and sugar became accomplices. As historian Herbert S. Klein explains, "It was only with the introduction of sugar production to the Atlantic islands and the opening up of the Western Hemisphere to European conquest at the end of the fifteenth century that a new and important use was found for slaves" (10). William J. Bernstein echoes this argument about the centrality of sugar to the development of the transatlantic slave trade:

> These fertile islands [Madeira, São Tomé, and Azores] had easy access to slave labor and provided plantation owners with far better conditions than those in the Middle East or the Mediterranean. Growers were particularly attracted to São Tomé, which was uninhabited when the Portuguese arrived in 1470, yet close to the heart of the central African slave trade. (206–207)

Thus, the economic structure of the slave trade that would pervade the Americas for the next three and a half centuries was first worked out in the islands of São Tomé, Madeira, and Canary in the 1490s (Klein 10, 14).[6] When the forest providing the fuel necessary for sugar production was depleted on these islands, it was a natural transition to the West Indian islands, where production of sugar soon became a "sugarocracy," especially in Cuba (Sommer, *Foundational Fictions* 357, note 16).[7] Historian Laird Bergad further clarifies:

> The slave/sugar complex has erroneously been seen in the popular imagination as a paradigm for understanding Latin American and Caribbean slavery in general. African slavery was well developed a century and a half prior to the onset of the Caribbean sugar cycle, and it was a very different institution, especially in Spanish colonies. (52–53)

Hence, the myth of the monocultural plantation slavery that predominates popular understandings of the enslavement of Africans in the Americas is not the full story. It is true that by the time Manzano wrote, in 1830, Cuba was a sugarocracy, but this development started in the seventeenth century. Before this, enslaved Africans cultivated a variety of crops (52).

Sugar left its residue in literature too. Two memorable uses of the sugar motif contextualize the politics around the sugar/slave complex in Cuba and the transnational interconnectedness of the trade in goods and Africans. Repentant of their domination of the slave trade in the eighteenth century, a group of British abolitionists launched a campaign to boycott the consumption of sugar in 1791 (Scoffern; Plasa 41). Led by women who called themselves the Anti-Saccharites, the society published an antislavery pamphlet featuring the shocking images of the cross section of the *Brookes* slave ship, showing how captured Africans were tightly packed for the Middle Passage.[8] Considered the first large-scale consumer boycott, the campaign pointed out to abolitionists the hypocrisy of lobbying for emancipation but simultaneously heaping sugar by the spoonful into their tea of choice, or adding it generously to their favorite cake recipes. These imported products—including coffee, rum, and tobacco, in addition to sugar—were no longer neutral.

The refined white powder became a political flash point and, by the end of the eighteenth century and beginning of the nineteenth, a theme worthy of fiction and poetry. In his second novel, *Melincourt* (1817), the English novelist Thomas Love Peacock (1785–1866) describes a sumptuous dinner party scene, an "anti-saccharine fête" for the social elite, at which absolutely no sugar is served or added to the food. The narrator describes the protagonist, Mr. Forester, the founder of the story's fictional antisugar society: "Mr. Forester thought to make luxury on this occasion subservient to morality, by showing what culinary art could effect without the intervention of West Indian produce." After the distinguished guests enjoy the "splendid dinner" without noticing the absence of sugar, the narrator curses the carbohydrate as the "abominable ingredient" and gives the moral imperative of the short sketch: "The produce of the labor of slavery should be banned from our shores." Mr. Forester argues that sugar embodies the worst elements of society as it is "superfluous," an indicator of "frivolous and wanton indulgence," "physically pernicious," and "morally atrocious" (Peacock 185–186, 189).[9] The message is clear: abstinence is best when it comes to consuming sugar.

Two other English authors poeticize sugar as a metonym for slavery. Robert Southey (1774–1843) famously denounces tea drinkers in Sonnet 3: "Oh ye who at your ease / Sip the blood-sweeten'd beverage!" while the enslaved African gasps as "that inhuman trader lifts on high / The mangling scourge" (110). While Southey rejects sugar as a pollutant to tea, the first two stanzas of English poet William Cowper's "Pity for Poor Africans" (1788) draw out this tension from the point of view of a speaker clearly torn between his taste buds and morality:[10]

> I own I am shocke'd at the purchase of slaves,
> and fear those who buy them and sell them are knaves;
> What I hear of their hardships, their tortures, and groans,
> Is almost enough to draw pity from stones.
>
> I pity them greatly, but I must be mum,
> For how could we do without sugar and rum?
> Especially sugar, so needful we see?
> What, give up our desserts, our coffee, and tea!
>
> Besides, if we do, the French, Dutch and Danes
> Will heartily thank us, no doubt, for our pains;
> If we do not buy the poor creatures, they will;
> And tortures and groans will be multiplied still.
>
> If foreigners likewise would give up the trade,
> Much more in behalf of your wish might be said;
> But, while they get riches by purchasing blacks,
> Pray tell me why we may not also go snacks? (455–456)

The *aabb* rhyme scheme gives the poem a frivolous air, perhaps offering a more honest picture of the conflict between opposing slavery in the abstract but questioning one's ability to forfeit the sweet taste of sugar: "For how could we do without sugar and rum?" Cowper's verses illustrate the way the distancing effect of living in England, so far away from the injustices occurring on West Indian soil, might allow a sympathizer to focus more on his "snacks," "our desserts, our coffee, our tea!" Cowper provides a more human reaction, in comparison to Peacock and Southey, to the abolitionist compulsion to condemn the West Indian produce. It is against this political background of England's antislavery and antisaccharine campaigns, which were moving into high gear in 1791, and of Haiti fighting for independence from the French, that Cuba rose to prominence as the primary exporter of sugar by the first third of the nineteenth century, when Manzano wrote his slave narrative.

TRANSCULTURACIÓN AND THE TESTIMONIAL

Nearly one hundred years after the 1840 publication of an English translation of Afro-Cuban Juan Francisco Manzano's *Autobiografía de un esclavo* [Autobiography of a Slave] in London, one of the only extant Latin American slave narratives, the fragmentary text was published in its original language.[11] In 1937, scholar José Luciano Franco restored Manzano's first-person account to Spanish, maintaining its nineteenth-century orthographic archaisms in "Juan Francisco Manzano, el poeta esclavo y su tiempo," in *Cuadernos de Historia Habanera* [Notebooks of the History of Havana].[12]

International critical attention surged when Black Studies proponents and Latin Americanists alike reclaimed the partial autobiography in the mid-1960s, securely placing it in their academic arsenals and anthologies.[13] Ivan A. Schulman's 1975 Spanish edition, and especially his modernized and en face bilingual (Spanish/English) 1996 edition, initiated a renewed wave of scholarship.[14] That it acted on an international stage in the antislavery movement a century before local Cuban recognition evidences this narrative's currency in a global circulation of texts and the transnational antislavery agenda, long before "Black Atlantic" and "the Americas" became prevailing interdisciplinary categories of analysis among academics.

Following the 1959 Cuban Revolution, encouraged by the fervor for Latin American slave narratives in the 1960s and the radical rise of the Black Studies movement, anthropologist Miguel Barnet, a student of José Luciano Franco, sought out a still-living formerly enslaved person in Cuba to document his life stories, in his work *Cimarrón: Historia de un esclavo* (published in English as *Biography of a Runaway Slave*).[15] Driven by a temporal urgency, the collection of these time-sensitive oral histories, much like the documentation of stories from Holocaust survivors, relates as much about the vicissitudes of memory over time as it does the discrete details in the personal accounts.

Barnet met, interviewed, and published a book about formerly enslaved Esteban Montejo. Unlike the comparatively conformist Manzano, Montejo's story is one of outright rebellion and victory. Montejo was a *cimarrón* or "wild Black," "an escaped African slave who often established independent settlements in inaccessible places and refused to recognize Spanish royal authority" (Rout xiv).[16] Although he lived to be 112 years old and occupied many identities in society—slave, *cimarrón* (runaway), soldier in the Cuban war of independence, revolutionary—Montejo never transcends his role as slave rebel in Barnet's interpretation of his life. Telling the tale of the *cimarrón* speaks to the readers' impulse to read an empowering story of an enslaved African who strikes back and wins. Much like the exemplary moment when Frederick Douglass defends himself and fights his slave driver Covey, the story of multiform sustained and effective slave resistance, on a grander scale, is the story of slavery in Latin America.

Since the 1960s, literary scholars have often studied the poetry and autobiography of Juan Francisco Manzano alongside a now familiar nineteenth-century Afro-Cuban antislavery corpus—Plácido's sonnets (1830s), Anselmo Suárez y Romero's *Francisco, el ingenio o las Delicias del Campo* (1838), Gertrudis Gómez de Avellaneda's *Sab* (1841), Antonio Zambrana's *Negro Francisco* (1875), Martín Morúa Delgado's *Sofía* (1891), and Cirilo Villaverde's *Cecilia Valdés* (1839)[17]—although it has rarely been juxtaposed with Esteban Montejo's dictated narrative. It is notable that although several of these texts feature female protagonists, the first attempts at Afro-Cuban canon formation resulted in anthologies with a heavily masculinist discourse and an absence of Afro-Cuban women authors. Only within the past forty-five years have literary scholars begun to study Barnet's *Cimarrón: Historia de un esclavo* as a testimonial novel, taking an approach similar to studies of Rigoberta Menchú's *I, Rigoberta* or Carolina Maria de Jesus's *Quarto de Despejo* (published in English as *Child of the Dark*), discussed in chapter 4. According to Edward Mullen, *Cuba poetica* (1861) was the "first true national anthology of Cuban poetry," which "presented some fifty authors, including the work of two Black poets: Plácido, and Juan Francisco Manzano (1797–1857)" and "were written in standard Castilian" (437).[18]

Interestingly, subsequent iterations of national anthologies banished Plácido and Manzano, well into the 1920s. While nineteenth-century anthologies focused on preservation of the past, an endeavor to codify "tradition," mid- to late twentieth-century anthologies attempted to "radicalize the traditional canon" (Mullen 449). Compare this to the US reception of these poets, and specifically the African American idealization of these poetic figures and the status of the "Negro" abroad.[19] In his 1922 preface to *The Book of American Negro Poetry,* James Weldon Johnson named Plácido and Manzano as exemplary poets:

> Mention of Dunbar brings up for consideration the fact that, although he is the most outstanding figure in literature among the Aframericans of the United States, he does not stand alone among the Aframericans of *the whole Western world.* There are Plácido and Manzano in Cuba; Vieux and Durand in Haiti; Machado de Assis in Brazil; and others still that might be mentioned, who stand on a plane with or even above Dunbar. Plácido and Machado de Assis rank as great in the literatures of their respective countries without any qualifications whatever. They are world figures in the literature of the Latin languages. (xxxvi; emphasis added)

Johnson expressed preoccupation with the task of establishing and anthologizing an illustrious tradition of what we might now call Black Atlantic or Afro-diasporic literature. What's more, he emphasizes the fact that Paul Laurence Dunbar possessed "unmixed Negro blood," to combat racist scientific beliefs about the inferiority of the "Negro race." Plácido and Manzano, then, along with Vieux, Durand, and Machado de Assis—"Aframericans" in the Western world—signify, in Johnson's effusively laudatory terms, "sheer genius," intellectual armor in this battle to provide proof of humanity.

Therefore, the measure of African blood, or the "Blackness" of an author, was a paramount consideration when compiling these anthologies at the time. Taken together, this corpus satisfied those intent on finding literary analogs to the classic Anglophone (primarily North American) slave narratives and a tentative answer to the puzzling question: Why are there no slave narratives penned by Afro-descendants in Latin America? Is this absence indicative of a public amnesia or willful resistance to remember? Manzano's testimony of his life, albeit fragmentary—or "unusual" and "disorderly," to borrow Gerard Aching's terms—fills the void (205, 201). Then, in 1966, Miguel Barnet's *Cimarrón: Historia de un esclavo* added to the conversation the voice of a man named Esteban Montejo, who had not only survived slavery but also rebelled, participated in the Cuban Revolution, and lived to be an old man to tell the story to the anthropologist, Barnet. The two voices—Manzano (mediated by R. R. Madden) and Montejo (as told to Miguel Barnet)—are the nodal points of this chapter's discussion of the poetics of slavery in Cuba.

Manzano's narrative comes more than three hundred years after the arrival of the first enslaved Africans in Cuba, around 1511 (Rout 288). Manzano writes during the period of colonial Spanish America, after the high-water mark of the Spanish empire's stronghold on the slave trade during the sixteenth and seventeenth centuries. This end date also coincides with the beginning of the Latin American wars of independence. From 1511 onward, forced importation of Africans to Cuba proceeded at a relatively slow pace. From 1740 to 1760, the Royal Havana Company forcibly transported approximately 4,000 to 11,000 Africans to Cuba, before its rapid dissolution due to accusations of illegal smuggling (Rout 58). Rout estimates that "all told, between 1511 and 1788 no more than 100,000 slaves are estimated to have been imported into the island," while G. Andrews surmises that "some 50,000 [Africans] arrived in Cuba in the 250 years prior to 1760" (Rout 289; G. Andrews 17). After the initial 250-year period, the forcible transportation of Africans to Cuba increased to 2,000 people per year. (G. Andrews 19). According to Paquette and Smith:

> While no consensus has emerged over exact figures for total imports from 1789 to 1867, David Eltis, the leading quantitative historian of the Atlantic slave trade, has estimated that more than 700,000 slaves entered Cuba, nearly doubling the number of slaves imported into the United States during its entire colonial and national history. (97)

Most striking, until 1774, the number of free persons of color, or *emancipados,* equaled the number of those enslaved (Knight 22).[20] In terms of the origins and ethnicities of the Africans brought to Cuba: "In Cuba the ubiquitous English traders helped to make the *lucumí* (from Lower Guinea) the most common black servitor" (Rout 27). The *lucumí,* or West Africans, represented 45 percent of the Cuban slave imports, while East Africans numbered 31 percent and Congo-Angolan's totaled 24 percent (G. Andrews 20).

Even more astonishing are the numerical estimates of Africans in the diaspora forcibly transported to locations south of the Gulf of Mexico. Although it is nearly impossible to reach international consensus on the exact figures, there is a drive to concretize the horrors through quantification.[21] Scholars estimate the Spanish American slave traffic to be around 1.5 million, including the Africans smuggled on unauthorized trips after the signing of the Treaty of Madrid, with some scholars estimating fewer than 1 million Africans.[22]

The irony is that predominant depictions and literary representations of slavery in the Americas often exclude or overlook the Spanish colonies and the Caribbean. The absences in the literary archives of the Cuban slave trade and the trafficking of humans in general reveal their ultimate unknowability. How does one compensate for the missing pieces, the absent birth and death records, and the disappearing texts? Moreover, how do the unknowable statistics of Africans transported to the Spanish Americas relate to present notions of afrolatinidad and the formation of racial identity?

Lack—a salient theme of this chapter, and discussed at length in the next section—specifically epistemological lack, stimulates the imagination. The impossibility of knowing the exact quantities of lives lost or those subjected to forced migration during the slave trade, for example, has paradoxically induced a filling-in and literary flourishing that is quite contrary to the sense of lack that Patricia D. Fox reacts against when she urges us to "rethink Blackness as a narrative not about slavery, lack, and open-ended neediness, but rather as a journey propelled by *uprootedness* and expressed with *improvisation,* responsively shaping life strategies as much as world views and behaviors" (4). This chapter makes the counterargument that, far from lack representing the negatively valued notion of inadequacy within the literary realm, it spurs transformative creation. For all of its omissions and perplexing silences, Manzano's *Autobiografía* supplies and inspires as much as it resists and denies. As Aching reminds us, it is a narrative that calls the reader to empathize with the "psychic life of an enslaved subject" (201). Further, it is a document that lays the foundation for defining an burgeoning "national" character.

A crucial consideration for a balanced understanding of Cuban literary treatments of slavery within the historical context of colonial Latin America, and of the Spanish Caribbean in particular, is the predominance of the sugar economy. Cuba evolved from a diversified agricultural labor system (which included tobacco, coffee, cattle, pigs, and of course sugar) into a sugar monoculture after 1800, and became one of the major hubs for sugar production, along with Brazil and Puerto Rico, culminating in the nineteenth-century sugar boom and the height of Cuban plantation slavery. Paquette and Smith connect this turn-of-the-century tumult to labor changes spurred by the largest slave rebellion in the Western Hemisphere: "It was precisely the results of the Haitian Revolution that drove sugar and coffee prices upward and thereby provided Cuban entrepreneurs with promising economic opportunities," despite "Great Britain's radical volte-face," from being the largest transporter of enslaved Africans in the eighteenth-century slave trade to "abolishing the British slave trade in 1807 and championing the abolitionist cause in the nineteenth century" (97).

Due to the fear of slave insurrection, Cubans did not even begin to fight for independence from the Spanish until the second half of the nineteenth century, ultimately obtaining it in 1889. Abolition came a few years before, in 1886, and coincided with the wars of independence (Andrews 10; Paquette and Smith 103). Fernando Ortiz's celebrated anthropology classic, *Contrapunteo cubano del tabaco y el azúcar* (or, *Cuban Counterpoint: Tobacco and Sugar*), also published one hundred years after the first publication of Manzano's *Autobiografía,* examines the sugar and tobacco industries: "Así en lo interno como en lo externo, estudiar la historia de Cuba es en lo fundamental estudiar la historia del azúcar y del tabaco como los sistemas viscerales de su economía" (Thus a study of the history of Cuba, both internal and external, is fundamentally a study of the history of sugar and tobacco as the essential bases of its economy) (*Contrapunteo* 138; *Counterpoint* 5).[23] In this study of "fenómenos económicos y de sus reflejos sociales" (economic phenomenon and its social reflexes), Ortiz's writing mixes the scientific, social, historical, and poetic. This baroque style embellishes the history of sugar and tobacco in the tone of a myth of origin:

> Blanca es la una, moreno es el otro. Dulce y sin olor es el azúcar; amargo y con aroma es el tabaco. ¡Contraste siempre! Alimento y veneno, despertar y adormecer, energía y ensueño, placer de la carne y deleite del espíritu, sensualidad e ideación, apetito que se satisface e ilusión que se esfuma, calorías de vida y humaredas de fantasía, indistinción vulgarota y anónima desde la cuna e individualidad aristocrática y de marca en todo el mundo, medicina y magia, realidad y engaño, virtud y vicio. El azúcar es ella; el tabaco es él . . . La caña fue obra de los dioses, el tabaco lo fue de los demonios; ella es hija de Apolo, él es engendro de Proserpina. (*Contrapunteo* 140)

> The one is White, the other dark. Sugar is sweet and odorless; tobacco bitter and aromatic. Always in contrast! Food and poison, waking and drowsing, energy and dream, delight of the flesh and delight of the spirit, sensuality and thought,

> the satisfaction of an appetite and the contemplation of a moment's illusion, calories of nourishment and puffs of fantasy, undifferentiated and commonplace anonymity from the cradle and aristocratic individuality recognized wherever it goes, medicine and magic, reality and deception, virtue and vice. Sugar is *she;* tobacco is *he.* Sugar cane was the gifts of the gods, tobacco of the devils; she is the daughter of Apollo, he is the offspring of Persephone. (*Counterpoint* 6)

Not only does this dialectical list point out the main differences between the two *yerbas tropicales* (tropical herbs) within the Cuban context, elevate the discussion of the economic to the poetic, and introduce Ortiz's gender- and race-infused rhetoric around sugar and tobacco, but also it foreshadows his elaborate metaphor as they become protagonists participating in a national drama throughout his introductory essay:

> El tabaco es oscuro, de negro a mulato; el azúcar es clara, de mulata a blanca. El tabaco no cambia de color, nace moreno y muere con el color de su raza. El azúcar cambia de coloración, nace parda y se blanquea; es almibarada mulata que siendo prieta se abandona a la sabrosura popular y luego se encascadilla y refina para pasar por blanca, correr por todo el mundo, llegar a todas las bocas y ser pagada mejor, subiendo a las categorías dominantes de la escala social. (*Contrapunteo* 143)

> Tobacco is dark, ranging from black to mulatto; sugar is light, ranging from mulatto to white. Tobacco does not change its color; it is born dark and dies the color of its race. Sugar changes its coloring; it is born brown and whitens itself; at first it is a syrupy mulatto and in this state pleases the common taste; then it is bleached and refined until it can pass for white, travel all over the world, reach all mouths, and bring a better price, climbing to the top of the social ladder. (*Counterpoint* 9)

Interestingly, sugar is the substance that crosses the color line and "passes" for white. Alternating passages about agriculture and the cultivation of these natural products with imaginative statements, Ortiz analogizes sugar and slavery in a description that moves beyond observations about color: "El azúcar nace sin apellido propio, como esclava" (Sugar comes into the world without a last name, like a [female] slave). Gendered and racialized as an enslaved woman, sugar lives an anonymous life: "El azúcar muere como nace y vive: anónima;

como avergonzada de vivir sin apellido, arrojada a un líquido o a una masa batida donde se diluye y desaparece como predestinada al suicidio en las aguas de un lago o en los turbiones de la sociedad" (Sugar dies as it is born and lives, anonymously; as though it were ashamed of having no name, thrown into a liquid or a dough where it melts and disappears as if predestined to suicide in the waters of a lake or in the maelstrom of society). In contrast to sugar, which undergoes a strenuous manufacturing process and multiple name changes, "el tabaco desde que nace ya es y se llama tabaco" (from birth tobacco was, and was called, tobacco) (*Contrapunteo* 187; *Counterpoint* 42).

The complex interaction between sugar and tobacco is articulated in Ortiz's famous neologism *transculturación* (transculturation), a theory embraced and expanded upon by scholars, which he defines as a concept:

> para expresar los variadísimos fenómenos que se originan en Cuba por las complejísimas transmutaciones de culturas que aquí se verifican, sin conocer las cuales es imposible entender la evolución del pueblo cubano, así en lo económico como en lo institucional, jurídico, ético, religioso, artístico, lingüístico, psicológico, sexual y en los demás aspectos de su vida. (*Contrapunteo* 254)
>
> [to express the highly varied phenomena that have come about in Cuba as a result of the extremely complex transmutations of culture that have taken place here, and without a knowledge of which it is impossible to understand the evolution of the Cuban folk, either in the economic or in the institutional, legal, ethical, religious, artistic, linguistic, psychological, sexual, or other aspects of its life.] (*Counterpoint* 98)

He argues that the "verdadera historia de Cuba es la historia de sus intricadísimas transculturaciones" (real history of Cuba is the history of its intermeshed transculturations) (254; 98). Ortiz's notion of transculturation sets the historical backdrop for Cuban literature and provides a theoretical framework for understanding the making of *mestizaje* in what Mary Louise Pratt calls the "contact zone."

While Ortiz's coinage of the term *transculturation* continues to function as a key theoretical concept, the proliferation of so-called errors in *Contrapunteo* also has garnered much scholarly attention. Indeed, Enrico Mario Santí notes in the introduction to his critical edition that Ortiz, Manzano, and Lezama Lima share "una afinidad común" (a common affinity) for producing texts replete with "errors" (108). Santí "corrected" what he deemed strange terms and dates in his edition. However, the "errors" in Manzano's text, Santí posits, represent "una parodia involuntaria del canon criollo blanco, estrategia de oposición típica de una literatura menor" (an involuntary parody of the white Creole canon, a typical oppositional strategy from a minor literature) (109). William Luis continues the rhetoric of error when he states, in the opening of his 2007 translation of Manzano's writings:

> Existen al menos dos versiones de la autobiografía de Juan Francisco Manzano: el manuscrito original que el poeta esclavo redactó con frecuentes errores ortográficos y la versión corregida por Anselmo Suárez y Romero. La autobiografía que doy a conocer proviene de esta última versión, que fue la que circuló entre los miembros de la tertulia delmontina y cuyo original se extravió en la segunda mitad del siglo XIX. La copia de esta autobiografía se halla en las *Obras completas de Juan Francisco Manzano esclavo de la Isla de Cuba,* cuaderno copiado con letra y puño de Nicolás Azcárate y hallado a mediados de la década de los ochenta en la Biblioteca Sterling de la Universidad de Yale.
>
> [There exist at least two versions of the autobiography of Juan Francisco Manzano: the original manuscript that the poet slave wrote with frequent orthographic errors and the corrected version by Anselmo Suárez y Romero. The autobiography that I reveal comes from this last version, which was the one circulated among members of the del Monte *tertulia* and whose original went missing in the second half of the nineteenth century. The copy of this autobiography is located in the *Obras completas de Juan Francisco Manzano esclavo de la Isla de Cuba,* a notebook Nicolás Azcárate copied by hand and has been located since the mid-1980s in the Yale University Sterling Library.] (Manzano, *Autobiografía* 11)[24]

The "corrected version" by Anselmo Suárez y Romero is another text altogether.[25] Moving beyond viewing the "frecuentes errores ortográficos" (frequent orthographic errors) as an "involuntary parody of the canon," I argue that the alleged "involuntary errors" are not errors at all but evidence of Manzano's poetic resistance as he has his way with the language of Cervantes.

▲▲▲▲▲

DISAPPEARING ACTS

Mas nada es para mí la cruda guerra
que en vano suspirar he soportado,
si la comparo, ¡oh Dios!, con lo que falta.

[But 'tis nothing the past—or the pains,
Hitherto I have struggled to bear,
When I think, oh, my God! on the chains,
That I know I'm yet destined to wear.]
—JUAN FRANCISCO MANZANO, "Treinta Años"

In 1835, Venezuelan-born Cuban abolitionist critic Domingo del Monte (1804–1853), leader of the prominent, eponymous literary group, commissioned Juan Francisco Manzano, later known as the *esclavo poeta* (poet slave), to write his memoirs. The members of the del Monte group and other sympathizers collectively purchased Manzano's freedom in 1836 for between 850 and 2,364 pesos.[26] Working closely with the Irish medical doctor Richard Robert Madden (1798–1886), del Monte entrusted Manzano with his antislavery portfolio, containing the literary works of many of the members of the group. By this time, Manzano had already published the poetry collections *Poesías líricas* (1821) and *Flores pasageras* (1830) (Jackson, "Slavery" 55).

Compare Manzano's epithet to *poeta dos escravos* (poet of the slaves), the Portuguese designation critics commonly use when describing Brazilian author Castro Alves. As we saw in chapter 4, Alves must speak for the enslaved Africans, as he does most notably in his canonical *O navio negreiro* [The Slave Ship], because he was not a slave himself and did not have any discernible African ancestry. It is important to note the word order in this compound noun *esclavo poeta* (poet slave). In the Spanish construction, *poeta* modifies *esclavo.* The syntactical accent is on the word *poeta;* thus, Manzano is a poet first, an identity that transcends his condition of enslavement. Manzano eliminates the interlocutor and speaks for himself; he reads and he composes his own poetry. To what extent were *slave* and *Black,* or *esclavo* and *negro,* considered synonymous at this time?[27]

It is his life narrative, along with original poems and letters, that R. R. Madden then translated into English, upon request of his friend del Monte, and published in England in 1840 under the lengthy descriptive title *Poems by a Slave in the Island of Cuba, Recently Liberated; Translated from the Spanish, by R. R. Madden, M.D. with the History of the Early Life of the Negro Poet, Written by*

Himself; to Which Are Prefixed Two Pieces Descriptive of Cuban Slavery and the Slave-Traffic, by R. R. M.[28] Whether Manzano was still enslaved or was recently liberated at the time of the composition (his manumission occurred in 1836), Madden incited British abolitionist readers with oxymoronic phrase "Poems by a Slave." To be at once enslaved and a poet were certainly two incongruous identities in 1840.

As a point of comparison, this was twelve years before Harriet Beecher Stowe's classic, *Uncle Tom's Cabin,* was published and translated into Spanish as *La cabaña del tío Tom,* which was influential among the Cuban abolitionist circles. This was also five years before Frederick Douglass's *Narrative of the Life of Frederick Douglass, An American Slave* and the commencement of his extensive lecturing tour in England. Although on his title page Madden cast Manzano as an unnamed, anonymous island poet slave ("a slave in the island of Cuba"), stripped of an individual identity and the possibility for an international rise to fame like Douglass's, the benefactor at least portrayed him as the author of the poems. What was the primary expression of this unnamed enslaved person's soul?

In the sonnet "Treinta Años" [Thirty Years], Manzano reflects on his life in captivity to age thirty with a revealing, strongly poetic "I."[29] Historians assert that, upon personal invitation, he recited this poem in the *tertulia* (literary circle) of Domingo del Monte, whom Jackson likens to Carl Van Vechten and sums up as a "wealthy, white critic-patron who sponsored black art" (Jackson, "Slavery" 54). This poem follows the Petrarchan form and is structurally divided into an octave and a sestet. Within these fourteen lines, the rhyme scheme of the octave is *abba, abba* and the sestet is *cde, cde.* Knowledgeable about the Western poetic tradition and its conventions, Manzano employs the form of the Italian sonnet to write about enslavement and a yearning for liberty instead of about unrequited love.

In Madden's rather liberal translation, the poem loses the Petrarchan conventions. Madden adds two lines, creating four quatrains, somewhat in the style of the English sonnet (a variation on three quatrains and a couplet), with the rhyme scheme *abab, cdcd, efef, ghgh.* The two opening lines set the reflective mode: "Cuando miro el espacio que he corrido / desde la cuna hasta el presente día, / tiemblo y saludo a la fortuna mía / más de terror que de atención movido" (When I think on the course I have run, / From my childhood itself to this day / I tremble and fain would I shun / The remembrance its horrors array). The word *mas* (but) at line 12 marks the turn in the poem, in which the speaker laments, crying out to God, that what he has managed to endure as a slave does not compare to what he lacks, or "lo que falta." Madden loosely translates Manzano's tercet to this closing quatrain: "But 'tis nothing the past—or the pains, / Hitherto I have struggled to bear, / When I think, oh, my God! on the chains, / That I know I'm yet destined to wear." The "cruda guerra" (harsh war) that Manzano describes become chains of slavery in Madden's version.

Jackson describes Manzano's implicit language in this sonnet as "oblique references" that "leave little doubt what his thirty years spent as a slave have been like" but concedes that even Manzano's *Autobiografía* is "underplayed" and "tragically controlled" (Jackson, "Slavery" 54, 59). The phrase "lo que falta" (what is lacking) in the original version closes the poem with a subtly vague intensity. Manzano never directly names what he lacks, and this gives the poem a universal appeal that transcends the specificity of the slavery theme.

"Lo que falta" fuels the charged transfigurations within the literary tradition of the Spanish colonial period and is the central motif in this chapter's exploration of the Cuban poetics of slavery. Most generally, "lo que falta" asks the question: Is the Latin American literary tradition lacking a memory of slavery? "Lo que falta" is textual lack, ambiguity, or absence, and in the case of Manzano's *Autobiografía,* the entire second half is missing. Sentences fade into ellipses.

The mysterious disappearance of the second half of the narrative is frustrating to scholars, and Madden's perhaps too liberal translation and clear antislavery agenda represent one strategy for dealing with textual ambiguity or absence: invention. Madden's nineteenth-century abolitionist-inspired, fill-in-the-blanks project precludes a faithful rendition of the artistry of Manzano's writing style, which one critic describes as "sencilla y emotiva" (simple and emotive) (Chang-Rodríguez 559). José Luciano Franco mentioned, in a footnote in his 1937 Spanish edition, that "en el original existen enmiendas y hasta tachaduras que no parecen hechas por Manzano" (in the original, there are amendments and even crossed-out words that do not seem to be made by Manzano). Max Henríquez Ureñas referred to these editorial additions as *impurezas* (impurities). It is unclear whether these "impurities" come from Madden's pen, but the unsourced annotations evidence a history of collective manipulation of the autobiography.

William Luis devotes the lengthy introduction in his comprehensive critical edition to parsing the "textual proliferation" of the autobiography, citing at least six distinct versions in circulation: Manzano's "original" manuscript (1836) and the basis of Franco's Spanish version (1937), Suárez y Romero's "correction"/rewriting (1839), Azcárate's liberal "copy" (1852), Francisco Calcagno's excerpted passages in his *Poetas de color* (1878), Madden's English translation (1840), and Schulman's modernization and bilingual edition (1975, 1996). With the multiplicity of Manzanos floating around in the world, the shifting levels of mediation in each subsequent correction and revision renders the idea of possessing an "original" text both dubious and distant.

Margarita Engle participates in the process of invention and communal transfiguration of the text with her twenty-first-century poetic fictionalization of Manzano's life, *The Poet Slave of Cuba.* Geared for the young adult reader, this lyrical embellishment based on Manzano's sketch of his life refuses the set of binary oppositions between the pure and impure text, memory and forgetfulness, or fact and fiction. In fact, Engle's poetic collection venerates the figure of Manzano and attempts to usher in a younger generation of readers. Assuming the voice of Manzano, Engle opens the book with a poem named after her protagonist, "Juan." It begins, "My mind is a brush made of feathers / painting pictures of words / I remember / all that I see / every syllable / each word a twin of itself / telling two stories / at the same time / one of sorrow / the other of hope" (3). Another poem, "Toribio," named after Manzano's father, probes the idea of imagination and what life in his son's place must feel like:

> Imagine
> how he must feel in that other home
> where he learns the words
> of verses, plays, sermons, sonnets
> now he's a parrot, not a poodle
> he listens, listens, listens
> repeats every sound he hears
> from every book in his godmother's library (24; emphasis added)

Manzano's biological father must "imagine" how his son "must feel in that other home," contemplating his son's life from afar. Subjugated by his station as an urban slave in the domestic sphere, Toribio here imagines his son enduring a particular kind of hell produced by sophisticated cognition of his condition. In Engle's riff on Manzano's narrative, memory and twinning emerge as dominant themes. Engle's poetic invention plays with the notion of memory ("I remember / all that I see") as readers of Manzano's narrative remember that his memory is selective; he at once brilliantly memorizes and recites poetry after hearing it only once, yet he omits crucial details of his life story. His intellectual abilities allow him to become a poet, but they also give him a glimpse of a life to which he will never have full access. In this manner, Engle expresses the gilded mental cage of Manzano's experience.

Manzano's narrative, then, represents the totipotent text, capacious, full of possibilities, prime for twisting and bending, a reflection of the desires of its reader and the agenda of its promoter.[30] This incomplete text has undergone numerous transformations, translations, and editorial interventions from around the globe. While Jackson notes that Manzano's text circulated in manuscript form before the official publication of the original Spanish version in 1937, Luis gives specifics of a complex circulation history in which two Spanish versions exist: "el manuscrito original que el poeta esclavo redactó con frecuentes errores ortográficos y la versión corregida por Anselmo Suárez y Romero" (the original manuscript that the slave poet wrote with frequent spelling errors and the corrected version by Anselmo Suárez y Romero) (W. Luis 11). Existing in competing and overlapping linguistic versions, the translation history of this text oscillates, from Spanish to English to Spanish to bilingual edition, invoking Benjamin's notion that "a translation, instead of resembling the meaning of the original, must lovingly and in detail incorporate the original's mode of signification, thus making both the original and the translation recognizable as fragments of a great language, just as fragments are part of a vessel."

Though Madden's translation fails to meet Benjamin's criterion of "refrain[ing] from wanting to communicate something," he reframes it for an abolitionist audience. It is precisely for this reason that he seems to approach the text lovingly, aware of the political potential of the original recast in antislavery terms. Just as Madden substitutes "chains" for "cruda guerra" (harsh war) in "Treinta Años," he draws on a poignant lexicon of slavery rhetoric throughout his translations, using word mnemonics that transform an innocuous and nuanced text into one that incorporates and consists of common tropes of the slave autobiography. Madden seems to resurrect and foreground the terror and brutality of slavery that Manzano attempts to encode in his poetry, and to trail off into ellipses in the autobiography.

The fragments of Manzano's text announce the simultaneous coming together and pulling apart of linguistic translations. Moreover, the vanishing text and the repetition of the ellipses indicate self-censorship through omission on Manzano's part, likely based on fear of repercussion. Formally, Manzano's "original" narrative, the version housed at the *Biblioteca Nacional de Cuba José*

Martí, is nonlinear and continuous; there are no chapter breaks, headings, or structural organization that make it adhere to the presentation of a "book." Resigned to fleeing from the abusive enslaver Don Nicolás and escaping from slavery, Manzano ends the first part of his *Autobiografía* by foreshadowing the second part, now absent to modern readers:

> Cuando iba a andar parar retirarme de la casa oí una voz que me dijo, "Dios te lleve con bien. Arrea duro." Yo creía que nadie me veía y todos me observaban, pero ninguno se me opuso como supe después. Lo que me sucedió luego lo veremos en la segunda parte que sigue a esta historia. (*Autobiografía* 134)

> [As I was about to ride away from the house, I heard a voice that said to me, "God be with you. Hurry along." I thought that nobody had seen me when everyone was watching me; but, as I later discovered, nobody tried to stop me. We shall see what happened to me later in the second part of this story which follows.] (*Autobiography* 135)

In the end, Manzano opts for the life of a *cimarrón* (maroon) in order to escape the cruelty of Don Nicolás. How does one read the silence and the missing second half of the text?

To be sure, the translation and publication history is testament to the generative fervor and resilience of this text touched by numerous hands. In a way, the text is all things to all who seek something within its pages. Similar to Anne Carson's project to represent visually the "missing matter" (xi) in her translation of the ancient Greek Sappho's poetic fragments—she uses brackets and dashes to represent torn papyrus of the ancient text—there is an archeology to Manzano's autobiography. The text vanishes into the promise for a conclusion, and only the silence of the "missing matter" of the second half remains—despite a resurgence in scholarly attention by scholars like Richard L. Jackson and its reclamation by Black Studies and by the local Cuban literary tradition. Miguel Barnet contributes to filling this archival lacunae with his recording, and perhaps quasi fictionalization, of Esteban Montejo's life. Although the profusion of editorial revisions attempt to mask the underlying uncertainty around the chronology and language of the narrative, the missing matter mirrors how Manzano himself fades into literary obscurity and ultimately dies an accused man. Like Plácido, who was mercilessly murdered during *La Escalera* (The Elevator) conflict, when alleged revolting enslaved Africans were tied to a ladder face down and punished, Manzano, too, died under suspicion of rebellious activities (Jackson 59). However, in his lasting and malleable autobiography, Manzano continues to live and reveal the tribulations of a young boy's forced labor in the master's house.

The two most important women in Manzano's life—his slave mistress and his mother—frame the opening paragraph and announce a text about mothers and mothering. Embedded in the theme of motherhood is the problem of racial mixing and how it both complicates and determines who is "allowed" to have a mother.

> La Señora Doña Beatriz de Justiz, Marquesa Justiz de Santa Ana, esposa del señor don Juan Manzano, cada vez que iba a su famosa hacienda el Molino gustaba de tomar *las más bonitas criollas* entre diez y once años. (*Autobiografía* 44; emphasis added)

> [Whenever Doña Beatriz de Justiz, the Marchioness Justiz de Santa Ana, wife of Don Juan Manzano, went to El Molino, her famous plantation, she liked to take with her *the most beautiful ten- and eleven-year-old Creole girls.*] (*Autobiography* 45; emphasis added)

Within the domestic space of her house—"la grandísima y hermosísima casa contigua a La Machina" (the enormous and very beautiful house next to La Machina)—his "Señora," the matriarch Doña Beatriz de Justiz, dictates the slave hierarchy (*Autobiografía* 46; *Autobiography* 47). Although her husband, Don Juan Francisco Manzano, the man after whom young Juan is named, rules El Molino plantation, Doña Beatriz is at the center of this domestic tale. Her predilection for "tomar las más bonitas criollas" (taking the most beautiful Creole girls) to the plantation reifies a hierarchical racial taxonomy that operates within the field (el Molino)/house dichotomy, in which the quantity of African blood a slave possesses and favorable work conditions are inversely proportional.[31] More African blood, then, relegates the slave to plantation fieldwork, and less African blood (and more European or Indian blood) makes room for achieving a higher station, characterized by the comparatively less arduous work of the domestic sphere, in the house.

That Doña Beatriz de Justiz selects the most beautiful Creole girls to enter the house indicates a process of humanization. Her recognition of their beauty, coupled with a willingness to educate them for their station in life, confers them with a bit of humanity and subjectivity: "Las traía consigo, dándoles una educación conforme a su clase y condición" (She took them along, providing them with an appropriate upbringing for their class and station in society) (44; 45). These beautiful girls represent more than pretty objects, like finely embroidered shawls or handcrafted wooden dolls; they form part of the early nineteenth-century Cuban class divisions and Latin American racial tabulations in which shades of Blackness and corresponding ranks existed. Compare this flexibility to the static racial divisions and slave classifications of the North American case, in which the "one-drop rule" reigned.[32] The Cuban societal structure, then, permits mixed-race girls, born on the island, to receive a reprieve from the rigors of outdoor field labor through employment in Doña Beatriz de Justiz's house.

Manzano's biological mother, one of the beautiful Creole girls, plays the maternal foil, albeit on the sidelines, to the impulses of a series of stringent mistresses into whose hands he falls. The final sentence of the opening paragraph introduces his mother: "Entre las escogidas fue una María del Pilar Manzano, *mi madre,* que de la servidumbre de mano de la señora Marquesa Justiz en su mayor edad, era una de las criadas de distinción, de estimación, o de razón, como quiera que se le llame" (Among the chosen few was one María del Pilar Manzano, *my mother,* who, as handservant in the marchioness's later years, was one of the maids of distinction, esteemed, or singled out for training, however one prefers to put it) (44; 45; emphasis added).

Remarkably, the phrase "mi madre" (my mother), as opposed to an "I" statement, gives the reader the first clue that this is a first-person narration instead of a seemingly objective, distant history. Defining himself through his mother's position in the house, Manzano reveals his identity as a slave, the son of a "chosen," beautiful *mulata* woman and a father named Toribio de Castro, also enslaved but living outside the house. Social position governs this intricate societal system in which a *criolla* (Creole) slave has the potential to become a "maid of distinction, esteemed . . . singled out for training" (*Autobiography* 45). After starting a sentence about his origins with "Cuando se verificó el matrimonio de Toribio de Castro con María del Pilar, a quienes debo el ser, saliendo a luz el año de. . . ." (And when the marriage of those to whom I owe my existence, Toribio de Castro and María del Pilar, came about, as I was born in the year. . . .) (*Autobiografía* 46; *Autobiography* 47), Manzano ends in ellipses, the first instance of "missing matter" in the text, and a lacuna that persists even in the latest edition. Although he knows both his mother and father, he does not know his birth date. Race and class intersect here as Manzano's mother's mixed-race status allows her to enter the world of domestic slave life and gain distinction, a feat achieved only through Doña Beatriz de Justiz's influence—her rank as marchioness is announced with each mention of her name. In this system, favor from and proximity to a mistress signify distance from the biological family. Doña Beatriz de Justiz's calls Manzano the "niño de su vejez" (child of my old age) and adopts him as her own child or "poodle"—"un género de entretenimiento" (a form of entertainment) (46; 47–48).

Manzano experiences a relatively carefree childhood and calls his mistress, who held him more than his own biological mother, *mama mía* (my mother). Stripped of parental rights, Toribio receives a reprimand from Doña Beatriz for beating his own son as punishment for misbehavior. She explains to Toribio the rights that correspond to him as father and those that correspond to her as *ama;* she occupies "el lugar de madre" (the role of mother) and owner (48; 49). In this slave community, then, motherhood becomes a double-edged position of power in which kindness can quickly turn to chastisement and relegation to the stocks. She also controls the womb of the enslaved women.

As the most "benevolent" mistress of the narrative, Doña Beatriz decrees that the subsequent children born to Maria del Pilar will be born with free status. Unfortunately, none of these children survives infancy. After Doña Beatriz dies, Manzano moves from his godmother's house to the care of the Marchioness de Prado Ameno, the most sadistic of his mistresses. Again he is dressed up in elaborate costume and "comía a los pies" (ate at the feet) of his mistress, like a trained dog (54; 55).

Margarita Engle adapts this theme of multiple mothers in her series of poems that alternate between the voices of the key characters in Juan's life. The poem "Juan" concludes this way:

She takes me with her wherever she goes
I become the companion of my owner, noble ghost
no, not a companion, remember?
a poodle, her pet
with my curly dark hair
and small child's brown skin
suitable
for the theater
and parties

While my sweet ghost-Mamá-owner
and all her friends
listen
they are forgetful
I am rememberful
I remember there is also one more mother
in my song
a bird-mother
caged
but winged (9)[33]

Manzano's slave status and the consequent uncertainty about who possesses him at any given moment underscore his anxiety about being considered living property. Ownership of Manzano transfers from the hands of one gloved mistress to another.

Although Manzano endures countless recorded and unrecorded moments of violence throughout his life, there are two salient scenes of resistance in which he fights back—on both occasions, to protect and uphold the honor of his biological mother, María del Pilar. Although Manzano often glosses over the daily horrors with elusive phrases like "Pasando por alto otros pormenores ocurridos durante los días que debía recibir el bautismo" (Passing over some other details that occurred during the days in which I was to be baptized) (50; 51), "Paso por alto algunos pasajes en los que se verificaría lo inestable de mi fortuna" (I am passing over some anecdotes that would verify the instability of my fortune) (56; 57), and "Saltando por encima de varias épocas, dejo atrás una multitud de lances dolorosos" (Skipping over several years, I will leave behind a multitude of painful episodes) (84; 85), which make the reader curious about his selective memory and censorship, Manzano manages to assert his boldness when protecting the woman who gave birth to him.

In the first scene of retaliation, Manzano's mother attempts to bargain with Señor Silvestre, the overseer, before he unleashes a punishment on her son for falling asleep at his post on the carriage, dropping a lantern outside the carriage, and then, after running to recover it, missing the carriage because it accelerated its speed. In response to María del Pilar's protests, "levantó la mano y dio a mi madre con el manatí" (he raised his hand and struck my mother with his whip) (70; 71). Although Manzano is often physically distant from his mother, because she lives in Matanzas and he must wait on and follow his mistress, he feels a psychic connection to her pain in this moment: "Este golpe lo sentí yo en mi corazón. Dar un grito y convertirme de manso cordero en un león todo fue una cosa. Me le zafé con un fuerte tirón del brazo por donde me llevaba y me le tiré encima con dientes y manos" (I felt this blow in my heart. All at once I screamed and was transformed from a gentle lamb into a lion. I wrenched myself loose from his grip with a strong yank of my arm and I attacked him with teeth and fists) (70; 71). Only an effort to protect the maternal figure who had been denied the opportunity to mother him sparks this transformation from meek little lamb to a fierce lion.

Of course, the overseer begins to beat Manzano almost to death, until his mother once more intervenes for his sake. Again, the narrative gives the reader a glimpse into this gruesome scene, but then Manzano pulls back:

> La culpa de mi madre fue que viendo que el mayoral me tiraba a matar, se le tiró encima y, haciéndose atender, pude ponerme en pie. Llegando los guardieros del tendal nos condujeron, y vi a mi madre puesta en el lugar de sacrificio por primera vez en su vida. Aunque ella estaba en la hacienda, estaba exenta del trabajo como mujer de un esclavo que se supo conducir y hacerse considerar de todos.
>
> Viendo yo a mi madre en este estado, suspenso, no podía ni llorar, ni discurrir, ni huir. Temblaba mientras que, sin pudor, los cuatro negros se apoderaron de ella y la arrojaron en tierra para azotarla. Pedía por Dios. Por ella todo lo resistí. Pero al oír estallar el primer fustazo, convertido en león, en tigre o en la fiera más animosa, estuve a pique de perder la vida a manos del citado Silvestre. Pero pasemos en silencio el resto de esta escena dolorosa. (*Autobiografía* 72)

> [My mother's mistake was that she assaulted the overseer when she saw he was about to kill me and, while he was dealing with her, I was able to stand up. When the watchmen arrived from the yard where the coffee beans are dried, they led us away and I saw my mother put in the sacrificial place for the first time in her life. Even though she lived on the plantation, as the wife of a slave who knew how to conduct himself and command respect from everyone, she was exempt from work.
>
> Bewildered, seeing my mother in this position, I could neither cry nor think nor flee. I was trembling as the four blacks shamelessly overpowered her and threw her on the ground to whip her. I prayed to God. For her sake I endured everything. But when I heard the first crack of the whip I became a lion,

> a tiger, the fiercest beast, and I was about to lose my life at the hands of the aforementioned Silvestre. But let us pass over the rest of this painful scene in silence.] (*Autobiography* 73)

Seeing his mother in this "lugar de sacrificio," the stocks, after she offered to take the lash of the whip intended for her son, in order to spare his life, Manzano rallies back and attacks the overseer again.[34] He loses the timidity of the fragile boy used to delicate indoor settings and rebels. As with other excised moments, witnessing the whipping of his mother in the stocks induces a forced silence about this brutality. The reader is left to imagine the conclusion of this violent scene.

Scenes of violence between enslavers and the enslaved typify the genre commonly known as the slave narrative. The discursive patterns and conventions of this genre are based almost wholly on the Anglo-African tradition. In his influential chapter "The Trope of the Talking Book," Gates theorizes about the function of slave narratives written in English in regions under British colonial rule:

> The slave, by definition, possessed at most a liminal status within the human community. To read and to write was to transgress this nebulous realm of liminality. The slave's texts, then, could not be taken as specimens of black literary culture. Rather, the texts of the slave could only be read as testimony of defilement: the slave's *representation* and reversal of the master's attempt to transform a human being into a commodity, and the slave's simultaneous verbal witness of the possession of a humanity shared in common with Europeans. (*Signifying* 128)

The assertion that a literate enslaved person represents a defiant and active transgression against codified legal and social literacy prohibition extends beyond the British Americas to include any region of the Western Hemisphere. However, for the purposes of this chapter, the question is: What conclusions, if any, may one draw from and about Manzano's autobiography in particular, and about the Latin American slave narrative in general, from the figure of a literate and published enslaved *mulato fino* on the largest island in Spanish America? What does the rhetorical figure of *praeteritio* signal with regard to the Latin American slave narrative, if such a generalization can be made?

A starting point for beginning to think through this problem may be found in exploring the particularities of the Spanish legal system in Cuba. If, as Gates argues, enslaved Anglo-Africans "had to represent themselves as 'speaking subjects' before they could even begin to destroy their status as objects, as commodities, with Western culture," and this process occurs "only by inscribing themselves in the written word" (*Signifying* 130), how does one interpret the Cuban case, in which enslaved Africans possessed, at least in theory and according to Castilian codes, the status of "legal subjects" through the practices of *coartación* (legal process of gradual manumission in Cuba) and *pedir papel* (literally, "to ask for paper"). Manzano mentions both of these *derechos* (rights) in his narrative, and they represent two pathways by which enslaved Cubans gained their manumission: either through making payments toward their freedom or by asking for paper to advertise for a new master. This indicates a legal system in which enslaved people were empowered, if even to the slightest degree, to understand the Castilian legal system and petition for their freedom.

Alejandro de la Fuente notes that "giving paper may have represented the possibility of selling a slave that was difficult to control," and he posits that "this custom developed in part as an extension of the widely practiced hiring-out system, by which a slave sought work, and therefore a temporary 'master,' with the authorization of his or her owner" (675). In this light, this was a legal practice that enslaved persons "managed to enforce, limiting in the process the dominium of the owners in fairly concrete terms" (de la Fuente and Gross 172). Implicit in this legal system is an acknowledgment that enslaved Africans may be able to use the paper and write these advertisements. How does this relate to the slave narrative? It seems that within colonial Spanish America the education of enslaved people was encouraged—to the degree that they became stylistic "parrots."

Let us return to the *Autobiografía* to examine the pivotal moments in which Manzano becomes an agent of both the literary and legal worlds. Not only does he memorize, recite, and copy, fulfilling the ventriloquist or parroting activities that his first mistress, Doña Beatriz, believes in, but also, timid as he may seem, he exercises his legal rights through the act of *pedir papel.* Unlike Montejo in *Cimarrón,* who dares to remove himself from the system entirely and live as a fugitive, Manzano attempts to work within the confines of slavery. This serves as an interesting comparison to the discussion of Carolina de Jesus's notebooks and her obsession with finding paper to write her diary, discussed in chapter 4. If reading and the pursuit of learning to read is the central trope of the autobiographies written by Anglo-Africans, then it seems that the moment of asking for paper (or *pedir papel*) becomes the dominant trope in Manzano's narrative. Whether this symbolic request for paper signifies the predominant trope across Latin American slave narratives remains to be uncovered, if more narratives are located, but it is clear that the theme of writing, in contrast to reading, signals the moment of transcendence.

As a young boy, Manzano exhibited great intellectual prowess, a strong statement against the common belief in the intellectual inferiority of enslaved Africans. By age ten, he could recite "todo el catecismo de memoria" (the entire catechism by heart) and he knew:

> casi todos los sermones de Fray Luis de Granada. Sabía además muchas relaciones, loas y entremeses, teoría regular y la colocación de las piezas. Me llevaron a la ópera francesa y vine remedando a algunos, por lo cual, aunque siempre era más por los sermones, mis padres recibían de mí la porción de galas que recogía en la sala. (*Autobiografía* 48)

> almost all of Fray Luis of Granada's sermons. I also knew many lengthy passages, short plays and interludes, dramatic theory, and stage sets. They took me to French operas, and I was good at imitating some of them, for which my parents used to receive the allotment of gifts from me that I would collect in the parlor, although it was always more from the sermons. (*Autobiography* 51)

While his ability to imitate might seem to verify his mistress's view of him as a trained parrot, he also learns to compose "de memoria muchas décimas" (several *décimas* by memory) (56; 57). During his adolescent years of melancholy, when he began to receive harsh punishments from his mistress regularly, Manzano composed verses without writing them down, because he did not yet know how to write: "Tenía un cuaderno de versos en la memoria" (I possessed a mental notebook of verses) (62; 63).

Manzano's library in his mind provides solace in the wake of the atrocious beatings and punishments he routinely receives for the slightest "offense" or accusation from his mistress. Such punishments included being sent to the stocks overnight in the cold, receiving twenty-five lashes, or being tied with a rope to a horse and forced to run, because of an accusation of stealing a chicken. In a poignant statement on the subjectivity of truth while enduring a beating, Manzano explains, "Se me mandaba a decir la verdad y yo no sabía cuál" (They were demanding I tell the truth and I did not know which truth they wanted)

(96; 97). Clearly, there is the truth of the enslaver and the truth of the enslaved and they do not intersect.

Manzano ultimately finds personal truth and intellectual liberation through his poetry. Interestingly, there is no "scene of instruction" around reading, in which Manzano painstakingly grapples with a book in the hopes that it will talk to him, as exists in the Anglophone tradition of slave narratives (Gates, *Signifying* 127–169). His travails around learning to read are omitted because his first mistress, Doña Beatriz, sent him to school "en casa de mi madrina de bautismo, Trinidad de Zayas" (at the home of my baptismal godmother, Trinidad de Zayas) (*Autobiografía* 48; *Autobiography* 49). Thus, learning to read, for Manzano, is not an act of transgression; in fact, his education is sanctioned and arranged by his mistress.

The emphasis here is on learning to write, which he accomplishes through imitation of the writing of his enslaver, Don Nicolás. Notably, in this narrative that centers prominently on the figure of the mistress/mother, it is from his enslaver's handwriting that Manzano learns to write, subtly revealing the gendering of the world of this intellectual space. He develops a system of independent study by using "algún pedazo de papel de los que mi señor botaba" (discarded sheet [of his master's]) as a template, and teaches himself to "formar letras" (fashion letters) (102; 103). Manzano's inventive method of self-teaching allows him to move from parroting others by simply memorizing their poetry to composing his own verses. He is no longer simply a consumer as reader (passive); he is now a producer as writer (active).

When he discovers Manzano's writing talent, the marquis at first prohibits further writing, a prohibition that Manzano defies. Finally, when Don Coronado finds scraps of paper on which Manzano has written décimas in the style of Arriaza, he "pronosticó que yo sería poeta, aunque se opusiera todo el mundo. Supo cómo aprendí a escribir y con qué fin, y aseguraba que con otro tanto han empezado los más" (predicted that I would be a poet, even though everyone was against it. He found out how I learned to write and why, and confirmed that most had begun the same way) (104; 105). The fact that Don Coronado even associates the position of poet with Manzano indicates a flexibility in his thinking about the capabilities of an enslaved person and their station that may have been less common in the US South of the same period. Manzano's literacy affords him the ability to write letters and notes (and even medical logs, while he cares for the sick), making him a valuable actor in the milieu of the enslaved domestic servant.

As a member of the literate world, Manzano attempts to work within the Spanish legal system to *pedir papel* and receive payment due for debt owed to his mother. Emboldened by his ability to write and by a filial desire to posthumously protect his biological mother (her death first appears in a footnote Manzano writes to clarify his nonsequential narration), he appeals to the system of *pedir papel* after his mistress comes to take him back, after a comparatively positive experience with Don Nicolás and his wife: "Me fui tan contrito y entre tanta reflexiones que por la mañana entre nueve y diez, me determiné a pedir papel para buscar amo. Se asombró mi señora de esto" (I went away contrite, thinking about so many things, that between nine and ten in the morning I decided to ask for the papers to solicit a master. My mistress was surprised by this) (108; 109). Although Manzano quickly expresses regret for *molestia* (bothering) his mistress with this matter, his attempt demonstrates a certain belief in the legal codes of the island as they pertain to the enslaved.

In addition to *pedir papel,* Manzano also gives his mistress receipts and promissory notes to request payment for unpaid debts and for his mother's money, which his mistress had in her possession and which was to be distributed to his mother's children. The second time Manzano inquires about this matter, his mistress replies angrily, "¿Estás muy apurado por la herencia? ¿No sabes que soy heredera forzosa de mis esclavos? En cuanto vuelvas a hablar de la herencia te pongo donde no veas el sol ni la luna. Marcha a limpiar las caobas" (Are you in a big hurry for your inheritance? Don't you know that I am the automatic heir of my slaves? If you as much as speak of the inheritance again, I will put you where you will see neither sunlight nor moonlight. Go clean the mahogany furniture) (118; 119). Hence, the precarious property rights of enslaved Africans, and other legal protections in place, nonetheless depended on the whims and discretion of the enslavers. When the attempts to contest slavery within the confines of the Castilian legal code break down, Manzano, like his autobiographical successor, Montejo, becomes a *cimarrón* (fugitive from slavery) and flees.

ESTEBAN MONTEJO BETWEEN FACT, FICTION, AND MEMORY

Two poignant images—the flying African and the enslaved African resurrected from the dead—set the tone for the series of *cuentos* (stories) that constitute the narrative now simply titled *Cimarrón: Historia de un esclavo.* These figures of dissent, first introduced at the end of the second chapter, "La vida en los barracones" [Life in the Barracoons], exemplify the theme of resilience that punctuates the oral history of Esteban Montejo, which he dictated to the anthropologist Miguel Barnet. Notably, the title of the English translation changed from *Autobiography of a Runaway Slave* (1968, 1973) to *Biography of a Runaway Slave*, the former possibly an effort to conform to the North American autobiographical mode of the so-called slave narrative. The Spanish title is pithier, directly translated as *Runaway: The Story of a Slave.*[35] Montejo's retelling of one of his *cuentos* begins with an aphorism:

> Una vez enterraron a un negro y levantó la cabeza. Y es que estaba vivito. Ese cuento me lo hicieron a mí en Santo Domingo, *después de la esclavitud.* Todo el barrio de Jicotea lo sabe. La cosa fue en un cachimbo que se llama el Diamante y era del padre de Marinello, el que habla mucho de Martí. En ese lugar enterraron a un congo y se levantó gritando. La gente se espantó y salió huyendo.
>
> Unos días más tarde el congo se apareció en el barracón; dicen que fue entrando despacito para no asustar a nadie. Pero cuando la gente lo vio se volvió a asustar. Entonces el mayoral le preguntó qué le había pasado y él dijo: "Me metieron en el hoyo por la cólera y cuando me curé, salí." Desde entonces cada vez que alguien cogía esa enfermedad o cualquier otra, lo dejaban días y días en la caja hasta que se enfriaba como un hielo. (*Cimarrón* 45–46; emphasis added)

> [Once they buried a black man, and he got up again. And truth is that he was alive and kicking. They told me that story in Santo Domingo, *after slavery.* The entire district of Jicotea knows it. The thing happened in a little sugarmill still called El Diamante that belonged to the father of Marinello, the one who talks about Martí a lot. In that place they buried a Congo, and he got up screaming. The people were scared and ran away.
>
> A few days later, the Congo man appeared in the barracoon. They say he came in slowly so as not to frighten anyone. But when people saw him they got scared all over again. Then the overseer asked him what had happened, and he said: "They put me in the ground because of cholera, and when I was better, I got out." Since then, every time someone got that disease or any other, they left him for days and days in the box until he was cold as ice.] (*Biography* 42; emphasis added)

This passage contains what I consider the driving and recurrent theme of Montejo's narrative: resistance to slavery through resurrection. The theme of resurrection presupposes that slavery is a form of "social death," as Orlando Patterson has brilliantly shown in *Slavery and Social Death,* in which the slave is introduced as a "nonbeing" who "can never be brought to life again as such"; except for "fictive rebirth, the slave will remain forever an unborn being (non-né)" (38). Montejo and other enslaved laborers are *cimarrones* (maroons), but they do not cowardly run away to the hills to achieve their "fictive rebirth" or resurrection. The sentence "Una vez enterraron a un negro y levantó la cabeza" (Once they buried a black man, and he got up again) emblematizes the defiant spirit of what is at once a counternarrative to and continuation of Manzano's *Autobiografía.* The powerful statement connotes the image of the oppressive enslavers, anonymous in this passage, heaping dirt and soil atop the lifeless body of an enslaved person, who rebelliously rises again from the earth, healed and transfigured.

The literal translation of the phrase "levantó la cabeza" (he lifted his head) metaphorically represents a body movement that contests the sorrowful, downtrodden symbolism of subordination associated with slavery. Far from remaining in the submissive position of head cast downward, the enslaved Black man raises his head and body from the grips of the grave to live again on earth, "*vivito*" (alive and kicking).[36] Lifting his head and rising from the dead signifies the persistent will to live and reclamation of humanity. The burial and symbolic resurrection simultaneously allude to New Testament parables about the dead miraculously rising (including Lazarus, the daughter of Jairus, and a young man during his funeral), which foreshadow the resurrection of Jesus Christ, and Montejo's invocation of the flying Africans.

Montejo claims that, unlike the Chinese in Cuba, the Africans rarely died by suicide; instead, they flew away. The dead Black man's springing forth from the ground mimetically anticipates the flying Africans jumping off the ground. Moreover, the phrase "levantó la cabeza" (he lifted his head) voices the ultimate resistance, even unto death, and represents this enslaved Black man's will to live, an instinct that cannot be quelled even under the demoralizing conditions of slavery. His salvation and redemption from the long suffering are not located in heaven. Instead, perhaps in a defiant posture toward Western religion, he experiences an earthly rebirth.

Striking, too, is the folkloric tone of this passage. The opening words *una vez* (once) evoke the orality of a children's fairy tale recounted from memory. Moreover, the prepositional phrase "después de la esclavitud" (after slavery) signifies that Montejo marks time in reference to slavery. This dating system positions slavery as the focal point and trauma par excellence against which all time and other life events are measured, and Montejo repeats this referential relationship to slavery through the narrative. For example, Montejo admits that most captive Africans did not know their age, so it was an approximation when they could stop serving in the field at age sixty.

The oral quality of Montejo's narrative, which Barnet endeavors to transfer into the written word, highlights the artificial circumstances surrounding the recording of this biography. Although Barnet does not render Montejo's speech in "dialect," he does retain several of Montejo's linguistic idiosyncrasies, such as his use of the verb *vide* (I seen) instead of *vi* (I saw) for the first person singular past tense of *to see,* to give the reader a sense of Montejo's speech patterns and use of colloquialisms. In the short introductory essay to the Spanish edition, "¿Quién es el Cimarrón?," Barnet admits that when they first met in 1963 and Montejo was 103 years old, Montejo initially expressed skepticism at the idea of documenting his story:

> Esteban me recibió con ciertas dudas; en realidad no sabía lo que yo iba a buscar en su vida y tuvo que pasar un tiempo para que se produjera entre nosotros una relación franca y espontánea. Más de tres años transcurrieron para que yo pudiera recoger de sus labios el rico tesoro de su larga y dramática existencia. Con paciencia de ambas partes pude indagar en la historia de su vida. Me serví de muchos libros de historia, de mapas, manuscritos, periódicos y revistas de la época.
>
> [Esteban received me with certain doubts; in reality, he did not know what I was going to look for in his life, and time had to pass so that it could produce a frank and spontaneous relationship between us. More than three years transpired so that I could gather this rich treasure of his long and dramatic existence from his lips. With patience on both sides, I was able to investigate the story of his life. I used many history books, maps, manuscripts, newspapers, and magazines of the time.] (*Cimarrón* 9)

Barnet's admission that he was looking for something in Montejo's life (buscar [algo] en su vida) and that he used secondary historical sources perhaps indicates that he approached this project with a certain agenda in mind. As an anthropologist and novelist, Barnet intercedes and becomes an undeniable presence in his rendering of the life narrative of an "illiterate" Cuban slave.

Couched in the 1960s scholarly context of reclamation of "marginalized" or "peripheral" voices, Barnet's ethnographic project to (re)assert the subjectivities and lost voices of enslaved Cubans brings to the foreground questions about the extent to which it was constructed to broadcast a particular image of the mighty and fearless *cimarrón*. As mentioned, throughout the narrative, Montejo refers to his recollections about his varied life experiences and the experiences of others as a series of *cuentos* (stories) or *historias* (histories or stories). The Spanish word *historias* contains the double significance of fact and fiction and problematizes a neat categorization of this text.

Is *Cimarrón* literature? A historical account? If so, who is the author? The clouded memories of our narrator and protagonist, Esteban Montejo, a playful and sometimes forgetful centenarian, obscure matters even further. It is interesting to note that Esteban Montejo's name does not appear in the title, nor does he receive any authorial credit in publications. In his afterword to the English translation, "The Alchemy of Memory," Barnet writes that he seeks to give voice to "the so-called 'people with no history'" who were both "everywhere" and "invisible in the eyes of the crafty ruler" through "the strength of testimony" (*Biography* 203).

In fact, Barnet names his work a "testimonial novel," which he defines as one that contains "a conjunction of styles, a coming together of approaches and a fusion of objectives, a confrontation with problems within the American context: violence, dependency, neocolonialism, the falsification of history by means of schematisms, applied and reapplied." Venerating the instructive possibilities of the testimonial novel, which he says "reworks . . . realism, autobiography, [and] the relationship between fiction and history," Barnet describes his work as "bring[ing] together sociological-anthropological interests and the literary, convinced that they travel together in underground caverns, seeking each other out and nourishing each other in joyful reciprocity" (204–205). This lyrical description of social science and the literary traveling together discloses the difficulty of parceling out disciplinary divisions.

The title of the essay "The Alchemy of Memory" itself suggests that Barnet enacts the role the alchemist, extracting gold from the rubble of Montejo's memories. Several scholars have argued that this is a polyphonic text (Ogundayo) that represents a fusion between Montejo's story and Barnet's writing, even going so far as to name a hybrid author "Bartejo" (Echevarría) or "Montenet" (Luis, "Politics"). In Barnet's structure, nearly two-thirds of the narrative is dedicated to the story of slavery, rebellion, and the period after abolition in

1886, with a short chapter at the end devoted to the war of independence, an organization that some historians surmise is politically motivated.[37]

Instead of dwelling on the question of authenticity, I presuppose that Montejo's experience is highly mediated through Barnet's politics and ethnographic project. Given the discontinuous temporality of the text and the composite narrative voice, the performance of Montejo relating his *cuentos* to Barnet, and Barnet's subsequent transfiguration of Montejo's oral stories into novelistic form, confirms the interpenetration of storytelling, memory, and the reciprocal relationship between personal narrative and public history. The issue is not about the authenticity of the narrative; rather, it is about what it teaches us about the interrelatedness of storytelling and memory.

In a manner characteristic of the oral quality of his often meandering narrative, Montejo later repeats the resurrection scene in much more muted terms, indicating his ambivalence toward "modern" technological advances:

> En muchas ocasiones se dio el caso de muertos que revivieron. Y es que los enterraban antes de tiempo. De ahí nació la idea de esperar veinticuatro horas para enterrarlos. Ese sistema es moderno. Aun así no he dado resultados, porque veinte veces he oído decir que ha habido muertos que después de estar cubiertos de tierra se han levantado flacos y enfermos y han seguido gritando. (*Cimarrón* 100)

> [On many occasions it happened that the dead came back to life. The thing is that they were buried too soon. Because of that they began waiting twenty-four hours to bury them. That's the modern system. Even so, it hasn't worked out because I've heard it said twenty times that there were dead men who, after being covered up with dirt, got up, skinny and sick, to go on screaming.] (*Biography* 93)

In this rewriting of the resurrection story, Montejo offers a more practical reason for the dead who seem to come back to life. They simply were not dead when buried. Gone is the parabolic tone and fervor of the first story. While the enslaved Congolese man featured in his first retelling of the story wrenches himself from a premature demise and fantastically rises from the dead, after slavery is abolished, the unnamed dead who come back to life in this tale prompt a "modern" system that requires a delay of twenty-four hours before burying the dead.[38] Implicit in the repetition of this story is Montejo's resistance to the cultural changes that accompany a country striving toward modernity.

In his introduction to *Culturas híbridas: Estrategias para entrar y salir de la modernidad,* Canclini offers a hypothesis about the uncertainty with which Latin America approaches the question of modernity: "La *incertidumbre* acerca del sentido y el valor de la modernidad deriva no sólo de lo que separa a naciones, etnias y clases, sino de los cruces socioculturales en que lo tradicional y lo moderno se mezclan" (The *uncertainty* about the direction and value of modernity derives not only from that which separates nations, ethnic groups, and classes, but also from sociocultural exchanges in which the traditional and the modern mix) (14; author's emphasis).

Montejo expresses this uncertainty about the incipient modernization of Cuba when he discusses in elaborate detail the process of mechanized sugar production. Born in an *ingenio* (sugarmill) in 1860, the *criollo* Montejo is the symbolic offspring of Fernando Ortiz's personification of sugar as *una esclava* (an enslaved Black woman).[39] In describing the mechanization of sugar production, he conveys ambivalent feelings:

> La verdad es que el adelanto causa admiración. Cuando yo veía todas esas máquinas moviéndose a la vez, me admiraba. Y de versa parecían ir solas. Yo nunca antes había visto tanto adelanto. Las máquinas eran inglesas o americanas. De España no vide ninguna. Ellos no sabían cómo de hacían. Los más revueltos con esa novedad eran los colonos. Se alegraban más que nadie, porque mientras más producción había en la casa de calderas, más caña les compraba el ingenio. (*Cimarrón* 108)
>
> [The truth is that progress is amazing. When I saw those machines moving all at once, I was impressed, and to tell the truth, they seemed to go by themselves. I never before had seen so much progress. The machines were English and American. I never seen a one from Spain. They didn't know how to make them. The tenant cane farmers were the most excited about the new things. They were happier than anybody else because more production in the boiler house meant that more cane was bought from them by the mill.] (*Biography* 101)

While he admired the progress of the sugar industry, on the one hand, Montejo also objected to the destruction of Cuba's natural landscape for the purposes of sugarcane cultivation, on the other: "Llegó la ambición de la caña y por poco no dejan ni montes en Cuba. Talaron los árboles de cuajo. Se llevaron caobas, *jiqui;* bueno, todo el monte se vino abajo" (The sugar cane fever arrived, and they left hardly any forest in Cuba. Trees were chopped down at the roots. They took out mahoganies, cedars, indigo trees. Well, the whole forest was cut down). Montejo asserts that "Se cultivó caña, pero se acabó con la belleza del país" (Cane was grown, but it destroyed the beauty of the country) (*Cimarrón* 109; *Biography* 102). It seems that Cuba must sacrifice her natural beauty as the price for the movement toward modernity.

Montejo calls forth memories of a "premodern" Cuba with the anaphora *me acuerdo* (I remember), which signals the beginning of one of his anecdotes of slavery, escape, or life after abolition in the protective shield of nature. Emphasizing the legitimacy of his memories, Montejo alternates the refrain "me acuerdo" with proclamations of the veracity of the stories he imparts. One might expect that Montejo's life from his birth in the sugarmill would revolve around his enslaved condition and his forced labor in the sugar industry, but surprisingly, his anecdotes about the barracoons and his experiences as a fugitive slave exhibit the vibrancy of enslaved people's lives and demonstrate how he exercised agency through resistance. Montejo summons the myth of the flying Africans in his account of slavery to provide another example of an action of dissent. Unlike the Indians in Cuba, who according to Montejo, died by suicide to escape forced conversion to Christianity, the Africans chose another path:

> Esas historias no son inventadas, lo que sí yo creo que es cuento, porque nunca lo vide, es que los negros se suicidaban . . . Pero los negros no hacían eso, porque ellos se iban volando, volaban por el cielo y cogían para su tierra. Los congos *musundi* eran los que más volaban, desaparecían por medio de la brujería. Hacían igual que las brujas isleñas pero sin ruido. Hay gentes que dicen que los negros se tiraban a los ríos; eso es falso. La verdad es que ellos se amarraban un *negocio* a la cintura que le decían *prenda* y estaba cargada. Ahí estaba la fuerza. Eso yo lo conozco palmo a palmo y es positivo. (*Cimarrón* 46)

> [These stories are not made up. What I do think is a fiction, because I never seen it ever, is that blacks committed suicide . . . But the blacks didn't do that because they went flying, flying in the sky, and headed off for their homeland. The Musundi Congo were the ones who flew the most. They disappeared through witchcraft. They did the same as Canary Island witches but without a sound. There are some who say that the blacks threw themselves into the rivers,

> but that's a lie. The truth is that they tied a doodad they called a prenda around their waist. That's where the power was. I know that like the palm of my hand, and it's a fact.] (*Biography* 43)

Montejo differentiates here between *historias* as fact and *cuentos* as fiction, although as mentioned, *historia* possesses the secondary meaning of "story" or "tale" in addition to signifying "history." Although he was not formally educated, Montejo's observation of and interaction with the diversity of ethnic groups living in Cuba, and particularly his encounters with Congolese and Lucumí elders, equipped him with a nuanced understanding of language. He plays with its ambiguity during his storytelling. For example, when Montejo affirms the veracity of a story—"la verdad es que . . ." (the truth is that . . .) and "es positivo" (it's a fact)—as he does in the passage above, he also undermines the listener/reader's confidence in his other stories. If this story is true, what are the other ones?

Beyond his employment of these rhetorical ruses, Montejo conjures the flying Africans not only to argue that enslaved Africans did not commit suicide or lie down and die but also to point out that they exercised independence. Many escaped. By emphasizing their strength, fortitude, and resilience, Montejo upends language of victimization with a discourse of thriving through ingenuity. It is no surprise, then, that Barnet ends the first section on slavery with this stirring account, predicting Montejo's own "flight."

Montejo is an expert storyteller and purveyor of Cuban collective memory, possessing what Barnet calls "un gran poder de expresión" (a great power of expression) (*Cimarrón* 9). He employs this rhetorical power to reshape memories through the process of narrative transmission, leaving the listener/reader enraptured by his magic. It is a text that straddles multiple boundaries, or as Rossana Nofal puts it, "Se sitúa en ese espacio intersticial que separa la ficción de la realidad y la mentira de la verdad" (It situates itself in the interstitial space the separates fiction from reality and lie from truth) (35). Montejo as storyteller maximizes the uncertainty of the interstitial space to simultaneously illuminate and obscure, mixing stories he witnessed with stories he heard.

However, the most significant and personal moment of resistance occurs after the previous failed attempt to flee, when he escapes from his overseer, in a violent episode. "A mí nunca se me ha olvidado la primera vez que intenté huirme" (I have never forgotten the first time I tried to run away), he explains, and he recalls the appearance of his *amo* (master):

> Me acuerdo de que era alto y nunca se quitaba el sombrero. Todos los negros lo respetaban, porque con un cuerazo que diera le arrancaba el pellejo a cualquiera. El caso es que ese día yo estaba caliente y no sé qué me pasó, pero tenía una rabia que de verlo nada más me encendía. (*Cimarrón* 49–50)
>
> [I remember that he was tall and never took his hat off. All the blacks had respect for him because one of the whippings he gave could strip the skin off of just about anybody. The thing is, one day I was riled up, and I don't know what got into me, but I was mad, and just seeing him set me off.] (*Biography* 44).

In a confrontation reminiscent of David's with Goliath, Montejo breaks the code of an enslaved person's expected subservient behavior by committing an act of violence against his overseer:

> Le silbé de lejos y él miró y se volvió de espaldas: ahí fue donde cogí una piedra y se la tiré a la cabeza. Yo sé que le dio, porque él gritó para que me agarraran. Pero no me vio más el pelo, porque ese día cogí el monte. (*Cimarrón* 50)
>
> [I whistled at him from a distance, and he looked around and then turned his back. That's when I picked up a rock and threw it at his head. I know it hit him because he shouted for someone to grab me. But he never saw me again because that day I made it into the woods.] (*Biography* 44–45)

By first whistling at him, an action of disrespect, Montejo transforms his "*amo*" into an animal and subjects him to the same degrading treatment Montejo has received. In a sense, it is the whistle, more than the rock thrown at his head, that challenges the power structure of the plantation. Of course, the rock inflicts physical pain, but the act of whistling attacks his social position and momentarily pulls the *amo* down to the degraded level of a slave. When Montejo emphatically states, "cogí el monte" (I made it into the woods), *el monte* (the woods) represents a site of liberation and independent living.[40] Montejo first hides in the corollary to Harriet Jacobs's confining hovel, or "the loophole of retreat," in *Incidents in the Life of a Slave Girl* (1861), a cave that he occupies for one and a half years, subsisting on stolen piglets and potatoes. Caves provide the perfect natural cloak for those escaping enslavement.

Montejo's account of his communion with nature as a *cimarrón* "en el monte" (in the woods) represents the most compelling section of the testimony precisely because he does not focus on his condition of enslavement. Montejo, via Barnet, devotes long sections of the text to explanations of leisure activities and entertainment, such as dances and fiestas on San Juan's day, courtship, and marriage. From detailed descriptions of the religious practices of the Congo or the theatrical performances of the Chinese to anecdotes about his voracious sexual appetite and vexed relationship with women, Montejo assumes Barnet's ethnographic voice and the narrative reads as an ethnography within an ethnography. As a skilled hunter and gatherer, Montejo learns to avoid poisonous snakes while living in the cave, to find nourishment and healing herbs in nature, and to identify the sounds of various birds based on their call. "Me acuerdo de todos" (I remember them all), he says (*Cimarrón* 60; *Biography* 53).

The birds and trees speak in the woods. Like the complementary relationship between the figure of the man resurrected from the dead and the flying Africans, Montejo's extensive delineation of spiritual exercises emphasizes syncretic religious practice on the island, in which Catholicism, Santería, and other dealings with spirits coexist: "Nadie es puro así de llano. Todas las religiones se han mezclado aquí en esta tierra. El africano trajo la suya, la más fuerte, y el español también trajo la suya, pero no tan fuerte. Hay que respetarlas todas. Ésa es mi política" (No one is so pure as all that. All the religions have become mixed up together in this country. The African brought his, the strongest, and the Spaniard also brought his, though not so strong. They all have to be respected. That's my way of doing things) (138; 130).[41] Leading up to his explication of the war of independence, he even offers three distinct versions of stories circulating around the death of infamous bandit Manuel García and revises the myth of the flying Africans.

What the listener/reader gleans from these stories is that the life of enslaved Africans is not solely made up of sorrow and pity, even for a *criollo* born on a sugar plantation. There are moments of singing and dancing, pleasure and recreation in the midst of the horrendous forced labor and living conditions. As a *cimarrón,* and even for some who were still living under the watchful eye of the overseer, it was possible to carve out a life that included dance, play, and healing, and through these moments, Montejo and others who were enslaved assumed the ultimate posture of defiance.

In a candid admission of fear at confronting his own mortality, Montejo expresses concern that the story of his life will be forgotten:

> Y yo digo que lo que hay es que no morirse, porque a los pocos días nadie se acuerda de uno, ni los mejores amigos. Es mejor no darles tanto cumplido a los muertos, como se hace ahora, porque la verdad que todo eso es hipocresía. Lo mismo antes que ahora. A mí, denme la fiesta en vida. (*Cimarrón* 101)
>
> [And I still maintain the thing is not to die because within a few days nobody remembers you, not even your best friends. The best thing is not to make such a fuss over the dead, as they do now, because the truth is that it's all hypocrisy. It was then and it is now. Give me the fiesta while I'm still alive.] (*Biography* 94)

Not only has Montejo avoided the fate of falling into oblivion, as his narrative has a secure place in the annals of the transatlantic memory of slavery, but also his name has become synonymous with *cimarrón,* a term now reappropriated by African descendants in the Spanish-speaking world much the way *quilombola* has been in Brazil. To be a *cimarrón* is a source of pride.

REMIXING SUGAR

When Jeffrey B. Ferguson argues, in his important book *Race and the Rhetoric of Resistance* (2021), that there are only two basic stories in African American discourse, "those of suffering and resistance," one may wonder whether this also holds true for representations of slavery in Latin America (1). We have seen in both Manzano's and Montejo's texts two different approaches to resistance: the first through deliberate omission of salient details, which allows Manzano to tell his story through allusion and charged absences in the text, and the second through Montejo's overt rebellion and rebirth as a maroon. Although I agree with Ferguson that oftentimes the "utter dominance" of the suffering/resistance duality becomes "an all too pat and unified picture of black life," I would suggest that the richness of differentiation might be found in the specificity of the text and national context (5, 8). In other words, not all stories of resistance are the same across the diaspora. Manzano resisted through his covert method of storytelling while Montejo resisted most obviously through running away, but also later, through refashioning his life story at the end of his life. Sometimes, resistance manifests itself as a transformation.

One of the most stunning of these transformations occurs with the transgressive reinscription of slavery in the sign of sugar. The celebrated salsa singer

Celia Cruz (1925–2003) famously reassigned the value of sugar from the negative, "abominable ingredient" of Peacock's sketch to a national chant of love, affection, unity, and *sabor* (flavor).[42] As we have discussed in relation to the Marvelous Sugar Baby (chapter 2) and to Jean Toomer wrestling with the specter of sugarcane in his modernist *Cane* (chapter 3), Cruz reappropriated the sign of sugar in her infectious cry "¡Azúcar!" When she sings her own lyrical autobiography—"Mi sangre es de azúcar negra / Es amor y es música" (My blood is made of brown sugar / It's love and it's music)—in her popular song "Azúcar Negra," she conveys to Cubans, whether on the island or exiled and living in the United States (as she was after Castro came into power in 1959),[43] that there is no shame in remembering the intertwined history of slavery.

In these varied genres—popular music, mediated Cuban pre- and postslavery (auto)biographies published a century apart, and sociopolitical narratives of sugar in the Caribbean—we apprehend a multiplicity of Afrodiasporic forms that provoke—indeed demand—novel approaches to comparative, interdisciplinary slavery studies. Cruz made the word *azúcar* one of the most ubiquitous reverberations of slavery in the popular imagination of Cubans and fans worldwide. Amazingly, she used music to allow the nation to mourn, accept, laugh, and dance because they had made it through, eschewing the "blood-sweeten'd beverage" for a collective Cuban *sabor* of which they can all shout happily, "¡Azúcar!"

Epilogue

A GATE OF RETURN

Toward an Infinite Sum of Afrodiasporic Forms

We need a place on earth, in America, in England, in France, in Spain, in Portugal or in Africa where we can meet History, set up memory and where we can talk to the spirits of slaves and pray for them, because there are three ways to die: lost memory, false memory and real death. We need such a place, we need a Gate of Return.

—JULIEN SINZOGAN

To commemorate the bicentennial of the 1807 British abolition of the transatlantic slave trade, Beninese artist Julien Sinzogan was commissioned to create an installation for the "Unforgettable Truths: The Shadow of Slave Trading on Contemporary Art" exhibit at the Victoria and Albert Museum in London. Acknowledging the haunting architectural structures of the "Gates of No Return" at slave castles, forts, and prisons scarring the West African coast, Sinzogan offered this polemic: "We talk of nothing but Gates of No Return. That is, there's no possibility, no way for those who ended up as slaves and their descendants to look back."

Sinzogan painted the captivating work *Gates of Return* (figure 7) to provide his artistic vision for Afrodiasporic return. In it, he unlocks the symbolic Gates of No Return and transforms them into revolving doors, beckoning Africans dispersed across the diaspora back home. Without succumbing to superficial sentimentality, this painting directly engages with the "unforgettable truth" of the transatlantic slave trade by constructing a visual portal through which descendants of enslaved Africans in the Americas might imagine returning to a long-lost homeland.

Sinzogan's *Gates of Return* wrestles with issues that are central to this book: the complex relationship among the historical memory of transatlantic slavery, its manifold literary and cultural renderings in postslavery literature and culture, and the challenge of apprehending its variegated representations across vast geographies, temporalities, cultures, and languages in the African diaspora. A symmetrical acrylic on canvas triptych, the painting depicts the cyclical motion of departure and return, with the left and right panels arranged spatially like mirror images of each other. The central, narrower panel represents the Gate of Return, aptly hung over the museum doors in the main foyer of the museum, beckoning visitors to cross the threshold to enter the exhibit—and to journey metaphorically back home. While the center of gravity of this immense painting is the symbolic gate for reentry, the two mammoth panels flanking the door depict the horrors of the capture and forced crossing to the Americas.

Moving beyond a merely decorative vision of a Pan-African "right of return" policy, Sinzogan's Yoruba-informed visual narrative highlights the tragic loss of returning spirits. The Yoruba belief in the cyclical movement from the unborn spirit world to this world and back to the spirit world as an ancestor figure is disrupted by slavery: "As long as the ancestors are properly remembered and venerated, all will be well on both sides of the divide, but an ancestor spirit scorned or, worse still, forgotten can wreak havoc on the inhabitants of this world" ("Gates of Return"). What has become of the spirits of those captured and enslaved in the New World?

J. Ọmọṣade Awolalu explains the significance of the spirit of the ancestors and the Egúngún masquerade that is alluded to in this painting:

> The Egúngún is an embodiment of the spirit of a deceased person who is believed to have returned from ọ̀run (the spirit world) to visit his children; hence he is called "ará ọ̀run" (the citizen of heaven) . . . The belief is that a living person who puts on the family Egúngún attire (*agò*) also puts on the spiritual powers of the ancestors whom he represents. In this materialised form, the Egúngún can speak to and pray for the living. (Awolalu 65–66)

The Egúngún figures appear on the left panel of *Gates of Return.* In the foreground, sketches of shackled, seminude male and female figures in shades of black, gray, and white exit the Gates of No Return to board the slave ship. These anonymous, faceless bodies—their backs face the viewer—extend into the infinity of the cascading waves with a vanishing point located deep in the Atlantic Ocean. This artistic subtlety registers as a poignant acknowledgment of the enslaved Africans who vanished during the Middle Passage—dying by suicide, or their sick bodies "disposed" of in the sea.

The ships shown on both the left and right panels are painted faintly, in the same grayscale colors as the African captives. The transparent ships highlight the vibrant red, green, blue, orange, and yellow colors of the traditional garb of the ancestors (Egúngún masquerade dancers), who tower over the enslaved figures in the foreground. Their rich, vibrant attire consumes them, and the viewer cannot discern individual faces as their elaborate costumes blend in with the colorful, high-flying sails billowing above the skeletal outline of the slave ships. The spirits of the enslaved Africans return to the African coastline as brightly adorned Egúngún masqueraders, triumphantly dancing to the drums that dot either side of the gate (Famule). The descendants of those enslaved do not return as strangers but as spirits of ancestors come home at last, remembered and venerated.

Yet Sinzogan complicates a facile, linear narrative of a painful grayscale past of enslavement overwritten by a colorful present and future of liberation. The exquisite colors of the Egúngún masquerade dancers collide with and overlay the transparency of the torturous slave ship and the abhorrent history of captivity on the left panel. As Michelle Wright argues, by denying the binary narrative of slavery-to-freedom progressing along a chronological timeline, Sinzogan provokes the viewer to recognize multiple visual frames and a layering of shapes, forms, and colors. Rather than erasing the horrors of slavery, this scene, which imagines a jubilant African return of the beautifully adorned spirits of the ancestors, requires us to apprehend the intertwined historical strands of the monstrous brutality of enslavement and the possibility of homecoming. As Eltis, Ferrer, Goyal, Hartman, Klein, Murphy, Sharpe, and a host of other scholars have observed, one "unforgettable truth" is that the global slave trade and the brutal afterlife of slavery hardly ended with legislation such as the Slave Trade Act of 1807 or the Emancipation Proclamation.

Gates of Return focuses on slavery's contemporaneous past and present, a temporal simultaneity that appears in literature of the African diaspora through foreshadowing, allusions, and textual echoes. Sinzogan's painting brilliantly illustrates Eyerman's notion of the "present as an unfolding of the past" (162) and Trouillot's gloss that "the past does not exist independently from the present" (151). As Claudia Rankine puts it, "You can't put the past behind you. It's buried in you; it's turned your flesh into its own cupboard" (63). The past burrows into the bone marrow, turning flesh into its hiding place.

Diasporic writers continue to contend with the buriedness of slavery's past, in poetry, prose, art, and song. The image of Africa—often mythologized and romanticized—becomes a focal point, as we saw in chapter 4 with Castro Alves's epic poem "O navio negreiro" [The Slave Ship] and his "Vozes d'África" [Voices of Africa], or in Esteban Montejo's testimonial version of history, which he remembers and relates in *Cimarrón.* As we have seen, the impulse to survive and create undergirds these vastly different literary engagements with trans-atlantic slavery and the legacy of racial violence.

Présence Africaine's provocation to map the literary sum of the monde noir registers as a worthwhile impossibility even as we acknowledge, as Clark argues, that diasporic coherence is elusive.[1] *Afrodiasporic Forms* makes a case for the project of comparative literary analysis in African diaspora studies, reading an archive of heterogenous literary and cultural production from Brazil, the United States, and Cuba—and from the historical periods that preceeded nation formation—that exposes ruptures and the intriguing imprints, withholdings, denials, and absences in the process of making and remaking of the multitudinous forms and genres of slavery. In these plural representations, from the canonical to the kitsch, we grasp the global dimensions of reckoning with modern racial slavery and its refraction through literary and artistic forms and genres of the African diaspora.

Consider the varied representational valences around Black womanhood that emerge, to varying degrees, in each chapter. We witness this in chapter 1 with the racial panic, scopic economies of enslavement, and disruption of the Brazilian slavocratic social order that emerge around Isaura's nearly white enslaved body in Guimarães's nineteenth-century novela and the globally exportable telenovela a century later. The infinite iterative possibilities of the US Mammy cult (chapter 2) highlight how, in contemporary renderings of the mythic figure, notably Kara Walker's *A Subtlety,* she has been reconfigured to oppose her own subjugation. The four-line reference to the pervasive sexual violation of the captive African woman on the slave ship, "the one they called The Guinea Rose," whom the captain and crew "cast lots and fought to lie with" (lines 56–59) in Hayden's "Middle Passage" (chapter 3), and the enslaved mother in Castro Alves's "O navio negreiro," whose breasts released blood instead milk (4.7–9) (chapter 4), likewise underscore disparate diasporic representations. Strikingly, there is the feminization of sugar in Fernando Ortiz's *Contrapunteo,* in which "she" becomes the fictionalized version of a dark woman passing for white (chapter 5), and, in that same chapter, the series of mothers and surrogate mothers in Juan Francisco Manzano's *Autobiografía.* Consider, too, Carolina Maria de Jesus, who dreams and writes a better life for her family out of poverty, and the Black woman performers mentioned in chapters 3 and 5, Billie Holiday and Celia Cruz, who transform the memory of slavery and legacy of racial violence into a performance of poignant beauty on stage.

Afrodiasporic Forms shows how transnational cross section of literary and cultural reverberations of modern racial slavery are inextricably connected to language and, as Brent Hayes Edwards argues, always emerge in translation (7). This translation, broadly conceived, reveals how the multiplicity of Afrodiasporic forms, through and across difference, raises questions regarding the intricacies of language (Can enslaved Africans speak?; What do they sound like?); scopic economies (What does an enslaved person look like?); location (Where have enslaved Africans been transported?; Why are the experiences of African descendants in some locations foregrounded and others silenced?); literacy (How does the enslaved person read and understand the world, given literacy prohibition?; How do we read them and they read us?); and temporality (Are African captives fixed in time?; What occurs in the postslavery moment?), and how are these linguistic nuances of the diaspora resulting from the transatlantic slave trade entangled in complex histories of new African diasporas and concepts of the monde noir (How might we create a summation of Afrodiasporic poetic production?). The "nouvelle somme de poésie du monde noir" approaches infinity.[2]

Notes

Introduction: "Traveling Through Fog"

1. To explore the diasporic connection to Africa as "our starting-place," and the global Black cultural production memorializing transatlantic slavery that proceeds from it, I draw from the buoyant concept of the "monde noir," or "Negro World," as it was translated in the 1960s English editions of *Présence Africaine,* one of the premier Francophone Pan-African journals, founded by Senegalese philosopher and editor Alioune Diop (1910–1980).

2. For an early use of this phrase, see Van Wyck Brooks, "On Creating a Usable Past" (1918), in *Van Wyck Brooks: The Early Years,* edited by Claire Sprague, 219–226.

3. Olakunle George, *African Literature and Social Change,* 48. George argues that the First International Conference of Negro Writers and Artists, which occurred in France in 1956, sponsored by the journal *Présence Africaine,* is one example of a "discursive juncture" within the domain if cultural criticism contemporarily considered "black Atlanticism" (48–49).

4. Marimba Ani discusses her critical term *Maafa,* from the Kiswahili word for "disaster," to delineate what she calls the "dehumanizing circumstance" of the "Afrikan holocaust" and its continuing effects on the African continent and the diaspora (12).

5. Emmanuel Akyeampong, "Africans in the Diaspora" notes that "the nature and composition of the African diaspora have undergone significant changes over time," including both forced migration of enslaved Africans and voluntary, ongoing emigration of Africans throughout the world, and rightly urges us not to "homogenize space and experience in the pre-nineteenth-century African diaspora" when, in addition to African captives, "free Africans travelled the slave routes as sailors, merchants, tourists, and students" (183, 191).

6. Lisa Lowe argues that one of the multivalent "emergent" meanings of intimacies is the "varieties of contacts between laboring peoples," which are "necessary for the production of bourgeois domesticity, as well as the intimacies of captured workers surviving together, the proximity and affinity that gives rise to political, sexual, intellectual collaborations, subaltern revolts and uprisings" (35). See also Paul Gilroy, *The Black Atlantic;* Robin D. G. Kelley, "How the West Was One"; and Michael A. Gomez, *Diasporic Africa: A Reader.*

7. Christel N. Temple, *Literary Spaces,* 20. See also Temple, "Rescuing the Literary in Black Studies" for an illuminating discussion of "the function of literature in the Black studies enterprise" (767).

8. The present study commences in the 1830s, for historiographical and archival reasons. For instance, Nat Turner's rebellion occurred in 1831, and slavery was abolished in the British colonies

in 1833. The 1830s serve as an important point of departure for this book's Afrodiasporic memorial studies of slavery, as the slave trade in the Spanish colonies, by contrast, flourished during this period.

9. See, for example, Rafael Ocasio for a compelling analysis connecting Manzano's "refined mulatto" (*mulato fino*) self-characterization and Costumbrista writing.

10. While Bhabha's introductory essay in *Nation and Narration* focuses specifically on discourses of nation and narration, his analysis of the interplay between ambivalence and liminality in the construction of nation is instructive here for the discussion of diaspora (1–7).

11. Yomaira Figueroa-Vásquez, *Decolonizing Diasporas,* 5. Figueroa-Vásquez relationally reads the literature of Equitorial Guinea and the Hispanophone Caribbean while also grappling with the fractures of domination and with "national, regional, and racial cartographies" (4, 7).

12. This range of configurations of Black being, as Sharpe suggests, riffs on the expansiveness of the prefix *trans-,* such as "translation, transatlantic, transgression, transgender, transformation, transmogrification, transcontinental, transfixed, trans-Mediterranean, transubstantiation" (30).

13. Goyal, "We Need New Diasporas," 641–642. The lens of transatlantic slavery is not intended to silence the new African diasporas of the last century that were not directly implicated in these legacies of slavery, but to show they are bound up together in the entwined legacies of colonization and enslavement. Regarding new waves of African immigrants in the United States, Baffour K. Takyi comments, "Increased immigration from Africa and other parts of the 'black world,' at a time of declining birth rates among native-born Americans of African ancestry, is helping to increase the diversity of the black community in the US" (251). For a discussion of the *longue durée* view of the African diaspora, see Emmanuel Akyeampong, "Africans in the Diaspora: The Diaspora and Africa," 183–215.

14. Aarthi Vadde's concept of "chimeras of form" calls into question "received understandings of coherence rather than affirming them" as a mode of ultimately arriving at "something real, long-standing, and urgent" (36).

15. In this moment of tenderness, Paul D holds the weight of Sethe's breasts after she recounts the story of her "stolen milk" and subsequent brutal whipping while pregnant for reporting the men who sexually abused her (17).

16. See also Mary Ann Doane on the "photographic afterimage" (71).

17. For two different twenty-first-century artistic examples of the corporeal repetitions of the scourged back, shifting gender, time, medium, and scale, see Arthur Jafa's 2017 *Ex-Slave Gordon,* a vacuum-formed plastic sculpture that brings the whipping scars of the well-known 1863 *Scourged Back* photograph first published in *Harper's Weekly* into shocking 3-D topographical formation, and the July/August 2020 *Vanity Fair* cover of Viola Davis, shot by Dario Calmese, the magazine's first Black photographer. Calmese describes his inspiration: "It's definitely not some, 'Oh, look how far we've come. . . . This reference image, for me, it's one that reimagines but also transmutes that pain. It's the transmuting of this gaze, and owning ourselves and owning our own beauty." In the cover photograph, Davis poses with her back toward the camera and left hand on her hip with her face in profile view, echoing Gordon's pose; yet, instead of bearing a map of scars or Sethe's tree, the sumptuously photographed image displays the smooth skin of her back—Davis is a self-proclaimed "dark-skinned Black woman"—as she is seated, adorned in a stunning midnight blue dress, with an impressively round Afro. See Konstantinides, "The First Black Photographer" for the complete Calmese interview. For a comprehensive study of slave ship icons and reimagined images of slavery, including Hank Willis Thomas's *The Chase Mastercard* (2004), which superimposes images

of Gordon's tortured, scarred back and the slave ship sketch onto a Chase credit card, see Finley, *Committed to Memory,* 190.

18. The 1966 edition (no. 57) of the new *Présence Africaine* is an exemplary case study. Its subtitle announces its towering mission: "Revue Culturelle Du Monde Noir" [Cultural Review of the Negro World]. The cover of the volume enacts with quadruplicate multilingual announcements—"New Sum of Poetry from the Negro World," "Nouvelle Somme de Poésie Du Monde Noir," "Nova Soma de Poesia do Mundo Negro," and "Nueva Suma de Poesía del Mundo Negro"—the poetic expression of the collective "Black world," doing much the same as W. E. B. Du Bois's never-realized *Encyclopedia Africana* would have done for "scientific" knowledge. Taking slavery as an organizing principle, I am interested in the multiple ways a transtemporal, transnational, cross-disciplinary literary and cultural review of Black artistic expression might take shape.

19. Monique A. Bedasse coins the term "trodding diaspora" to indicate the Rastafarian sense of *trod* as travel or a journey, particularly physical and spiritual movements between the Caribbean and Africa, from the watery spaces to the terrestrial.

20. One of these geographies that has been privileged within the US context is the space of the plantation, which tends to pervade discussions of the environment of enslaved people's daily lives. In the introduction to the 2019 special issue of *American Literature,* on the plantation and postplantation, Gwen Bergner asserts that the most salient theme in the essays collected is "less the brutality and persistence of the plantation and its permutations than the creative agency black people have deployed despite them" (455).

21. Although I employ the phrase "symbolic sites of slavery" to refer to various geographies and critical cartographic possibilities of the African diaspora, I do so advisedly, aware of the implications and risks of metaphorizing slavery. This book aims to provide aesthetic, formalist readings of texts while also attending to the transtemporal historical event of the Atlantic slave trade involving an estimated 12.7 million Africans forcibly transported to the Americas. Salamishah Tillet, *Sites of Slavery* uses the concept of "sites of slavery," which I have reworked here from her thematic use in relation to post–civil rights African American memory to a more diasporic, geographic focus, playing with *sites* and *sights* as a homophonic pair.

22. In his foundational text, Gilroy continues the maritime metaphors by likening the reading of his book to "embark[ing] on a sea voyage" and famously describes his methodological practice as being "rooted in" and "routed through," later echoed in the anthropological work of James Clifford, ushering in a theoretical reorientation in multiple fields (xi). Matory describes this effect as "reverse flow" and calls for research attentive to "both local meaning and transnational context" (5, 8).

23. Paul Tiyambe Zeleza, "Rewriting the African Diaspora" notes that the "tendency to privilege the Atlantic, or rather the Anglophone, indeed the American branch of the African diaspora" is clear in Gilroy's germinal book (36). See Tölölyan, "Rethinking Diaspora(s)" for a history of the word *diaspora,* from its roots in Greek antiquity to Jewish diaspora as the paradigmatic case, to the Armenian diaspora, to its more modern uses.

24. For a sampling of books with this disciplinary focus, see *Diasporic Africa,* edited by Michael Gomez; *African Diasporas in the New and Old Worlds,* edited by Genevieve Fabre and Klaus Benesch; *African Roots/American Cultures: Africa in the Creation of the Americas,* edited by Sheila Walker; *The African Diaspora: African Origins and New World Identities,* edited by Isidore Okpewho, Carol Boyce Davies, and Ali A. Mazrui; and Brent Hayes Edwards, *The Practice of Diaspora: Literature, Translation, and the Rise of Black Internationalism.*

25. See Warren, 2.

26. I am indebted to the work of Salamishah Tillet, who brilliantly develops this term "sites of slavery" in her book *Sites of Slavery: Citizenship and Racial Democracy in the Post-Civil Rights Imagination,* drawing from the classic, oft-referenced theories of Pierre Nora, *Les Lieux de mémoire* and Toni Morrison, "The Site of Memory." These geographic categories, from literature to film, monument, sculpture, and song, are unevenly valued and circulated within diaspora studies. In describing the diaspora, I use the convention of speaking of the continent of Africa, though I do not wish to suggest an equivalency to the geographic regions of the Caribbean archipelago or the country of Brazil, or to the United States, nor to collapse the immense diversity (of resources, languages, nations, traditions, cultures, and literatures) of the African continent or suggest an undifferentiated singularity or essentialism, as was the troubling case in African historiography for nearly the first half of the twentieth century. While remaining aware of the "imaginary" nature of the nation-state and the linguistic and cultural complexity of each site, I simplified the units of comparison by focusing on three countries in particular (Brazil, Cuba, and the United States). Although, for the sake of sentence structure, I occasionally use the adjective *American* to refer to literature from the United States, one of the central aims of this research is to displace the primacy of the United States in studies of the Americas. Moreover, I use *African* to refer to various writers and theorists as a collective, though I am aware of the vastly different cultural, social, linguistic, and political contexts of each of the nations that compose the continent.

27. For comparative emancipation time lines, see Bergad.

28. Wainaina's article is a widely circulated parodic critique of the generalizing condescension often found in writings about Africa.

29. See Essien, Brazilian-African Diaspora in Ghana.

30. I am interested in how the notion of "collective memory" or "cultural memory" plays out across the African diaspora. See Paul Ricoeur, *Memory, History, Forgetting;* Michel-Rolph Trouillot, *Silencing the Past;* and Maurice Halbwachs, *On Collective Memory.*

31. In *Afro-Fabulations,* Tavia Nyong'o speculates on the ways in which "black aesthetics and expressivity may have always already been queer" (4). Omise'eke Natasha Tinsley, "Black Atlantic, Queer Atlantic" expounds on the queerness of the Black Atlantic: "Yet regardless of whether intimate sexual contact took place between enslaved Africans in the Atlantic or after landing, relationships between shipmates read as queer relationships" in the sense of "praxis of resistance," which emerges from "loving your own kind when your kind was supposed to cease to exist" (199).

32. For a discussion of nonlinear diasporic frameworks, see Nyong'o, *Afro-Fabulations,* 4; and Michelle M. Wright, *Physics of Blackness,* 37–65.

33. As Stuart Hall, "Cultural Identity and Diaspora" reminds us, "We all write and speak from a particular place and time, from a history and a culture which is specific. What we say is always 'in context,' positioned" (222). Scholars like Patricia Hill Collins and William Merrill Decker, for example, have foregrounded their positionality in their work.

34. While this book does not engage extensively with the vast historiography and theoretical work of Francophone studies of memory and slavery, particularly the rich scholarship on Haiti, this would be a crucial critical voice to bring more often into cross-disciplinary conversation with diasporic literary studies in other languages. We find serious attention to the stakes of diasporic literacy in the work of scholars such as Toyin Falola, Gwendolyn Midlo Hall, Marcus Wood, Ana Lucia Araújo, and Michelle Commander.

35. Although Stephen Best employs "wanton" specifically in the context of "the idea of the fugitive," I too draw upon the significations of this term, denoting "unrestrained," "rebellious," and

"ungoverned," to convey a diasporic archive of slavery that strays in multiple directions at once and refuses to cohere.

1. "White Skin, Black Slavery"

1. Bernardo Guimarães, *A Escrava Isaura, Romance* (São Paulo, Difusão Cultural do Livro, 2006). All citations refer to this edition of the text. Translations are mine unless otherwise noted.

2. Statistics can be found on the *Memória Globo* website, memoriaglobo.globo.com, which records historical information about all of its productions. While they share common roots, the main differences between the soap opera of the United States and Britain, on the one hand, and the telenovela of Latin America, on the other, are duration (telenovelas typically last four to seven months, emphasizing closure of the narrative structure, whereas US and British soap operas may continue for decades); broadcast time (telenovelas are broadcast during prime-time evening hours, during family dinnertime, while US and British soap operas are broadcast during the daytime and are targeted toward women viewers); and natural settings (telenovelas film scenes in nature, outdoors, and on actual locations, while US soap operas tend to rely on studio sets). There are, of course, Spanish-language networks based in the United States, such as Univision and Telemundo, both of which import telenovelas from the Latin American world and create original programming marketed toward US-born Latinos. For more of these distinctions, see Nico Vink, *Telenovela and Emancipation,* especially page 11 and chapter 6. As is general practice, the terms *telenovela* and its abbreviated form, *novela,* are used interchangeably to refer to these television narratives. To avoid confusion with novella or short novel, which describes Guimarães's original text, I only use the term *telenovela* throughout to reference the television production.

3. Describing the creative collaboration between Brazilian and Chinese film producers, Lucélia Santos noted that Chinese filmmakers "queriam ter a escrava Isaura numa história deles" (wanted to have escrava Isaura in one of their stories). "'Escrava Isaura,' originou projeto," E7.

4. According to a 1997 *Variety* article, *A Escrava Isaura* was the "first foreign TV show to enter China after the Cultural Revolution." Bill Hinchberger, "Actress Has Int'l Spirit." Another article claims that the telenovela had more than 500 million views in China and that viewers in Hungary "collected the equivalent of $75,000 and sent it to the Brazilian embassy to purchase the heroine's freedom." Ross Anderson, "Betty the Latin American Superstar." See also Robert Stam, *Tropical Multiculturalism,* 78; Artur da Távola, *A telenovela brasileira;* Ismael Fernandes, *Memória da telenovela brasileira* ; and Joel Zito Araújo, *A negação do Brasil.*

5. It is also reported that the Cuban government suspended the rationing of energy so that the public would not miss any episodes. *Toronto Star,* February 27, 1990: B3; Vink, *Telenovela and Emancipation,* 21. See also memoriaglobo.globo.com.

6. See also Kate Baldwin, "Montezuma's Revenge," 285–300.

7. For a sampling of studies focusing on the Latin American telenovela, see Thomas Tufte; Jesús Martín-Barbero; José Ignacio Cabrujas; Samira Campadelli; Michèle Mattelart; Jose Marques de Melo; Ana M. Lopez; and Robert C. Allen.

8. Harold E. Hinds Jr., "A Holistic Approach to the Study of Popular Culture ," 164.

9. Both Vink, in *Telenovela and Emancipation,* and Ibsen Martínez, in "Romancing the Globe," argue that these telenovelas tend to target socioeconomically disadvantaged communities, while Venezuelan author Arturo Uslar Pietri derided the immensely popular genre as "the opium of the poor" (Martínez 53).

10. For example, some versions of the telenovela available on YouTube are overdubbed in Russian for TV-6-Moskva, with the Portuguese language audible faintly in the background and with English subtitles. I obtained from an independent seller on eBay a complete copy of the series *La esclava Isaura* in Spanish. Most of the episodes in the original Portuguese are posted on YouTube.

11. As João José Reis and Flávio dos Santos Gomes explain, the African influence in Brazil is apparent in "sua agricultura, culinária, religião, língua, música, artes, arquitetura . . . a lista é longa e já estamos cansados de ouvi-la" (her architecture, cuisine, religion, language, music, art, arquitecture . . . the list is long and we are already tired of hearing it) (9). This mock exhaustion with repeatedly hearing the litany of African influences in Brazilian culture underscores the embeddedness of this concept in cultural consciousness. See also, for example, Elisa Larkin Nascimento's edited volume, *A matriz africana no mundo.*

12. I call upon the theorizations of Beverley Skeggs and Judith Roof on scopic economies to interrogate the politics of looking and being seen, viewing, evaluating, (re)valuing, and assessing racialized, gendered bodies as a form of economic, social, cultural, and political capital, dynamics particularly resonant during slavery's era. Roof, for example, argues that "gender regimes have a scopic dimension insofar as genders are modes of both unconscious and conscious display" (171). See Skeggs; and Roof 23–34, 171–195.

13. This censorship was in effect from 1964 to 1985, and writers of many of Globo's telenovelas were forced to change words and plotlines to project Christian morals and political stability.

14. On the untranslatability of the elusive Portuguese and Galician word *saudade,* see, for instance, Jasmine Garsd, "Saudade: An Untranslatable, Undeniably Potent Word," which cites seventeenth-century author Francisco Manuel de Mello's definition of the term as "a pleasure you suffer, an ailment you enjoy." See also George Monteiro, *There's No Word for Saudade.*

15. For an in-depth analysis of these images, see Wood, *Black Milk;* Sadlier, 112–114; and Araújo, *Brazil through French Eyes.*

16. Brandão, "Mutantes e vampiros atacam clássicos nacionais." Similarly, author Pedro Vieira transformed Machado de Assis's classic *Memórias póstumas de Brás Cubas* [The Posthumous Memoirs of Brás Cubas] into *Memórias desmortas de Brás Cubas* [The Undead Memoirs of Brás Cubas].

17. Often these texts are called literary "mash-ups," a term also used frequently in the world of new media.

18. For an insightful study on this notion of "culture under capital" and Marxism in the twenty-first century, see Mathias Nilges, 66–89.

19. For more extensive biographical information, see Paes and Moisés, *Pequeno dicionário de literatura brasileira,* 181–183; Verity Smith, *Encyclopedia of Latin American Literature,* 396–397; Stephen M. Hart, *A Companion to Latin American Literature,* 118–119; and Haberly, "The Brazilian Novel from 1850 to 1900."

20. Norwood Andrews Jr., 233–272. See also Paes and Moisés, 182.

21. Sayers, *O negro* (316–317), for instance, surmises that Guimarães appropriated the entire Isaura in flight to the North (Recife) and fugitive section from chapter 8, "Eliza's Escape," in Harriet Beecher Stowe's *Uncle Tom's Cabin.*

22. Sollors, *Anthology of Interracial Literature,* 8–53. Perhaps it resonates more strongly with the birthmark in novels like Pauline Hopkins's serialized novel *Of One Blood* (1902–1903), in which the biracial characters all share a "lotus-lily mark" to indicate their mixed-race status (429).

23. Isaura's description of despair here invites an association with Cain.

24. Several passages from Nathaniel Hawthorne's *The Scarlet Letter* (1850) intimate similar scopic anxieties of overexposure and shame around a sign on the body legible to the public:

> But the point which drew all eyes and, as it were, transfigured the wearer—so that both men and women, who had been familiarly acquainted with Hester Prynne, were now impressed as if they beheld her for the first time—was that Scarlet Letter, so fantastically embroidered and illuminated upon her bosom. It had the effect of a spell, taking her out of the ordinary relations with humanity and enclosing her in a sphere by herself. (61)

> The unhappy culprit sustained herself as best a woman might, under the heavy weight of a thousand unrelenting eyes, all fastened upon her and concentered at her bosom. (64)

> But in their great mercy and tenderness of heart, they have doomed Mistress Prynne to stand only a space of three hours on the platform of the pillory, and then and thereafter, for the remainder of her natural life, to wear a mark of shame upon her bosom. (69)

25. There is an obvious parallel here with Harriet Jacobs's 1861 *Incidents in the Life of a Slave Girl,* and the marital choice of one white man over another provides, if not agency, then a way to exit the most pernicious domestic environment. See Gomes 167–171.

26. Callaway, 91, note 131.

27. Maria Manuel Lisboa advances the argument that Isaura is forced from the slave market to the marriage market and notes the racial identitarian sacrifices Isaura must make in this exchange: "At the end she is stripped of her black heritage (whitened by marriage to [Álvaro]), and, by implication, deprived also of other dimensions of freedom and right to identity, namely the freedom to be black and a slave, and the right to a black identity without stigma or oppression" (396–397).

28. Sollors, *Neither Black nor White yet Both,* 127, 202, 211, 220–245, 333–334. See also Raimon; Bogle; and Fredrickson, 277. For one of the first critical treatments of the "tragic mulatto" stereotype, see Sterling A. Brown, *Negro Poetry and Drama* , 145. For the specifics of the stereotype in the Brazilian context, see Teófilo de Queiroz Júnior, *Preconceito de cor e a mulata na literatura brasileira;* and Giovana Xavier, 78–82.

29. Hanciau, "A representação da mulata na literatura brasileira."

30. These are typical plots one finds in narratives of interracial unions. For an extensive sampling of these stories, see Sollors, *Anthology of Interracial Literature.* One wonders to what extent the tragic mulatto becomes the "bela mulata" (beautiful mulatto woman) stereotype in the Brazilian context, in which *mulata* represents an inoffensive description of the mixed-race woman whose beauty and sun-kissed, perpetually tanned intermediary skin color is glorified above all other versions of femininity as the standard of beauty and sensuality. The female protagonists of many of Jorge Amado's novels solidify this stereotype. For example, the actress Sônia Braga played the eponymous Gabriela in the 1975 telenovela adaption of his famous 1958 novel, *Gabriela, cravo e canela* [Gabriela, Clove and Cinnamon]. There is the famous Rio de Janeiro carnival song by João de Barro e Antônio Almeida (1948), praising the beauty of the *mulata:* "Branca é branca, preta é preta / Mas a mulata é a tal, é a tal" (The white woman is white, the black woman is black / But the *mulata* is the real thing, the real thing). For an insightful analysis of this stereotype, see Patai; and Mendes.

31. Joel Zito Araújo, *A negação do Brasil* 45.

32. Although Isaura's actions do not appear to be motivated by the internal conflict of racial belonging, perhaps because notions of "race" in Brazil were already more pliant than in the United

States, departing from the definitional limits of the tragic mulatto stereotype, the market success of this particular tale of slavery confirms Brown's notion of "race flattery" as observed by Sollors. Brown would likely not be surprised by its commercial success, although he would perhaps be a little miffed.

33. Brown, "Negro Character as Seen by White Authors," 179–203.

34. Interestingly, in 1978, just one year after the final broadcast of the telenovela, Black activists established November 20 as the Dia Nacional da Consciência Negra (National Day of Black Consciousness), commemorating the date the hero of the Quilombo dos Palmares, Zumbi, was assassinated and celebrating African origins and the commitment to fight against oppression, racism, and prejudice. For more on this celebration and the movement, see www.palmares.gov.br; and Sansone.

35. Sollors, Neither Black nor White yet Both, 232.

36. For examples of the literary figure of the quadroon, see, for example, Lydia Maria Child, "The Quadroons" (1842); Henry Wadsworth Longfellow, "The Quadroon Girl" (1842); "The Quadroon's Story" chapter in Harriet Beecher Stowe's *Uncle Tom's Cabin* (1852); William Wells Brown, *Clotel; or, The President's Daughter* (1853); and Mayne Reid, *The Quadroon* (1856). For an analysis of these texts, see Sollors, *Neither Black nor White Yet Both,* 208–219. In these literary narratives, there is often one lasting physical remnant belying the "black blood" of the young woman in question. Consider this famous line about the appearance of Xarifa, the ill-fated mixed-race child and daughter of Rosalie, in Child's short story "The Quadroons": "The iris of her large, dark eye had the melting, mezzotinto outline, which remains *the last vestige of African ancestry,* and gives that plaintive expression, so often observed, and so appropriate to that docile and injured race" (Sollors, *Interracial Literature,* 233, my emphasis). Although Child refers to both mother and daughter as quadroons, or one-quarter black, the text suggests that Rosalie's enslaved mother was herself biracial, since Rosalie herself is referred to as a quadroon, therefore technically making her daughter, Xarifa, an "octoroon," according to the racial classifications of the time. In the telenovela version of *A Escrava Isaura,* the heroine possesses no such legible phenotypic African vestige.

37. For more on this motif, see "The Bluish Tinge in the Half-Moon," in Sollors, *Neither Black nor White yet Both,* 142–161.

38. The verb *retirar* corresponds to the English verbs "to withdraw," "to draw back," "to pull back," or "to pull away," while the intransitive form, *retirar-se,* means "to retreat" or "to leave." I use "migrants" as a convenient translation of *retirantes,* but it loses the sense of hopelessness in literary uses of *retirante.* For an insightful discussion of the distinction between *migrante* and *retirante* in the work of José Américo and Jorge Amado, see Sudha Swarnakar.

39. This captivating opening refrain, "Lerê lerê le rê rê rê rê rê," has seeped into the collective consciousness of the Brazilian people and fans of the show worldwide. Thirty-five years later, Essinger's article in the Brazilian newspaper *O Globo* calls the composer, Waltel Branco, "the creator of the 'lerê lerê'" and observes that "o lerê" has become a colloquialism for tiring, difficult work.

40. Although the enslaved Yoruba in Brazil were grouped together under the term *Nagô,* Olatunji Ojo notes that "sub-ethnic differences in the Yoruba homeland re-echoed in Bahia and manifested themselves in the survival of identities such as those of Oyo, Ijesa, Ketu, Egba, and Ijebu among others" (54). *Nagô* was also used in the French colony of Saint-Domingue (present-day Haiti). The strongest example of a pan-Yoruba identity around the Nagô designation occurred with the slave uprising in Bahia in 1835. See also Law, "Ethnicity and the Slave Trade"; Lovejoy and Ojo; and Reis, *Slave Rebellion in Brazil.*

41. In *Introdução à História da Literatura Brasileira* (1882), Sílvio Romero describes the funda-

mental combination of "três fatores" (three factors) or three races that are necessary for an understanding of Brazilian literature and national identity.

42. Strikingly missing from the lithographs displayed in the title sequence in many versions is the element of violence in the life of enslaved Brazilians, or scenes of "slavery pornography," such as the prolonged whipping scenes in *Roots*. Debret documented this violence in other ethnographic illustrations. In my fourth chapter, on the pillory and the memory of slavery in Brazilian literature, I return to the art of Debret to examine the shocking *L'exécution de la Punition du Fouet* [Execution of the Punishment of the Whip] and other paintings of violence. In some imported versions of the telenovela, however, the opening credits included three images of violence and punishment, including *L'exécution de la Punition du Fouet*, an image of enslaved Africans in stocks, and one of a man crouching down in the moment before he bears the lash of the whip.

43. See, for example, *Famille d'un Chef Camacan se préparant pour une Fête* [Family of a Camacan Chief Preparing for a Festival] or *Danse d'indiens de la mission Saint-Jose* [Indians Dancing at the São José Mission].

44. Despite the complexities of racial casting, the telenovela produced two breakout international stars: the lead actress, then-newcomer Lucélia Santos, who played the titular role and in 1985 was the first foreign actress to win the Prêmio Águia de Ouro (Golden Eagle Award) for Chinese television, awarded by popular vote, for her acting performance, and Rubens de Falco, the legendary actor who portrayed the diabolical and lecherous *fazenda* owner, Leôncio, whose indelible performance as one of the most rancorous villains to grace the small screen rivals the best dramatic performances of Shakespeare's character of Iago. According to *Memória Globo*, after the broadcast of the telenovela in China in 1985, 500 million copies of Bernardo Guimarães's text, translated into Chinese, were sold. See Hu.

45. This narrative structure is vaguely reminiscent of Victor Séjour's play *La tireuse des cartes*.

46. Isaura's mother rejected the sexual advances of Comendador Almeida, who then banished her to hard field labor. There, Juliana was rescued by Miguel, the Portuguese *feitor*, who fathered her child, Isaura. Unfortunately, when the comendador found out, he fired Miguel, and Juliana died shortly after childbirth.

47. Although Emily A. Owens's analysis of consent focuses on the US legal framework, the inability of an enslaved woman to consent to sex and reproductive labor holds true in the systems of slavery across the Americas. See also Fuentes; Jessica Marie Johnson; Carneiro; and Joshua Bennett.

48. Nearly twenty-five years earlier, a Vera Cruz major studio film, *Sinhá Moça*, brought the period directly before abolition of slavery to the big screen and attempted to tell the story from the perspective of both the enslaved and the enslavers. For more on race in Brazilian cinema, and this film in particular, see Stam 138–150. *Sinhá Moça* was adapted into a telenovela in 1986, patterned after *A Escrava Isaura* and also starring Lucélia Santos.

2. Subtle Resistance

1. Throughout this chapter, I use *A Subtlety* and *Marvelous Sugar Baby* interchangeably to refer to the sugar-coated sculpture. The Mammy monument proposal bill (S. 4119) was first introduced to Congress on December 8, 1922, by Senator John Sharp Williams (1854–1932), a Democrat from Mississippi. It was not until January 1923, however, that Charles Manly Stedman (1841–1930), from North Carolina, introduced an identical bill to the House of Representatives and delivered the monologue referenced here.

2. In response to critical reaction to her use of racist imagery, Walker, "Un-Private Collection" asks, "What happens when you, yourself, an artist, claims some agency over these images?" Walker's work also includes drawings, watercolors, and projections.

3. I use the term "floating signifier" to refer to the emptiness of the Mammy sign. See Stuart Hall, "Race: The Floating Signifier." See also Claude Levi-Strauss, especially this passage explaining the "signifier-surfeit": "So, in man's effort to understand the world, he always disposes of a surplus of signification" and also the explication of the "floating signifier" as "the disability of all finite thought (but also the surety of all art, all poetry, every mythic and aesthetic invention)" (62–63).

4. See Peterson, 21; and Carol E. Henderson, *America and the Black Body,* 17.

5. For three book-length projects focused exclusively on the figure of the Mammy, see McElya; Wallace-Sanders, *Mammy;* and Charlotte Hawkins Brown. See also Lisa M. Anderson; Patricia A. Turner; Corbould; Trudier Harris; Jewell; Manring; and Harris-Perry.

6. Walker has remarked that the "subtlety" usage also plays on the notion of medieval "subtleties" or "sotiltees," which were special small dishes, often disguised to resemble something else, to delight and entertain during a feast. These subtleties often were not intended to be consumed. As is noted in many of the handwritten medieval cookery manuscripts, "The most visually alluring pieces at the table were special sugar sculptures know as sotiltees (or subtleties). These sculptures came in all sorts of curious forms—castles, ships, famous philosophers, or scenes from fables. Sotiltees were also known as 'warners,' as they were served at the beginning of a banquet to 'warn' (or notify) the guests of the approaching dinner." Bovey, "Middle Ages." This tradition continued into the early modern period.

7. "Through a Sugar Refinery," 607–609. A summary of the intricate sugar refinement process details a fascinating transformation in color from "bone black" to "pure white," adding another intriguing, subtle layer to Walker's playful color reversals in *A Subtlety.* See also Dunlap; and Cardwell. For a stunning photographic archive of the iconic refinery, see Raphaelson.

8. "Creative Time Presents Kara Walker." In 2019, Walker reflected that the team construction of *A Subtlety* "was a little too removed from my hand" (Mitter).

9. The exhibition was open on Fridays, Saturdays, and Sundays from May 10 through July 6, 2014. A total of 130,554 visitors attended. Social media images show crowds numbering in the thousands, with lines wrapped around the block.

10. For the art historical contexts and major contributions of each of these artists, see Michael D. Harris, 83–124; Sharon F. Patton, 183–210; Farrington, 168; and Gwendolyn DuBois Shaw, 31–36. For insightful readings of Faith Ringgold's work, see Wallace-Sanders, *Skin Deep, Spirit Strong;* and Kimberly Juanita Brown.

11. The first wave of subversive Aunt Jemimas include, among others, Jeff Donaldson, *Aunt Jemima and the Pillsbury Doughboy* (1963); Joe Overstreet, *New Jemima* (1964); Murray DePillars, *Aunt Jemima* (1968); Jon Onye Lockard, *No More* (1972); and Betye Saar, *The Liberation of Aunt Jemima* (1972). These remarkable examples reconfigure Aunt Jemima into an empowered, rebellious figure and include imagery of active resistance, often alluding to violent (sometimes rifle-toting) retaliation against her white enslavers. Faith Ringgold's 1983 quilt narrative, *Who's Afraid of Aunt Jemima?,* also reimagines the advertising icon. Notably, it was Saar who embarked on a letter-writing campaign after pronouncing Walker's work "revolting" and "a form of betrayal to the slaves, particularly women and children; that it was basically for the amusement and the investment of the white art establishment." PBS Video, *I'll Make Me a World.* The pressing concern about whether

Walker's art reinforces and perpetuates rather than transgresses derogatory images is commonly posed by her critics and detractors. For Mammy's advertising image makeover, see Staples.

12. Keizer, "Gone Astray," 1671. In addition to Keizer, scholars such as Glenda Carpio, Lisa E. Farrington, Michael D. Harris, Amber Musser, Tavia Nyong'o, Rebecca Peabody, and Christina Sharpe, to name a few, have written compellingly and extensively on the postmodern sensibilities, flesh, black female sexuality, fabulation, and "postmemorial" aspects of Walker's art.

13. Marshall, 21.

14. For an excellent comparative study of slavery's visual archive in North America and Brazil, see Marcus Wood, *Black Milk,* which correlates the popular Mãe Preta figure in Brazil to the Black Mammy figure in the United States. Wood notes that sculptural art depicting Mãe Preta often represents her as a fertility goddess, Iemanjá, the goddess of the sea in the Afro-Brazilian Candomblé religion, displaying ample breasts, through which the Black wet nurse becomes "goddess of mammary abundance" (435). In addition, Mãe Preta is presented as a Black Madonna with child.

15. Stedman. All quotes are from this text. For an excellent historical overview of the proposal, see Joan Marie Johnson.

16. Consider contemporary controversies, debates, and occurrences concerning the fate of the Confederate flag and monuments, including, for example, the 2015 removal of the Confederate flag from the South Carolina State House grounds following twenty-one-year-old white supremacist gunman Dylann Roof's murder of nine African American parishioners inside the historic Emanuel African Methodist Episcopal Church; the 2017 nighttime removal of the Liberty Place Monument, which commemorated white citizens' attempts to thwart Reconstruction government in New Orleans, Louisiana; the 2017 white supremacist Unite the Right rally in Charlottesville, Virginia, held to protest the removal of a Confederate General Robert E. Lee statue; and the sixty Confederate monuments toppled or removed in the wake of the killing of George Floyd in 2020. See, for an overview, Karen L. Cox; "Whose Heritage?"; and Burnett and McDaniel.

17. See, for example, "'Mammy' Story of Gassaway Starts Protest." See also "Senate OK's 'Mammy' Monument, Insults Race"; "Mammy Statue Disgraceful Insult"; and "Oppose Monument."

18. As Amy Louise Wood notes in a footnote to *Lynching and Spectacle,* "Although over sixteen antilynching bills were written in the early 1920s, only the Dyer bill reached a vote; it passed in the House but was blocked in the Senate. Lynching opponents were more successful in the mid-1930s, however, as a number of bills came to votes and two passed the House. Again, their bills failed to overcome Senate filibustering" (304).

19. Sollors, Neither Black nor White yet Both, 278.

20. Bill "Bojangles" Robinson (May 25, 1878–November 25, 1949), descended from enslaved grandparents, was a famous African American tap dancer and actor who starred in vaudeville, musicals, and several films with Shirley Temple. Audiences remember his memorable line in *The Little Colonel* (1935), delivered while teaching Shirley Temple to dance: "Now, honey, all you gotta do is listen with your feet." He was known for his facial expressions—typically a huge, fixed smile and bright eyes—and complicated footwork of skipping and tapping up and down a flight of stairs during his dance routines. Despite his success as a dancer, Robinson never learned to read or write and, after giving away much of his fortune to the needy, he died penniless at the age of seventy-one. A December 12, 1949, *Life* magazine article, "Goodby to Bojangles," reported that forty-five thousand people attended his funeral. In modern usage, *Bojangles* is a derogatory term (much like *Mammy* or *Uncle Tom*) to describe an African American who appeases or "performs" in front of

white audiences in order to achieve success and acceptance. See Haskins and Mitgang; and Marks and Edkins.

21. Lynchings spiked during the period after Reconstruction, with more than 150 reported in 1892. "Lynchings: By Year and Race."

22. "'Mammy' Story of Gassaway Starts Protest."

23. "Old Mammy Stuff."

24. "Black Mammies."

25. "While Rome Burns."

26. "Senate OK's 'Mammy' Monument"; "Mammy Statue Disgraceful Insult"; "Oppose Monument."

27. "'Mammy' Statue Not Race Issue."

28. "Mammy."

29. "A Monument That Mammy'd Like To View."

30. "'Mammy' Statue Not Race Issue."

31. These critics have included Betye Saar, Faith Ringgold, Howardena Pindell, and Juliette Bowles, among others. See Gwendolyn DuBois Shaw; and Keizer, "Gone Astray in the Flesh" for an illuminating discussion.

32. Walker's art titles are in conversation with Glenn Ligon's *Untitled* series from *Narratives* (1993), which also riffs on nineteenth-century frontispieces.

33. Throughout this chapter, I employ the gender pronouns *she* and *her* to personify *A Subtlety* in her embodied representation as a female and feminine figure.

34. The foregrounding of the large breasts also echoes the breast-feeding imagery prevalent in Walker's earlier silhouette work, including *A Means to an End . . . A Shadow Drama in Five Acts* (1995) and *The End of Uncle Tom and the Grand Allegorical Tableau of Eva in Heaven* (1995).

35. In many ways, Walker reworks one of her earlier cyclorama silhouette pieces, *The End of Uncle Tom,* which illustrates a series of interconnected suckling Mammy figures, which Walker describes as a metaphor for her "constant need to suckle from history, as though history could be seen as a seemingly endless supply of mother's milk represented by the big black mammy of old." Sharpe, *Monstrous Intimacies,* 161. See also Roberts, for an informative analysis of infant mortality rates linked to malnutrition and disease due to the inability of breast-feeding enslaved women to care for their children because they were forced to labor in the fields.

36. See Abdur-Rahman, 163, for a thought-provoking discussion of nineteenth-century medical discourses and the black body. See also Marcus Wood, 2, for a fascinating reading of the correlation between "Black milk" and "slave mother's milk."

37. Alice Randall's *The Wind Done Gone* (2001), an "unauthorized parody" of Margaret Mitchell's *Gone with the Wind* (1936), cleverly debunks the notion of Mammy's asexuality by retelling the original narrative from the point of view of a new protagonist, Cynara, the illegitimate child of Mammy and Planter, the father of Scarlett O'Hara, who is referred to as Other in Randall's text.

38. With the signifier of the handkerchief tied around her forehead, the *Marvelous Sugar Baby* recuperates silenced histories, with her facial features visually signaling sub-Saharan African heritage, reinscribing the oft-debated missing nose of the Egyptian Sphinx while also referencing the tradition of Black scholars citing ancient Egyptian civilization (Kemet) as source and evidence of black genius and anodyne to anti-Black racial prejudice. Gomez, *Reversing Sail* points out that a long tradition of scholars—from nineteenth-century thinkers (David Walker and Frederick Douglass) to early twentieth-century scholars (W. E. B. Du Bois, Carter G. Woodson, St. Clair Drake) to

Cheikh Anta Diop and later Afrocentrists—consider the illustrious civilizations of Egypt, Nubia, and Ethiopia "exemplars of black accomplishment and creativity" (7–8). See Diop for scientific research on the history of precolonial Africa and the origins of civilization, which counters prevailing racial designations and contends that "ancient Egyptians were Negroes" (xiv). One recalls, too, Du Bois's famous pronouncement in "Of Our Spiritual Strivings," in *The Souls of Black Folk,* about the flitting "shadow of a mighty Negro past" encoded in "the tale of Ethiopia the Shadowy and of Egypt the Sphinx," which represents the ultimate striving, that is, "to be a co-worker in the kingdom of culture" (9). Afrocentrists likewise locate in Kemet, or ancient Egypt, glorious evidence of a rich and varied precolonial African history. See also Keita.

39. See Gomez, *Reversing Sail;* and Fabre, "Slave Ship Dance."

40. For more on the terrors of the Middle Passage, the slave ship, and its media representations, see Smallwood; Rediker; Mustakeem; and Green.

41. For a captivating discussion of performance, Black women's bodies, "ontological ambiguity," and the concept of "Mammy memory," see McMillan, 24–34.

42. An oft-cited example is the tragic life of the Khoikhoi woman Saartjie Baartman, pejoratively labeled the "Hottentot Venus," who was exhibited in Europe to display her anatomy in the early nineteenth century and whose genitalia remained locked in glass jars on display in a French museum until her remains were finally repatriated to South Africa in 2002.

43. For excellent theories on the stakes of trauma, art, and memory, see, for example, Joseph A. Young; and Caruth, *Unclaimed Experience.*

44. Pinckney recalls the surprise of his experience viewing and walking around *A Subtlety:* "And as you walked around the rear of the Mammy figure, maybe expecting a big fig leaf or a blank, neutral area, there were the folds of a huge vulva. It was beautiful that Walker had not lost her nerve" (57).

45. Act XII, Laws of Virginia, December 1662. See Hening 170. For more on the significance of this 1662 law concerning slavery, hereditary, kinship, and property, see, for example, Gwendolyn DuBois Shaw 61; Abdur-Rahman 35; Carby 31; and Spillers, "Mama's Baby," 75–76.

46. For a sampling of historical perspectives of sugar and the slave trade, see Eltis, Lewis, and Richardson, 673–700; Carrington; and Dunn.

47. Led by Nadia Williams, Black women later planned and organized the "We Are Here" event to promote the attendance of people of color at the exhibit; see, for example, Jamilah King. For a book-length examination of this topic, see also Cooks.

48. Creative Time created #KaraWalkerDomino to create a digital space for viewers to engage with *A Subtlety.* Part of their social media marketing campaign was a dedicated "Digital Sugar Baby" page on their website, where visitors could share photos using the hashtag to create "an interactive 3D version of Kara Walker's marvelous artwork!" and an evolving "living tribute" to her work.

49. For a synopsis of the "politics of spectatorship" around the piece, see Russell.

50. bell hooks, *Black Looks,* 4, 7. See also Hobbs, 110.

51. See Saal for an insightful blog post situating the public work in its historical context, referencing sugar, capitalism, and Mammy iconography, with numerous theoretical interventions, including those from bell hooks and Vincent Brown.

52. For the complete notebook sketches, see creativetime.org.

53. See also Kara Walker, "Sweet Talk."

54. The *Oxford English Dictionary* traces an early literary reference to a "mammy" in John Skelton's 1523 *A Goodly Garlande or Chapelet of Laurell,* where it denotes one's mother, without racial

designation. It was not until nineteenth-century texts set in the US South that *mammy* strictly refers to African American women caring for white children.

55. For an instructive discussion of narrative voice, see Ursin, 91.

56. For a brilliant reading of the politics of breast-feeding in this text, see Davies. Basu also offers an analysis of how the interracial intimacy between mother and infant displaces the transgression of interracial heterosexual desire, and perhaps even lesbian desire between Rufel and Dessa.

57. Interestingly, there is a body of scholarship around nineteenth-century division of reproductive labor and breast-feeding practices that verifies that more white women were breast-feeding their own babies than the Mammy myth or Old Plantation southern lore would suggest. See, for starters, Weiner; and McMillen.

58. As noted earlier, another subversive permutation of the Mammy motif related to practices of lactation can be found in an image in Kara Walker's *The End of Uncle Tom* (1995). Rendered in Walker's characteristic cutout silhouette style, this image shows a group of three women and a child simultaneously breast-feeding one another, playing with the notion of Mammy as wet nurse and the multidirectional sexual desire in the setting of the antebellum South. For more on the controversy generated by this image, see Seidl, 24–39. For an insightful close reading of this image, see Gwendolyn DuBois Shaw, 47–53. For an excellent discussion of the deconstruction of Mammy mythology in the art of Robert Colescott and Kara Walker, see Carpio, 140–190.

3. "Black Flesh After Flame"

1. For literary, historical, and photographic studies of lynching as US white supremacist "communal rituals," "execution rituals," and "a family affair, a ritual celebration of white supremacy," see, for example, Jacquelyn Hall; Cone; Trudier Harris, *Exorcising Blackness;* Goldsby; Koritha Mitchell, *Living with Lynching;* Rushdy, *American Lynching;* Gunning; James Allen; and Barnes.

2. See also Raboteau.

3. According to Margolick, *Strange Fruit: Biography of a Song,* the poem "Strange Fruit" first appeared as "Bitter Fruit" in the *New York Teacher* in January 1937. Billie Holiday's account in her autobiography, *Lady Sings the Blues,* which many critics consider a greatly embellished characterization of her life, implicitly argues that Lewis Allan wrote the song especially for her and that she even had a hand in writing it: "It was during my stint at Café Society that a song was born which became my personal protest—'Strange Fruit.' The germ of the song was in a poem written by Lewis Allen [*sic*]. I first met him at Café Society. When he showed me that poem, I dug it right off. It seemed to spell out all the things that had killed Pop" (84).

However, scholars disagree over the extent to which the jazz singer exerted control over the songs she sang and what role she played in the composition of "Strange Fruit." See Chilton; and Clarke for a biographic narrative of Holiday's incomprehension of the song's content: "Allan played it for her, and later wrote that she didn't know what 'pastoral' meant. . . . Lady was non-political; when she first looked at 'Strange Fruit' she didn't know what to make of it. She never read anything but comic books—promoter Ernie Anderson brought her bundles of them—and she was used to learning songs, not reading poetry" (163). Robert O'Meally also argues that though no one would ever sing "Strange Fruit" like Holiday, she fabricated details around the composition and production of the song, including the claim that she had written it or that it was written for her (45). See also the work of Angela Y. Davis; Griffin, *If You Can't Be Free;* and Blackburn. For an insightful discussion of the life, works, and revision of the tragic narrative surrounding Billie Holiday, see Griffin, *If You Can't Be Free.*

Although various artists, including Nina Simone, Tori Amos, Sting, and Lou Rawls, have interpreted and recorded this tragically beautiful song, Billie Holiday's inimitable interpretation of "Strange Fruit" remains the definitive version. Angela Y. Davis explains that Columbia records refused to record "Strange Fruit" because of the fear of backlash from white southerners, so a new independent label, Commodore Records, recorded the song (95).

4. Consider this recollection in *Lady Sing the Blues:* "A lot of the real dicty people with talent used to come and hear me. They were wonderful to sing to, but as usual it only took one cracker in the audience to wreck things. I had just started doing 'Strange Fruit' then; the record was selling and I always got a request for it in about every show. I remember the night this white boy stayed around just to bug me. When I started singing it, he'd start kicking up a storm of noise, rattling glasses, calling me a nigger, and cursing nigger singers" (92–93).

5. Newspaper articles drew attention to the racial mingling of the era; see, for example, Abe Hill. The "black and tan" clubs, integrated by definition, still operated along entrenched racial and class hierarchies: the musicians, performers, and staff were African American but the patrons were white. The iconic Cotton Club catered to an upscale all-white audience and directly appropriated the romanticized fiction of the Old South as its theme, even painting the set like a plantation house surrounded by slave quarters. All the entertainers were Black, including the "tall, tan, and terrific" dancers, who were required to project a certain aesthetic: light skin, tall, and under the age of twenty-one. For more on this history, see Haskins.

6. For more on the legal restrictions of the Black gaze and the denial of Black sexual freedom, see Berry, which details the specific legal case of Matt Ingram. His charge was "reckless eyeballing," or assault on a white woman without any touching, in the form of visual assault, or an inappropriate, suggestive, and/or threatening gaze.

7. James Allen argues that the long history of lynching in the United States, including a period with mob law, was not driven, at least exclusively, by notions of Black and white racial difference.

8. Excluding the graphic lynching photograph here follows the arguments of Hartman and others who refuse to perform the work of complicity and reproduce the "routinized," quotidian violence and "spectacular character of black suffering" (*Scenes of Subjection* 3–4).

9. The lynching survivor, activist, and founder of America's Black Holocaust Museum lived to be ninety-two years old and died in 2006. Having received national recognition for his bravery, courage, and commitment to educating youth about the racial violence and brutality of this period in American history, he treasured the official pardon he received from the State of Indiana in 1993 as his crowning achievement. "Since Indiana had forgiven me, I, in turn, forgive Indiana." "Strange Fruit: Anniversary of a Lynching." See Cameron; and Kaplan.

10. Patterson argues that a certain class of lynchings represent a "blood-sacrifice" and "brutal rite of passage enacted . . . for the community," which fits squarely within a larger historical tradition of sacrifice practices (175).

11. Goldsby clarifies that the definition of lynching changed over time and originally was correlated with nonfatal forms of public punishment, such as tar and feathering, but by the end of the nineteenth century it became "murderous." For the "feast of blood" reference, see Patterson, *Rituals of Blood,* 171.

12. See also Madison; and lynching data sets from the National Association for the Advance-

ment of Colored People. From January 1882 onward, the *Chicago Tribune* published an annual list of lynchings by state. "Lynchings: By State and Race, 1882–1968" of the Archives at Tuskegee Institute lists 3,446 lynchings of African Americans from 1882 to 1968. Trudier Harris, *Exorcising Blackness* uses the figure of an estimated 4,951 people from 1882 to 1927 (7). Tolnay and Beck underscore the importance of including the record of lynching threats in official tabulations of "racialized terrorism."

13. African American women writers such as Mary Burrill, Alice Dunbar-Nelson, Angelina Weld Grimké, and Georgia Douglas Johnson were positioned at the forefront of the production of lynching plays. Koritha Mitchell, *Living with Lynching*, 2.

14. For an examination of the complexity of Toomer's racial designation, see Byrd and Gates. See also Fabre and Feith; and Diana Williams, 188–201.

15. This is the "vital question" that Rudolph Byrd and Henry Louis Gates Jr. investigate in their afterword to a 2011 edition of *Cane,* drawing on United States Federal Census records, marriage certificates, and draft registries to reach this conclusion: "It is our carefully considered judgment, based upon an analysis of archival evidence previously overlooked by other scholars, that Jean Toomer—for all of his pioneering theorizing about what today we might call a multicultural or mixed-raced ancestry—was a Negro who decided to pass for white. Here we respectfully disagree with Toomer's biographers Kerman and Eldridge, who claim that Toomer never attempted 'to pass' in a racial sense." Toomer, *Cane,* 236–237. For a counterreading, see Hutchinson's introduction to *Cane:* "Contrary to some later narratives, Toomer was not attempting to 'pass' as white. He would adhere to his own self-understanding while allowing others to make of him what they would. He considered himself the first conscious member of a 'new race' coming into existence in the United States" (xxviii).

16. See Hutchinson, "Jean Toomer and the 'New Negroes' of Washington"; Kerman and Eldridge; and Nellie McKay. Hutchinson argues that the divide between Toomer and the African American intelligentsia has been overstated and that Toomer did maintain correspondence and social visits with Alain Locke and Georgia Douglas Johnson.

17. Biographers Kerman and Eldridge used Toomer's stated quest for an "intelligible scheme" as the theme and title of their book: "I had been, I suppose, unconsciously seeking—as a man must ever seek—an intelligible scheme of things, a sort of whole into which everything fit, or seemed to fit, a body of ideas which held a consistent view of life and which enabled one to see and understand as one does when he sees a map" (67). See also Byrd, 68.

18. Toomer tries out these themes of a new race of America in the poem "The First American" (no longer extant), and reworks them in the later, longer 1936 poem "The Blue Meridian."

19. Toomer also seemed not to give much credence to the institution of marriage, as he had the regrettable habit of having affairs with the wives of his friends and mentors. For more on his affairs with Margaret Naumberg and Georgia O'Keeffe, see Kerman and Eldridge, 213–214; Whalan, xxxiii.

20. "Cultural criticism finds itself faced with the final stage of the dialectic of culture and barbarism. To write poetry after Auschwitz is barbaric. And this corrodes even the knowledge of why it has become impossible to write poetry today." Adorno, 34.

21. Frank directed the publication of *Cane* with Boni and Liveright. This advising relationship and friendship would be irreparably breached in 1924 when Toomer had an affair with Frank's wife, Margaret Naumburg, a prominent educator and one of the first proponents of art therapy. For more on this, see Jean Toomer papers; and Whalan, x.

22. Aside from the pervasive imminent threat of white mob violence, much of the tension in "Kabnis" derives precisely from perceived regional differences between southern and northern Negroes, who maintain a mutual disdain for each other, with the southerners perceiving the northerners to be uppity, unable to perform physical labor, and reluctant to associate with Black southerners, while the northern Blacks (Kabnis and Lewis, the two northern visitors in town) assume their southern counterparts are provincial, overly spiritual, clannish, poorly educated peasants with little hope for the future. Note the doom in Lewis's thoughts about Carrie K., Halsey's sister: "Her soft rolled words are fresh pain to Lewis. He wants to take her North with him" (104).

23. It is also noteworthy that Toomer completed "Kabnis" the day before his grandfather, Pinckney Benton Stewart Pinchback, died.

24. In an earlier letter to Lola Ridge, dated late January or early February 1923, Toomer provides the inspirational "source" for two of his biracial characters: "Lew, in point of origin, is as authentic as Kabnis. For I myself am frankly the source of both of them. Lewis has the sense of direction and the intelligent grip of things that Kabnis lacks. Whereas Kabnis has the emotion which I could not possibly give to Lewis without bringing Lewis into the foreground more than I care to in this instance." Whalan, 124–125.

25. One significant challenge to the lynching photograph souvenir as the ultimate insignia of power was the publication—in *Jet* magazine on September 15, 1955, and in the *Chicago Defender* on September 17, 1955—of photographs of fourteen-year-old Emmett Till's brutally beaten and disfigured corpse in an open casket. The shocking photographs show close-up images of the severely mutilated body and the crushed, bloated head of this young African American man from Chicago who had traveled to the Mississippi Delta to visit relatives. He was viciously beaten and shot in the back of the head, and then a seventy-five-pound cotton gin fan was strapped to his neck and his body was dumped in a river, as punishment for allegedly whistling at or flirting with a white woman. His mother, Mamie Till Bradley, insisted on the open-casket funeral (more than fifty thousand people attended and viewed the corpse), exclaiming that she "wanted the world to see what they did to my boy." By allowing publication of the photographs of her son's horribly disfigured and brutalized corpse, she insisted that her son's death would not be ignored or forgotten, that she would tell her own story of the consequences of racial violence from the perspective of the mother of a lynching victim who must bury the mutilated body of her child. Mamie Till Bradley's use of the photographic medium to persuade worked because it sparked national outrage, despite the fact that the perpetrators were convicted of no crime. For an engaging discussion of the contested narratives around Till's murder, see Rubin; Whitfield; Metress; Pollack and Metress; and Till-Mobley.

One twenty-first-century attempt to reverse the hegemony of violent artifacts of visual culture (in this case, lynching photographs and the Confederate flag) surfaced with artist John Sims's controversial installation "The Proper Way to Hang a Confederate Flag," in which he erected a thirteen-foot gallows to stage a mock lynching of the Confederate flag. He stated that the purpose of the exhibit was "to say that this [the Confederate flag] has caused me major problems. I'm lynching it. And then I'm going to resurrect it and bring it back on my terms." The "Recoloration Proclamation: The Gettysburg Redress" exhibit, featuring a Confederate flag hanging from a noose, which was installed on September 25, 2004, at Gettysburg College, caused such strong objections from Sons of Confederate Veterans, Civil War relic shop owners, the Gettysburg Battlefield Preservation Association, and the Civil War community that the iconoclastic installation was moved to the inside of the Schmucker Art Gallery at Gettysburg College, though it was originally intended for installation in outdoors gallows. Sims also displayed Confederate flags refashioned with different colors, such as the black, red, and green of the African liberation movement, and lavender and pink with glitter and fur, to represent "drag flags."

The response to white artist Dana Schutz's 2016 abstract painting *Open Casket,* which reinterprets the open-casket funeral photograph of Emmett Till, at the Whitney Biennial elicited contempt from scholars and artist-activists like Parker Bright, who protested the promotion of the "Black Death Spectacle" with a custom T-shirt. In her open letter to the Whitney Biennial, Hannah Black urgently demanded the removal and destruction of the painting: "It is not acceptable for a white person to transmute Black suffering into profit and fun, though the practice has been normalized for a long time." See Calvin Tomkins; Kennedy; Livingstone and Gyarkye; Black; and johnsimsprojects.com/john-sims.

26. This moment prefigures the opening of Richard Wright's *Native Son* (1940), when Bigger Thomas slaughters with an iron skillet a huge black rat that intrudes in his family's one-room residence.

27. The first chapter of Trudier Harris, *Exorcising Blackness* offers a reading of the prolonged torture and gruesome lynching scene in Sutton Griggs's *The Hindered Hand* (1905).

28. As Darwin T. Turner asserts in his introduction to the 1975 edition of *Cane,* the fictional double murder of Mame Lamkins and her unborn child seems to be loosely based on the lynching of eight-month-pregnant Mary Turner in Lowndes County, Georgia, on May 17, 1918. According to Julie Buckner Armstrong, Turner "was hung, set on fire, and shot multiple times in front of a crowd of five hundred to one thousand people" during a rash of lynchings in Brookes and Lowndes Counties following the death of a white farmer, Hampton Smith, and his wife, Mary (38). However, Armstrong argues that the multiple competing narratives of Mary Turner's lynching deemphasize the labor abuse the farm workers endured. See also National Association for the Advancement of Colored People, *Thirty Years of Lynching in the United States: 1889–1918.*

29. Most reported lynchings of Black women also involved rape, and many of the women lynched were also pregnant. For analyses of racial and sexual violence, see Delongoria; Feimster; and Koritha Mitchell, *Living with Lynching.*

30. According to Philip Dray, "death at the hands of person unknown" was a common euphemism, ensuring impunity for the white lynch mob or perpetrators of extralegal punishments, whose identities were protected and kept anonymous in official documents, including coroner's reports and death certificates (ix).

31. An interesting comparison emerges between Toomer's Father John figure and the recurring figure of Uncle Julius, also formerly enslaved, who features prominently in the fiction of Charles W. Chesnutt. Chesnutt referred to the stock character in an 1889 letter as "the old Negro who serves as mouthpiece." Sollors, "Note on the Texts," 924.

32. Toomer explains the architecture of the book in a letter to Waldo Frank on December 12, 1922: "From three angles, CANE's design is a circle. Aesthetically, from simple forms to complex ones, and back to simple forms. Regionally, from the South up into the North, and back into the South again. Or, from the North down into the South, and then a return North. From the point of view of the spiritual entity behind the work, the curve really starts with Bona and Paul (awakening), plunges into Kabnis, emerges in Karintha etc. swings upward into Theatre and Box Seat, and ends (pauses) in Harvest Song." Whalan, 101.

33. Richard Wright's "Between the World and Me" (excerpted in this chapter's epigraph) recounts "the sooty details" of a lynching and ritualistic burning of the body. The description of ashes and "white bones slumbering forgottenly" functions similarly to the ashes in Toomer's "Portrait in

Georgia," that is, as an erasure of identity. Notably, the first line of the poem repeats the "thingification" of the charred lynching victim: "And one morning while in the woods, I stumbled / suddenly upon the thing." Similarly, the final six lines of McKay's fourteen-line poem "The Lynching" depict a crowd of women and young children complicit in the grisly sociopolitical terror of lynching. Here, the corpse is a "dreadful thing," signaling that the mob succeeded in "thingifying" a former human being, to draw on William I. Oliver's use of the term *thingification* as a "form of dying" (197).

34. Also quoted in Koritha Mitchell, "James Baldwin," 56.

35. For an article on the significance of the site of the 135th Street Library, see Sarah A. Anderson.

36. The investment in Locke's concept of the New Negro was not unilateral. Consider, for example, this reaction:

> Let is [*sic*] be repeated finally that there is no New Negro. What the Negro is doing today in a cultural, economic and civic way he has always been doing. The basis of all this unceasing chatter about the New Negro lies in fact that what he has always been doing he is now doing better.
>
> In other words, there are now more Negroes with something to say, more capable of saying it convincingly, and possessed of more media through which to say it. What else is to be expected after a half-century of education and intelligent contact with western civilization? Negroes are today more articulate than they were ten, twenty-five years ago.
>
> They have in their own press a medium of incalculable force, while increasingly the columns of metropolitan monthlies, of erudite quarterlies are opening to them. Publishing houses solicit their manuscripts, prominent colleges invite them to lecture, great absorbed audiences tumultuously applaud as they sing, speak or act.
>
> They are being heard and seen and felt and understood as never before. But a New Negro? Hardly! (Stewart)

37. As Darwin T. Turner points out in his 1975 introduction to *Cane,* the great irony of Toomer's literary career is that he is the most renowned writer of the Harlem Renaissance or Black Arts Movement, yet he later completely rejects this racial mantle (122).

38. For an extended biographical sketch of Robert Hayden's life, see Pontheolla T. Williams; and Mark A. Sanders, "Hayden, Robert."

39. See Pontheolla T. Williams, 3–36; and Gates and McKay, 1497–1499.

40. See Woodson for a catalog of Hayden's literary influences.

41. All citations are taken from "Middle Passage," from Glaysher's 2013 edition of Hayden's *Collected Poems.* There are three sections in the poem. References are to section and line.

42. Regarding the question of influence, Woodson notes that Hayden appropriates "the narrator who is a 'floating singer,' the catalogs of the names of ships, and some of the vocabulary (e.g., 'corposant')."

43. Although adopted and raised in a Christian family, Hayden converted to the Baha'i faith in 1943. For more on Hayden's religious conversion, see Pontheolla T. Williams.

4. Os Laços de Lembrança e Esquecimento

1. See Fundação de Casa Jorge Amado, www.jorgeamado.org.br.

2. The substantive, *lembrança,* denotes both "recollection" and "remembrance" in the English sense of *remembering,* but it also connotes "relic," "memorial," or "souvenir."

3. For an analysis of the "open-air museum,"see Straile, 211. See Amado, *Tenda dos Milagres* for the book blurb reference to "território do saber popular."

4. Leys calls this "mimesis," by which she means "an experience of hypnotic imitation or identification . . . an experience that, because it appeared to shatter the victim's cognitive-perceptual capacities, made the traumatic scene unavailable for a certain kind of recollection" (8–9).

5. See Amado, *Tent of Miracles* for English translation and *Tenda dos Milagres* for the original Portuguese. Interestingly, the English translation adds the word *Pelourinho,* which the original only gives as "território livre." It is noteworthy, too, that this novel, along with several others, including *Dona Flor e Seus Dois Maridos* (1966), was adapted for television and film. For many critics, the early novels of Jorge Amado—such as *O país do carnaval* (1931), *Juabiabá* (1935), and *Mar Morto* (1936)—marked the period when Amado most concerned himself with "the plight of the miserable." These represent his "proletarian novels." Others criticized his "old-fashioned Dickensian style" and "populism." Stavans xi–xii, xiv.

6. This could be linked to what Carl Jung calls the "collective unconscious." See Jung 112.

7. *The Masters and the Slaves* [Casa-Grande & Senzala] and *New World in the Tropics* represent definitive sociological scholarship on the repercussions of slavery in the formation of Brazilian society. Contemporary scholars continue to debate Freyre's work. Compare Freyre's concept of the interpenetration of cultures to Fernando Ortiz's "transculturación" (transculturation), discussed in chapter 5.

8. Although the numbers are often shifting, Conrad cites these statistics:

> The number of slaves in Brazil in 1798 is said to have been about 1,582,000. Between 1800 and 1850 probably 1,600,000 were imported into that country. If, therefore, the population had been maintained through natural reproduction (which of course was difficult owing to a low ratio of females to males), the slaves of Brazil should have numbered close to 3 million in 1871, the year of the Free Birth Law. Yet only 1,541,819 slaves were registered under the provisions of that legislation. (150–151)

For the most updated estimates of the embarkation, disembarkation, and human toll of the transatlantic and inter-American slave trades, see the Slave Voyages database, slavevoyages.org. For further history on slavery in Brazil, see Casimiro:

> Dentre as atividades econômicas da sociedade baiana (naturalmente com sua articulação à metrópole, Portugal), é necessário evidenciar o papel do tráfico e do comércio de escravos, que além de ter sido uma das formas mais lucrativas, foi também a mais cruel e injusta das formas de ideologia e de mentalidade da referida sociedade.
>
> [Among the economic activities of Bahian society (naturally linked to the metropolis, Portugal), it is necessary to highlight the role of the slave traffic and trade, which besides being one of the most profitable forms, was also the most cruel and unjust of the forms of ideology and mentality of that society.] (35)

9. Matory explains *brasilidade* in relation to the Candomblé religion: "With the best of intentions, Candomblé's intellectual and journalistic admirers, like those of the Carnaval, regularly misread Candomblé as the model of every cultural or political reform they desire, as the inversion and antitype of every story of social oppression and psychological distress suffered by Euro-Brazilians" (166).

10. From 1991 to 2010, the Indigenous population expanded from 34.5 percent to 80.5 percent

in two counties in Brazil, according to data from Instituto Brasileiro de Geografia e Estatística, www.ibge.gov.br/home/default.php.

11. While the fate of the Indigenous populations in this region of Brazil is beyond the scope of my study, Schwartz provides an excellent history on this subject.

12. For comparative reading of Pelourinho and Williamsburg County, see Straile. For comparative slave historiographies of the Americas, see Bergad, *Comparative Histories;* Ramos, 69–71. Ramos traces the three relocations of the pillory before it was permanently removed in 1835. She notes, "This is now the main place for musical events to take place" (71).

13. Alexandra K. Brown points out that 1835 is also the year of the Muslim uprising in Bahia. See also João José Reis, *Slave Rebellion.*

14. See Daniel Defoe's "Hymn to the Pillory" (1703), which he wrote before serving three days in the pillory for writing the satiric pamphlet *The Shortest Way with Dissenters.*

15. Other literary groups formed during this time included Vida de Artista, Folha de Rosto, and Nuvem Cigana. See Moisés, *História,* 399.

16. All quoted material is from Alvim, *O metro nenhum* (Campanhia das Letras, 2011). Translations are mine.

17. For illuminating discussions of Debret's art in Brazil, see Marcus Wood, *Black Milk;* Ana Lucia Araújo, *Brazil through French Eyes.*

18. Quilombo dos Palmares was a seventeenth-century maroon community, or an interior settlement of fugitive and free Blacks. It was usually surrounded by palm trees; hence the name, Palmares. Existing as an autonomous republic for almost fifty years, Palmares has become a potent symbol of Black resistance in Brazil and the African diaspora. As Bergad points out, there is no historiography of slavery in Brazil that does not devote some attention to the maroon community of Palmares in Pernambuco, which is "the most famous example of a large-scale *quilombo* that survived for much of the seventeenth century. . . . It had a sophisticated state structure, a taxation system, and even a standing army for defense. Repeated Portuguese military campaigns finally destroyed it in the 1690s" (45). See Bergad; Price; and the prolific work of Ana Lucia Araújo on public memory, slavery, and Brazil.

19. Castro Alves's immense national popularity is evidenced by the countless public commemorations and memorials in his honor: Teatro Castro Alves; O Parque Histórico Castro Alves (established March 8, 1971, at Cabaceiras do Paraguaçu in Bahia, where patron Edivaldo Boaventura, as Secretário de Educação e Cultura do governo de Luiz Viana Filho, restored the home in which Castro Alves was born and transformed it into a cultural center); and Praça Castro Alves in Salvador, where a sepulchre for his remains is located. These memorials underscore the polemics of institutions and publicly sanctioned or "official" memories.

20. I use the term *Afro-Brazilian* cautiously, as taxonomies of color and race in Brazil rely on an ever-expanding range of terms. As Sansone argues, "Black Brazilian identities have an internal logic and forms of representation of their own rather than being simple replicas of what happens in other regions of the Black Atlantic" (166). For example, the spectrum of terms used in the self-identification of color includes *moreno, pardo, white, preto, negro, light moreno, mulato, sarará* (fair-skinned, but with clear Negroid features), *blond, ruivo* (reddish), *amarelo* (yellow), and the list continues. Sansone, 39.

21. All citations of the English translation of "O navio negreiro" are from *Major Abolitionist Poems,* edited and translated by Amy A. Peterson (Garland, 1990).

22. *Saudade* is a "longing, yearning (for someone), fond remembrance," or "homesickness, nostalgia."

23. These colors are, generally, "black," "dark," "mulatto," "creole," and "brown."

24. Noteworthy are Esmeralda Ribeiro's "Continente Sem Fim" [Endless Continent], Geni Guimarães's "Leveza" [Lightness], and Lourdes Dhytta's "Trem Ilusão" [Illusion Train], to name a few excellent poems in this anthology that foreground the process of writing and self-reflection.

25. Given the elasticity of Brazilian racial categories, some critics would be reluctant to designate Machado de Assis as an Afro-Brazilian (*mulato*). For a case in favor of this distinction, see Eduardo de Assis Duarte.

26. For more contemporary Afro-Brazilian literature, see, for example, Jônatas Conceição da Silva; Afolabi, Barbosa, and Ribeiro; and Elio Ferreira de Souza.

27. Rufino, 40–41.

28. Portuguese citations are from Carolina Maria de Jesus, *Quarto de Despejo* (Editora Francisco Alves, 1960), which duplicates Carolina's syntactical idiosyncrasies and distinctive writerly style. English translations are from *Child of the Dark,* translated by Nancy P. S. Naro and Cristina Mehrtens (Rutgers, 1999). Throughout, I refer to the author as Carolina de Jesus, or simply Carolina, just as it is standard practice to refer to Machado de Assis as Machado as opposed to de Assis.

29. See also Joseph and Szuchman, 167.

30. Subsequent research indicates that Carolina de Jesus may have been cheated out of a significant portion of the profits from her book sales and the royalties. She ultimately died in obscurity.

31. Although the British House of Lords passed An Act for the Abolition of the Slave Trade on March 25, 1807, and attempted to block the importation of captive Africans on other slave ships, to preserve the economic stronghold of the British Empire, Brazil did not abolish the slave trade until 1831. Thus, according to the narrative time scheme, Norambo has the "*sorte*" (luck) to be smuggled on an illegal slave ship, "o ultimo navio negreiro a ancorar no porto de Salvador" (the last slave ship to dock in the port of Salvador) (13). Although Norambo/Felipe does not return to his ancestral home in Africa, he nevertheless carries his given name, Norambo, with him spiritually even as he lives in Brazil, speaks Portuguese, and is commonly known by Felipe.

32. It is also significant that Dudda Seixas changed his name. Dudda sounds like the word *black* in Yoruba.

33. See Hartman, *Lose Your Mother.*

34. To listen to the audio of this song, see "Quando eu venho de Luanda–Mestre Toni Vargas," uploaded June 4, 2008, www.youtube.com/watch?v=MXsmsmBMbPY&feature=emb_logo.

5. Azúcar, (Auto)biografía, and Absence

1. Dr. John Scoffern (1814–1882) was a professor of forensic medicine and chemistry at the Aldersgate College of Medicine. He was a lecturer on chemistry and medicine and also maintained a private practice. He wrote several scientific textbooks for a general audience and more than twenty journal articles. In his essay on the history of sugar, its manufacture, and the sugar tariff, he denounces the slave trade and the sufferings of the enslaved "dark souls" in the Americas. For more on Scoffern's biography, see Darby, 527–544.

2. Scoffern alludes to the early Christian theologian and prolific writer St. Origen of Alexandria (184/185–253/254). He compares the enslaved Africans in Cuba to this early Christian, who, according to Eusebius, castrated himself in order to better serve God, following the recommendation in Matthew 19:12. For more on this saint and father of the Church, see Heine.

3. Klein notes that the forced relocation of Africans did not "drop below the 50,000 range until

the 1840s, and even then 43,000 Africans were still arriving every year up to midcentury. . . . Though Cuba still kept bringing Africans in the next two decades, the trade had diminished to just 14,000 per annum in the 1850s and slowly petered out in the next decade" (47). When the Ten Years' War (1868–1878) began, just four years later, it would be the first of three wars of independence Cubans fought against Spain. The last would end with US intervention, in the Spanish-American War (1898). See Sommer, *Foundational Fictions,* 249.

4. The production of sugar also played a significant role in Brazil, in the Caribbean slavocratic economies of Puerto Rico, Haiti, the Dominican Republic, and in the southern United States.

5. There has been increasing critical interest in comparative readings of these two narratives, particularly within Latin American studies, focusing on a range of topics, including religious practice, orality, sociopolitical contexts of slavery, testimony, voice, and space. See, for example, DeCosta-Willis, "Self and Society," 6–15; Bergad, 64–95; Luis; Ocasio; Campuzano; and Tsouroukdissian. I comparatively read these two narratives to consider the nexus of sugar, autobiography, and absence from an Afrodiasporic comparative perspective.

6. Another key difference in this structure was the enslavement of non-Christianized, non-Europeanized Africans, *bozales,* as opposed to the *ladinos* or Christianized, Europeanized Africans laboring in captivity in Europe.

7. The Cuban "sugarocracy" allowed owners of the sugar mills, land, and the enslavers of Africans to thrive. Cuba's boom in sugar production resulted from the Haitian Revolution, during which time Haiti's production collapsed. Regarding this sugarocracy, Karl Marx argues in an 1848 speech, "You believe, perhaps, gentlemen, that the production of coffee and sugar is the natural destiny of the West Indies. Two centuries ago, Nature, which does not trouble herself about commerce, had planted neither sugar-cane nor coffee trees there" (207).

8. So effective was this pamphlet that this sketch is now one of the most recognizable images of the antislavery movement. Even the descriptions of the Middle Passage, including phrases like "tightly packed," became clichés in the abolitionist literature and may have lost their poignancy for the modern reader.

9. This novel explores and condemns the follies of human behavior, and in this excerpt, it shows that a scrumptious dinner can and should be prepared for polite society without the use of sugar.

10. William Cowper (1731–1800), who suffered from long bouts of depression during his life, is perhaps best known as the coauthor, with John Newton, of the *Olney Hymns* (including "Amazing Grace" and others). Cowper also wrote a number of antislavery poems, including "The Negro's Complaint" (1788), "The Morning Dream" (1788), and "Sweet Meat Has Sour Sauce: Or, the Slave Trader in the Dumps" (1788).

11. All references to *Autobiografía* in this chapter are from the bilingual *Autobiography of a Slave,* modernized by Ivan A. Schulman (Wayne State, 1996), and the digitized version of the original Spanish, accessed through the national archive, Biblioteca Nacional de Cuba José Martí. I refer to Manzano using the general term *Afro-Cuban,* though scholars such as W. Luis, R. Jackson, and Ocasio describe his mixed-race ancestry, based on Cuban racial taxonomy, as "*pardo*" (brown) and "*mulato fino.*" On the complexities of "Afro-Latinx subjectivity," see Valdés, who asserts, "The construction of *afrolatinidad* remains unsatisfying and inadequate because it does not yet convey that Africanness was constitutive of the Latinx in the Western Hemisphere" (15). Luis notes that the antislavery publications produced from Domingo del Monte's literary circle were not published in their original language until many years later, when the *sistema represivo* (repressive system) of the

Spanish crown had disappeared and "la escritura no representara un peligro para el Estado" (the writing no longer represented a danger to the state) (Manzano, *Autobiografía,* 16).

12. Professor, researcher, and editor José Luciano Franco (1891–1989) made it his life's work to investigate the slave trade and Africans in the "New World," particularly the Caribbean. A sample of his prolific work on this subject includes *Afroamérica* (1961), *La presencia negra en le Nuevo Mundo* (1968), *Facetas del esclavo africano en América Latina* [Introduction to African culture in Latin America] (1970), *Comercio clandestino de esclavos negros en el siglo XIX, Los Palenques de los negros cimarrones* (1971), and *Las Minas de Santiago del Prado y la Rebelión de los Cobreros: 1530–1800* (1975). See Franco's interview with Fernando Ortiz in the prologue of an updated and posthumous edition of the classic sociological text *Los negros esclavos,* which, when it was first published in 1916, initiated the field of Afro-Cuban studies.

13. For scholarship centering Blackness within Latin American and Afrodiasporic literary studies, see, for example, the influential works of Richard L. Jackson; DeCosta-Willis; Mullen; Lorna V. Williams; Tillis; Valdés; and Figueroa-Vásquez.

14. See Molloy, 393, for important questions around the use of modernized Spanish translations and what she calls Manzano's "manicured" prose.

15. Compare Barnet's ethnographic work with Montejo to the US Federal Writers' Project of the 1930s, during which elderly, formerly enslaved African Americans were interviewed and related their stories.

16. For an insightful study on the importance of slavery and revolution in the United States, see Sundquist, *To Wake the Nations.*

17. This list includes the five classic nineteenth-century Cuban antislavery novels. See Lorna V. Williams; and Moreno. For a theoretical study of the transatlantic Black community, see Nwankwo.

18. Notice the conflicting death year for Manzano, reflecting a lack of scholarly consensus on his birth and death dates. I use the dates cited in Schulman.

19. For instance, consider transnational literary relationships, such as the well-documented alliance between Langston Hughes and Nicolás Guillén. For an early comparative study, see Cobb.

20. For more on the free people of color in Cuba, see the extensive work of Pedro Deschamps Chapeaux and Maria del Carmen Barcia.

21. The scholarly debate around the dedication in Toni Morrison's *Beloved,* "Sixty Million and more," sheds light on what is at stake in quantifying trauma and suffering. In an interview, Morrison explains:

> "Q. *Beloved* is dedicated to the 60 million who died as a result of slavery. A staggering number—is this proved historically?
>
> A. Some historians told me 200 million died. The smallest number I got from anybody was 60 million. There were travel accounts of people who were in the Congo—that's a wide river—saying, 'We could not get the boat through the river, it was choked with bodies.' That's like a logjam. A lot of people died. Half of them died in those ships" (Angelo).

For a synopsis of the critical response to the dedication, see Mandel.

22. Rout gives the higher figure of 1.5 million, which takes into account illegal, unauthorized slave ships (66); Andrews gives the lower figure in comparison to Brazil, which he estimates received 2.5 million Africans by the year 1800 (14). Historians' interest in quantifying the numbers of enslaved Africans captured and forcibly transported, and locating the sites of embarkment and disembarkment, has intensified in the past fifty years. Aided by digital technology, Herbert S. Klein,

David Eltis, David Richardson, Stephen Behrendt, and other scholars and institutions have combined independent archives of slave trading voyages, ultimately culminating in the Trans-Atlantic Slave Trade database, which now exists at www.slavevoyages.org, a searchable database of nearly thirty-six thousand voyages.

23. For a Marxist treatment of Cuba's sugar economy, see Fraginals, *El ingenio.*

24. Nicolás Azcárate (1826–1894) was another key figure in the literary circles and Cuban intelligentsia. He founded the New Lyceum of Havana and hosted events in which men gave papers, which he later published. See Willis Fletcher Johnson; and Marilyn Miller.

25. Although R. R. Madden read Anselmo Suárez y Romero's *Francisco, el ingenio o las Delicias del Campo* and wrote to Domingo del Monte, "Tho there is literary merit of but small account in this piece, there is life and truth in every line of it," he did not publish the novel in England and chose instead to publish Manzano's *Autobiografía.* See Ruiz, iv.

26. See also the chronology and introduction in Luis, *Autobiografía* for dates and historical estimates around the cost of purchasing Manzano's freedom. Although some critics consider the title of Manzano's second poetry collection, *Flores pasageras,* to be misspelled, I argue that this and other so-called errors, especially given Manzano's memorization abilities, are evidence of Manzano's poetic style.

27. Compare this to the controversy around New South Book's decision to expunge the "N-word" from its 2012 edition of Mark Twain's classic novel *The Adventures of Huckleberry Finn* and replace it with the word *slave.* See, for example, Bosman; and Kurutz.

28. For a book-length study on the relationship between Madden and Manzano from a postcolonial perspective, see Burton.

29. The English version of Manzano's "Treinta Años" [Thirty Years], translated by R. R. Madden, appears in the University of North Carolina, Chapel Hill collection *Documenting the American South,* https://docsouth.unc.edu/neh/manzano/manzano.html#p101.

30. I borrow the word *totipotent* from biology, where it refers to a cell that is capable of developing into a complete organism or becoming another, related kind of cell.

31. Schulman's footnote indicates that *criollo* was "a term used in the literature of the period to refer to the enslaved person of African descent born on the island" (45).

32. For influential historical studies on the complexities of studying the Caribbean, see Torres-Saillant; Dash; and Benítez-Rojo.

33. Note the echoes in the last stanza from Paul Laurence Dunbar's 1899 poem "Sympathy":

> I know why the caged bird sings, ah me,
> When his wing is bruised and his bosom sore,—
> When he beats his bars and he would be free;
> It is not a carol of joy or glee,
> But a prayer that he sends from his heart's deep core,
> But a plea, that upward to Heaven he flings—
> I know why the caged bird sings! (*Lyrics of the Hearthside* 40)

34. For an analysis of the "ethereal presence" and religious syncretism in Manzano's narrative, see Pettway.

35. See Barnet, *Cimarrón: Historia de un esclavo.* For the English translation, see Barnet, *Biography of a Runaway Slave,* translated by W. Nick Hill. The title of the original publication in Cuba was *Biografía de un cimarrón.* For a sampling of texts that address the "myth of the flying Africans,"

see, for example, Morrison, *Song of Solomon;* Georgia Writers' Project; Colbert; and Jason R. Young. Montejo's narrative inspired a recital for four musicians by German composer Hans Werner Henze, which premiered at the Berlin Festival in 1970.

36. The complete phrase is "vivito y coleando," which translates to the colloquial "alive and kicking."

37. For a discussion of the curious omission of the Cuban Revolution of the late 1950s and Barnet's political affiliation at the time, see Graden.

38. For a reading of the later narratives that link early Congolese traditions and vengeance against the enslavers, see Finch.

39. Historically, *criollo* (Creole) refers to those of European descent born in Spanish America. Here, it holds the special meaning of "children born in slavery and, thus, to Africans born in Cuba." Barnet, *Biography* 216.

40. Hill translates *el monte* as "woods," therefore interpreting the phrase "cogí el monte" as "I made it into the woods." Another gloss on this phrase uses the primary meaning of *el monte* as "hill" or "mountain," which translates the phrase "cogí el monte" as "I climbed the mountain," resonating with the liberating language of the Moses motif.

41. For instructive theory on "translocal dialogues" and Africa in the Americas in relation to religion, see Matory.

42. World-renowned Cuban salsa singer Celia Cruz would often shout to her fans the catchphrase "¡Azúcar!" (Sugar!) during concerts or in passing, and they would shout it back to her in response:

> "Azúcar!" was Celia Cruz's battle cry. It literally means "sugar." It was her way of energizing and injecting the music with that extra serving of *sabor* (flavor). It was also the way she made the music her own. Sugar is an essential agricultural product in Cuba's history, directly linked both to the vibrant diversity of Cuban culture and to the violence of slavery. Celia Cruz's throaty cry evoked those associations. ("¡Azúcar! The Life and Music of Celia Cruz")

43. Celia Cruz received news via telegram that her mother had died, after the revolution of 1959, but she was not allowed to return to Cuba to attend the funeral. For more on Cruz's life, see Cruz and Reymundo.

Epilogue. A Gate of Return

1. See also McKittrick, *Dear Science:* "Diasporic literacy signals ways of being and ways of living (memories, imaginations, mnemonics) that we know and share in order to collectively struggle against suffocating racial logics" (6).

2. For the scholarship on twenty-first-century iterations of the economic logics of slavery in literature and society, see Murphy; and Goyal.

Bibliography

Abdur-Rahman, Aliyyah I. *Against the Closet: Black Political Longing and the Erotics of Race.* Duke UP, 2012.

Abreu, Martha. "Outras histórias de Pai João: Conflitos raciais, protesto escravo e irreverência sexual na poesia popular, 1880–1950." *Afro-Ásia* 31 (2004): 235–276.

Aching, Gerard. *Freedom from Liberation: Slavery, Sentiment, and Literature in Cuba.* Indiana UP, 2015.

Adams, Clementina R. *Common Threads: Themes in Afro-Hispanic Women's Literature.* Ediciones Universal, 1998.

Adler, Tony. "A Lynching Deconstructed, in Charles Smith's *The Gospel According to James.*" *Reader,* May 26, 2011.

Adorno, Theodor W. "Cultural Criticism and Society." In *Prisms,* translated by Samuel and Shierry Weber, 17–34. MIT P, 1967.

Afolabi, Niyi. *Afro-Brazilians: Cultural Production in a Racial Democracy.* U of Rochester P, 2009.

Afolabi, Niyi, Marcio Barbosa, and Esmeralda Ribeiro, eds. *Cadernos negros: Literatura afro-brasileira contemporânea* [Black Notebooks: Contemporary Afro-Brazilian Literature]. Translated by Niyi Afolabi. Africa World P, 2008.

"Africans and Afro-Americans." "The Mail." *Harvard Crimson,* May 9, 1963.

Aguiar, Maciel de. *História dos quilombolas: Serie história dos quilombolas.* São Mateus: Memorial, 2007.

Akyeampong, Emmanuel. "Africans in the Diaspora: The Diaspora and Africa." *African Affairs* 99, no. 395 (April 2000): 183–215.

———. "History, Memory, Slave-Trade and Slavery in Anlo (Ghana)." *Slavery and Abolition* 22, no. 3 (December 2001): 1–24.

Alexander, Elizabeth. *Crave Radiance: New and Selected Poems 1990–2010.* Graywolf, 2010.

———. "Dunbar Lives!" *African American Review* 41, no. 2 (Summer 2007): 395–401.

Alexander, Michelle. *The New Jim Crow: Mass Incarceration in the Age of Colorblindness.* New Press/Perseus, 2010.

Aljoe, Nicole N., and Ian Finseth, eds. *Journeys of the Slave Narrative in the Early Americas.* U of Virginia P, 2014.

Allahar, Anton. *Ethnicity, Class, and Nationalism: Caribbean and Extra-Caribbean Dimensions.* Lexington Books, 2005.

Allen, James. *Without Sanctuary: Lynching Photography in America.* Twin Palms, 2000.

Allen, Marlene D., and Seretha D. Williams, eds. *Afterimages of Slavery: Essays on Appearances in Recent American Films, Literature, Television and Other Media.* McFarland, 2012.

Allen, Robert Clyde, ed. *To Be Continued: Soap Operas around the World.* Routledge, 1995.

Allen, William Francis, Charles Pickard Ware, and Lucy McKim Garrison, compilers. *Slave Songs of the United States.* Books for Libraries P, 1971.

Als, Hilton. "The Sugar Sphinx." *New Yorker,* May 8, 2014, www.newyorker.com/culture/culture-desk/the-sugar-sphinx.

Alves, Castro. *The Major Abolitionist Poems.* Edited and translated by Amy A. Peterson. Garland, 1990.

———. *Os Escravos.* Rio de Janeiro: Livraria F. Alves Editora, 1988.

———. *Poesias completas.* Edited by Jamil Almansur Haddad. São Paulo: Companhia Editôra Nacional, 1966.

Alves, Castro, and Antônio José Chediak. *O Navio Negreiro: Tragédia no Mar.* Rio de Janeiro: Academia Brasileira de Letras, 2000.

Alves, Castro, and Aldemir Martins. *O Navio Negreiro.* São Paulo: Studioma, 1992.

Alves, Kleberson da Silva. "Escravistas *versus* emancipacionistas na prosa romântica: As representações senhoriais no romance *A Escrava Isaura.*" *Afro-Ásia* 43 (2011): 155–194.

Alves, Miriam, ed. *Enfim—Nós: Escritoras negras brasileiras contemporâneas* [Finally—Us: Contemporary Black Brazilian Women Writers]. Translated by Carolyn Richardson Durham. Three Continents P, 1995.

Alves, Miriam, and Maria Helena Lima. *Women Righting: Afro-Brazilian Women's Short Fiction* [Mulheres escre-vendo: Uma antologia bilingüe de escritoras afro-brasileiras contemporâneas]. London: Mango, 2005.

Alvim, Francisco. *O metro nenhum.* São Paulo: Campanhia das Letras, 2011.

Amado, Jorge. *Gabriela, cravo e canela.* Lisbon: Publicações Europa-América, 1970.

———. *Jubiabá: Romance.* Rio de Janiero: Record, 1995.

———. *Tenda dos Milagres.* Rio de Janeiro: Record, 1998.

———. *Tent of Miracles.* Translated by Barbara Shelby Merello. U of Wisconsin P, 2003.

Anderson, Lisa M. *Mammies No More: The Changing Image of Black Women on Stage and Screen.* Rowman and Littlefield, 1997.

Anderson, Ross. "Betty the Latin American Superstar." *The Times,* January 4, 2007, www.thetimes.co.uk/article/betty-the-latin-american-superstar-g6nzqz33nqr.

Anderson, Sarah A. "'The Place to Go': The 135th Street Branch Library and the Harlem Renaissance." *Library Quarterly* 73, no. 4 (October 2003).

Andrade, Mário de. *A escrava que não é Isaura: Discurso sobre algumas tendências da poesia modernista.* São Paulo: Livraria Lealdade, 1925.

Andrews, George Reid. *Afro-Latin America, 1800–2000.* Oxford UP, 2004.

Andrews, Norwood, Jr. "Nineteenth-Century Brazilian Polemics: A Critical Appraisal of

Bernardo Guimarães: *A Escrava Isaura* and *Rosaura, A Enjeitada.*" *Revista de Letras* 8/9 (1966): 233–272.

Andrews, William L., ed. *African American Autobiography: A Collection of Critical Essays.* Prentice Hall, 1993.

———. *The Portable Charles W. Chesnutt.* Penguin Classics, 2008.

Andrews, William L., Frances Smith Foster, and Trudier Harris, eds. *The Oxford Companion to African American Literature.* Oxford UP, 1997.

Andrews, William L., and Henry Louis Gates Jr., eds. *The Civitas Anthology of African American Slave Narratives.* Civitas/Counterpoint, 1999.

Angelo, Bonnie. "Toni Morrison: The Pain of Being Black." *Time,* May 22, 1989.

Ani, Marimba. *Let the Circle Be Unbroken: The Implications of African Spirituality in the Diaspora.* Nkonimfo Publications, 1997.

Anquandah, Kwesi J. *Castles and Forts of Ghana.* Atalante: Ghana Museums and Monuments Board, 1999.

Anquandah, James Kwesi, Naana Jane Opoku-Agyemang, and Michel R. Doortmont, eds. *The Transatlantic Slave Trade: Landmarks, Legacies, Expectations.* Accra: Sub-Saharan Publishers, 2007.

Anton, Danilo J. *Diversity, Globalization, and the Ways of Nature.* Ottawa: International Development Research Centre, 1995.

"Antônio de Castro Alves." *Revista Hispánica Moderna* 12, no. 1/2 (January–April 1946): 189–190.

Apel, Dora, and Shawn Michelle Smith. *Lynching Photographs.* U of California P, 2007.

Appiah, Anthony, and Henry Louis Gates Jr., eds. *Africana: The Encyclopedia of the African and African American Experience.* Oxford UP, 2005.

———. *Encyclopedia of Africa.* 2 vols. Oxford UP, 2010.

Araújo, Ana Lucia. *Brazil through French Eyes: A Nineteenth-Century Artist in the Tropics.* U of New Mexico P, 2015.

———. *Politics of Memory: Making Slavery Visible in the Public Space.* Routledge, 2013.

———. *Shadows of the Slave Past: Memory, Heritage, and Slavery.* Routledge, 2014.

———. *Slavery in the Age of Memory: Engaging the Past.* Bloomsbury Academic, 2021.

Araújo, Ana Lucia, Mariana Pinho Candido, and Paul E. Lovejoy, eds. *Crossing Memories: Slavery and African Diaspora.* African World P, 2011.

Araújo, Emanoel, Francisco C. Weffort, Fernando Henrique Cardoso, and Abigail Moura, eds. *Para nunca esquecer: Negras memórias: memórias de negros.* Rio de Janeiro: Museu Histórico Nacional; Ministério da Cultura, 2002.

Araújo, Joel Zito. *A negação do Brasil: O negro na telenovela brasileira.* São Paulo: Editora Senac São Paulo, 2000.

Araújo, José Goes de. *Da velha cidade da Bahia: História & estórias.* Salvador: Secretaria da Cultura e Turismo do Estado da Bahia, Fundação Cultural, 1998.

Arguedas, José M., and Pérez F. Amezcua. *Arguedas: Entre La Antropología Y La Literatura.* México: Ediciones Taller Abierto, 2000.

Arhin, Kwame, A. D. C. Hyland, and Samuel S. Quarcoopome. *The Cape Coast and Elmina Handbook: Past, Present, and Future.* Legon: Institute of African Studies, University of Ghana, 1995.

Armah, Ayi Kwei. *Remembering the Dismembered Continent.* Popenguine: Per Ankh, 2010.

Armstrong, Julie Buckner. *Mary Turner and the Memory of Lynching.* U of Georgia P, 2011.

Arndt, Susan. "African Gender Trouble and African Womanism: Chikwenye Ogunyemi and Wanjira Muthoni." *Signs* 25, no. 3 (Spring 2000): 709–726.

Ashe, Bertram D., and Ilka Saal, eds. *Slavery and the Post-Black Imagination.* U of Washington P, 2020.

Auspitz, Josiah Lee. "A Milder View." *Harvard Crimson,* May 10, 1963.

Austin, J. L. *How to do Things with Words.* Harvard UP, 1975.

Awolalu, J. Ọ. *Yoruba Beliefs and Sacrificial Rites.* Longman, 1979.

Axiotou, Georgia. *Breaking the Silence: West African Authors and the Transatlantic Slave Trade.* PhD diss., University of Edinburgh, 2008.

"¡Azúcar! The Life and Music of Celia Cruz." National Museum of American History, Kenneth E. Behring Center, Smithsonian Institution.

Bailey, Anne C. *African Voices of the Atlantic Slave Trade: Beyond the Silence and the Shame.* Beacon, 2005.

Bailey, Dale S. *Slavery in the Novels of Brazil and the United States: A Comparison.* PhD diss., Indiana University, 1961.

Bal, Mieke, Jonathan V. Crewe, and Leo Spitzer. *Acts of Memory: Cultural Recall in the Present.* Dartmouth College/UP of New England, 1999.

Baldwin, James. *Notes of a Native Son.* Beacon, 1955.

Baldwin, Kate. "Montezuma's Revenge: Reading *Los ricos también lloran* in Russia." In *To be Continued: Soap Operas around the World,* edited by Robert C. Allen, 285–300. Routledge, 1995.

Banks, Mary Moss. *Bright Days in the Old Plantation Time.* Lee and Shepard, C.T. Dillingham, 1882.

Baraka, Imamu Amiri (LeRoi Jones). *Blues People: Negro Music in White America.* 1963. Perennial, 2002.

Barbosa, Lucia Maria de Assunção, Petronilha Beatriz Gonçalves e Silva, and Valter Roberto Silvério. *De preto a afro-descendente: Trajetos de pesquisa sobre o negro, cultura negra e relações étnico-raciais no Brasil.* São Carlos: EdUFSCar, 2003.

Barcia Paz, Manuel. *Con el látigo de la ira: Legislación, represión, y control en las plantaciones cubanas, 1790–1870.* Havana: Ciencias Sociales, 2000.

———. *Seeds of Insurrection: Domination and Resistance on Western Cuban Plantations, 1808–1848.* Louisiana State UP, 2008.

Barcia Zequeira, María del Carmen. *La otra familia: Parientes, redes, y descendencia de los esclavos en Cuba.* La Habana: Cubanas Ediciones, 2004.

Barnes, Natasha. "On *Without Sanctuary.*" *Nka: Journal of Contemporary African Art* 20, no. 1 (2006): 86–91.

Barnet, Miguel. *Biografía de un cimarrón.* La Habana: Instituto del Libro, 1966.
———. *Biography of a Runaway Slave.* Translated by W. Nick Hill. Curbstone, 2003.
———. *Cimarrón: Historia de un esclavo.* 1967. 3rd ed., Madrid: Ediciones Siruela, 2009.
Bartra, Roger. *La jaula de la melancolía: Identidad y metamorfosis del mexicano.* México: Grijalbo, 1987.
Basu, Biman. "Hybrid Embodiment and an Ethics of Masochism: Nella Larsen's *Passing* and Sherley Anne Williams's *Dessa Rose.*" *African American Review* 36, no. 3 (Autumn 2002): 383–401.
Bathrick, David, Brad Prager, and Michael D. Richardson, eds. *Visualizing the Holocaust: Documents, Aesthetics, Memory.* Camden House, 2008.
Battenfeld, Mary. "'Been Shapin Words T Fit M Soul': *Cane,* Language, and Social Change." *Callaloo* 25, no. 4 (August 2002): 1238–1249.
Baucom, Ian. *Specters of the Atlantic: Finance Capital, Slavery, and the Philosophy of History.* Duke UP, 2005.
Baudrillard, Jean. *Simulacres et Simulation* [Simulacra and Simulation]. U of Michigan P, 1994.
Beaulieu, Elizabeth Ann. *Black Women Writers and the American Neo-Slave Narrative: Femininity Unfettered.* Greenwood P, 1999.
Beckles, Hilary, and Elsa V. Goveia, eds. *Inside Slavery: Process and Legacy in the Caribbean Experience.* Canoe/U of the West Indies, 1996.
Beckles, Hilary, and Verene Shepherd. *Caribbean Slavery in the Atlantic World: A Student Reader.* James Currey/M. Weiner, 2000.
Bedasse, Monique A. *Jah Kingdom: Rastafarians, Tanzania, and Pan-Africanism in the Age of Decolonization.* U of North Carolina P, 2017.
Beer, Janet, and Bridget Bennett, eds. *Special Relationships: Anglo-American Affinities and Antagonisms, 1854–1936.* Manchester UP, 2002.
Behn, Aphra. *Oroonoko, or, The Royal Slave,* edited by Catherine Gallagher and Simon Stern. Bedford/St. Martin's, 2000.
Benesch, Klaus, and Geneviève Fabre, eds. *African Diasporas in the New and Old Worlds: Consciousness and Imagination.* Rodopi, 2004.
Benét, Stephen Vincent. "John Brown's Body." In *Selected Works of Stephen Vincent Benét.* Vol. 1, *Poetry.* Farrar and Rinehart, 1942.
Benítez-Rojo, Antonio. *The Repeating Island: The Caribbean and the Postmodern Perspective.* Duke UP, 1997.
Benjamin, Walter. *Illuminations.* Edited by Hannah Arendt. Translated by Harry Zorn. Pimlico, 1999.
Bennett, Herman L. *African Kings and Black Slaves: Sovereignty and Dispossession in the Early Modern Atlantic.* U of Pennsylvania P, 2019.
Bennett, Joshua. *Being Property Once Myself: Blackness and the End of Man.* Belknap Press of Harvard UP, 2020.
Bennett, Michael, and Vanessa D. Dickerson. *Recovering the Black Female Body: Self-Representations by African American Women.* Rutgers UP, 2001.

Benston, Kimberly W. "Black Hauntologies, Slavery, Modernity, Photography." Alain LeRoy Locke lecture delivered at W. E. B. Du Bois Institute for African and African American Research, Harvard University, April 20, 2011.

Bercovitch, Sacvan. *The American Jeremiad.* U of Wisconsin P, 1978.

———. *The Cambridge History of American Literature.* Vol. 4, *Nineteenth-Century Poetry, 1800–1910.* Cambridge UP, 2008.

Bergad, Laird W. *The Comparative Histories of Slavery in Brazil, Cuba, and the United States.* Cambridge UP, 2007.

Bergad, Laird W., Fe Iglesias García, and María del Carmen Barcia. *The Cuban Slave Market, 1790–1880.* Cambridge UP, 1995.

Bergner, Gwen. "Introduction: The Plantation, the Postplantation, and the Afterlives of Slavery." Special issue, edited by Gwen Bergner and Zita Cristina Nunes: *American Literature* 91, no. 3 (September 2019): 447–652.

Bergreen, Laurence. *As Thousands Cheer: The Life of Irving Berlin.* Viking, 1990.

Berlin, Ira. *American Slavery in History and Memory.* La Trobe University History Programme, 2004.

———. "Coming to Terms with Slavery." In *Slavery and Public History: The Tough Stuff of American Memory,* edited by James Oliver Horton and Lois E. Horton. W. W. Norton, 2006.

Berlin, Ira, Marc Favreau, and Steven F. Miller. *Remembering Slavery: African Americans Talk About Their Personal Experiences of Slavery and Freedom.* New Press; Library of Congress, 1998.

Berman, Carolyn Vellenga. *Creole Crossings: Domestic Fiction and the Reform of Colonial Slavery.* Cornell UP, 2006.

Bernd, Zilá. *Introdução à literatura negra.* São Paulo: Editora Brasiliense, 1988.

———. *Negritude e literatura na América Latina.* Porto Alegre: Mercado Aberto, 1987.

Berner, Robert L. *World Literature Today* 55, no. 1 (Winter 1981): 162.

Bernier, Celeste-Marie. *African American Visual Arts: From Slavery to the Present.* U of North Carolina P, 2008.

Bernier, Celeste-Marie, and Hannah Durkin, eds. *Visualising Slavery: Art across the African Diaspora.* Liverpool UP, 2016.

Bernstein, William J. *A Splendid Exchange: How Trade Shaped the World.* Atlantic Monthly/Publishers Group West, 2008.

Berry, Ian, Darby English, Vivian Patterson, and Mark Reinhardt, eds. *Kara Walker: Narratives of a Negress.* MIT P, 2003.

Berry, Mary Frances. "'Reckless Eyeballing': The Matt Ingram Case and the Denial of African American Sexual Freedom." *Journal of African American History* 93, no. 2 (2008): 223–234.

Best, Stephen M. *The Fugitive's Properties: Law and the Poetics of Possession.* U of Chicago P, 2004.

———. *None Like Us: Blackness, Belonging, Aesthetic Life.* Duke UP, 2018.

Best, Stephen, and Sharon Marcus. "Surface Reading: An Introduction." *Representations* 108 (Fall 2009): 1–21.

Beverley, John, and Hugo Achugar. *La voz del otro: Testimonio, subalternidad y verdad narrativa.* Guatemala: Universidad Rafael Landívar, 2002.

Bhabha, Homi K. *The Location of Culture.* Routledge, 2004.

———, ed. *Nation and Narration.* Routledge, 1990.

Black, Hannah. "Open Letter to the Curators and Staff of the Whitney Biennial." *Black Contemporary Art,* March 21, 2017, blackcontemporaryart.tumblr.com/post/158661755087/please-read-share-hannah-blacks-open-letter-to.

Blackburn, Julia. *With Billie.* Pantheon, 2005.

"Black Mammies." *New York Amsterdam News,* March 21, 1923.

Blackmon, Douglas A. *Slavery by Another Name: The Re-Enslavement of Black People in America from the Civil War to World War II.* Anchor, 2008.

Blassingame, John W. *The Slave Community: Plantation Life in the Antebellum South.* Oxford UP, 1979.

Blight, David W., ed. *Passages to Freedom: The Underground Railroad in History and Memory.* Washington, DC: Smithsonian Books, 2004.

———. *Race and Reunion: The Civil War in American Memory.* Belknap Press of Harvard UP, 2001.

———. *A Slave No More: Two Men Who Escaped to Freedom—Including their Own Narratives of Emancipation.* Harcourt, 2007.

Bloom, Harold, ed. *Bloom's Modern Critical Views: Robert Hayden.* Chelsea House, 2005.

Boaventura, Edivaldo M. *Castro Alves: Um parque para o poeta.* Salvador: Empresa Gráfica da Bahia, 2006.

Bogle, Donald. *Toms, Coons, Mulattoes, Mammies, and Bucks: An Interpretive History of Blacks in American Films.* Continuum, 2001.

Bolles, Edmund Blair. *Remembering and Forgetting: An Inquiry into the Nature of Memory.* Walker, 1988.

Bontemps, Arna Wendell. *Black Thunder.* Beacon, 1968.

The Bookman: An Illustrated Magazine of Literature and Life, August 1902–February 1903. Dodd Mead and Company.

Borim, Dário. "Retrato social às avessas: A inserção classista e sexista em *A Escrava Isaura.*" *Revista de Crítica Literária Latinoamericana* 27, no. 54 (2001): 67–75.

Bosi, Alfredo. *História concisa da literatura brasileira.* São Paulo: Editora Cultrix, 1994.

Bosman, Julie. "Publisher Tinkers with Twain." *New York Times,* January 4, 2011, www.nytimes.com/2011/01/05/books/05huck.html.

Bourne, H. R. Fox. *Slave Traffic in Portuguese Africa: An Account of Slave-Raiding and Slave-Trading in Angola and of Slavery in the Islands of San Thome and Principe.* London: P. S. King and Son, 1908.

Bovey, Alixe. "The Middle Ages: The Medieval Diet." British Library, April 30, 2015, https://www.bl.uk/the-middle-ages/articles/the-medieval-diet.

Bowdich, T. Edward. *Mission from Cape Coast Castle to Ashantee, with a Descriptive Account of that Kingdom.* London: Griffith and Farran, 1873.

Boyd, Valerie. *Wrapped in Rainbows: The Life of Zora Neale Hurston.* Scribner, 2003.

Boym, Svetlana. *The Future of Nostalgia.* Basic Books, 2001.

Bradley, Adam Francis. *Liberation of Perception: Evil's Emergence in 20th Century African American Literature.* PhD diss., Harvard University, 2003.

Brandão, Lívia. "Mutantes e vampiros atacam clássicos nacionais." *O Globo,* September 13, 2010.

Braxton, Joanne M., and Maria Diedrich, eds. *Monuments of the Black Atlantic: Slavery and Memory.* Münster: LIT Verlag, 2004.

Brayman Hackel, Heidi, and Catherine E. Kelly. *Reading Women: Literacy, Authorship, and Culture in the Atlantic World, 1500–1800.* U of Pennsylvania P, 2008.

Bröck-Sallah, Sabine. *White Amnesia—Black Memory?: American Women's Writing and History.* Peter Lang, 1999.

Brodber, Erna. *The Continent of Black Consciousness: On the History of the African Diaspora from Slavery to the Present Day.* New Beacon, 2003.

Brooks, Gwendolyn. "From *Books Noted.*" In *Robert Hayden: Essays on the Poetry,* edited by Laurence Goldstein and Robert Chrisman, 58–60. U of Michigan P, 2001.

Brooks, Joanna, and John Saillant. *"Face Zion Forward": First Writers of the Black Atlantic, 1785–1798.* Northeastern UP, 2002.

Brooks, Van Wyck. *Van Wyck Brooks, the Early Years: A Selection from His Works, 1908–1925.* Edited by Claire Sprague. Northeastern UP, 1993.

Brown, Alexandra K. "'A Black Mark on Our Legislation': Slavery, Punishment, and the Politics of Death in Nineteenth-Century Brazil." Special issue: *State, Society, and Political Culture in Nineteenth-Century Brazil: Luso-Brazilian Review* 37, no. 2 (Winter 2000): 95–121.

Brown, Caroline A. *The Black Female Body in American Literature and Art: Performing Identity.* Routledge, 2012.

Brown, Charlotte Hawkins. *Mammy: An Appeal to the Heart of the South; and, the Correct Thing to do—to Say—to Wear.* G. K. Hall, 1995.

Brown, Kimberly Juanita. *The Repeating Body: Slavery's Visual Resonance in the Contemporary.* Duke UP, 2015.

Brown, Michael Joseph. *Blackening of the Bible: The Aims of African American Biblical Scholarship.* Trinity P International, 2004.

Brown, Sterling A. "The Negro Character as Seen by White Authors." *Journal of Negro Education* 2, no. 2 (April 1933): 179–203.

———. *Negro Poetry and Drama, and the Negro in American Fiction.* Atheneum, 1969.

Brown, William Wells. *Clotel; Or, the President's Daughter.* Modern Library, 2000.

Browne, Simone. *Dark Matters: On the Surveillance of Blackness.* Duke UP, 2015.

Brown-Guillory, Elizabeth, ed. *Middle Passages and the Healing Place of History: Migration and Identity in Black Women's Literature.* Ohio State UP, 2006.

Burnett, John, and Piper McDaniel. "Confederate Statues Come Down around US, but Not Everywhere." *Morning Edition*, NPR, October 6, 2020. www.npr.org/2020/10/06/919193176/confederate-statues-come-down-around-u-s-but-not-everywhere.

Burton, Gera. *Ambivalence and the Postcolonial Subject: The Strategic Alliance of Juan Francisco Manzano and Richard Robert Madden.* Peter Lang, 2004.

Butler, Kim. "Defining Diaspora, Refining a Discourse." *Diaspora: A Journal of Transnational Studies* 10, no. 2 (2001): 189–219.

Byrd, Rudolph P. Afterword. In *Essentials: Timeless Truths for Living in Today's World,* edited by Rudolph P. Byrd and Henry Louis Gates Jr. Hill Street, 1999.

Byrd, Rudolph P., and Henry Louis Gates Jr. "Jean Toomer's Conflicted Racial Identity." *Chronicle of Higher Education,* February 6, 2011, www.chronicle.com/article/jean-toomers-conflicted-racial-identity.

Cabrujas, José Ignacio, Vicencio González-Azuaje, and Leonardo Padrón. *Y Latinoamérica inventó la telenovela.* Caracas: Alfadil Ediciones, 2002.

Callahan, Allen Dwight. *The Talking Book: African Americans and the Bible.* Yale UP, 2006.

Callahan, John F. *In the African-American Grain: Call-and-Response in Twentieth-Century Black Fiction.* Wesleyan UP, 2001.

Callahan, Monique-Adelle. *Between the Lines: Literary Transnationalism and African American Poetics.* Oxford UP, 2011.

Callaway, Jessica G. *Mothers, Orphans, and the Law of the Free Womb: The Rhetoric of Brazilian Abolition in the Fiction of Aluísio Azevedo, Machado de Assis, and their Contemporaries.* PhD diss., Harvard University, 2008.

"Call to Eradicate Discrimination and Intolerance Marks Conclusion of World Conference against Racism." Press release RD/D/45, September 8, 2001. World Conference against Racism, Racial Discrimination, Xenophobia and Related Intolerance, Durban, South Africa, August 31–September 7, 2001. www.un.org/WCAR/pressreleases/rd-d45.htm.

Cameron, James. *A Time of Terror: A Survivor's Story.* LifeWrites, 2016.

Campadelli, Samira. *A telenovela.* São Paulo: Ático, 1985.

Campbell, Lewis D. *Speech of Hon. L. D. Campbell, of Ohio: On Southern Aggression, the Purposes of the Union, and the Comparative Effects of Slavery and Freedom, with a Facsimile of the Signatures to the Articles of Association of the Continental Congress, in the House of Representatives, February 19, 1850.* Washington: Buell & Blanchard, 1850.

Campt, Tina, and Deborah A. Thomas. "Gendering Diaspora: Transnational Feminism, Diaspora and Its Hegemonies." *Feminist Review* 90 (2008): 1–8.

Campuzano, Betina Sandra. "Revelaciones y Silencios: *Autobiografía de un esclavo,* de Juan Francisco Manzano y *Biografía de un cimarrón,* de Miguel Barnet." *Mitologías hoy* 12 (Winter 2015): 147–162.

Canclini, Néstor García. *Culturas híbridas: Estrategias para entrar y salir de la modernidad.* Ciudad de México: Grijalbo: Consejo Nacional para la Cultura y las Artes, 1990.

Cape Coast Castle. *Cape Coast Castle Record Book, 1777–1803.* Ghana, n.d.

Carby, Hazel V. *Reconstructing Womanhood: The Emergence of the Afro-American Woman Novelist.* Oxford UP, 1987.

Cardoso, Gerald. *Negro Slavery in the Sugar Plantations of Veracruz and Pernambuco, 1550–1680: A Comparative Study.* UP of America, 1983.

Cardoso, Luiz Antonio Fernandes, Adriana Almeida Couto, Pedro Mocair Maia, Sérgio Simões, Domingos Linheiros, Edson Fogaça, et al., eds. *Centro histórico de Salvador, Bahia, Brasil* [Historic Center of Salvador, Bahia, Brazil]. São Paulo: Horizonte Geográfico, 2000.

Cardwell, Diane. "Familiar Domino Sugar Refinery Will Shut Down Much of Its Operation." *New York Times,* August 21, 2003, www.nytimes.com/2003/08/21/nyregion/familiar-domino-sugar-refinery-will-shut-much-of-its-operation.html.

Carneiro, Cristina Helena. "A Dupla Objectificação da Mulher em *A Escrava Isaura:* Uma Amostragem do Poder Patriarcal." *Revista Urutágua: Revista Acadêmica Multidisciplinar* 7 (2004): 1–12.

Carpio, Glenda. *Laughing Fit to Kill: Black Humor in the Fictions of Slavery.* Oxford UP, 2008.

Carretta, Vincent. *Unchained Voices: An Anthology of Black Authors in the English-Speaking World of the Eighteenth Century.* UP of Kentucky, 1996.

Carretta, Vincent, and Philip Gould. *Genius in Bondage: Literature of the Early Black Atlantic.* UP of Kentucky, 2001.

Carrington, Selwyn H. H. *The Sugar Industry and the Abolition of the Slave Trade, 1775–1810.* UP of Florida, 2002.

Caruth, Cathy. *Trauma: Explorations in Memory.* Johns Hopkins UP, 1995.

———. *Unclaimed Experience: Trauma, Narrative, and History.* Johns Hopkins UP, 1996.

Carybé, and Odorico Tavares. *Pelourinho, 27 Desenhos De Carybé* [Pseud.] *Texto: Odorico Tavares.* Salvador: Progresso, 1955.

Casey, Edward S. *The Fate of Place: A Philosophical History.* U of California P, 1998.

Casimiro, Ana Palmira Bittencourt Santos. *Mentalidade e Estética na Bahia Colonial.* Salvador: As Letras Da Bahia, 1996.

Castro-Klarén, Sara. *A Companion to Latin American Literature and Culture.* Blackwell, 2008.

Castronovo, Russ. *Fathering the Nation: American Genealogies of Slavery and Freedom.* U of California P, 1995.

Cerqueira, Nelson, Bruno Furrer, and Jorge Amado, eds. *Pelourinho, centro histórico de Salvador, Bahia: A grandeza restaurada* [Pelourinho, Historic District of Salvador, Bahia]. 3rd ed. Salvador: Fundação Cultural do Estado da Bahia, 1995.

Chadbourn, James Harmon. *Lynching and the Law.* U of North Carolina P, 1933. Reprint, Johnson Reprint Corp., 1970.

Chaney, Michael A. *Fugitive Vision: Slave Image and Black Identity in Antebellum Narrative.* Indiana UP, 2008.

Chang-Rodríguez, Raquel. Book review. *Hispania* 59, no. 3 (September 1976): 558–559.

Chapeaux, Pedro Deschamps. *El negro en la economía habanera del siglo XIX.* Havana: Unión de Escritores y Artistas de Cuba, 1971.

Chase, Bill. "'Strange Fruit' Hits at Mob Law." *New York Amsterdam News,* July 22, 1939.

Chesnutt, Charles W. *Frederick Douglass.* Boston: Small, Maynard, 1899. Reprint, Johnson Reprint Corp., 1970.

———. *Stories, Novels, & Essays.* Library of America/Penguin Putnam, 2002.

Chilton, John. *Billie's Blues: Billie Holiday's Story 1933–1959.* Stein and Day, 1975.

Christopher, Emma. *Slave Ship Sailors and Their Captive Cargoes, 1730–1807.* Cambridge UP, 2006.

Christopher, Emma, Cassandra Pybus, and Marcus Buford Rediker, eds. *Many Middle Passages: Forced Migration and the Making of the Modern World.* U of California P, 2007.

Clark, VèVè Amasasa. "Developing Diaspora Literacy and Marasa Consciousness." In *Comparative American Identities,* edited by Hortense J. Spillers, 40–61. Routledge, 1991.

Clarke, Donald. *Wishing on the Moon: The Life and Times of Billie Holiday.* Viking, 1994.

Clarkson, Thomas. *An Essay on the Comparative Efficiency of Regulation or Abolition as Applied to the Slave Trade: Shewing that the Latter Only Can Remove the Evils to Be Found in that Commerce.* London: J. Phillips, 1789.

Clifford, James. *Routes: Travel and Translation in the Late Twentieth Century.* Harvard UP, 1997.

Cobb, Martha. *Harlem, Haiti, and Havana: A Comparative Critical Study of Langston Hughes, Jacques Roumain, Nicolás Guillén.* Three Continents P, 1979.

Cohen, David William, and Jack P. Greene, eds. *Neither Slave nor Free: The Freedman of African Descent in the Slave Societies of the New World.* Johns Hopkins UP, 1972.

Colbert, Soyica Diggs. *Black Movements: Performance and Cultural Politics.* Rutgers UP, 2017.

Colbert, Soyica Diggs, Robert J. Patterson, and Aida Levy-Hussen, eds. *The Psychic Hold of Slavery: Legacies in American Expressive Culture.* Rutgers UP, 2016.

Coleman, Willie Mae. *Keeping the Faith and Disturbing the Peace: Black Women, from Anti-Slavery to Women's Suffrage.* PhD diss., University of California, Irvine, 1982.

Collins, John F. "Melted Gold and National Bodies: The Hermeneutics of Depth and the Value of History in Brazilian Racial Politics." *American Ethnologist* 38, no. 4 (November 2011): 683–700.

———. *Revolt of the Saints: Memory and Redemption in the Twilight of Brazilian Racial Democracy.* Duke UP, 2015.

Collins, Patricia Hill. *Black Feminist Thought: Knowledge, Consciousness, and the Politics of Empowerment.* Routledge, 2009.

Commander, Michelle D. *Afro-Atlantic Flight: Speculative Returns and the Black Fantastic.* Duke UP, 2017.

Cone, James H. *The Cross and the Lynching Tree.* Orbis, 2011.

Congresso de História da Bahia (4th: 1999: Salvador, Brazil). *Anais do IV Congresso de História da Bahia: Salvador 450 anos.* Salvador, Instituto Geográfico e Histórico da Bahia; Fundação Gregório de Mattos, 2001.

Conniff, Michael L., and Thomas J. Davis. *Africans in the Americas: A History of the Black Diaspora.* St. Martin's, 1994.

Conrad, Robert. "Nineteenth-Century Brazilian Slavery." In Robert Brent Toplin, *Slavery and Race Relations in Latin America,* 146–174. Greenwood, 1974.

"The Cook Whose Cabin Became More Famous than Uncle Tom's." Advertisement. *Evening World,* January 29, 1920.

Cook, William W. Book review. *New England Review* 1, no. 2 (Winter 1978): 241–246.

Cooks, Bridget R. *Exhibiting Blackness: African Americans and the American Art Museum.* U of Massachusetts P, 2011.

Corbould, Clare. *Becoming African Americans: Black Public Life in Harlem, 1919–1939.* Harvard UP, 2009.

Corliss, Richard. "That Old Feeling: A Berlin Bio-pic." *Time,* December 30, 2001.

Counihan, Clare. "Reading the Figure of Woman in African Literature: Psychoanalysis, Difference and Desire." *Research in African Literatures* 38, no. 2 (Summer 2007): 161–180.

Coutinho, Afrânio, José Galante de Sousa, and OLAC. *Enciclopédia de literatura brasileira.* Rio de Janeiro: Ministério da Educação, Fundação de Assistência ao Estudiante, 1990.

Cowper, William. *The Poems of William Cowper.* London: Methuen, 1905.

Cox, Karen L. "Why Confederate Monuments Must Fall." *New York Times,* August 15, 2017, www.nytimes.com/2017/08/15/opinion/confederate-monuments-white-supremacy-charlottesville.html.

Cox, Timothy J. *Postmodern Tales of Slavery in the Americas: From Alejo Carpentier to Charles Johnson.* Taylor and Francis, 2001.

Crafts, Hannah, and Henry Louis Gates Jr., eds. *The Bondwoman's Narrative.* Warner Books, 2002.

Crane, Susan A., ed. *Museums and Memory.* Stanford UP, 2000.

Creative Time. "Creative Time Presents Kara Walker." March 20, 2017, www.creativetime.org/projects/karawalker.

Cruz, Celia, with Ana Cristina Reymundo. *Celia: Mi Vida—Una autobiografía.* HarperCollins, 2004.

Cummings, Brian, ed. *The Book of Common Prayer: The Texts of 1549, 1559, and 1662.* Oxford UP, 2011.

Cunha, Fausto. *O Romantismo no Brasil, de Castro Alves a Sousândrade.* Rio de Janeiro, Paz e Terra, 1971.

Cuno, James B., et al. *Change the Joke and Slip the Yoke: A Series of Conversations on the Use of Black Stereotypes in Contemporary Visual Practice: March 18–19, 1998.* Videorecording. 1998.

Cuti, Luiz Silva. *Literatura negro-brasileira.* São Paulo: Selo Negro, 2010.

Damrosch, David. *What Is World Literature?* Princeton UP, 2003.

Darby, Robert. "The Benefits of Psychological Surgery: John Scoffern's Satire on Isaac Baker Brown." *Medical History* 51, no. 4 (October 2007): 527–544.

Dash, J. Michael. *The Other America: Caribbean Literature in a New World Context.* U of Virginia P, 1998.

David, Mary T. "The Theme of Regeneration in Selected Works by Wole Soyinka." *Black American Literature Forum* 22, no. 4, Wole Soyinka issue, part 2 (Winter 1988): 645–661.

Davies, Carole Boyce. "Mother Right/Write Revisited: *Beloved* and *Dessa Rose* and the Construction of Motherhood in Black Women's Fiction." In *Narrating Mothers: Theorizing Maternal Subjectivities,* edited by Brenda O. Daly and Maureen T. Reddy, U of Tennessee P, 1991.

Davis, Angela Y. *Blues Legacies and Black Feminism: Gertrude "Ma" Rainey, Bessie Smith, and Billie Holiday.* Pantheon, 1998.

Davis, Charles T., and Henry Louis Gates Jr., eds. *The Slave's Narrative.* Oxford UP, 1990.

Davis, Darién J. *Slavery and Beyond: The African Impact on Latin America and the Caribbean.* SR Books, 1995.

Davis, David Brion. *Challenging the Boundaries of Slavery.* Harvard UP, 2003.

———. *Inhuman Bondage: The Rise and Fall of Slavery in the New World.* Oxford UP, 2006.

———. *The Problem of Slavery in the Age of Revolution, 1770–1823.* Oxford UP, 1998.

———. *The Problem of Slavery in Western Culture.* Oxford UP, 1988.

———. *Slavery and Human Progress.* Oxford UP, 1984.

Davis, Natalie Zemon. *Slaves on Screen: Film and Historical Vision.* Harvard UP, 2000.

Davis, Robert Con, and Ronald Schleifer. *Contemporary Literary Criticism: Literary and Cultural Studies.* Longman, 1994.

Dawson, Michael C. *Behind the Mule: Race and Class in African American Politics.* Princeton UP, 1994.

Deandrea, Pietro. *Fertile Crossings: Metamorphoses of Genre in Anglophone West African Literature.* Amsterdam: Rodopi, 2002.

Decker, William Merrill. *Geographies of Flight: Phillis Wheatley to Octavia Butler.* Northwestern UP, 2020.

DeCorse, Christopher R. *An Archaeology of Elmina: Africans and Europeans on the Gold Coast, 1400–1900.* Washington, DC: Smithsonian Institution P, 2001.

DeCosta-Willis, Miriam. *Blacks in Hispanic Literature: Critical Essays.* Kennikat, 1977.

———. "Self and Society in the Afro-Cuban Slave Narrative." *Latin American Literary Review* 16, no. 32 (July–December 1988): 6–15.

Defoe, Daniel. *The Shortest Way with the Dissenters: Or Proposals for the Establishment of the Church.* London, 1702.

de Jong, Ferdinand, and Michael Rowlands, eds. *Reclaiming Heritage: Alternative Imaginaries of Memory in West Africa.* Taylor and Francis, 2007.

de la Fuente, Alejandro. "Slaves and the Creation of Legal Rights in Cuba: Coartación and Papel." *Hispanic American Historical Review* 87, no. 4 (2007).

de la Fuente, Alejandro, and Ariela J. Gross. *Becoming Free, Becoming Black: Race, Freedom, and Law in Cuba, Virginia, and Louisiana.* Cambridge UP, 2020.

Delongoria, Maria. *'Stranger Fruit': The Lynching of Black Women—The Cases of Rosa Richardson and Marie Scott.* PhD diss., University of Missouri–Columbia, 2006.

Deutsch, Otto Erich. *Music Review* 1 (February 1940).

DeWolf, Thomas Norman. *Inheriting the Trade: A Northern Family Confronts its Legacy as the Largest Slave-Trading Dynasty in US History.* Beacon, 2008.

Diedrich, Maria, Henry Louis Gates Jr., and Carl Pedersen, eds. *Black Imagination and the Middle Passage.* Oxford UP, 1999.

Diop, Cheikh Anta. *The African Origin of Civilization: Myth or Reality.* Edited and translated by Mercer Cook. Chicago Review P, 1974.

Diouf, Sylviane A. *Dreams of Africa in Alabama: The Slave Ship Clotilda and the Story of the Last Africans Brought to America.* Oxford UP, 2007.

———. *Fighting the Slave Trade: West African Strategies.* Ohio UP/James Currey, 2003.

Doane, Mary Ann. *The Emergence of Cinematic Time: Modernity, Contingency, the Archive.* Harvard UP, 2002.

Domínguez, Jorge I., ed. *Race and Ethnicity in Latin America.* Garland, 1994.

Doriani, Beth Maclay. "Black Womanhood in Nineteenth-Century America: Subversion and Self-Construction in Two Women's Autobiographies." *American Quarterly* 43, no. 2 (June 1991): 199–222.

Douglass, Frederick. *Narrative of the Life of Frederick Douglass, an American Slave.* Laurel, 1997.

———. *Prose Works. Selections; Autobiographies.* Library of America/Penguin Books, 1996.

Dow, George Francis. *Slave Ships and Slaving.* Negro UP, 1970.

Dray, Philip. *At the Hands of Persons Unknown: The Lynching of Black America.* Random House, 2002.

Drescher, Seymour. *From Slavery to Freedom: Comparative Studies in the Rise and Fall of Atlantic Slavery.* Macmillan, 1999.

Drescher, Seymour, and Stanley L. Engerman. *A Historical Guide to World Slavery.* Oxford UP, 1998.

Dresser, Madge, and Sue Giles. *A Respectable Trade? Bristol & Transatlantic Slavery.* Exhibition catalog, City Museum and Art Gallery, Bristol (March 6–September 2, 1999). Bristol Museums and Art Gallery with the University of the West of England, 2000.

Du Bois, W. E. B. *Black Reconstruction in America 1860–1880.* 1935. Free Press, 1998.

———. "The Economics of Negro Emancipation in the United States." *Sociological Review* 4, no. 3 (October 1911): 303–313.

———. *The Gift of Black Folk: The Negroes in the Making of America.* 1924. Edited by Henry Louis Gates Jr. Oxford UP, 2007.

———. "The Talented Tenth." In *The Negro Problem: A Series of Articles by Representative American Negroes of Today.* James Pott, 1903.

———. *The Souls of Black Folk: Authoritative Text, Contexts, Criticism.* Edited by Henry Louis Gates Jr. and Terri Hume Oliver. W. W. Norton, 1999.

Duarte, Constância Lima. "Gênero e etnia no nascente romance brasileiro." *Revista Estudos Feministas* 13, no. 2 (2005): 443–444.

Duarte, Eduardo de Assis, ed. *Machado de Assis afro-descendente: Escritos de Caramujo (antologia).* Belo Horizonte: Crisálida, 2007.

DuBois, Page. *Slaves and Other Objects.* U of Chicago P, 2003.

Dunbar, Paul Laurence. *In His Own Voice: The Dramatic and Other Uncollected Works of Paul Laurence Dunbar.* Edited by Herbert Woodward Martin and Ronald Primeau. Ohio UP, 2002.

———. *In Old Plantation Days.* New York: Dodd, Mead and Company, 1903.

———. *Lyrics of the Hearthside.* Dodd, Mead and Company, 1899.

Duncan, Quince. *El negro en la literatura costarricense.* San José: Editorial Costa Rica, 1975.

Dunlap, David W. "Relics of the Domino Sugar Refinery, Frozen in Time and Syrup." *New York Times,* October 23, 2013.

Dunn, Richard S. *Sugar and Slaves: The Rise of the Planter Class in the English West Indies, 1624–1713.* U of North Carolina P, 2000.

Dzidzienyo, Anani, and Suzanne Oboler, eds. *Neither Enemies nor Friends: Latinos, Blacks, Afro-Latinos.* Palgrave Macmillan, 2005.

Ebron, Paulla A. *Performing Africa.* Princeton UP, 2002.

Echávez-Solano, Nelsy, and Kenya Dworkin y Méndez. *Spanish and Empire.* Vanderbilt UP, 2007.

Echevarría, Roberto González. "*Biografía de un cimarrón* and the Novel of the Cuban Revolution." In *The Voice of the Masters: Writing and Authority in Modern Latin American Literature,* 110–123. U of Texas P, 1985.

Eckstein, Lars. *Re-Membering the Black Atlantic: On the Poetics and Politics of Literary Memory.* Rodopi, 2006.

Edwards, Brent Hayes. *The Practice of Diaspora: Literature, Translation, and the Rise of Black Internationalism.* Harvard UP, 2003.

Eichstedt, Jennifer, and Stephen Small. *Representations of Slavery: Race and Ideology in Southern Plantation Museums.* Smithsonian Institution P, 2002.

Elam, Harry J., Jr., and Kennell Jackson, eds. *Black Cultural Traffic: Crossroads in Global Performance and Popular Culture.* U of Michigan P, 2005.

Ellison, Brian D., and Melissa Lee. "Black Student Life at Harvard: Black History Month." *Harvard Crimson,* February 23, 1993.

Eltis, David. "The Volume and Structure of the Transatlantic Slave Trade: A Reassessment." *William and Mary Quarterly* 58, no. 1 (January 2001): 17–46.

Eltis, David, Frank D. Lewis, and David Richardson. "Slave Prices, the African Slave Trade, and Productivity in the Caribbean, 1674–1807." *Economic History Review* 58, no. 4 (November 2005): 673–700.

Eltis, David, Frank D. Lewis, and Kenneth L. Sokoloff, eds. *Slavery in the Development of the Americas.* Cambridge UP, 2004.

Eltis, David, and David Richardson. *Atlas of the Transatlantic Slave Trade.* Yale UP, 2010.

Emmer, P. C., ed. *Colonialism and Migration: Indentured Labour before and after Slavery.* Dordrecht: Martinus Nijhoff, 1986.

Engerman, Stanley L. *Slavery, Emancipation, and Freedom: Comparative Perspectives.* Louisiana State UP, 2007.

———. *Terms of Labor: Slavery, Serfdom, and Free Labor.* Stanford UP, 1999.

Engle, Margarita. *The Poet Slave of Cuba: A Biography of Juan Francisco Manzano.* Henry Holt, 2006.

Equiano, Olaudah, Mary White Rowlandson, and Gordon M. Sayre. *American Captivity Narratives: Selected Narratives with Introduction.* Houghton Mifflin, 2000.

"'Escrava Isaura' originou projeto de minissérie para TV chinesa e filme." *Folha De S. Paulo,* December 30, 2007: E7.

Espino, Gonzalo, ed. *Tradición oral, culturas peruanas: invitación al debate.* Lima: Fondo Editorial, Universidad Nacional Mayor de San Marcos, Ciencias Humanas, 2003.

Essien, Kwame. *Brazilian-African Diaspora in Ghana: The Tabom, Slavery, Dissonance of Memory, Identity, and Locating Home.* Michigan State UP, 2016.

Essinger, Silvio. "A musicalidade do criador do 'lerê lerê.'" *O Globo,* January 7, 2012.

Evaristo, Conceição. "Da representação à auto-apresentação da mulher negra na literatura brasileira." *Palmares* 1, no. 1 (August 2005): 52–57.

Eyerman, Ron. "The Past in the Present: Culture and the Transmission of Memory." *Acta Sociologica* 47, no. 2 (June 2004): 159–169.

Fabre, Geneviève. "The Slave Ship Dance." In *Black Imagination and the Middle Passage,* edited by Maria Diedrich, Henry Louis Gates Jr., and Carl Pedersen, 33–46. Oxford UP, 1999.

Fabre, Geneviève, and Michel Feith, eds. *Jean Toomer and the Harlem Renaissance.* Rutgers UP, 2000.

Fabre, Geneviève, and Robert G. O'Meally, eds. *History and Memory in African-American Culture.* Oxford UP, 1994.

Fadipe, Ashamu Sewanu. *Slave Trade and Western Civilisation in Badagry* [Le commerce d'esclaves et la civilisation occidentale à Badagry]. Ikeja: Media Ace, 2000.

Faery, Rebecca Blevins. *Cartographies of Desire: Captivity, Race, and Sex in the Shaping of an American Nation.* U of Oklahoma P, 1999.

Falconbridge, Alexander. *An Account of the Slave Trade on the Coast of Africa.* London: J. Phillips, 1788.

Falola, Toyin. *The African Diaspora: Slavery, Modernity, and Globalization.* U of Rochester P, 2013.

Falola, Toyin, and Matt D. Childs, eds. *The Yoruba Diaspora in the Atlantic World.* Indiana UP, 2004.

Falola, Toyin, and Steven J. Salm. *Globalization and Urbanization in Africa.* Africa World P, 2004.

Falola, Toyin, and Aribidesi Adisa Usman. *Movements, Borders, and Identities in Africa.* U of Rochester P, 2009.

Famule, Olawole. *The Ijumu-Yoruba Egungun Masquerades: Art and Spirituality in an African Culture.* VDM Verlag, 2009.

Fanon, Frantz. *Black Skin, White Masks* [Peau noire, masques blancs]. Grove, 2008.

Farrington, Lisa E. *Creating Their Own Image: The History of African-American Women Artists.* Oxford UP, 2005.

Faulkner, William. *Absalom, Absalom!: The Corrected Text.* Vintage, 1990.

Feelings, Tom. *The Middle Passage: White Ships/Black Cargo.* Dial, 1995.

Feimster, Crystal Nicole. *Southern Horrors: Women and the Politics of Rape and Lynching.* Harvard UP, 2009.

Felder, Cain Hope. *Stony the Road We Trod: African American Biblical Interpretation.* Fortress, 1991.

Felman, Shoshana, and Dori Laub. *Testimony: Crises of Witnessing in Literature, Psychoanalysis, and History.* Routledge, 1992.

Feracho, Lesley. *Linking the Americas: Race, Hybrid Discourses, and the Reformulation of Feminine Identity.* State U of New York P, 2005.

Ferguson, Jeffrey B. *Race and the Rhetoric of Resistance.* Rutgers UP, 2021.

———. *The Sage of Sugar Hill: George S. Schuyler and the Harlem Renaissance.* Yale UP, 2005.

Fernandes, Florestan. "Beyond Poverty: The Negro and the Mulatto in Brazil." In Robert Brent Toplin, *Slavery and Race Relations in Latin America,* 277–297. Greenwood, 1974.

Fernandes, Ismael. *Memória da telenovela brasileira.* São Paulo: Editora Brasiliense, 1987.

Fernandes Dias, Maria Suzette, ed. *Legacies of Slavery: Comparative Perspectives.* Cambridge Scholars Publishing, 2007.

Ferreira, Carlos Antero. *Castelo da Mina: Da fundação às representações iconográficas dos séculos XVI e XVII.* Lisboa: Livros Horizonte, 2007.

Ferreira, Débora R. S. "Na obra de Carolina Maria de Jesus, um Brasil esquecido." *Luso-Brazilian Review* 39, no. 1 (Summer 2002): 103–119.

Ferreira de Souza, Elio. *Poesia negra: Solano Trinidade e Langston Hughes.* Curitiba: Appris Editora, 2017.

Ferrer, Ada. *Freedom's Mirror: Cuba and Haiti in the Age of Revolution.* Cambridge UP, 2014.

Figueroa-Vásquez, Yomaira. *Decolonizing Diasporas: Radical Mappings of Afro-Atlantic Literature.* Northwestern UP, 2020.

Finch, Aisha K. *Rethinking Slave Rebellion in Cuba: La Escalera and the Insurgencies of 1841–1844.* U of North Carolina P, 2015.

Finkelman, Paul, ed. *Comparative Issues in Slavery.* Garland, 1989.

Finley, Cheryl. *Committed to Memory: The Art of the Slave Ship Icon.* Princeton UP, 2018.

Fleischner, Jennifer. *Mastering Slavery: Memory, Family, and Identity in Women's Slave Narratives.* New York UP, 1996.

Foley, Barbara. *Jean Toomer: Race, Repression, and Revolution.* U of Illinois P, 2014.

Fomin, E. S. D. *A Comparative Study of Societal Influences on Indigenous Slavery in Two Types of Societies in Africa.* Edwin Mellen, 2002.

Foner, Laura, and Eugene D. Genovese, eds. *Slavery in the New World: A Reader in Comparative History.* Prentice Hall, 1969.

Foreman, P. Gabrielle, et al. "Writing About Slavery? Teaching About Slavery?" Community-sourced document. docs.google.com/document/d/1A4TEdDgYslX-hlKezLodMIM71My3KTNozxRvoIQTOQs/mobilebasic. Accessed May 11, 2020.

Foster, Frances Smith. *Witnessing Slavery: The Development of Ante-bellum Slave Narratives.* 2nd ed. U of Wisconsin P, 1979.

———. *Written by Herself: Literary Production by African American Women, 1746–1892.* Indiana UP, 1993.

Fox, Patricia D. *Being and Blackness in Latin America: Uprootedness and Improvisation.* UP of Florida, 2006.

Fox-Genovese, Elizabeth, and Eugene D. Genovese. *The Mind of the Master Class: History and Faith in the Southern Slaveholders' Worldview.* Cambridge UP, 2005.

———. *Slavery in White and Black: Class and Race in the Southern Slaveholders' New World Order.* Cambridge UP, 2008.

Fraga Filho, Walter. *Encruzilhadas da liberdade: Histórias de escravos e libertos na Bahia, 1870–1910.* Campinas: Editora da Unicamp, 2006.

Fraginals, Manuel Moreno. *El ingenio: Complejo económico-social cubano del azúcar.* 3 vols. La Habana: Editorial Ciencias Sociales, 1978.

———. *El ingenio* [The Sugar Mill]. Barcelona: Crítica, 2001.

França, Jean Marcel Carvalho. *Imagens do negro na literatura brasileira (1584–1890).* São Paulo: Editora Brasiliense, 1998.

Franco, José Luciano. *La diáspora africana en el nuevo mundo.* La Habana: Editorial Ciencias Sociales, 1975.

———. *Las minas de Santiago del Prado y la rebelión de los cobreros, 1530–1800.* La Habana: Editorial Ciencias Sociales, 1975.

———. *A presença negra na América Latina.* Lisboa: Prelo, 1971.

———. *Rebeldías negras en los siglos XVIII y XIX.* La Habana: Centro de Información Científica y Técnica, Universidad de la Habana, 1975.

Franklin, John Hope, and Evelyn Brooks Higginbotham. *From Slavery to Freedom: A History of African Americans.* 10th ed. McGraw-Hill, 2021.

Fredrickson, George M. *The Black Image in the White Mind: The Debate on Afro-American Character and Destiny, 1817–1914.* Harper and Row, 1971.

Freeman, Mark Philip. *Rewriting the Self: History, Memory, Narrative.* Routledge, 1993.

French, Scot. *The Rebellious Slave: Nat Turner in American Memory.* Houghton Mifflin, 2004.

Freud, Sigmund. *Moses and Monotheism.* Vintage, 1955.

Frey, Sylvia R., and Betty Wood, eds. *From Slavery to Emancipation in the Atlantic World.* Frank Cass, 1999.

Freyre, Gilberto. *Americanidade e latinidade da América Latina e outros textos afins,* edited by Edson Nery da Fonseca. São Paulo: Imprensa Oficial, 2003.

———. *Brazil: An Interpretation.* Alfred A. Knopf, 1947.

———. *Casa-Grande & Senzala.* Rio de Janeiro: Editora Record, 2002.

———. *The Masters and the Slaves: A Study in the Development of Brazilian Civilization.* 1933. Translated by Samuel Putnam. U of California P, 1986.

———. *New World in the Tropics: The Culture of Modern Brazil.* Greenwood, 1959.

Fuentes, Marisa J. *Dispossessed Lives: Enslaved Women, Violence, and the Archive.* U of Pennsylvania P, 2016.

Furtado, Jú. *Chica Da Silva: A Brazilian Slave of the Eighteenth Century.* Cambridge UP, 2009.

Gabbin, Joanne V., ed. *The Furious Flowering of African American Poetry.* UP of Virginia, 1999.

Gál, Hans. "The Riddle of Schubert's Unfinished Symphony: A Contribution to the Psychology of Musical Creative Work." *Music Review* 2, no. 1 (1941): 63–67. http://www.hansgal.com/storage/writings/riddle.pdf.

Galland, China. *Love Cemetery: Unburying the Secret History of Slaves.* HarperOne, 2007.

Galler, Robert. "From 'Three Recent Volumes.'" In *Robert Hayden: Essays on the Poetry,* edited by Laurence Goldstein and Robert Chrisman, 61–62. U of Michigan P, 2001.

García Rodríguez, Gloria. *Voices of the Enslaved in Nineteenth-Century Cuba: A Documentary History.* Translated by Nancy L. Westrate. U of North Carolina P, 2011.

García Salazar, Juan. *La poesía negrista en el Ecuador.* Esmeraldas: Banco Central del Ecuador, 1982.

Garland, Caroline. *Understanding Trauma: A Psychoanalytical Approach.* Duckworth, 1998.

Garsd, Jasmine. "Saudade: An Untranslatable, Undeniably Potent Word." *Alt.Latino: Latinx Arts and Culture,* NPR, January 8, 2015, https://www.npr.org/sections/altlatino/2014/02/28/282552613/saudade-an-untranslatable-undeniably-potent-word.

Garuba, Harry. "Masked Discourse: Dramatic Representation and Generic Transformation in Wole Soyinka's *A Dance in the Forests.*" *Modern Drama* 45, no. 3 (Fall 2002): 378–394.

Garvey, Marcus. "First Message to the Negroes of the World from Atlanta Prison." *Negro World,* February 10, 1925.

———. *Philosophy and Opinions of Marcus Garvey, Or, Africa for the Africans.* Compiled by Amy Jacques Garvey. Routledge, 2006.

Gates, Henry Louis, Jr., ed. *Lincoln on Race and Slavery.* Princeton UP, 2009.

———. *"Race," Writing, and Difference.* U of Chicago P, 1986.

———. *The Signifying Monkey: A Theory of Afro-American Literary Criticism.* 25th anniversary ed. Oxford UP, 2014.

Gates, Henry Louis, Jr., and Nellie Y. McKay, eds. *The Norton Anthology of African American Literature.* W. W. Norton, 2004.

"Gates of Return, Julien Sinzogan." London: Victoria and Albert Museum, 2007. www.vam.ac.uk/content/articles/g/gates-of-return-julien-sinzogan.

Gault, Robert H. "Lynchings in 1912." *Journal of the American Institute of Criminal Law and Criminology* 4, no. 1 (May 1913): 130.

Geary, Christraud. "The Body of a Myth: Embodying the Black Mammy Figure in Visual Culture." In *Black Womanhood: Images, Icons, and Ideologies of the African Body,* edited by Barbara Thompson and Ifi Amadiume, 163–180. U of Washington P, 2008.

Geary, Christraud M., and Andrea Nicolls. *Elmina: Art and Trade on the West African Coast.* National Museum of African Art, Smithsonian Institution, 1992.

Genette, Gérard. *Palimpsests: Literature in the Second Degree.* Translated by Channa Newman and Claude Doubinsky. U of Nebraska P, 1997.

Genovese, Eugene D. *Roll, Jordan, Roll: The World the Slaves Made.* Pantheon, 1974.

George, Olakunle. *African Literature and Social Change: Tribe, Nation, Race.* Indiana UP, 2017.

Georgia Writers' Project. *Drums and Shadows: Survival Studies among the Georgia Coastal Negroes.* 1940. U of Georgia P, 1986.

Ghana Ministry of Information and Broadcasting. *Historic Elmina: A Brief Account of the History and Structure of Elmina Castle.* Accra, n.d.

Gibbs, James, Ketu H. Katrak, and Henry Louis Gates Jr., eds. *Wole Soyinka: A Bibliography of Primary and Secondary Sources.* Greenwood, 1986.

Gibney, Mark, ed. *The Age of Apology: Facing Up to the Past.* U of Pennsylvania P, 2008.

Gielow, Martha S. *Mammy's Reminiscences, and Other Sketches.* New York: A. S. Barnes, 1898.

Gikandi, Simon. *Encyclopedia of African Literature.* Routledge, 2003.

———. *Slavery and the Culture of Taste.* Princeton UP, 2011.

Gilroy, Paul. *The Black Atlantic: Modernity and Double Consciousness.* Harvard UP, 1993.

Glissant, Édouard, and J. M. Dash. *Caribbean Discourse: Selected Essays.* UP of Virginia, 1989.

Goldberg, Andrew V., and Peter N. Yianilos. "Towards an Archival Intermemory." *Proceedings IEEE International Forum on Research and Technology Advances in Digital Libraries,* April 22–24, 1998, 147–156.

Goldsby, Jacqueline. *A Spectacular Secret: Lynching in American Life and Literature.* U of Chicago P, 2006.

Goldstein, Laurence, and Robert Chrisman, eds. *Robert Hayden: Essays on the Poetry.* U of Michigan P, 2001.

Gomes, Heloisa Toller. "Silences and Voices of Slavery: *A escrava Isaura* and *Incidents in the Life of a Slave Girl.*" In *Comparative Perspectives on the Rise of the Brazilian Novel,* edited by Ana Cláudia Suriani da Silva and Sandra Guardini Vasconcelos, 161–179. U College London P, 2020.

Gomez, Michael A., ed. *Diasporic Africa: A Reader.* New York UP, 2006.

———. *Exchanging our Country Marks: The Transformation of African Identities in the Colonial and Antebellum South.* U of North Carolina P, 1998.

———. *Reversing Sail: A History of the African Diaspora.* 2nd ed. Cambridge UP, 2020.

Gonçalves, Marco Antonio. "Um mundo feito de papel: Sofrimento e estetização da vida (os diários de Carolina Maria de Jesus)." *Horizontes Antropológicos* 20, no. 42 (2014): 21–47.

Goodheart, Lawrence B., Richard D. Brown, and Stephen Rabe, eds. *Slavery in American Society.* D. C. Heath, 1993.

Goodrick, Edward W., and John R. Kohlenberger III, eds. *The NIV Complete Concordance: The Complete English Concordance to the New International Version.* Zondervan, 1981.

Gordon, Avery. *Ghostly Matters: Haunting and the Sociological Imagination.* U of Minnesota P, 1997.

Goyal, Yogita. *Romance, Diaspora, and Black Atlantic Literature.* Cambridge UP, 2010.

———. *Runaway Genres: The Global Afterlives of Slavery.* New York UP, 2019.

———. "We Need New Diasporas." *American Literary History* 29, no. 4 (2017): 640–663.

Graden, Dale T. "Miguel Barnet's *Biography of a Runaway Slave:* Testimonial Literature as History." Review. *Humanities and Social Sciences Online, H-Ethnic,* October 1996.

Green, Tara T. *Reimagining the Middle Passage: Black Resistance in Literature, Television, and Song.* Ohio State UP, 2018.

Greene, David, Marvin J. Chomsky, John Erman, and Gilbert Moses, dirs. *Roots: The Saga of an American Family.* 1977. Burbank: Warner Bros. Entertainment, 2018.

Griffin, Farah Jasmine. *If You Can't Be Free, Be a Mystery.* Free P, 2001.

———. *"Who Set You Flowin'?": The African-American Migration Narrative.* Oxford UP, 1995.

Griffiths, Jennifer L. *Traumatic Possessions: The Body and Memory in African American Women's Writing and Performance.* U of Virginia P, 2009.

Gruesser, John Cullen. *Confluences: Postcolonialism, African American Literary Studies, and the Black Atlantic.* U of Georgia P, 2005.

Gubar, Susan. *Racechanges: White Skin, Black Face in American Culture.* Oxford UP, 2000.

Guenther, Christina, and Beth A. Griech-Polelle, eds. *Trajectories of Memory: Intergenerational Representations of the Holocaust in History and the Arts.* Cambridge Scholars, 2008.

Gueye, Abdoulaye, and Johann Michel, eds. *A Stain on Our Past: Slavery and Memory.* Africa World P, 2018.

Guillén, Nicolás. *Yoruba from Cuba: Selected Poems.* Leeds: Peepal Tree, 2005.

Guimarães, Bernardo. *Dois romances.* Rio de Janeiro: Editora Nova Aguilar, 1976.

———. *A Escrava Isaura, Romance.* São Paulo: Difusão Cultural do Livro, 2006.

Gunning, Sandra. *Race, Rape, and Lynching: The Red Record of American Literature, 1890–1912.* Oxford UP, 1996.

Gysin, Fritz, and Christopher Mulvey, eds. *Black Liberation in the Americas.* Münster: LIT Verlag, 2001.

Haberly, David T. "The Brazilian Novel from 1850 to 1900." In *The Cambridge History of Latin American Literature.* Vol. 3, *Brazilian Literature; Bibliographies,* edited by Roberto Gonzalez Echevarría and Enrique Pupo-Walker, 137–156. Cambridge UP, 1996.

Habert, Angeluccia Bernardes. *A Bahia de outr'ora, agora: Leitura de artes & artistas, uma revista de cinema da década de 20.* Salvador: Academia de Letras da Bahia, Assemblia Legislativa do Estado da Bahia, 2002.

Haehnel, Birgit, and Melanie Ulz, eds. *Slavery in Art and Literature: Approaches to Trauma, Memory and Visuality.* Berlin: Frank and Timme GmbH, 2009.

Halbwachs, Maurice. *On Collective Memory.* Edited and translated by Lewis A. Coser. U of Chicago P, 1992.

Haley, Alex. *Roots: The Saga of an American Family.* Doubleday, 1976.

Hall, Catherine. *Civilising Subjects: Colony and Metropole in the English Imagination, 1830–1867.* U of Chicago P, 2002.

Hall, Gwendolyn Midlo. *Slavery and African Ethnicities in the Americas: Restoring the Links.* U of North Carolina P, 2005.

Hall, Jacquelyn. *Revolt against Chivalry: Jesse Daniel Ames and the Women's Campaign against Lynching.* Columbia UP, 1979.

Hall, Stuart. "Cultural Identity and Diaspora." In *Identity: Community, Culture, Difference,* edited by Jonathan Rutherford, 222–237. Lawrence and Wishart, 1990.

———. *Race, the Floating Signifier.* Transcript. Media Education Foundation, 1997. https://www.mediaed.org/transcripts/Stuart-Hall-Race-the-Floating-Signifier-Transcript.pdf.

Halloran, Vivian Nun. *Exhibiting Slavery: The Caribbean Postmodern Novel as Museum.* U of Virginia P, 2009.

Halperin, Paula. "Então ela é escrava? *Escrava Isaura,* History and National Identity." *Significação* 47, no. 53 (2020): 162–183.

Hamilton, Douglas, and Robert J. Blyth, eds. *Representing Slavery: Art, Artefacts and Archives in the Collections of the National Maritime Museum.* London: Lund Humphries, 2007.

Hammond, Eli Shelby, Orlando Davis Hammond, and Justin Winsor. *Slave-Life on a Plantation before the War.* Manuscript, April 4, 1893.

Hanciau, Nubia. "A representação da mulata na literatura brasileira: Estereótipo e preconceito." *Cadernos Literários* 7 (2002): 57–64.

Handley, George B. *Postslavery Literatures in the Americas: Family Portraits in Black and White.* UP of Virginia, 2000.

Harper, Frances Ellen Watkins. *A Brighter Coming Day: A Frances Ellen Watkins Harper Reader,* edited by Frances Smith Foster. Feminist P at the City U of New York, 1990.

———. *Complete Poems of Frances E. W. Harper,* edited by Maryemma Graham. Oxford UP, 1988.

———. *Moses: A Story of the Nile.* Merrihew and Son, 1869.

Harris, Michael D. *Colored Pictures: Race and Visual Representation.* U of North Carolina P, 2003.

Harris, Trudier. *Exorcising Blackness: Historical and Literary Lynching and Burning Rituals.* Indiana UP, 1984.

———. *From Mammies to Militants: Domestics in Black American Literature.* Temple UP, 1982.

Harris-Perry, Melissa V. *Sister Citizen: Shame, Stereotypes, and Black Women in America (for Colored Girls Who've Considered Politics When Being Strong Isn't Enough).* Yale UP, 2011.

Harrison, William. "A New Negro Voice." *Opportunity* 19, no. 3 (March 1941), 91.

Hart, Stephen M. *A Companion to Latin American Literature.* Tamesis, 2004.

Hartman, Saidiya V. *Lose Your Mother: A Journey along the Atlantic Slave Route.* Farrar, Straus and Giroux, 2007.

———. *Scenes of Subjection: Terror, Slavery, and Self-Making in Nineteenth-Century America.* Oxford UP, 1997.

———. "Venus in Two Acts." *Small Axe* 12, no. 2 (2008): 1–14.

Haskins, James. *The Cotton Club.* Random House, 1977.

Haskins, James, and N. R. Mitgang. *Mr. Bojangles: The Biography of Bill Robinson.* William Morrow, 1988.

Hatcher, John. *From the Auroral Darkness: The Life and Poetry of Robert Hayden.* George Ronald, 1984.

Hawthorne, Nathaniel. *The Scarlet Letter: A Romance.* 1850. New American Library, 1959.

Hayden, Robert. *Collected Poems: Robert Hayden,* edited by Frederick Glaysher. Liveright, 2013.

———. "Preface to *The New Negro.*" In *Collected Prose,* edited by Frederick Glaysher, 62–67. U of Michigan P, 1984.

Heine, Robert E. *The Commentaries of Origen and Jerome on St. Paul's Epistle to the Ephesians.* Oxford UP, 2002.

Henderson, Carol E. *America and the Black Body: Identity Politics in Print and Visual Culture.* Fairleigh Dickinson UP, 2009.

———, ed. *Imagining the Black Female Body: Reconciling.* Palgrave Macmillan, 2005.

Hening, William Waller. *The Statutes at Large; Being a Collection of All the Laws of Virginia from the First Session of the Legislature, in the Year 1619.* Bartow, 1823.

Henze, Hans Werner. *El Cimarrón: Biographie des geflohenen Sklaven Esteban Montejo* [Biography of the Runaway Slave Esteban Montejo]. Mainz: B. Schott's Söhne, 1976.

Herman, Judith Lewis. *Trauma and Recovery: The Aftermath of Violence—from Domestic Abuse to Political Terror.* Basic, 1997.
Herskovits, Melville J. *The Myth of the Negro Past.* Harper and Bros., 1941.
Heywood, Linda Marinda, and John Kelly Thornton. *Central Africans, Atlantic Creoles, and the Foundation of the Americas, 1585–1660.* Cambridge UP, 2007.
Hill, Abe. "52nd Street NY's Real 'Melting Pot': Problem—Yes? No?" *New York Amsterdam News,* July 15, 1944.
Hill, Patricia Liggins. "'Let Me Make the Songs for the People': A Study of Frances Watkins Harper's Poetry." *Black American Literature Forum* 15, no. 2 (Summer 1981): 60–65.
Hill, Telenia. *Castro Alves e o poema lírico.* 2nd ed. Rio de Janeiro: Tempo Brasileiro, 1986.
Hinchberger, Bill. "Actress Has Int'l Spirit." Special report, *Focus: Brazil: Variety* (October 20, 1997–October 26, 1997): 46.
Hinds, Harold E., Jr. "A Holistic Approach to the Study of Popular Culture: Context, Text, Audience, and Recoding." In *Popular Culture Theory and Methodology: A Basic Introduction,* edited by *Harold E. Hinds* Jr., Marilyn F. Motz, and Angela M. S. Nelson, 163–179. U of Wisconsin P, 2006.
Hinds, Harold E., Jr., Marilyn F. Motz, and Angela M. S. Nelson, eds. *Popular Culture Theory and Methodology: A Basic Introduction.* U of Wisconsin P, 2006.
Hine, Darlene Clark. "Rape and the Inner Lives of Black Women in the Middle West: Preliminary Thoughts on the Culture of Dissemblance." *Signs* 14, no. 4 (1989): 912–920.
Hine, Darlene Clark, and Jacqueline McLeod, eds. *Crossing Boundaries: Comparative History of Black People in Diaspora.* Indiana UP, 1999.
Hobbes, Thomas. *Leviathan.* Edited by J. C. A. Gaskin. Oxford UP, 1998.
Hobbs, Robert. "Reading Black Through White: Kara Walker and the Question of Racial Stereotyping. A Discussion between Michael Corris and Robert Hobbs." In *Differences and Excess in Contemporary Art: The Visibility of Women's Practices,* edited by Gill Perry, 104–123. Blackwell, 2004.
Hobson, Janell. "Everybody's Protest Song: Music as Social Protest in the Performances of Marian Anderson and Billie Holiday." *Signs* 33, no. 2 (2008): 443–448.
Hodgson, Adam. *A Letter to M. Jean-Baptiste Say, on the Comparative Expense of Free and Slave Labour.* Liverpool: Hatchard and Son, 1823.
Hoetink, H. *Slavery and Race Relations in the Americas: Comparative Notes on their Nature and Nexus.* Harper and Row, 1973.
Holiday, Billie, with William Dufty. *Lady Sings the Blues.* Doubleday, 1956.
Holsey, Bayo. *Routes of Remembrance: Refashioning the Slave Trade in Ghana.* U of Chicago P, 2008.
hooks, bell. *Black Looks: Race and Representation.* South End, 1992.
———. *Feminism Is for Everybody: Passionate Politics.* South End, 2000.
Hopkins, Pauline. *Of One Blood, or, the Hidden Self.* Washington Square P, 2004.
Horton, James Oliver. *Landmarks of African American History.* Oxford UP, 2005.

Horton, James Oliver, and Lois E. Horton. *Slavery and Public History: The Tough Stuff of American Memory.* W. W. Norton, 2006.

Howlett, Jacques. "*Présence Africaine* 1947–1958." *Journal of Negro History* 43, no. 2 (April 1958): 140–150.

Hoy, David Couzens, ed. *Foucault: A Critical Reader.* B. Blackwell, 1986.

Hu, Zhihua, and Maria Teresa Roberto. "A introdução e recepção da 'A Escrava Isaura' na China." *Gláuks—Revista de Letras e Artes* 20, no. 2 (2020): 99–123.

Hubbard, Dolan. *Recovered Writers/Recovered Texts: Race, Class, and Gender in Black Women's Literature.* U of Tennessee P, 1997.

Hughes, Carl Milton. *The Negro Novelist: A Discussion of the Writings of American Negro Novelists, 1940–1950.* Citadel, 1953.

Hughes, Derek. *Versions of Blackness: Key Texts on Slavery from the Seventeenth Century.* Cambridge UP, 2007.

Hughes, John Milton Charles. *The Negro Novelist: A Discussion of the Writings of American Negro Novelists, 1940–1950.* Ayer, 1967.

Humphries, Jefferson, ed. *Southern Literature and Literary Theory.* U of Georgia P, 1990.

Hurston, Zora Neale. "How It Feels to Be Colored Me." *The World Tomorrow,* May 1928.

———. *Moses, Man of the Mountain.* Harper Perennial, 2009.

———. *Mules and Men.* Harper Perennial, 2008.

———. *Their Eyes Were Watching God.* Perennial Classics, 1998.

Hutchinson, George B. Introduction. *Cane.* Penguin Books, 2019.

———. *The Harlem Renaissance in Black and White.* Belknap Press of Harvard UP, 1995.

———. "Jean Toomer and the 'New Negroes' of Washington." *American Literature* 63, no.4 (December 1991): 683–692.

———. "Toomer and American Racial Discourse." *Texas Studies in Literature and Language* 35, no. 2 (Summer 1993): 226–250.

Huyssen, Andreas. *Present Pasts: Urban Palimpsests and the Politics of Memory.* Stanford UP, 2003.

Ingersoll, Thomas N. *Mammon and Manon in Early New Orleans: The First Slave Society in the Deep South, 1718–1819.* U of Tennessee P, 1999.

Irele, F. Abiola. *The African Imagination: Literature in Africa and the Black Diaspora.* Oxford UP, 2001.

———. "The African Imagination." *Research in African Literatures* 21, no. 1 (Spring 1990): 49–67.

Irele, F. Abiola, and Biodun Jeyifo, eds. *The Oxford Encyclopedia of African Thought.* 2 vols. Oxford UP, 2010.

Irwin, Graham W. *Africans Abroad: A Documentary History of the Black Diaspora in Asia, Latin America, and the Caribbean during the Age of Slavery.* Columbia UP, 1977.

Jackson, Richard L. *The Black Image in Latin American Literature.* U of New Mexico P, 1976.

———. *Black Literature and Humanism in Latin America.* U of Georgia P, 1988.

———. *Black Writers and the Hispanic Canon.* Twayne, 1997.
———. *Black Writers and Latin America: Cross-Cultural Affinities.* Howard UP, 1998.
———. "Slavery, Racism and Autobiography in Two Early Black Writers: Juan Francisco Manzano and Martín Morúa Delgado." In *Voices from Under: Black Narrative in Latin America and the Caribbean,* edited by William Luis, 55–64. Greenwood, 1984.
Jacobs, Harriet A. *Incidents in the Life of a Slave Girl: Written by Herself.* Edited by L. Maria Child. Boston, 1861.
"James Cameron, Human-Rights Activist, Dies." *All Things Considered,* NPR, June 13, 2006. www.npr.org/templates/story/story.php?storyId=5482946.
James, Conrad, and John Perivolaris, eds. *The Cultures of the Hispanic Caribbean.* UP of Florida, 2000.
Jean Toomer Papers. James Weldon Johnson Collection. Beinecke Rare Book and Manuscript Library. Series 1, Correspondence (box 26). archives.yale.edu/repositories/11/resources/950.
Jesus, Carolina Maria de. *Child of the Dark: The Diary of Carolina Maria de Jesus.* Translated by David St. Clair. New American Library, 2003.
———. *Quarto de Despejo.* Edited by Audálio Dantas. São Paulo: Editora Francisco Alves, 1960.
———. *The Unedited Diaries of Carolina Maria de Jesus.* Edited by Robert M. Levine and José Carlos Sebe Bom Meihy. Translated by Nancy P. S. Naro and Cristina Mehrtens. Rutgers UP, 1999.
Jewell, K. Sue. *From Mammy to Miss America and Beyond.* Routledge, 1993.
Jeyifo, Biodun, ed. *Conversations with Wole Soyinka.* UP of Mississippi, 2001.
———. *Modern African Drama: Backgrounds and Criticism.* W. W. Norton, 2002.
———. "Okonkwo and His Mother: Things Fall Apart and Issues of Gender in the Constitution of African Postcolonial Discourse." *Callaloo* 16, no. 4 (1993): 847–858.
———. *The Truthful Lie: Essays in a Sociology of African Drama.* New Beacon, 1985.
John, Catherine A. *Clear Word and Third Sight: Folk Groundings and Diasporic Consciousness in African Caribbean Writing.* Duke UP, 2003.
Johnson, Barbara. *Moses and Multiculturalism.* U of California P, 2010.
Johnson, James Weldon. *The Autobiography of an Ex-Coloured Man.* Vintage, 1989.
———. *The Book of American Negro Poetry.* Harcourt, Brace, 1922.
Johnson, Jessica Marie. *Wicked Flesh: Black Women, Intimacy, and Freedom in the Atlantic World.* U of Pennsylvania P, 2020.
Johnson, Joan Marie. "'Ye Gave them a Stone': African American Women's Clubs, the Frederick Douglass Home, and the Black Mammy Monument." *Journal of Women's History* 17, no. 1 (Spring 2005): 62–86.
Johnson, Willis Fletcher. *The History of Cuba.* 5 vols. B. F. Buck, 1920.
Johnston, Alison M. *Is the Sacred for Sale?: Tourism and Indigenous Peoples.* Earthscan, 2006.
Jones, Eldred Durosimi, ed. *Women in African Literature Today.* Africa World P, 1987.

Joseph, G. M., and Mark D. Szuchman. *I Saw a City Invincible: Urban Portraits of Latin America.* SR Books, 1996.

Jung, C. G. *The Collected Works of C. G. Jung.* Vol. 8, *The Structure and Dynamics of the Psyche.* Edited and translated by Gerhard Adler and F. C. Hull. Princeton UP, 1966.

Kaplan, Fran. "Dr. James Cameron, Museum Founder and Lynching Survivor." America's Black Holocaust Museum. https://www.abhmuseum.org/about/dr-cameron-founder-lynching-survivor.

Keita, Maghan. *Race and the Writing of History: Riddling the Sphinx.* Oxford UP, 2000.

Keizer, Arlene R. *Black Subjects: Identity Formation in the Contemporary Narrative of Slavery.* Cornell UP, 2004.

———. "Gone Astray in the Flesh: Kara Walker, Black Women Writers, and African American Postmemory." *PMLA* 123, no. 5 (2008): 1649–1672.

Kelley, Mary. *Private Woman, Public Stage: Literary Domesticity in Nineteenth-Century America.* U of North Carolina P, 2002.

Kelley, Robin D. G. "How the West Was One: The African Diaspora and the Re-Mapping of US History." *Black Scholar* 30, no. 3–4 (2000): 31–35.

Kendi, Ibram X. *Stamped from the Beginning: The Definitive History of Racist Ideas in America.* Bold Type Books, 2017.

Kennedy, Randy. "White Artist's Painting of Emmett Till at Whitney Biennial Draws Protests." *New York Times,* March 21, 2017, www.nytimes.com/2017/03/21/arts/design/painting-of-emmett-till-at-whitney-biennial-draws-protests.html.

Kerman, Cynthia Earl, and Richard Eldridge. *The Lives of Jean Toomer: A Hunger for Wholeness.* Louisiana State UP, 1987.

Kimball, Robert, and Linda Emmet, eds. *The Complete Lyrics of Irving Berlin.* Alfred A. Knopf, 2000.

King, Jamilah. "The Overwhelming Whiteness of Black Art." *Colorlines,* May 21, 2014, www.colorlines.com/articles/overwhelming-whiteness-black-art.

King, Martin Luther, Jr. *A Testament of Hope: The Essential Writings and Speeches of Martin Luther King, Jr.* Edited by James Melvin Washington. Harper San Francisco, 1991.

Klein, Herbert S. *The Atlantic Slave Trade.* Cambridge UP, 2010.

———. *Slavery in the Americas: A Comparative Study of Virginia and Cuba.* U of Chicago P, 1967.

Knight, Franklin W. *Slave Society in Cuba During the Nineteenth Century.* U of Wisconsin P, 1970.

Konstantinides, Anneta. "The First Black Photographer to Shoot a Vanity Fair Cover Shares the Power Story behind His Picture of Viola Davis." *Insider,* July 15, 2020, www.insider.com/viola-davis-vanity-fair-cover-first-by-a-black-photographer-2020-7.

Koolish, Lynda, and June Jordan. *African American Writers: Portraits and Visions.* UP of Mississippi, 2001.

Kossoy, Boris, and Maria Luiza Tucci Carneiro. *O olhar europeu: O negro na iconografia brasileira do século XIX.* São Paulo: Edusp, 1994.

Kowaleski-Wallace, Elizabeth. *The British Slave Trade and Public Memory.* Columbia UP, 2006.

Kulka, Tomáš. *Kitsch and Art.* Pennsylvania State UP, 1996.

Kurutz, Steven. "A Twain Scholar Reacts to the New, Censored Version 'Huckleberry Finn.'" *Wall Street Journal,* January 9, 2011, www.wsj.com/articles/BL-SEB-58698.

Lackey, Michael. "Moses, Man of Oppression: A Twentieth-Century African American Critique of Western Theocracy." *African American Review* 43, no. 4 (Winter 2009): 577–588.

Landers, Jane, and Barry Robinson. *Slaves, Subjects, and Subversives: Blacks in Colonial Latin America.* U of New Mexico P, 2006.

La Pastina, Antonio C., and Joseph D. Straubhaar. "Multiple Proximities between Television Genres and Audiences: The Schism between Telenovelas' Global Distribution and Local Consumption." *Gazette: The International Journal for Communication Studies* 67, no. 3 (June 2005): 271–288.

Lauter, Paul. *Canons and Contexts.* Oxford UP, 1991.

Law, Robin. "Ethnicity and the Slave Trade: 'Lucumi' and 'Nago' as Ethnonyms in West Africa." *History in Africa* 24 (1997): 205–219.

———, ed. *From Slave Trade to "Legitimate" Commerce: The Commercial Transition in Nineteenth-Century West Africa.* Cambridge UP, 1995.

Leão, Angela Vaz, ed. *Contatos e ressonâncias: Literaturas africanas de língua portuguesa.* Belo Horizonte: Editora PUC Minas, 2003.

Leary, Joy DeGruy. *Post Traumatic Slave Syndrome: America's Legacy of Enduring Injury and Healing. Newly revised and updated edition.* Joy DeGruy Publications, 2017.

Lee, Julia Sun-Joo. *The American Slave Narrative and the Victorian Novel.* Oxford UP, 2010.

Leitch, Vincent B. *The Norton Anthology of Theory and Criticism.* W. W. Norton, 2001.

León, Yansert Fraga. *Poetas esclavos en Cuba: El trinatario Ambrosio Echemendía.* Sanctí Spíritus: Ediciones Luminaria, 2009.

Levin, Amy K., ed. *Defining Memory: Local Museums and the Construction of History in America's Changing Communities.* AltaMira, 2007.

Levine, Lawrence W. *Black Culture and Black Consciousness: Afro-American Folk Thought from Slavery to Freedom.* Oxford UP, 2007.

Levine, Robert M. "The Cautionary Tale of Carolina Maria de Jesus." *Latin American Research Review* 29, no. 1 (1994): 55–83.

Levine, Robert M., and John J. Crocitti, eds. *The Brazil Reader: History, Culture, Politics.* Duke UP, 1999.

Lévi-Strauss, Claude. *Introduction to the Work of Marcel Mauss.* Translated by Felicity Baker. Routledge, 1987.

Levinson, Sanford. *Written in Stone: Public Monuments in Changing Societies.* Duke UP, 1998.

Lewis, Bernard. *Race and Slavery in the Middle East: An Historical Enquiry.* Oxford UP, 1990.

Leys, Ruth. *Trauma: A Genealogy.* U of Chicago P, 2000.

Lima, Luciano Rodrigues. "Poesia negra contemporânea: O redescobrimento do Brasil: Discurso poético, consciência e atitude." In *Estampa de letra: Literatura, lingüística and outras linguagens ensaios,* edited by Márcia Rios da Silva and Rosa Helena Blanco, 105–124. Salvador: Quarteto Editora, 2004.

Limeira, José Carlos, and Éle Semog. *O Arco-Íris Negro.* São Paulo, 1978.

Lisboa, Maria Manuel. "A escrava Isaura: Novel by Bernardo Guimarães." In *Encyclopedia of Latin American Literature,* edited by Verity Smith, 396–397. Fitzroy Dearborn, 1997.

Livingstone, Josephine, and Lovia Gyarkye. "The Case against Dana Schutz." *New Republic,* March 22, 2017, newrepublic.com/article/141506/case-dana-schutz.

Locke, Alain LeRoy. *The New Negro: Voices of the Harlem Renaissance.* Simon and Schuster, 1997.

Lopez, Ana M. "Our Welcomed Guests: Telenovelas in Latin America." In *To Be Continued: Soap Operas around the World,* edited by Robert C. Allen, 256–274. New York, 1995.

López Springfield, Consuelo, ed. *Daughters of Caliban: Caribbean Women in the Twentieth Century.* Indiana UP, 1997.

Lorini, Alessandra. *Rituals of Race: American Public Culture and the Search for Racial Democracy.* UP of Virginia, 1999.

Lott, Eric. *Love and Theft: Blackface Minstrelsy and the American Working Class.* Oxford UP, 1993.

Lovejoy, Henry B., and Olatunji Ojo. "'Lucumí,' 'Terranova,' and the Origins of the Yoruba Nation." *Journal of African History* 56, no. 3 (2015): 353–372.

Lovejoy, Paul E. *Transformations in Slavery: A History of Slavery in Africa.* Cambridge UP, 1983.

Lowe, Lisa. *The Intimacies of Four Continents.* Duke UP, 2015.

Luis, William. "The Politics of Memory and Miguel Barnet's 'The Autobiography of a Runaway Slave.'" *Modern Language Notes* 104, no. 2 (1989): 475–491.

———, ed. *Voices from Under: Black Narrative in Latin America and the Caribbean.* Greenwood, 1984.

Luminet, Olivier, and Antonietta Curci, eds. *Flashbulb Memories: New Issues and New Perspectives.* Psychology P, 2009.

"Lynchings: By State and Race, 1882–1968." Archives at the Tuskegee Institute. http://archive.tuskegee.edu/repository/digital-collection/lynching-information. Accessed May 11, 2020.

"Lynchings: By Year and Race." University of Missouri–Kansas City School of Law. http://law2.umkc.edu/faculty/projects/ftrials/shipp/lynchingyear.html. Accessed July 2, 2021.

Mack, Angela D., and Stephen G. Hoffius, eds. *Landscape of Slavery: The Plantation in American Art.* U of South Carolina P, 2008.

Madison, James H. *A Lynching in the Heartland: Race and Memory in America.* Palgrave, 2001.

Makward, Edris. "The Poet of Négritude." *African Arts* 35, no. 2 (Summer 2002): 4–7.

Malafala, E. B. de Ataíde. *Pelourinhos portugueses.* Lisboa: Imprensa Nacional-Casa de Moeda, 2005.

"Mammy." *Chicago Defender,* February 3, 1917.

"Mammy Statue Disgraceful Insult." *Afro-American,* July 20, 1923.

"'Mammy Statue Not Race Issue Says Dixieites: Same Thing as Kitchen Door Handouts, According to South Carolina Paper." *Chicago Defender,* December 24, 1923.

"'Mammy' Story of Gassaway Starts Protest: Oklahoma Senator's Address over Radio Station Resented." *Philadelphia Tribune,* May 9, 1935.

Mandel, Naomi. "'I Made the Ink': Identity, Complicity, 60 Million, and More." *MFS: Modern Fiction Studies* 48, no. 3 (2002): 581–613.

Manring, M. M. *Slave in a Box: The Strange Career of Aunt Jemima.* UP of Virginia, 1998.

Mansour, Mónica. *La poesía negrista.* México: Ediciones Era, 1973.

Manuel, Peter, Kenneth M. Bilby, and Michael Largey. *Caribbean Currents: Caribbean Music from Rumba to Reggae.* Temple UP, 1995.

Manzano, Juan Francisco. *Autobiografía del esclavo poeta y otros escritos.* Edited by William Luis. Madrid: Iberoamericana, 2007.

———. *The Autobiography of a Slave* [Autobiografía de un esclavo]. Modernized by Ivan A. Schulman. Wayne State UP, 1996.

———. *Poems by a Slave in the Island of Cuba.* Translated by R. R. Madden. London: Thomas Ward, 1840.

Marfo, Florence. "Marks of the Slave Lash: Black Women's Writing of the 19th Century Anti-Slavery Novel." *Diáspora: Journal of the Annual Afro-Hispanic Literature and Culture Conference* 11 (2001): 80–86.

Margolick, David. *Strange Fruit: Billie Holiday, Café Society, and an Early Cry for Civil Rights.* Running P, 2000.

———. *Strange Fruit: The Biography of a Song.* Running P, 2000.

Maria das Neves, Cylaine. *A vila de São Paulo de Piratininga: Fundação e Representação.* São Paulo: Annablume, 2007.

Markovitz, Jonathan. *Legacies of Lynching: Racial Violence and Memory.* U of Minnesota P, 2004.

Marks, Carole, and Diana Edkins. *The Power of Pride: Stylemakers and Rulebreakers of the Harlem Renaissance.* Crown, 1999.

Marotti, Giorgio. *Negro nel romanzo brasiliano: Black Characters in the Brazilian Novel.* University of California, Center for Afro-American Studies, 1987.

Marshall, Paule. "The Negro Woman in Literature." *Freedomways* 6, no. 1 (Winter 1966): 20–25.

Martin, Gertrude. "Review of *Heart-Shape in the Dust.*" In *Robert Hayden: Essays on the Poetry,* edited by Laurence Goldstein and Robert Chrisman, 49. U of Michigan P, 2001.

Martín-Barbero, Jesús, and Germán Rey. *Los ejercicios del ver: Hegemonía audiovisual y ficción televisiva.* Barcelona: Gedisa, 1999.

Martínez, Ibsen. "Romancing the Globe." *Foreign Policy* 151 (November–December 2005): 48–56.

Martínez Montiel, Luz M. *Negros en América.* Madrid: Editorial MAPFRE, 1992.

Martins, Wilson. *História da Inteligência Brasileira.* 7 vols. São Paulo: Editora Cultrix, 1976.

Marx, Karl. "Address on the Question of Free Trade." In *The Poverty of Philosophy.* Martin Lawrence, 1933.

Matory, J. Lorand. *Black Atlantic Religion: Tradition, Transnationalism, and Matriarchy in the Afro-Brazilian Candomblé.* Princeton UP, 2005.

Mattelart, Michèle, and Armand Mattelart. *The Carnival of Images: Brazilian Television Fiction.* Translated by David Buxton. Bergin and Garvey, 1990.

Mattos, Waldemar. *A Bahia de Castro Alves.* São Paulo: Instituto Progresso Editorial, 1948.

Mays, Benjamin E. *The Negro's God, as Reflected in His Literature.* Negro UP, 1969.

Mbembe, Achille. "African Modes of Self-Writing." Translated by Steven Rendall. *Public Culture: Special Issue on New Imaginaries* 14, no. 2 (2002): 239–273.

———. *Critique of Black Reason.* Translated by Laurent Dubois. Duke UP, 2017.

———. *Necropolitics.* Translated by Steve Corcoran. Duke UP, 2019.

McClaurin, Irma, ed. *Black Feminist Anthropology: Theory, Politics, Praxis, and Poetics.* Rutgers UP, 2001.

McDowell, Deborah E., and Arnold Rampersad. *Slavery and the Literary Imagination.* Johns Hopkins UP, 1989.

McElroy, Guy C., and Christopher C. French, eds. *Facing History: The Black Image in American Art, 1710–1940.* Bedford Arts, 1990.

McElya, Micki. *Clinging to Mammy: The Faithful Slave in Twentieth-Century America.* Harvard UP, 2007.

McGlynn, Frank, and Seymour Drescher, eds. *The Meaning of Freedom: Economics, Politics, and Culture After Slavery.* U of Pittsburgh P, 1992.

McKay, Claude. *Harlem Shadows: The Poems of Claude McKay.* Harcourt, Brace, 1922.

McKay, Nellie. "Jean Toomer in His Time: An Introduction." In *Jean Toomer: A Critical Evaluation,* edited by Therman B. O'Daniel, 3–13. Howard UP, 1988.

McKittrick, Katherine. *Dear Science and Other Stories.* Duke UP, 2021.

———. *Demonic Grounds: Black Women and the Cartographies of Struggle.* U of Minnesota P, 2006.

McMillan, Uri. *Embodied Avatars: Genealogies* of *Black Feminist Art and Performance.* New York UP, 2015.

McMillen, Sally G. *Southern Women: Black and White in the Old South.* Wiley, 2017.

Meihy, José Carlos Sebe Bom, and Robert M. Levine. *Cinderela negra: A saga de Carolina Maria de Jesus.* Rio de Janeiro: Editora UFRJ, 1994.

Mellafe R., Rolando. *Negro Slavery in Latin America.* U of California P, 1975.

Melo, José Marques de. *As telenovelas da Globo: Produção e exportação.* São Paulo: Summus Editorial, 1988.

Menchú, Rigoberta. *Me llamo Rigoberta Menchú y así me nació la conciencia.* [I, Rigoberta Menchú: An Indian Woman in Guatemala]. Edited by Elisabeth Burgos-Debray. Verso, 1984.

Mendelsohn, Isaac. *Slavery in the Ancient Near East: A Comparative Study of Slavery in Babylonia, Assyria, Syria, and Palestine from Middle of the Third Millennium to the End of the First Millennium.* Greenwood, 1978.

Mendes, Miriam Garcia. *O negro e o teatro brasileiro.* São Paulo: Fundação Cultural Palmares, 1993.

Menezes, Raimundo de. *Dicionário literário brasileiro.* Rio de Janeiro: Livros Técnicos e Científicos Editora, 1978.

Mérimée, Prosper. *The Writings of Prosper Mérimée, Comprising his Novels, Tales, and Letters to an Unknown.* Translated by Emily Mahy Waller and Biahy Helena Dey. Holby, 1905.

Messeder, Carlos Alberto. *Retrato de época: Poesia marginal anos 70.* Rio de Janeiro, Funarte, 1981.

Metress, Christopher. *The Lynching of Emmett Till: A Documentary Narrative.* U of Virginia P, 2002.

Miller, Christopher L. *The French Atlantic Triangle: Literature and Culture of the Slave Trade.* Duke UP, 2008.

Miller, Joseph Calder. *Slavery, a Comparative Teaching Bibliography.* Crossroads, 1977.

Miller, Marilyn. "Rebeldía narrativa, resistencia poética y expresión 'libre' en Juan Francisco Manzano." *Revista Iberoamericana* 71, no. 211 (April–June 2005): 417–436.

Mitchell, Angelyn. *The Freedom to Remember: Narrative, Slavery, and Gender in Contemporary Black Women's Fiction.* Rutgers UP, 2002.

———. *Within the Circle: An Anthology of African American Literary Criticism from the Harlem Renaissance to the Present.* Duke UP, 1994.

Mitchell, Koritha. "James Baldwin, Performance Theorist, Sings the *Blues for Mister Charlie.*" *American Quarterly* 64, no. 1 (March 2012): 33–60.

———. *Living with Lynching: African American Lynching Plays, Performance, and Citizenship, 1890–1930.* U of Illinois P, 2011.

Mitchell, Margaret. *Gone with the Wind.* 1936. Macmillan, 1975.

Mitchell, Robin. *Vénus Noire: Black Women and Colonial Fantasies in Nineteenth-Century France.* U of Georgia P, 2020.

Mitter, Siddhartha. "Kara Walker Takes Monumental Jab at Britannia." *New York Times,* September 30, 2019, www.nytimes.com/2019/09/30/arts/design/kara-walker-tate-turbine-hall.html.

Moisés, Massaud. *História da literatura brasileira: Modernismo.* 1st ed. São Paulo: Editora Cultrix, 1983–1989.

Molloy, Sylvia. "From Serf to Self: The Autobiography of Juan Francisco Manzano." In

At Face Value: Autobiographical Writing in Spanish America, 36–54. Cambridge UP, 1991.

Monteiro, George. *There's No Word for Saudade: Perspectives on the Literature and Culture of Portuguese America.* Peter Lang, 2017.

Montejo, Esteban, and Miguel Barnet. *Biografía de un cimarrón: Novela.* La Habana: Editorial Letras Cubanas, 1993.

Montejo, Esteban, Miguel Barnet, and W. N. Hill. *Biography of a Runaway Slave.* Curbstone, 1994.

Montez, Angela Barros. *Autores brasileiros: Biobibliografias.* Rio de Janeiro: Ministério da Cultura, Fundação Biblioteca Nacional, Departamento Nacional do Livro, 1998.

"A Monument That Mammy'd Like to View." *Chicago Defender,* June 21, 1941.

Moore, Niamh, and Yvonne Whelan, eds. *Heritage, Memory and the Politics of Identity: New Perspectives on the Cultural Landscape.* Ashgate, 2007.

Morales, Ed. *The Latin Beat: The Rhythms and Roots of Latin Music from Bossa Nova to Salsa and Beyond.* Da Capo, 2003.

Morales, Jorge Luis. *Poesía afroantillana y negrista: Puerto Rico, República Dominicana, Cuba.* Río Piedra: Editorial Universitaria, Universidad de Puerto Rico, 1981.

Moreno, Elena. *El discurso del poder y la lucha de contrarios en la narrativa de la esclavitud en Cuba y Estados Unidos.* PhD diss., Florida International University, 2006.

Morgan, Jennifer L. *Laboring Women: Reproduction and Gender in New World Slavery.* U of Pennsylvania P, 2004.

———. *Reckoning with Slavery: Gender, Kinship, and Capitalism in the Early Black Atlantic.* Duke UP, 2021.

Morgan, Kenneth. "Slave Women and Reproduction in Jamaica, ca. 1776–1834." In *Women and Slavery.* Vol. 2, *The Modern Atlantic,* edited by Gwyn Campbell, Suzanne Miers, and Joseph C. Miller, 27–53. Ohio UP, 2008.

Morgan, Robin. *Sisterhood Is Global: The International Women's Movement Anthology.* Anchor/Doubleday, 1984.

Morrison, Toni. *Beloved.* Plume, 1998.

———. *The Origin of Others.* Harvard UP, 2017.

———. "The Site of Memory." In *Inventing the Truth: The Art and Craft of Memoir,* edited by William Zinsser, 83–102. 2nd ed. Houghton Mifflin, 1995.

———. *Song of Solomon.* Knopf, 1995.

Morton, Patricia, ed. *Discovering the Women in Slavery: Emancipating Perspectives on the American Past.* U of Georgia P, 1996.

Mudimbe, V. Y. *The Surreptitious Speech: Présence Africaine and the Politics of Otherness, 1947–1987.* U of Chicago P, 1992.

Mufti, Aamir R. "Global Comparativism." *Critical Inquiry* 31, no. 2 (Winter 2005): 472–489.

Mullen, Edward. "The Emergence of Afro-Hispanic Poetry: Some Notes on Canon Formation." *Hispanic Review* 56, no. 4 (Autumn 1988): 435–453.

Murphy, Laura T. *Metaphor and the Slave Trade in West African Literature.* Ohio UP, 2012.

———. *The New Slave Narrative: The Battle over Representations of Contemporary Slavery.* Columbia UP, 2019.

Musser, Amber Jamilla. "Queering Sugar: Kara Walker's Sugar Sphinx and the Intractability of Black Female Sexuality." *Signs* 42, no. 1 (2016): 153–174.

Mustakeem, Sowande' M. *Slavery at Sea: Terror, Sex, and Sickness in the Middle Passage.* U of Illinois P, 2016.

Nascimento, Elisa Larkin, ed. *A matriz africana no mundo.* São Paulo: Selo Negro, 2008.

Nasta, Susheila. *Motherlands: Black Women's Writing from Africa, the Caribbean, and South Asia.* Rutgers UP, 1992.

National Association for the Advancement of Colored People. "Lynchings in the United States." *Crisis* (February 1922): 168–169.

———. *Thirty Years of Lynching in the United States: 1889–1918.* 1919.

National Underground Railroad Freedom Center. *Unchained Memories: Readings from the Slave Narratives.* Bulfinch, 2002.

National Woman's Rights Convention. *Proceedings of the Eleventh National Woman's Rights Convention, Held at the Church of the Puritans, New York, May 10, 1866: Phonographic Report.* Robert J. Johnston, 1866.

Nazer, Mende, and Damien Lewis. *Slave.* Public Affairs, 2003.

Nehl, Markus. *Transnational Black Dialogues: Re-Imagining Slavery in the Twenty-First Century.* Transcript Verlag, 2016.

Neira, Luz García. "Abertura de Telenovela: O Designo em Movimento" [The Soap-Opera Title Sequence: The Design in Movement]. Paper presented at 8° Congresso Brasileiro de Pesquisa e Desenvolvimento em Design, October 8–11, 2008, São Paulo, Brazil.

Nelson, Charmaine. *The Color of Stone: Sculpting the Black Female Subject in Nineteenth-Century America.* U of Minnesota P, 2007.

Nilges, Mathias. "Marxism and Form Now." *Meditations* 24, no. 2 (Spring 2009): 66–89.

Nishida, Mieko. *Slavery and Identity: Ethnicity, Gender, and Race in Salvador, Brazil, 1808–1888.* Indiana UP, 2003.

Nofal, Rossana. "*Biografía de un cimarrón* de Miguel Barnet: 'La construcción de una voz.'" *Revista Chilena de Literatura* 40 (November 1992): 35–39.

Nora, Pierre. *Rethinking France: Les Lieux de Mémoire.* Vol. 1, *The State.* Translated by Mary Trouille. U of Chicago P, 2001.

Northrup, David, ed. *The Atlantic Slave Trade.* D. C. Heath, 1994.

"Noted Author Talks at 135th St. Library: Clement Wood Urges Race to Change White Man's 'Stereotype.'" *New York Amsterdam News,* February 21, 1923.

Nunes, Jovane. *A Escrava Isaura e o Vampiro.* Lua de Papel, 2010.

Nwankwo, Ifeoma Kiddoe. *Black Cosmopolitanism: Racial Consciousness and Transnational Identity in the Nineteenth-Century Americas.* U of Pennsylvania P, 2005.

Nyong'o, Tavia. *Afro-Fabulations: The Queer Drama of Black Life.* New York UP, 2019.

Ocasio, Rafael. *Afro-Cuban Costumbrismo: From Plantations to the Slums.* UP of Florida, 2012.

Ogundayo, 'BioDun J. "Polyphony in Miguel Barnet's *Biografía de un cimarrón.*" *Nebula* 3.2–3.3 (September 2006): 189–204.

Ogundiran, Akinwumi, and Toyin Falola. *Archaeology of Atlantic Africa and the African Diaspora.* Indiana UP, 2010.

Ojo, Olatunji. "The Root Is Also Here: The Nondiaspora Foundations of Yoruba Ethnicity." In *Movements, Borders, and Identities in Africa,* edited by Toyin Falola and Aribidesi Usman, 53–80. U of Rochester P, 2009.

Okpewho, Isidore. *African Oral Literature: Backgrounds, Character, and Continuity.* Indiana UP, 1992.

———. "Oral Tradition: Do Storytellers Lie?" *Journal of Folklore Research* 40, no. 3 (September–December 2003): 215–232.

———. "The Primacy of Performance in Oral Discourse." *Research in African Literatures* 21, no. 4 (Winter 1990): 121–128.

Okpewho, Isidore, Carole Boyce Davies, and Ali A. Mazrui, eds. *The African Diaspora: African Origins and New World Identities.* Indiana UP, 1999.

———. *The New African Diaspora.* Indiana UP, 2009.

Oldfield, J. R. *"Chords of Freedom": Commemoration, Ritual and British Transatlantic Slavery.* Manchester UP, 2007.

"The 'Old Mammy' Market." *New York Times,* January 9, 1908.

"An Old Mammy's Bread—Bettered." Advertisement. *Washington Times,* February 27, 1918.

"Old Mammy Stuff." *Philadelphia Tribune,* December 2, 1937.

Oliver, Paul, dir. *Songsters and Saints: Vocal Traditions on Race Records.* Badminton: Matchbox Records, 1984. 2 sound discs.

Oliver, William I. "After Absurdity." *Educational Theatre Journal* 17, no. 3 (October 1965): 196–205.

Oliveira, Emanuelle K. F. *Writing Identity: The Politics of Contemporary Afro-Brazilian Literature.* Purdue UP, 2008.

Olivieri-Godet, Rita, and Lícia Soares de Souza. *Identidades e representações na cultura brasileira.* João Pessoa: Idéia, 2001.

Olszewski Filha, Sofia. *A fotografia e o negro na cidade do Salvador, 1840–1914.* Salvador: Empresa Gráfica da Bahia, 1989.

Oluoch-Olunya, Garnette. "East Africa: A Confiscated History." *Africa News,* February 28, 2005.

O'Meally, Robert G. *Lady Day: The Many Faces of Billie Holiday.* Arcade, 1991.

———. "Slavery's Shadow." *Callaloo* 20 (Winter 1984): 157–158.

Opoku-Agyemang, Kwadwo. *Cape Coast Castle.* Accra: Afram, 1996.

———. "Ghana Speaking (1): The 'Living Wound' at Cape Coast Castle." Interview. Radio Open Source: Arts, Ideas and Politics with Christopher Lydon. http://www.radioopensource.org/ghana-speaking-the-living-wound-at-cape-coast-castle/.

Opoku-Agyemang, Naana, Paul E. Lovejoy, and David V. Trotman, eds. *Africa and Trans-Atlantic Memories: Literary and Aesthetic Manifestations of Diaspora and History.* Africa World P, 2008.

"Oppose Monument." *New York Amsterdam News,* February 7, 1923.

Orser, Charles E., ed. *Race and the Archaeology of Identity.* U of Utah P, 2001.

Ortiz, Fernando. *Contrapunteo cubano del tabaco y el azúcar.* Caracas: Biblioteca Ayacucho, 1978.

———. *Cuban Counterpoint: Tobacco and Sugar.* Translated by Harriet de Onís. Duke UP, 1995.

———. *Los negros esclavos.* La Habana: Editorial Ciencias Sociales, 1996.

Osagie, Iyunolu Folayan. *The Amistad Revolt: Memory, Slavery, and the Politics of Identity in the United States and Sierra Leone.* U of Georgia P, 2000.

Owen, Hilary. *Mother Africa, Father Marx: Women's Writing of Mozambique, 1948–2002.* Bucknell UP, 2007.

Owen, Mary Alicia. *Voodoo Tales as Told among the Negroes of the Southwest: Collected from Original Sources.* 1893. Negro Universities Press, 1969.

Owens, Emily A. "Consent." *differences* 30, no. 1 (2019): 148–156.

Paes, José Paulo, and Massaud Moisés, eds. *Pequeno dicionário de literatura brasileira.* São Paulo: Editora Cultrix, 2001.

Page, Thomas Nelson. *Red Rock: A Chronicle of Reconstruction.* C. Scribner's Sons, 1898.

Palmer, Colin A. "The African Diaspora." *Black Scholar* 30, no. 3/4 (Fall–Winter 2000): 56–59.

———. "Defining and Studying the Modern African Diaspora." *Journal of Negro History* 85, no. 1–2 (Winter–Spring 2000): 27–32.

Panish, Jon. *The Color of Jazz: Race and Representation in Postwar American Culture.* UP of Mississippi, 1997.

Paquette, Robert L., and Mark M. Smith, eds. *The Oxford Handbook of Slavery in the Americas.* Oxford UP, 2010.

"'Part in *Imitation* Is Not Real Me,' says Fredi." *Chicago Defender,* national ed., January 19, 1935, 9.

Parekh, Pushpa, and Siga Fatima Jagne, eds. *Postcolonial African Writers: A Bio-Bibliographical Critical Sourcebook.* Routledge, 1998.

Patai, Daphne. "Jorge Amado: Champion of Women's Sexual Freedom." In *Confronting Change, Challenging Tradition: Women in Latin American History,* edited by Gertrude M. Yeager, 55–65. Scholarly Resources, 1994.

Patterson, Orlando. *Rituals of Blood: Consequences of Slavery in Two American Centuries.* Basic Civitas Books, 1998.

———. *Slavery and Social Death: A Comparative Study.* Harvard UP, 1982.

———. *The Sociology of Slavery: An Analysis of the Origins, Development, and Structure of Negro Slave Society in Jamaica.* Fairleigh Dickinson UP, 1967.

Patton, June O. "Moonlight and Magnolias in Southern Education: The Black Mammy Memorial Institute." *Journal of Negro History* 65, no. 2 (Spring 1980): 149–155.

Patton, Sharon F. *African-American Art.* Oxford UP, 1998.

PBS Video. *I'll Make Me A World: A Century of African-American Arts.* Blackside, February 1, 1999.

Peabody, Rebecca. *Consuming Stories: Kara Walker and the Imagining of American Race.* U of California P, 2016.

Peacock, Thomas Love. *Melincourt.* 2 vols. Philadelphia: Moses Thomas, 1817.

Pereira, Carlos Alberto M. *Retrato de época: Poesia marginal anos 70.* Rio de Janeiro: Edição Funarte, 1981.

Pereira, Edimilson de Almeida. "Survey of African-Brazilian Literature." *Callaloo* 18, no. 4 (1995): 875–880.

Perry, John Jasiel. *Freedom National—Slavery Sectional Speech of Hon. John J. Perry, of Maine, on the Comparative Nationality and Sectionalism of the Republican and Democratic Parties; Delivered in the House of Representatives, May 1, 1856, the House being in Committee of the Whole on the State of the Union.* Washington: Congressional Globe Office, 1856.

Petersen, Kirsten Holst, ed. *Criticism and Ideology: Second African Writers Conference, Stockholm.* Uppsala: Scandinavian Institute of African Studies, 1988.

Peterson, Carla L. *Doers of the Word: African-American Women Speakers and Writers in the North, 1830–1880.* Oxford UP, 1995.

Pettway, Matthew. *Cuban Literature in the Age of Black Insurrection: Manzano, Plácido, and Afro-Latino Religion.* UP of Mississippi, 2020.

Phillips, William D. *Slavery from Roman Times to the Early Transatlantic Trade.* U of Minnesota P, 1985.

Picard, David, and Mike Robinson. *Festivals, Tourism and Social Change: Remaking Worlds.* Channel View, 2006.

Pinckney, Darryl. "Black Lives Matter." *New York Review of Books* (November 9, 2017): 55–57. www.nybooks.com/articles/2017/11/09/kara-walker-black-lives-matter.

Pinheiro, Délio José Ferraz, and Maria Auxiliadora da Silva. *Visões imaginárias da cidade da Bahia:* Um *diálogo entre a geografia e a literatura.* Salvador: EDUFBA, 2004.

Pinho, Patricia de Santana. *Mama Africa: Reinventing Blackness in Bahia.* Translated by Elena Langdon. Duke UP, 2010.

———. *Reinvenções da África na Bahia.* São Paulo: Annablume, 2004.

Pinto, Samantha. *Difficult Diasporas: The Transnational Feminist Aesthetic of the Black Atlantic.* Duke UP, 2013.

Plasa, Carl. *Slaves to Sweetness: British and Caribbean Literatures of Sugar.* Liverpool UP, 2009.

Plasa, Carl, and Betty J. Ring. *The Discourse of Slavery: Aphra Behn to Toni Morrison.* Routledge, 1994.

Pollack, Harriet, and Christopher Metress, eds. *Emmett Till in Literary Memory and Imagination.* Louisiana State UP, 2008.

Poplawski, Paul, ed. *Encyclopedia of Literary Modernism.* Greenwood, 2003.

Powell, Richard J., and David A. Bailey. *Rhapsodies in Black: Art of the Harlem Renaissance.* U of California P, 1997.

Powers, Nicholas. "Why I Yelled at the Kara Walker Exhibit." *The Indypendent,* June 30, 2014, indypendent.org/2014/06/why-i-yelled-at-the-kara-walker-exhibit.

Pratt, Mary Louise. "Arts of the Contact Zone." *Profession* 91 (1991): 33–40.

———. *Imperial Eyes: Travel Writing and Transculturation.* Routledge, 2008.

Price, Richard. *Maroon Societies: Rebel Slave Communities in the Americas.* Johns Hopkins UP, 1996.

Prince, Mary. *The History of Mary Prince: A West Indian Slave.* Penguin, 2000.

Public Opinion: A Comprehensive Summary of the Press Throughout the World on All Important Current Topics 26 (January 1899–June 1899).

Pupo-Walker, Enrique, and Roberto González Echevarría. *The Cambridge History of Latin American Literature.* 3 vols. Cambridge UP, 1996.

Purbrick, Louise, Jim Aulich, and Graham Dawson, eds. *Contested Spaces: Sites, Representations and Histories of Conflict.* Palgrave Macmillan, 2007.

Queiroz Júnior, Teófilo de. *Preconceito de cor e a mulata na literatura brasileira.* São Paulo: Editora Ática, 1975.

Raboteau, Albert J. *"The Invisible Institution": The Origins and Conditions of Black Religion before Emancipation.* University Microfilms International, 1975.

Raimon, Eve Allegra. *The "Tragic Mulatta" Revisited: Race and Nationalism in Nineteenth-Century Antislavery Fiction.* Rutgers UP, 2004.

Ramos, Denise Geminez. "Creativity and Art as Part of the Elaboration of Trauma and Creativity as Brought on by Slavery." In *Cultures and Identities in Transition: Jungian Perspectives,* edited by Murray Stein and Raya A. Jones, 66–79. Routledge, 2010.

Rampersad, Arnold. Afterword. In *Robert Hayden, Collected Poems,* edited by Frederick Glaysher, 167–212. W. W. Norton, 2013.

Randall, Alice. *The Wind Done Gone.* Houghton Mifflin, 2001.

Rankine, Claudia. *Citizen: An American Lyric.* Graywolf, 2014.

Raphaelson, Paul. *Brooklyn's Sweet Ruin: Relics and Stories of the Domino Sugar Refinery.* Schiffer, 2017.

Rawick, George P. *From Sundown to Sunup: The Making of the Black Community.* Greenwood, 1972.

Raymond, James. *Prize Essay, on the Comparative Economy of Free and Slave Labour, in Agriculture.* J. P. Thompson, 1827.

Redding, J. Saunders. *To Make a Poet Black.* Cornell UP, 1988.

Rediker, Marcus. *The Slave Ship: A Human History.* Viking, 2007.

Reed, Ishmael. *Flight to Canada.* Random House, 1976.

Reinhardt, Catherine A. *Claims to Memory: Beyond Slavery and Emancipation in the French Caribbean.* Berghahn, 2006.
Reis, João José. *Slave Rebellion in Brazil: The Muslim Uprising of 1835 in Bahia.* Translated by Arthur Brakel. Johns Hopkins UP, 1993.
Reis, João José, and Flávio dos Santos Gomes, eds. *Liberdade por um fio: História dos quilombos no Brasil.* São Paulo, Companhia das Letras, 1996.
Rela, Walter. *Diccionario de escritores brasileños contemporáneos.* Montevideo: Editorial Relieve, 1994.
Ribeiro, Esmeralda. "Fato." In *Enfim—Nós: escritoras negras brasileiras contemporâneas* [Finally—Us: Contemporary Black Brazilian Women Writers], translated by Carolyn Richardson Durham, edited by Miriam Alves, 86–87. Three Continents P, 1995.
Rice, Anne P, ed. *Witnessing Lynching: American Writers Respond.* Rutgers UP, 2003.
Ricoeur, Paul. *Memory, History, Forgetting.* Translated by Kathleen Blamey and David Pellauer. U of Chicago P, 2004.
Riss, Arthur. *Race, Slavery, and Liberalism in Nineteenth-Century American Literature.* Cambridge UP, 2006.
Roberts, Dorothy. *Killing the Black Body: Race, Reproduction, and the Meaning of Liberty.* Vintage, 1997.
Robinson, Angelo Rich. "'Mammy Ain't Nobody Name': The Subject of Mammy Revisited in Shirley [*sic*] Anne Williams's *Dessa Rose.*" *Southern Quarterly* 49, no. 1 (2011): 50–68.
Rocha, Carlos Eduardo da. *O Barroquismo na poesia de Castro Alves.* Salvador: Academia de Letras da Bahia, 1998.
Roche, Emma Langdon. *Historic Sketches of the South.* Knickerbocker, 1914.
Rodman, Selden. "Negro Poets." In *Robert Hayden: Essays on the Poetry,* edited by Laurence Goldstein and Robert Chrisman, 51. U of Michigan P, 2001.
Rodríguez, Ileana. *Transatlantic Topographies: Islands, Highlands, Jungles.* U of Minnesota P, 2004.
Rodríguez, Junius P. *The Historical Encyclopedia of World Slavery.* 2 vols. ABC-CLIO, 1997.
Romero, Sílvio. *Introdução à história da literatura brasileira.* 1888. 5th ed., 5 vols. Rio de Janeiro: Livraria Olympio Editora, 1953.
Roof, Judith. *What Gender Is, What Gender Does.* U of Minnestoa P, 2016.
Rosell, Sara V. *La novela antiesclavista en Cuba y Brasil, siglo XIX.* Vol. 125. Madrid: Editorial Pliegos, 1997.
Rosenthal, Debra J. *Race Mixture in Nineteenth-Century US and Spanish American Fictions: Gender, Culture, and Nation Building.* U of North Carolina P, 2004.
Rossano, Herval, and Milton Gonçalves, dirs. *A Escrava Isaura.* Rede Globo, October 11, 1976–February 5, 1977. Telenovela.
Rout, Leslie B. *The African Experience in Spanish America.* Markus Wiener, 2003.
Rubin, Anne Sarah. "Reflections on the Death of Emmett Till." *Southern Cultures* 2, no. 1 (Fall 1995): 45–66.

Rufino, Alzira. "Verídico." In *Enfim—Nós: Escritoras negras brasileiras contemporâneas* [Finally—Us: Contemporary Black Brazilian Women Writers], translated by Carolyn Richardson, edited by Miriam Alves, 40–41. Three Continents, 1995.

Ruiz, Fernando Díaz. Introduction. In Anselmo Suárez y Romero, *Francisco, el ingenio o las delicias del campo,* i–viii. Sevilla: Editorial Doble J, 2007.

Rushdy, Ashraf H. A. *American Lynching.* Yale UP, 2012.

———. "Reading Mammy: The Subject of Relation in Sherley Anne Williams' *Dessa Rose.*" *African American Review* 27, no. 3 (1993): 365–389.

Russell, Francey. "Kara Walker: A Subtlety at the Domino Sugar Factory." *Los Angeles Review of Books,* June 20, 2014, lareviewofbooks.org/article/kara-walker-subtlety-domino-sugar-factory.

Saal, Ilka. "The Taste for Whiteness: Kara Walker's Marvelous Sugar Baby (2014)." *Food, Fatness and Fitness,* April 27, 2015, www.foodfatnessfitness.com/2015/04/27/the-taste-for-whiteness-kara-walkers-marvelous-sugar-baby-2014.

Sadlier, Darlene J. *Brazil Imagined: 1500 to the Present.* U of Texas P, 2008.

Sáenz de Tejada, Cristina. "Raza y género en la narrativa femenina afro-brasileña." *Revista de Crítica Literaria Latinoamericana* 23, no. 4 (1997): 269–285.

Sampaio, Consuelo Novais. *50 anos de urbanização: Salvador da Bahia no século XIX.* Rio de Janeiro: Odebrecht, 2005.

Sanders, Mark. *Complicities: The Intellectual and Apartheid.* Duke UP, 2002.

Sanders, Mark A. "Hayden, Robert." In *The Oxford Companion to African American Literature,* edited by William L. Andrews, 193–194. Oxford UP, 1997.

Sansone, Livio. *Blackness without Ethnicity: Constructing Race in Brazil.* Palgrave Macmillan, 2003.

Santos, Fabiano Rodrigo da Silva. *Lira dissonante: Considerações sobre aspectos do grotesco na poesia de Bernardo Guimarães e Cruz e Sousa.* São Paulo: Cultura Acadêmica, 2009.

Sappho. *If Not, Winter: Fragments of Sappho.* Translated by Anne Carson. Vintage, 2002.

Saraiya, Sonia. "Viola Davis: 'My Entire Life Has Been a Protest.'" *Vanity Fair,* July 14, 2020, www.vanityfair.com/hollywood/2020/07/cover-story-viola-davis.

Savage, Kirk. *Monument Wars: Washington, DC, the National Mall, and the Transformation of the Memorial Landscape.* U of California P, 2009.

———. *Standing Soldiers, Kneeling Slaves: Race, War, and Monument in Nineteenth-Century America.* Princeton UP, 2018.

Savali, Kirsten West. "From Mammy to 'The Marvelous Sugar Baby': The Art of Black Womanhood." *Huffington Post,* June 10, 2014, www.huffpost.com/entry/the-art-of-black-womanhood_b_5463766.

Savary, Claude, and Gilles Labarthe. *Mémoires d'esclaves.* Genève: Musée d'ethnographie, 1997.

Sayers, Raymond S. *The Negro in Brazilian Literature.* Hispanic Institute in the United States, 1956.

———. *O negro na literatura brasileira.* Edições o Cruzeiro, 1958.

Scarborough, W. S., and Michele V. Ronnick, eds. *The Autobiography of William Sanders Scarborough: An American Journey from Slavery to Scholarship.* Wayne State UP, 2005.

Scarry, Elaine. *The Body in Pain: The Making and Unmaking of the World.* Oxford UP, 1985.

Schmidt-Linsenhoff, Viktoria. "On and Beyond the Colour Line: Afterimages of Old and New Slavery in Contemporary Art Since 1990." In *Slavery in Art and Literature: Approaches to Trauma, Memory, and Visuality,* edited by Birgit Haehnel and Melanie Ulz, 59–92. Berlin: Frank & Timme, 2010.

Schuyler, George Samuel. *Black No More: Being an Account of the Strange and Wonderful Workings of Science in the Land of the Free, AD 1933–1940.* Modern Library, 1999.

Schwarcz, Lilia Moritz. *Nem preto, nem branco, muito pelo contrário: cor e raça na sociabilidade brasileira.* São Paulo: Claro Enigma, 2012.

Schwartz, Stuart B. *Sovereignty and Society in Colonial Brazil: The High Court of Bahia and its Judges, 1609–1751.* U of California P, 1973.

Scoffern, John. "Sugar." *The St. James's Magazine* 10. London: W. Kent, 1864.

Scott, Rebecca J. *Abolition of Slavery and the Aftermath of Emancipation in Brazil.* Duke UP, 1988.

Scruggs, Charles, and Lee VanDemarr. *Jean Toomer and the Terrors of American History.* U of Pennsylvania P, 1998.

"Secção Escolar Portuguesa." *Revista Hispánica Moderna* 12, no. 1/2 (January–April, 1946): 189–190.

Seidl, Monika. "Racial Stereotypes and the Art of Kara Walker." *Revue LISA* 7, no. 1 (2009): 24–39.

Seixas, Dudda. *Mãe África Pai Brasil.* Salvador: JM Gráfica e Editora, 2007.

Séjour, Victor. *La tireuse de cartes: drame en cinq actes et un prologue, en prose.* Paris: Michel Lévy frères, 1860.

"Senate OK's 'Mammy' Monument, Insults Race—Monument to 'Mammy' Wins Senate Pays Respect to Uncle Tom's Wife; Refuses to Give a Man's Job to W. L. Cohen." *Chicago Defender,* March 10, 1923.

Senghor, Léopold Sédar. *Negritude: Black Poetry from Africa and the Caribbean.* Edited and translated by Norman Shapiro. London, 1970.

Sernett, Milton C. *Harriet Tubman: Myth, Memory, and History.* Duke UP, 2007.

Shapiro, Norman R. *Négritude: Black Poetry from Africa and the Caribbean.* October House, 1970.

Sharpe, Christina. *In the Wake: On Blackness and Being.* Duke UP, 2016.

———. *Monstrous Intimacies: Making Post-Slavery Subjects.* Duke UP, 2010.

Sharpe, Jenny. *Ghosts of Slavery: A Literary Archaeology of Black Women's Lives.* U of Minnesota P, 2003.

———. *Immaterial Archives: An African Diaspora Poetics of Loss.* Northwestern UP, 2020.

Sharpless, Rebecca. *Cooking in Other Women's Kitchens: Domestic Workers in the South, 1865–1960.* U of North Carolina P, 2010.

Shaw, Gwendolyn DuBois. *Seeing the Unspeakable: The Art of Kara Walker.* Duke UP, 2004.

Shaw, Rosalind. *Memories of the Slave Trade: Ritual and the Historical Imagination in Sierra Leone.* U of Chicago P, 2002.

Sheppard, Moses. *African Slave Trade in Jamaica, and Comparative Treatment of Slaves; Read before the Maryland Historical Society, October 1854.* John D. Toy, 1854.

Shockley, Evie. "pantoum: landing, 1976." In *a half-red sea,* 4. Carolina Wren P, 2006.

Shuffelton, Frank, ed. *A Mixed Race: Ethnicity in Early America.* Oxford UP, 1993.

"Sick with the Excess of Sweetness: A Great Poet's Brushes with the World's First Consumer Boycott." *Economist,* December 19, 2006, www.economist.com/special-report/2006/12/19/sick-with-excess-of-sweetness.

Sidbury, James. *Becoming African in America: Race and Nation in the Early Black Atlantic.* Oxford UP, 2007.

Silva, Alberto da Costa e. *Um Rio Chamado Atlântico: A África no Brasil e o Brasil na África.* Rio de Janeiro: UFRJ, 2003.

Silva, Jônatas Conceição da. *Vozes quilombolas: Uma poética brasileira.* Salvador: Edufba-Ile Aiye, 2006.

Silva, Leonardo Dantas, and Raymundo Nina Rodrigues. *Estudos sobre a escravidão negra.* 2 vols. Recife: Fundação Joaquim Nabuco, Editora Massangana, 1988.

Simmons, Roscoe. "The Mammy Statue," *Chicago Defender,* February 24, 1923.

Singleton, Theresa A., ed. *The Archaeology of Slavery and Plantation Life.* Routledge, 1985.

Skeggs, Beverley. *Formations of Class and Gender: Becoming Respectable.* Sage, 1997.

Smallwood, Stephanie E. *Saltwater Slavery: A Middle Passage from Africa to American Diaspora.* Harvard UP, 2007.

Smith, Christen A. *Afro-Paradise: Blackness, Violence, and Performance in Brazil.* U of Illinois P, 2016.

Smith, Derik. *Robert Hayden in Verse: New Histories of African American Poetry and the Black Arts Era.* U of Michigan P, 2018.

Smith, James McCune. *The Works of James McCune Smith: Black Intellectual and Abolitionist,* edited by John Stauffer. Oxford UP, 2006.

Smith, Robert C. "Colonial Towns of Spanish and Portuguese America." *Journal of the Society of Architectural Historians* 14, no. 4 (December 1955): 3–12.

Smith, Verity, ed. *Encyclopedia of Latin American Literature.* Routledge, 1997.

Sollors, Werner, ed. *An Anthology of Interracial Literature: Black–White Contacts in the Old World and the New.* New York UP, 2004.

———. *Beyond Ethnicity: Consent and Descent in American Culture.* Oxford UP, 1986.

———, ed. *Interracialism: Black-White Intermarriage in American History, Literature, and Law.* Oxford UP, 2000.

———. *Neither Black nor White yet Both: Thematic Explorations of Interracial Literature.* Harvard UP, 1999.

———, ed. "Note on the Texts." In *Charles W. Chesnutt: Stories, Novels, and Essays,* 924–928. Library of America, 2002.

Sollors, Werner, and Maria Diedrich, eds. *The Black Columbiad: Defining Moments in African American Literature and Culture.* Harvard UP, 1994.

Sommer, Doris. *Foundational Fictions: The National Romances of Latin America.* U of California P, 1991.

———. *Proceed with Caution, when Engaged by Minority Writing in the Americas.* Harvard UP, 1999.

Sontag, Susan. *Against Interpretation, and Other Essays.* Farrar, Straus and Giroux, 1966.

———. *Regarding the Pain of Others.* Picador, 2003.

Sousa, Avanete Pereira. *Salvador, capital da colônia.* São Paulo: Atual, 1995.

Southern, Eileen. *The Music of Black Americans: A History.* W. W. Norton, 1983.

Southey, Robert. *The Complete Poetical Works of Robert Southey, LL.D. (Later Poet Laureate).* D. Appleton, 1846.

Souza, Florentina da Silva. *Afro-descendência em Cadernos Negros e Jornal do MNU.* Belo Horizonte: Autêntica Editora, 2006.

Souza, Florentina, and Maria Nazaré Lima, eds. *Literatura Afro-Brasileira.* Centro de Estudos Afro-Orientais: Fundação Cultural Palmares, 2006.

Soyinka, Wole. "Between Truths and Indulgences." *The Root,* July 21, 2010, https://www.theroot.com/between-truths-and-indulgences-1790880336.

———. *The Burden of Memory, the Muse of Forgiveness.* Oxford UP, 1999.

———. *Five Plays: A Dance of the Forests; The Lion and the Jewel; The Swamp Dwellers; The Trials of Brother Jero; The Strong Breed.* Oxford UP, 1964.

———. *Myth, Literature and the African World.* Cambridge UP, 1976.

Spencer-Walters, Tom, ed. *Memory and the Narrative Imagination in the African and Diaspora Experience.* Bedford Publishers, 2011.

Spillers, Hortense J., ed. *Comparative American Identities: Race, Sex, and Nationality in the Modern Text.* Routledge, 1991.

———. "Mama's Baby, Papa's Maybe: An American Grammar Book." *Diacritics* 17, no. 2 (1987): 64–81.

Sprague, Claire, ed. *Van Wyck Brooks: The Early Years.* Northeastern UP, 1993.

St. Clair, William. *The Door of No Return: The History of Cape Coast Castle and the Atlantic Slave Trade.* BlueBridge, 2007.

Stam, Robert. *Tropical Multiculturalism: A Comparative History of Race in Brazilian Cinema and Culture.* Duke UP, 1997.

Staples, Brent. "Aunt Jemima Gets a Makeover." *New York Times,* October 19, 1994, www.nytimes.com/1994/10/19/opinion/editorial-notebook-aunt-jemima-gets-a-makeover.html.

Stark, Seymour. *Men in Blackface: True Stories of the Minstrel Show.* Xlibris, 2000.

Stavans, Ilan. Introduction. In Jorge Amado, *Tent of Miracles,* translated by Barbara Shelby, xi–xv. U of Wisconsin P, 2003.

Stedman, C. Manly. *A Monument in Commemoration of the Faithful Colored Mammies of the South: Speech of Hon. Charles M. Stedman of North Carolina on H.R. 13672 in the House of Representatives, January 9, 1923.* Government Printing Office, 1923.

Stein, Murray, and Raya A. Jones, eds. *Cultures and Identities in Transition: Jungian Perspectives.* Routledge, 2010.

Stepto, Robert B. *From behind the Veil: A Study of Afro-American Narrative.* U of Illinois P, 1991.

Stewart, Gustavus A. "Afro Readers Say." *Afro-American,* May 5, 1928.

Stier, Oren Baruch, and J. Shawn Landres, eds. *Religion, Violence, Memory, and Place.* Indiana UP, 2006.

Stowe, Harriet Beecher. *The Annotated Uncle Tom's Cabin.* Edited by Henry Louis Gates Jr. and Hollis Robbins. W. W. Norton, 2007.

———. *Uncle Tom's Cabin, Or, Life among the Lowly.* Edited by Ann Douglas. Penguin Books, 1986.

Straile, Paula. "The Pillory/Pelourinho in Open-Air Museums in the US and Brazil: A Site of Racism and Racial Reconciliation." In *Erasing Public Memory: Race, Aesthetics, and Cultural Amnesia in the Americas,* edited by Joseph A. Young and Jana Evans Braziel, 209–242. Mercer UP, 2007.

"Strange Fruit: Anniversary of a Lynching." *All Things Considered,* NPR, August 6, 2010. www.npr.org/templates/story/story.php?storyId=129025516.

Suárez y Romero, Anselmo. *Francisco, el ingenio; o, Las delicias del campo.* 1880. Sevilla: Editorial Doble J, 2007.

Sue, Eugène. *Works of Eugène Sue.* 7 vols. Current Literature Publishing, 1912.

Suleiman, Susan Rubin. *Crises of Memory and the Second World War.* Harvard UP, 2006.

———. *Exile and Creativity: Signposts, Travelers, Outsiders, Backward Glances.* Duke UP, 1998.

Sundquist, Eric J. *Empire and Slavery in American Literature, 1820–1865.* UP of Mississippi, 2006.

———. *Strangers in the Land: Blacks, Jews, Post-Holocaust America.* Belknap Press of Harvard UP, 2005.

———. *To Wake the Nations: Race in the Making of American Literature.* Belknap Press of Harvard UP, 1993.

Swarnakar, Sudha. "Drought, Misery and Migration: The Fictional World of José Américo de Almeida's *A bagaceira* and Jorge Amado's *Seara vermelha* and *Gabriela, cravo e canela.*" Presented at Latin American Studies Association Conference, Dallas, Texas, March 27–29, 2003.

Takyi, Baffour K. "Africans Abroad: Comparative Perspectives on America's Postcolonial West Africans." In *The New African Diaspora,* edited by Isidore Okpewho and Nkiru Nzegwu, 236–254. Indiana UP, 2009.

Tannenbaum, Frank. *Slave and Citizen: The Negro in the Americas.* Vintage, 1946.

Tatar, Maria, ed. *The Classic Fairy Tales: Texts, Criticism.* W. W. Norton, 1999.

Tate, Claudia. *Domestic Allegories of Political Desire: The Black Heroine's Text at the Turn of the Century.* Oxford UP, 1992.

Tate, Katherine. *From Protest to Politics: The New Black Voters in American Elections.* Harvard UP, 1994.

Távola, Artur da. *A telenovela brasileira: História, análise e conteúdo.* São Paulo: Editora Globo, 1996.

Teelock, Vijaya, and Edward A. Alpers, eds. *History, Memory and Identity.* Mauritius: Nelson Mandela Centre for African Culture, University of Mauritius, 2001.

Temple, Christel N. *Literary Spaces: Introduction to Comparative Black Literature.* Durham, NC: Carolina Academic P, 2007.

———. "Rescuing the Literary in Black Studies." *Journal of Black Studies* 36, no. 5 (2006): 764–785.

Thomas, Hugh. *The Slave Trade: The History of the Atlantic Slave Trade, 1440–1870.* Picador, 1997.

Thornton, John Kelly. *Africa and Africans in the Making of the Atlantic World, 1400–1680.* Cambridge UP, 1992.

"Through a Sugar Refinery." *Illustrated American* 15 (1894).

Tidwell, John Edgar, and Steven C. Tracy, eds. *After Winter: The Art and Life of Sterling A. Brown.* Oxford UP, 2009.

Till-Mobley, Mamie. *Death of Innocence: The Story of the Hate Crime that Changed America.* Random House, 2003.

Tillet, Salamishah Margaret. *Sites of Slavery: Citizenship and Racial Democracy in the Post–Civil Rights Imagination.* Duke UP, 2012.

Tillis, Antonio D., ed. *Critical Perspectives on Afro-Latin American Literature.* Routledge, 2012.

Tinsley, Omise'eke Natasha. "Black Atlantic, Queer Atlantic: Queer Imaginings of the Middle Passage." *GLQ* 14, no. 2–3 (2008): 191–215.

Tolnay, Stewart E., and E. M. Beck. "'Racialized Terrorism' in the American South: Do Completed Lynchings Tell an Accurate Story?" *Social Science History* 42, no. 4 (July 2018): 677–701.

Tölölyan, Khachig. "Rethinking Diaspora(s): Stateless Power in the Transnational Moment." *Diaspora: A Journal of Transnational Studies* 5, no. 1 (1996): 3–36.

Tompkins, Calvin. "Why Dana Schutz Painted Emmett Till." *New Yorker,* April 10, 2017, www.newyorker.com/magazine/2017/04/10/why-dana-schutz-painted-emmett-till.

Tompkins, Jane P. *Sensational Designs: The Cultural Work of American Fiction, 1790–1860.* Oxford UP, 1985.

Toomer, Jean. *Cane: Authoritative Text, Contexts, Criticism.* Edited by Rudolph P. Byrd and Henry Louis Gates Jr. W. W. Norton, 2011.

———. *Essentials: Definitions and Aphorisms.* J. Toomer, 1931.

———. *A Jean Toomer Reader: Selected Unpublished Writings.* Edited by Frederik L. Rusch. Oxford UP, 1993.

———. *The Wayward and the Seeking: A Collection of Writings by Jean Toomer.* Edited by Darwin T. Turner. Howard UP, 1980.

Toplin, Robert Brent. "Abolition and the Issue of the Black Freedman's Future in Brazil." In *Slavery and Race Relations in Latin America,* 253–276. Greenwood, 1974.

———. *Slavery and Race Relations in Latin America.* Greenwood, 1974.

Torres-Saillant, Silvio. *An Intellectual History of the Caribbean.* Palgrave Macmillan, 2005.

Townsend, Hannah, and Mary Townsend. *The Anti-Slavery Alphabet.* Printed for the Anti-Slavery Fair, Philadelphia, 1846.

Trouillot, Michel-Rolph. *Silencing the Past: Power and the Production of History.* Beacon, 1995.

Tsouroukdissian, Carolina Rodríguez. "Codificación espacial de la dominación: Los no-hogares del esclavo en la Cuba del siglo XIX." *Afro-Hispanic Review* 36, no. 1 (Spring 2017): 37–57.

Tuden, Arthur, and Vera D. Rubin, eds. *Comparative Perspectives on Slavery in New World Plantation Societies.* New York Academy of Sciences, 1977.

Tufte, Thomas. *Living with the Rubbish Queen: Telenovelas, Culture and Modernity in Brazil.* U of Luton P, 2000.

Turner, Darwin T., ed. Introduction. In *Cane: An Authoritative Text, Backgrounds, Criticism.* W. W. Norton, 1988.

Turner, Patricia A. *Ceramic Uncles and Celluloid Mammies: Black Images and Their Influence on Culture.* Anchor, 1994.

Tutuola, Amos. *Yoruba Folktales.* Nigeria: Ibadan UP, 1986.

"The Un-Private Collection: Kara Walker and Ava DuVernay." *The Broad,* October 11, 2014, www.thebroad.org/events/un-private-collection-kara-walker-and-ava-duvernay.

Ursin, Reanna A. "Cultural Appropriation for Mainstream Consumption: The Musical Adaption of Dessa Rose." *Mosaic* 47, no. 1 (March 2014): 91–109.

"Uzodinma Iweala—Natural-Born Writer." *Africa News* 22 (May 2007).

Vadde, Aarthi. *Chimeras of Form: Modernist Internationalism Beyond Europe, 1914–2016.* Columbia UP, 2017.

Valdés, Vanessa K. *Diasporic Blackness: The Life and Times of Arturo Alfonso Schomburg.* State U of New York P, 2017.

Van Deburg, William L. *Slavery and Race in American Popular Culture.* U of Wisconsin P, 1984.

Van Sertima, Ivan. *They Came before Columbus: The African Presence in Ancient America.* 1976. Random House, 2003.

Verger, Pierre. *Centro histórico de Salvador: 1946 a 1952.* São Paulo: Corrupio, 1989.

Vergès, Françoise. *La mémoire enchaînée: Questions sur l'esclavage.* Paris: Albin Michel, 2006.

Viana Filho, Luís. *O negro na Bahia.* Rio de Janeiro: Editora Nova Fronteira, 1988.

Vicente de Azevedo, Vicente de Paulo. *O poeta da liberdade.* São Paulo: Clube do Livro, 1971.

Vink, Nico. *The Telenovela and Emancipation: A Study on Television and Social Change in Brazil.* Amsterdam: Royal Tropical Institute, 1988.

Wainaina, Binyavanga. "How to Write About Africa." *Granta* 92 (2005). https://granta.com/how-to-write-about-africa.

Waldrep, Christopher. *Lynching in America: A History in Documents.* New York UP, 2006.

Walker, Alice. "In Search of Our Mothers' Gardens." In *In Search of Our Mothers' Gardens: Womanist Prose,* 231–243. Harcourt, 1983.

Walker, Kara. "Sweet Talk." Lecture, Radcliffe Institute for Advanced Study, Harvard University. Uploaded December 18, 2014. www.youtube.com/watch?v=jiDU024R7lI.

Walker, Sheila S., ed. *African Roots/American Cultures: Africa in the Creation of the Americas.* Rowman & Littlefield, 2001.

Wallace, Michele. *Black Macho and the Myth of the Superwoman.* 1978. Verso, 2015.

Wallace-Sanders, Kimberly. *Mammy: A Century of Race, Gender, and Southern Memory.* U of Michigan P, 2008.

———, ed. *Skin Deep, Spirit Strong: The Black Female Body in American Culture.* U of Michigan P, 2002.

Walton, William. *Present State of the Spanish Colonies: Including a Particular Report of Hispañola, Or the Spanish Part of Santo Domingo; with a General Survey of the Settlements on the South Continent of America, as Relates to History, Trade, Population, Customs, Manners, &c., with a Concise Statement of the Sentiments of the People on their Relative Situation to the Mother Country, &c.* London: Printed for Longman, Hurst, Rees, Orme, and Brown, 1810.

Warnock, Mary. *Memory.* Faber, 1987.

Warren, Kenneth. *What Was African American Literature?* Harvard UP, 2012.

Washington, Booker T., ed. *The Negro Problem: A Series of Articles by Representative American Negroes of Today.* J. Pott, 1903.

Weheliye, Alexander G. *Habeas Viscus: Racializing Assemblages, Biopolitics, and Black Feminist Theories of the Human.* Duke UP, 2014.

Weiner, Marli Frances. *Mistresses and Slaves: Plantation Women in South Carolina, 1830–80.* U of Illinois P, 1997.

Wells-Barnett, Ida. *Selected Works of Ida B. Wells-Barnett.* Edited by Trudier Harris. Oxford UP, 1991.

Westrup, C. W. *Some Notes on the Roman Slave in Early Times: A Comparative Sociological Study.* København: I kommission hos Munksgaard, 1956.

Whalan, Mark, ed. *The Letters of Jean Toomer, 1919–1924.* U of Tennessee P, 2006.

"While Rome Burns." *New York Amsterdam News,* March 7, 1923.

White, Deborah Gray. *Ar'n't I a Woman?: Female Slaves in the Plantation South.* W. W. Norton, 1999.

White, Linda M. "Oh, the Irony of It: Analysis of African American Heteroglossia in Robert Hayden's *Elegies for Paradise Valley.*" *Zora Neale Hurston Forum* 12 (1998): 22–32.

White, Newman Ivey. "American Negro Poetry." *South Atlantic Quarterly* 20, no. 4 (October 1921): 304–322.

Whitehead, Anne. *Memory.* Routledge, 2008.

Whitfield, Stephen J. *A Death in the Delta: The Story of Emmett Till.* Free Press, 1988.

Whittemore, Katharine, and Gerald Marzorati, eds. *Voices in Black and White: Writings on Race in America from Harper's Magazine.* Franklin Square, 1993.

"Whose Heritage?: Public Symbols of the Confederacy." Southern Poverty Law Center, February 1, 2019, www.splcenter.org/20190201/whose-heritage-public-symbols-confederacy.

Wiggins, William H. *O Freedom!: Afro-American Emancipation Celebrations.* U of Tennessee P, 1987.

Wilkes, Donald E., Jr. "The Last Lynching in Athens." *Flagpole Magazine,* September 10, 1997.

Williams, Diana I. "Building the New Race: Jean Toomer's Eugenic Aesthetic." In *Jean Toomer and the Harlem Renaissance,* edited by Geneviève Fabre and Michel Feith, 188–201. Rutgers UP, 2000.

Williams, Lorna V. *The Representation of Slavery in Cuban Fiction.* U of Missouri P, 1994.

Williams, Pontheolla T. *Robert Hayden: A Critical Analysis of His Poetry.* U of Illinois P, 1987.

Williams, Sherley Anne. *Dessa Rose.* Harper Perennial, 1986.

Williams, Tom. "The Gospel According to James." Review. *Chicago Critic,* May 18, 2011, chicagocritic.com/the-gospel-according-to-james.

Willis, Deborah. *Family History Memory: Recording African American Life.* Hylas, 2005.

Winks, Robin W., ed. *Slavery: A Comparative Perspective: Readings on Slavery from Ancient Times to the Present.* New York UP, 1972.

Womack, Autumn. "Visuality, Surveillance, and the Afterlife of Slavery." *American Literary History* 29, no. 1 (Spring 2017): 191–204.

Wood, Amy Louise. *Lynching and Spectacle: Witnessing Racial Violence in America, 1890–1940.* U of North Carolina P, 2009.

Wood, Marcus. *Black Milk: Imagining Slavery in the Visual Cultures of Brazil and America.* Oxford UP, 2013.

———. *Blind Memory: Visual Representations of Slavery in England and America, 1780–1865.* Routledge, 2000.

Wood, Nancy. *Vectors of Memory: Legacies of Trauma in Postwar Europe.* Berg, 1999.

Wood, Rebecca S. *Slavery's Visual and Literary Legacy: Trauma Studies and Recent Reconfigurations of Slave Bodies.* PhD diss., Indiana University, 2004.

Woodson, Jon. "Consciousness, Myth, and Transcendence: Symbolic Action in Three Poems on the Slave Trade." In *The Furious Flowering of African American Poetry,* edited by Joanne V. Gabbin, 154–168. UP of Virginia, 1999.

Woolfork, Lisa. *Embodying American Slavery in Contemporary Culture.* U of Illinois P, 2009.

Wright, Derek. "African-American Tensions in Black Writing of the 1960s." *Journal of Black Studies* 19, no. 4 (June 1989): 442–458.

Wright, Michelle M. *Becoming Black: Creating Identity in the African Diaspora.* Duke UP, 2004.

———. *Physics of Blackness: Beyond the Middle Passage Epistemology.* U of Minnesota P, 2015.

Wright, Richard. "Between the World and Me." *Partisan Review* 2, no. 8 (July–August 1935): 18–19.

———. *Native Son.* 1940. Harper Perennial Modern Classics, 2008.

Xavier, Giovana. "Entre personagens, tipologias e rótulos da "diferença": A mulher escrava na ficção do Rio de Janeiro no século XIX." In *Mulheres negras no Brasil escravista e do pós-emancipação,* edited by Giovana Xavier, Juliana Barreto Farias, and Flavio Gomes. São Paulo: Selo Negro Edições, 2012.

Xavier, Nilson. "Novelas que conhecemos nas reprises." Uploaded September 20, 2019. www.youtube.com/watch?v=8gR2tc2qkuw.

Yaeger, Patricia. "Circum-Atlantic Superabundance: Milk as World-Making in Alice Randall and Kara Walker." *American Literature* 78, no. 4 (2006): 769–798.

Yeager, Gertrude M., ed. *Confronting Change, Challenging Tradition: Women in Latin American History.* Scholarly Resources, 1994.

Yelvington, Kevin A., ed. *Afro-Atlantic Dialogues: Anthropology in the Diaspora.* School of American Research P/James Currey, 2006.

Yerxa, Donald A., ed. *Recent Themes in the History of Africa and the Atlantic World: Historians in Conversation.* U of South Carolina P, 2008.

Young, Harrison. "Summer 'Advocate.'" *Harvard Crimson,* October 30, 1964.

Young, Jason R. "All God's Children Had Wings: The Flying African in History, Literature, and Lore." *Journal of Africana Religions* 5, no. 1 (2017): 50–70.

Young, Joseph A., and Jana Evans Braziel, eds. *Erasing Public Memory: Race, Aesthetics, and Cultural Amnesia in the Americas.* Mercer UP, 2007.

Zeleza, Paul Tiyambe. "African Diasporas: Toward a Global History." *African Studies Review* 53, no. 1 (April 2010): 1–19.

———. "Rewriting the African Diaspora: Beyond the Black Atlantic." *African Affairs* 104, no. 414 (2005): 35–68.

Index